The Food and Wine Lover's Companion to Tuscany

THE FOOD AND WINE LOVER'S Companion to

TUSCANY

Completely Revised, Updated, and Expanded

BY CARLA CAPALBO

CHRONICLE BOOKS
SAN FRANCISCO

Library of Congress Cataloging-in-Publication Data available.

ISBN 0-8118-3380-1

Printed in the United States of America.

Tuscan maps based on Touring Club Italiano's Toscana: 1:200,000, by kind permission.

Front cover photographs, clockwise from top left, by Roger Sherman, Steven Rothfeld, Andy Katz, and Christopher Hirsheimer; back cover photo by Steven Rothfeld.

The author and the publisher have taken due care to ensure that all the information in the book was correct at press time. They cannot be held responsible for any errors or inaccuracies. Readers' comments and suggestions for further editions are welcome. Write to the author care of the publisher, or email carla.capalbo@tin.it

Cover design by Ayako Akazawa

Book design by Margery Cantor

Distributed in Canada by Raincoast Books
9050 Shaughnessy Street
Vancouver, BC V6P 6E5

10 9 8 7 6 5 4 3 2 1

Chronicle Books LLC
85 Second Street
San Francisco, California 94105

www.chroniclebooks.com

For Sandro and for Dr. Martha Skinner and Dr. Raymond Comenzo
and the brilliant team of doctors and nurses at Boston University Medical Center
who saved my sister Isabelle's life

Acknowledgments

It has taken me several years to research and write this book. I spent months at a time on the road, driving alone from one end of Tuscany to the other. Many people, most of whom I did not know at the outset, helped me along the way, offering everything from a bed for the night to much-needed moral support. Each of them made this fascinating but complex project a little bit easier and a lot more enjoyable. Thank you all—I couldn't have done it without you.

In Tuscany:

MASSA CARRARA: Mauro and Eugenia Giannarelli, Michele and Gabriella Giannarelli, Avvocato Carletti, Lilia Borghetti and family, Valentina Harris. LUCCA: Fabio Tognetti, Andrea Bertucci, Enzo Pedreschi, Gabriele Bertucci, Gabriele Mazzei, and Arnaldo Poli. PISTOIA: Giannina Verreschi, the Montecatini APT, and Paolo Bresci of the Pistoia APT. FIRENZE: Maresciallo Rovida of the Carabinieri, Franca Michon Pecori, Aldo and Grazia Capobianco, Leonardo Romanelli, Vito Lacerenza. PISA: Carlo Gazzarrini, Simonetta Fehr, Walter Surbone, and Diliano Stefanini. LIVORNO: Ernesto Gentili, Claudio Mollo, Penny Murray, Ulisse Mibelli of the Livorno APT. ELBA: Donatella Moro and Gherardo Frassa, Fabio Picchi. CHIANTI: Leo Codacci, Barbara Poole, Ladislas Rice, Sylvie Haniez and Roberto Melosi, Bernadette and the late Renzo Bolli. GROSSETO: Roberto Santini and Carlo Pascini of Grosseto Export, Antonio Perico, Rita Presenti and Attilio Barbero, Alberto Pellegrini and Nolberto Palla. AMIATA: the two Paola Coppis of the Amiata apt, Claudia Perguidi and Valentina Perguidi of the Heimat Cooperative. MONTALCINO: Franco Biondi Santi, Roberto Cipresso. AREZZO: Nancy Harmon Jenkins, Barbara and Julian Sachs, Burton and Nancy Anderson, Silvio Ristori and the Arezzo chapter of the Sommeliers d'Italia, Massimo Rossi, Pietro Bartoli and the AICOO, Luca Fabbri, Dott. Baldesi of the Arezzo APT, Marco Noferi and Tamara Scarpellini.

Beyond Tuscany:

MILAN: James Siddall, Paola Bonfanti at the Touring Club, Giorgio Albonetti at Techniche Nuove, Carlo Galante, Ermanno Tritto, Alessandra Zucchi, Giacomo Ghidelli, Aldo Petillo. POLLINO: Luigina and Giulio Aiello, Christa and Mike Irdmann. LONDON: Carole Clements and Tim Garland, Wallace Heim, Mary Fedden, John Hubbard, Eileen and Tim Tweedy. NEW YORK: Douglas Harry Elliott, Beth Gerowitz, Donna Gorman, Dianne Janis, Joni Hughes and Antoine Bootz, Carla and Eddie Bigelow, and Tracy Tynan McBride.

I am very grateful to Dott. Roberto Melis at the Touring Club Italiano for allowing its excellent map of Tuscany to be used as the basis for the maps in this book.

Dott. Luciano Panci of the Regione Toscana offered early assistance with the project. Piero Pesenti of the Amiata APT was an eager host in his area. Many thanks go to Stefano Campatelli and Marta Ripaccioli at the Consorzio del Vino Brunello di Montalcino for their willing cooperation, and to Silvia Formentini and Ursula Thurner at the Consorzio di Chianti Classico for their invaluable organizational help and good cheer.

My literary agent, Colleen Mohyde, brought immediate enthusiasm to this project; I am also grateful for her sensitivity and support as a friend during the writing of this book. The book's early editor at Chronicle, Bill LeBlond, was encouraging from the start, as was Amy Treadwell on the second edition. Thanks also to Margery Cantor, the book's original designer, and Jeff Campbell, its first copy editor. I am very grateful to Alexander Fyjis-Walker of Pallas Athene, the book's London publisher, for his British edition. Karen Kaplan and Mara Papatheodorou of *Bon Appétit* magazine helped make the second edition possible.

Special thanks go to Maria-Teresa Giannarelli for being my first Tuscan friend and for getting me through the first day; Anna and Fabrizio Galli for endlessly putting me up; Sophie and Valdo Verreschi and Giuliana and Enrico Galli for their generous hospitality; Franco Guerrieri for keeping my VW on the road; Bruno, Elyane, and Booboo Moos and the *club des cinq* for sharing their house and everything else; Graziano Mannozzi for the anemones and for his extraordinary support during my sister's illness. Judy and Nino, Cosmo and Toto MacDonald gave me a home away from home on many occasions; Harriet Shapiro was in on it from the beginning; Harvey Sachs was my first friend in Tuscany and my first editor; Alberto Biagetti and David Zuman were cheerful and tireless map-men. Thanks go to Mark Edmonds at the London *Daily Telegraph* for being instructive about "color" in writing; to Anne Mendelson for being the book's fairy godmother and to my uncle, Leonard A. Stevens, for introducing me to her.

The idea for this book came out of a conversation with Henrietta Green, whose *Food Lover's Guide to Britain* has been an inspiration throughout. Fred Nijhuis and Nicolas Belfrage have been unfailingly generous in sharing their wine expertise with me. My brother-in-law, Adam Sodowick, helped change the course of my sister Isabelle's life and thus my own. I am grateful to my sister Sandra Lousada, who took my photograph for the cover. Thanks to my brother, Sebastian Lousada, for setting an example to us all by being an organic grower, and to my 102-year-old grandmother, Marie McBride (née Giuditta Camera), for her support and faith in me. The late Gary Nikolis, who had long been my champion, was an enthusiastic fan of the project. Lauren Crow has been a welcome friend and helpful early reader of the manuscript. A very special thank-you to my father, Carmen Capalbo, who read almost every word of the text and offered an infallible ear for language, a wealth of bookish wisdom, and quite a few laughs.

I almost invariably dined alone when reviewing the restaurants for this book, but I amused myself by taking along a group of "virtual" companions whose opinions I liked to "consult": Peter Frank lent me his fine eye for detail at all of the grandest restaurants; Elizabeth Heyert brought her sensitive appreciation and her exceptions to many dietary rules; my mother, Patricia Lousada, was everpresent with her standards of excellence in cooking and her discerning (but not uncritical) palate. My sister Isabelle Lousada was always with me, bringing her joy of eating out and her sense of style; so was my brother Marco Capalbo, with whom I first learned to love eating in Tuscany.

Two people followed the course of the making of this book on a daily (and usually distant) basis: my loyal friend and unofficial editor, Nicola Rudge Iannelli, whose intelligent attention and solidarity helped me to get through it, and Alessandro Guerriero, whose love, generosity of spirit, and faith in me were the gifts that left me free to go off alone and take on the world of Tuscany.

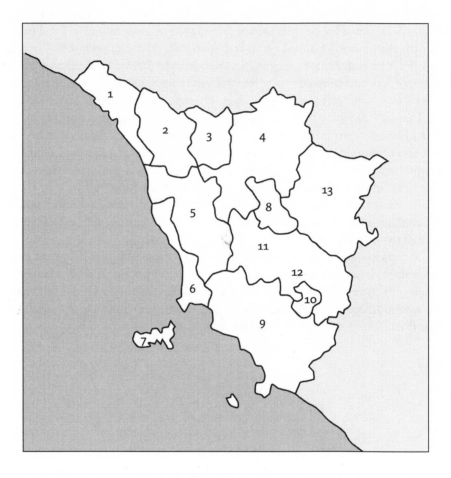

Contents

Introduction

*P*icture yourself in Tuscany. You are in the heart of Italy, surrounded by medieval hill towns, gray-green olive groves, and sloping vineyards. You appreciate good food, and you are in the mood to cook or to enjoy a leisurely lunch in the country. But where should you go to buy the finest bread or cheeses, extra-virgin olive oil, or estate-bottled wine? When is market day in the nearest village? And which are the nicest family-run trattorias?

The Food and Wine Lover's Companion to Tuscany tells you. This practical guide leads you to the best foods and wines in Tuscany. It suggests which products to buy, explains how they are made, and tells you where to find them. And it offers insight into the complex gastronomic culture of one of Italy's most fascinating and diverse regions.

To research this book I drove thousands of kilometers, on and off the beaten track. I interviewed hundreds of people: shepherds in the Maremman hills, mushroom gatherers in the mountains above Carrara, fishermen along the Mediterranean coast. I visited historic wine castles in Chianti as well as tiny vineyards in less famous locations whose wines are just as noteworthy. I searched for unpretentious trattorias serving genuine home cooking and more ambitious restaurants whose chefs are reinterpreting Tuscany's culinary traditions. To uncover the best food products, I sampled dozens of gelati and chocolates, *salumi* and cheeses, baked goods and bottled preserves. Along the way, I learned a lot about the people who make them.

This book is a love letter to Tuscany's food artisans—to the bakers and cheese-makers, wine producers and *salumieri* who have devoted their lives to doing one thing with passion and pride. They are as much a part of Italy's cultural heritage as the Duomo in Florence or Botticelli's *Venus*. But many of them are fighting to survive in a world of convenience foods and one-stop shopping. And sadly, the elderly *salumiere* in his medieval village or the dedicated young couple producing handmade goat's cheeses in the Apennine mountains are not only struggling against the evils of mass marketing and globalization. They may also be battling overzealous bureaucracies intent on industrial standardization, whose respect for individual artisans is often not what it could be.

Luckily, there still are people who understand the difference between a loaf of bread that is factory made with bleached flours and preservatives and one crafted of stone-ground grains, leavened with natural yeasts, and baked on chestnut leaves in a wood-burning oven. These foods still exist, although they often qualify as "endangered species."

In the few years since the first edition of this book, there has been increasing concern around the world about many food issues. Italy's Slow Food movement has been instrumental in raising awareness about the plight of small local producers in Italy and beyond and has fought to protect them and their unique products. It is well worth becoming a member, wherever you live. Go to: www.slowfood.com.

Like most Italians, the Tuscans treasure their "secret" food sources. As a sign of hospitality they proudly offer guests slices of hand-cured local prosciutto, a glass of a favorite estate wine, or a taste of freshly pressed olive oil bought at a nearby *frantoio*. These precious resources have been carefully sought out and tested by the Tuscans, and by me. They are valued for their genuine quality and for the link they maintain with the honored traditions of the past. Often they are to be found within a stone's throw of a town or supermarket. You just have to know where to look.

An early-morning outing to a fish market or a tour of the cellars of a stately wine *castello* may be as memorable an experience as a trip to a landmark frescoed church. They represent complementary aspects of Italian culture: one frozen in the past, the other still very much alive today.

With this *Companion* as your guide, your visits to Tuscany should be full of pleasurable, delicious, and informative gastronomic adventures. Mine certainly have been!

How to Use This Book

For the sake of this book, I have divided Tuscany into thirteen sections (and chapters); most correspond to official province boundaries (such as Pistoia or Livorno), but in three (Lunigiana and Versilia, Chianti Classico, and Mount Amiata), entries belonging to more than one province are grouped together for greater consistency of subject matter or ease of travel. The island of Elba, part of the province of Livorno, has a chapter of its own, as does the wine town of Montalcino.

The Maps

Each chapter begins with a map showing the area's key towns. Names printed in boldface indicate towns in which an entry appears. These maps are intended to help you organize your visits to foodmakers, but I strongly recommend obtaining Touring Club Italiano's Toscana 1:200,000 map (with a green cover) to anyone planning to do much driving in rural Tuscany. It is readily available within Italy and is the only map I have found that shows the smaller roads in enough detail to be useful.

The Entries and Their Categories

Towns and villages containing entries are listed alphabetically within each chapter. Within each town, the entries are grouped by category—by food type (bread, cheese, olive oil, wine) or establishment type (bar, olive mill, restaurant)—and within these categories, the listings are arranged alphabetically by key words: within one town, a bar will be listed before a restaurant or winery. Some entries have more than one category. Others may suggest additional products within the text: for instance, most wineries also produce fine olive oil.

How to Read an Entry

In addition to the town and category, each entry begins with the full NAME AND ADDRESS of the business, including the postal code. (When writing, always add the town and province name after this code. For example: Macelleria Marini. Via Selva, 313. Ferruccia. 51030 Agliana. Pistoia.) Note, too, that in Italy, house numbers are written after the street name.

OPENING HOURS are given, but they may vary by season or whim: if you are planning a long trip, phone first to check whether the establishment will be open.

Many wineries and other private artisan producers are open only by appointment; phone before going to confirm whether they are able to receive drop-in visitors. For restaurants, meals served, rather than business hours, are given.

CLOSING DAYS are given whenever possible; holiday closures, when known, are indicated by month, although the establishment may not be closed for the entire month.

If an establishment accepts CREDIT CARDS, they are indicated: Visa, Master-Card (MC), American Express (Amex), and Diners Club (DC).

DIRECT-SALE information is included for farms and estates that sell directly to the public. When direct sale is not possible, a nearby seller is noted. Mail-order information is included for those companies that provide this service.

Each entry also tells WHETHER ENGLISH IS SPOKEN.

FEATURES such as "summer garden terrace" apply mainly to restaurants, so you can see at a glance if outdoor dining is possible.

RESERVATIONS apply only to restaurants, indicating when reservations are required. However, it is always best to reserve.

The PRICE CATEGORY is also used only for restaurants, and it gives the average cost per person of a three- or four-course meal without wine, beverages, or service and cover charges (prices accurate as of summer 2001). Here are the ranges used:

$	up to 18 euros
$$	18–26 euros
$$$	26–38 euros
$$$$	38–52 euros
$$$$$	52–72 euros
$$$$$$	72 euros and over

These price ranges should be used as a guide only. Meals may cost less if fewer courses are ordered, or they may cost more, depending on the wines you choose.

The "OTHER" category indicates aspects of an establishment that are not directly connected to food, such as apartments for holiday rentals or a museum on the grounds.

DIRECTIONS are given to help you locate the entries, and they should be used in conjunction with a good road map. In rural Tuscany, few roads have names (and of those, few have street signs). The most important visible indicators are the blue-and-white signs pointing to the next town or village. When an entry's directions say "go toward" a village, I am referring to these signs. They are usually the only indication that you are going in the right direction. All distances are given in kilometers. When directions say "in the town center," that means within the *centro storico*, or historic center. They are easy to find, always indicated on the outskirts of town by the symbol of black concentric circles on a white ground. Within large towns or cities, cross streets or nearby landmarks are given, but almost every village has a large map in the main square showing its landmarks and streets. For

Firenze and other large towns, I suggest buying a map with a street index. They are sold at every newspaper stand or bookstore.

What You Will Find in the Entries

I have personally visited every address of the more than five hundred included in this book, looking for the best in each category. I tried to choose places that are fun to visit—where the food is great, the people are charming, and the locations are lovely. The entries include food and wine producers, restaurants, food shops, and table crafts.

The Food Entries

These entries describe fine food producers and some of their products. I have included information about how the products are made and descriptions of those I was able to taste or liked best. Other products are also often available.

The Wine Entries

This book describes more than one hundred quality wine estates throughout Tuscany. Many more exist, far too many for any one book. No matter how detailed the tasting notes on a particular wine may be, they rarely offer much insight into the personality of the winery that produced it. I felt it was more important to bring out the characteristics of the winemakers and their estates than to analyze their wines. After all, you will have a chance to visit some of these wineries and judge their products yourself; read about the estates listed here and visit those that sound the most interesting. There is no substitute for the experience of tasting a fine wine in the cellars that made it.

Wines may be bought directly from most estates at prices that are the same or slightly lower than nearby wine shops. At all but the biggest wineries (which may have permanent staff on hand to show you around), it is best to phone ahead to arrange a visit. All are hospitable and keen on receiving interested visitors—novices and experts alike—so don't miss out on this wonderful, fascinating opportunity.

In the listings, the wine entries are alphabetized by the key word in their company titles: Castello dei Rampolla is under R.

The Restaurant Reviews

I have reviewed restaurants offering well-cooked food in all price ranges and styles. Some specialize in traditional Tuscan cuisine; others take a more modern approach. Since some foods are seasonal, I mention the time of year I visited.

This book does not give scores or grades; I did not visit the restaurants anonymously. I describe a meal in each restaurant rather than list its complete menu. These necessarily subjective accounts should help visitors choose the restaurants best suited to their tastes.

Boxed Inserts

These offer detailed information about some of Tuscany's most important foods and wines.

Also

These are shorter mentions at the end of a town's entries; the reduced length does not imply that the products are less interesting.

Tuscan Market Days (see p 377)

This is an alphabetical list, divided by chapter, of the towns and villages and their weekly or monthly market days.

Glossary (see p 383)

This provides translations of Italian (and some French) food and wine terms commonly used in Tuscany and in this book. It also will help in translating menus written in Italian.

Index (see p 391)

At the end of the book you will find a comprehensive general index that also lists the entries and their foods by category. For example, you can see where chocolate is made throughout Tuscany, and thus read about the chocolate makers before deciding which ones to visit. There are also separate indexes of wines (see p 392) and wine grape varietals (see p 394).

PART ONE

The Foods of Tuscany

Tuscany's food is rooted in *cucina povera*, poor or peasant cookery, a rural cuisine based on available natural ingredients: olive oil, unsalted bread, vegetables and pulses, wild leaves and mushrooms, and salt-cured or simply cooked meats. Many dishes are purely seasonal, looked forward to and eaten only when their ingredients make their annual appearance. But Tuscany's noble families also favored elaborate dishes of Renaissance origin.

Tuscan antipasti include *crostini* (canapés topped with chicken livers or vegetables), *salumi* (salt-cured pork meats such as prosciutto and *salame*), and *bruschetta* (grilled bread topped with olive oil or tomatoes). *Primi*, first courses, feature hearty soups more than pasta, such as the two popular bread-thickened *zuppe: la ribollita* and *pappa al pomodoro*. Each province's favorites are discussed in the entries. *Secondi*, main courses, include grilled meats, game, country rabbit stewed with olives, and, on the coast, fish. *La Fiorentina* is the Tuscan T-bone steak, served rare and best made from Chianina beef. (Note: As a result of recent health concerns about beef in Europe, all cattle in Italy are now slaughtered before they are old enough to carry disease.) Vegetarians will find stewed or sautéed vegetables, salads, and egg dishes like frittata. Desserts are simple: Vin Santo with *cantucci* cookies is a classic, but there are often gelati, rather dry cakes, or the ubiquitous tiramisù. Locally grown fruit and berries are always good options.

Much of this book is devoted to Tuscany's artisan food producers. Many still work using traditional methods—water-powered stone mills for grinding, or hand-stirred milk for cheesemaking—adapted now to a modern world dominated by industry and impersonal production regulations.

The quality of these foods sets them apart from their industrial counterparts. Only the experience of a perfectionist (and all the artisans are that) can judge whether the meat for *salame* has been kneaded enough or the dough for an organic loaf needs more time to rise. These artisans are justly proud of their work. Many sell directly from farms and workshops and welcome visitors. If possible, phone before you go, especially if you are interested in seeing how they work: otherwise they may be in the fields or barns.

Restaurants and Eating Out

Tuscany offers many options for eating out. A *bar* sells drinks, coffee, and snacks; some even serve several courses at lunchtime. *Enoteche* are wine bars; many also serve food. *Trattorias* and *osterie* feature rustic home cooking and are often family run. *Ristoranti* (restaurants) include world-class establishments and are usually well appointed. I have grouped them all under the category "restaurant."

Mealtimes in Italy respect a well-defined timetable. Lunch is normally served from 12:30 to 14:30 and dinner from 19:30 to 21:30. Some kitchens may stay open later, but they are the exception, especially in the countryside. Do not expect restaurants to serve a meal in mid-afternoon, though a simple *panino* (sandwich) can usually be found in a bar.

Italians traditionally eat three or four courses at each meal: antipasto (hors d'oeuvres), *primo* (pasta or soup), *secondo* (meat or fish main course with a *contorno* of vegetables), and *dolce* (dessert). These habits are changing, and it is now usually acceptable to have just two or three courses. Some restaurants may not look favorably on those wanting only a pasta and salad, but others understand that not everyone eats as many courses as the Italians. Those restaurants that require diners to order a full four-course meal are indicated.

Not all restaurants have printed menus; in some the proprietor recites the day's offerings. If you want a full meal, many restaurants offer a *menu degustazione,* or tasting menu. In a good restaurant, this can be a good value, offering a chance to taste dishes in each category at a predetermined price.

To avoid disappointment it is always advisable to make a phone reservation: popular restaurants may be fully booked, and country trattorias sometimes close off-season if no customers have reserved.

Food Markets

Most villages and towns in Tuscany host a weekly market in addition to any permanent market structures they have. These are great to visit not only for shopping—prices are usually lower than in the supermarkets, and the produce is fresher—but also to see what is in season. Vegetables and fruits are priced and sold by weight: either by the kilogram (2.2 lbs) or the *etto* (100 grams, or 3.5 ounces). Any item sold and priced singly will be marked *cadauno* or *cad.* (each).

For a listing of Tuscany's principal market days, see p 377.

Food Festivals

At least once a year, almost every village in Tuscany holds a food fair, which may be called a *sagra* or *festa* and may be big or small. On summer weekends many villages hold fairs on the same day. *Sagre* are usually dedicated to one particular food or dish: *sagra della bistecca* (steak festival), *della fragola* (strawberry), *del cinghiale* (wild boar), *del pecorino* (sheep's cheese), and so on. They range from elaborate events with costumes, music, and a rich assortment of foods to very local village affairs with a few tables set up in the main square. Whatever their size, they are usually fun to attend and offer an insight into rural life in Tuscany. Usually, local cooks prepare the village's specialties using the seasonal ingredient the fair is dedicated to. Visitors pay a modest fee and sit at large communal tables for their meal.

The best way to find out about food fairs is to look for posters, which are put up a week or two before the fair. If attending a fair involves much traveling, phone the commune or the local Azienda Promozione Turistica (APT) that is holding it to make sure it is really happening. I once drove three hundred kilometers to attend an onion fair I saw advertised, only to discover it had been cancelled!

Table Crafts and Kitchen Shops

For those who collect handmade table crafts—ceramics, baskets, and linens—Tuscany has some to offer, though there are fewer artisans now than in the past. Several Tuscan towns (Montelupo Fiorentino, Vinci, Monte San Savino, Impruneta) produce ceramics using local clay and traditional and Renaissance designs. Be careful in souvenir shops, however, which often sell hand-painted ceramics signed underneath with the name of their town. Most of this pottery is made semi-industrially in Deruta (in Umbria) or in Italy's south. There is nothing wrong with it, but it probably was not produced in the town where it is being sold. Unless you see the potter sitting at the wheel, the pieces may have been factory made elsewhere.

I found some fine Tuscan linens (at Arezzo and Anghiari), hand-woven baskets for drying figs or picking olives (San Gimignano and San Casciano), and beautiful alabaster objects (Volterra). See the index under individual crafts if you are looking for something specific.

Well-stocked kitchen shops offer good presents to take home: individual espresso makers, olive-wood cutting boards or cheese graters, wedges for dividing Parmesan, or any of the modern design objects the Italians are brilliant at producing.

Olive Oil

The olive tree is a bushy evergreen with pointy gray-green leaves. It lives to a great age when not attacked by disease or severe cold. Until relatively recently the Tuscan landscape was characterized by enormous, sculptural olive trees more than a hundred years old. The freak winter of 1985, with heavy snow and temperatures of -20°C/-4°F in areas accustomed to only light frosts, killed the majority of Tuscany's oldest olive trees. The great trunks, many measuring several feet across, were cut down. Luckily, the olive tree sends up new shoots if its roots are not dead. Look carefully at the olive trees now growing in Tuscany and you often will see two or three young plants growing around a large cut stump.

The olive is a fruit. At its purest and best, olive oil is the "juice" of this fruit—just crush and press the olives and it will drip free. Unfortunately, the process is rarely kept that simple. There is a world of difference between industrial extra-virgin olive oil and estate-bottled oil made from homegrown, hand-picked olives. The latter will more than repay itself in quality. An aromatic, fruity oil can turn a good meal into a great one.

It is worth knowing that industrial extra-virgin oil is bought as "crude extra virgin" from many Mediterranean countries, regardless of where the bottler is located. It is always a blend, often including seed oils—though companies are not obliged to declare that on the label. Industrially refined "virgin olive oils" and "light" olive oils have been stripped of their natural taste and defects by chemical solvents.

Tuscany is one of Italy's most important producers of high-quality extra-virgin olive oil. As with all natural products, each oil's particular characteristics are determined by plant type, climate, and geography. Lucca's coastal oils, like Liguria's, are light in color and sweet in taste; they go well with seafood. Oils from Tuscany's central hills are more decisive in flavor, with a peppery aftertaste and agreeable bitterness; they are best on salads and vegetables or drizzled on grilled bread.

Reputable small producers are attentive to each stage of the (necessarily costly) process. To make the best oil, healthy olives are hand-picked early in the season, before they are ripe enough to fall to the ground. (Falling means bruising, and the likelihood of rotting or fermentation.) They are carried in airy crates to the *frantoio*, or mill, and preferably milled within thirty-six hours of being picked. There are currently two nonindustrial systems for extracting the oil: the traditional stone mill and the modern continuous cycle plant.

"Until recently, everyone agreed that stone-ground oil was the finest," explained Marco Chiletti, a Tuscan oil producer. "It certainly is the most picturesque system—nothing could be more dramatic than to watch the great round stones as they crush the olives, with the air full of a fine mist of aromatic olive oil."

The washed olives are ground to a dark brown pulp. This is usually heated very slightly, or it would not release its oil, and then kneaded before being spread onto circular woven mats. The mats are stacked onto a steel pole, sandwiching the paste between them. A hydraulic press squeezes the mats together, forcing the oil out. A final spin in a centrifuge separates the oil from its accompanying vegetal water. The residue of the paste, a hard brown substance that looks a bit like cork, is called *sansa*. It may be burned as a fuel or sold to refineries that extract more oil from it using chemical solvents. This *Olio di Sansa* should be avoided.

"Nowadays, the modern 'continuous cycle' system is increasingly popular," said Chiletti. "It has several advantages. It is more hygienic: the olives and pulp are worked entirely in stainless-steel containers, which are easily cleaned and reduce the risk of contamination from one batch of olives to the next. Each client can tailor the machinery to his needs, as it is temperature controlled at every stage. In some types the olives are not crushed but cut with a series of fine blades, enabling the oil to drip away by gravity. This is definitely the way of the future."

Many fine wine producers also make olive oil: the terrain required to grow olives is similar to that for grapes, and the harvesting seasons are staggered, the grapes being picked in September and October, the olives from late October through December.

There has been a lot of talk about acidity levels and cold pressing in olive oils. Although an oil must have less than 0.1 percent acidity to be considered extra virgin, low acidity levels alone do not guarantee good flavor (industrial oils may be manipulated chemically to "correct" acidity), and some experts claim that the difference between 0.02 and 0.06 percent acidity cannot even be distinguished by the tongue. Even the word *cold* is relative: unless the olive paste is at least 15°C/ 59°F, little oil can be extracted; below 8°C/46°F, the oil freezes. The most important factor for the layperson is the reputation of the producer—all the rest is personal preference.

A bottle of artisan-made, pure extra-virgin olive oil may seem expensive, but used sparingly, its wonderful fresh flavor will enhance any meal, and it will last much longer than a comparably priced bottle of wine.

How to Store Your Oil

Pure extra-virgin olive oil is a delicate natural product. Keep it away from its principal enemies, heat and light. Oil is also easily contaminated by bad odors, so never refill your oil cruet unless it has been perfectly cleaned and dried. Even a little oxidized residue is enough to ruin the taste of fresh oil.

Unlike wine, oil does not improve with age. Use it within a year of its being made.

Several associations are dedicated to the appreciation of fine olive oils, and they organize tastings and publish literature. Contact Corporazione dei Mastri Oleari, www.mastrioleari.org; Associazione Italiana Conoscere l'Olio d'Oliva (AICOO), tel/fax 0577 40334.

Wine

Tuscany is one of Italy's most important wine-producing regions, and its best wines are among the world's finest. Tuscany contains many subzones that have been granted a nationally recognized winemaking status: DOC (*Denominazione di Origine Controllata*) or the more recent and more stringent DOCG, which adds *e Garantita* to the DOC. These denominations are similar to France's *appellation* system: wines made within a circumscribed area must comply with set standards in order to be accredited with the DOC or DOCG label. Grape varieties, a maximum grape yield per hectare (2.47 acres), and vinification and aging specifications are established for each type of wine. Ideally, these specifications are strict enough to keep standards high and discourage fraud while still affording producers some flexibility of interpretation.

Winemakers within a DOC region may make wines outside these regulations, but they may not be classified as DOC or DOCG wines. Indeed, in the last twenty-five years there has been a revolution in Tuscany's winemaking as progressive estates have created new wines outside the DOC categories. At first, these wines had no official name, so they adopted the simple "table wine" description given to Italy's humblest wines. These *vini da tavola* were christened "super-Tuscans" (see below, p 26). These powerful, *barrique*-aged, and often expensive wines are modeled on the great wines of Bordeaux and have gained an international following. The Tuscan wine that sparked this revolution was Sassicaia (see Tenuta San Guido, p 150).

Recently a new denomination has been created, IGT (*Indicazione Geografica Tipica*). A large and increasing number of wines fall into this category, and they range from the simplest table wines to the greatest super-Tuscans. The IGT can suggest a regional wine style, but is more often used for wines whose grape varieties exclude it from the local DOC or DOCG. It should not in itself be taken as a guarantee of quality.

Vin Santo, or Holy Wine, is a Tuscan specialty, the perfect ending to any meal. This amber dessert wine ranges from dry and sherrylike to sweet and opulent. It is made of white grapes partially dried on cane mats or hung from wires or rafters. After several months, when their sugars have been concentrated, the grapes are pressed and sealed into *caratelli*, small wooden casks, for three years or more. The kegs are stored in the *vinsantaia*, a room under the roof where the wine's temperature may rise and fall with the seasons. Vin Santo is traditionally dunked with *cantucci* biscuits; the finest Vin Santi are complex, rich wines better savored on their own.

But What Is Wine?

I recently heard a foreign visitor ask a winery owner, "So what is in this wine, aside from grapes, sugar, and water?" The question was fair, but it clearly surprised the winemaker—he assumed everyone knew that wine was made only from grapes. So, for those new to winemaking, here is a simplified description of the process.

Wine is an alcoholic drink made from fermented grape juice—ideally without water or sugar. Red wine is made from red grapes, getting its deep color from the skins (the pulp of red grapes has little color): red grapes are fermented with their skins, white grapes are usually not. The stalks and seeds contain bitter tannins, and although red wines need some tannins to help them age and give them character, too many are not good, so the stalks are removed. In Tuscany, where most grapes are picked by hand, a machine that looks like a giant corkscrew presses the pulp, skins, and seeds through, leaving the stalks behind; what comes out is called "must."

The must is pumped into large tanks of stainless steel, vitrified cement, or wood, where it begins to ferment. Yeasts (either naturally present or added) heat the mass as they convert the grapes' natural sugar into alcohol, giving off carbon dioxide. The heat must be controlled and should not exceed 25° to 32°C (77° to 89°F). (Winemakers used to cool tanks by hosing them down with cold water, but modern steel tanks have built-in coolers.) As the gas rises to the top of the tank, it pushes the skins up into a thick layer called the "cap." This should be pushed back down to the bottom of the tank, usually twice a day, to keep the skins in contact with the fermenting juice. That is now done by pumping juice up from below and over the cap, forcing it back down. This fermentation process "on the skins" may last from one to several weeks, depending on the style of wine being made. For red wines that are intended to be drunk young, and that do not require excessive tannins, the fermenting juice may be separated from the skins and seeds after just a few days and put into another tank to finish its fermentation.

At this point, a second, "malolactic" fermentation may occur naturally or be induced—a bit of ambient heat starts the wine fermenting again. La malolattica, as it is called in Italy, transforms malic acid (as in apples) into lactic acid (as in milk), and the result is a mellower, softer wine. The wine may then be kept in steel vats until bottling or aged in wooden barrels, large or small. Large Tuscan casks (botti) were often made of chestnut but are now usually Slavonian oak. Large casks hardly impart any of the wood's character to the wine, as the ratio of wood to liquid is very low. Modern-style wines such as the super-Tuscans are usually put in small French oak barrels called barriques. These barrels do affect the wine's flavor and structure, giving it added tannins and a woody taste.

Wine may be aged for anything from a few months to a hundred years—depending on the grape type and structure—in steel, old or new wood, glass, or a mixture of them all. The aging process continues in the bottle, which is why many "big" red wines need prolonged cellaring to give their best.

Dry white wine (which may also be made from red grapes) is made somewhat differently, as contact with the skins (and their tannins) is not usually desirable. Here the grapes are softly pressed to separate the juice from the skins and seeds. The juice is filtered before being fermented at slightly lower temperatures than red wine in order to keep its flavors fresh and aromatic, usually for ten to fourteen days. The wine is then run off the sludge of dead yeasts; it may or may not undergo the secondary malolactic fermentation. Some modern-style Tuscan Chardonnays are fermented in barriques to give them more complex flavors and the ability to age longer than normal white wines.

WHAT ARE THE SUPER-TUSCANS?

"The original super-Tuscan was Sassicaia," explained Burton Anderson, an American wine expert who has lived in Tuscany for many years. "When in 1968 Mario Incisa put that wine on the market, and it was a big success, it inspired the use in Tuscany of Cabernet, which in turn inspired Piero Antinori in 1975 to make a wine from Sangiovese and Cabernet, Tignanello. Giacomo Tachis, the enologist for both Antinori and Sassicaia, was the prime mover."

This revolution came about because most Sangiovese vines planted in Tuscany in the 1960s and 1970s were inferior clones grown in the wrong way: too few vines per hectare, too much growth per vine. "The result was that Chianti was basically a wishy-washy wine by the end of the 1970s, with very few exceptions. It was pale not only because of the added white grapes but because the Sangiovese was inferior." Some producers familiar with the great red wines of Bordeaux felt that Tuscany ought to be capable of producing wines of similar intensity and style.

Sassicaia also inspired the use of *barriques*, the small barrels of French oak, for aging the wine. "If you start with the right wine, *barriques* are a way of making it more appealing to the so-called international market. And not just because of the wood: if it has the right structure, a wine in *barriques* matures to become more complex and interesting," Anderson said.

"The first pure Sangiovese super-Tuscan was Sergio Manetti's Le Pergole Torte, which also started a school. Before that people believed that without Cabernet, their wines would not have enough to them. But Sergio proved that Sangiovese did have enough to it to benefit from the *barriques*." Most super-Tuscans are now made primarily from Sangiovese, often blended with Cabernet or Merlot, or even Syrah. Many are now classified within the new IGT category (see p 24).

PART TWO

CHAPTER 1

The Lunigiana and Versilia

*D*riving into Tuscany from Parma you come across the Apennines into the Lunigiana, on what was the CISA—one of the earliest roads through these imposing mountains. The Lunigiana was named for Luni, a Roman town now in neighboring Liguria. The *autostrada* curves down past the rustic villages of Pontremoli, Aulla, and Bagnone before straightening out along the sea. There it runs a spectacular course between the dramatic marble mountains of Carrara, the Apuan Alps, and the Mediterranean coast, known here as Versilia. The most famous Riviera town is Viareggio; it hosts an elaborate winter carnival.

Carrara's quarries have for centuries provided Italy's sculptors and architects, including Michelangelo, with marble; the extraction of the monumental blocks is now mostly mechanized. Years ago it represented one of the hardest and most dangerous manual jobs. This part of Tuscany may be less "typically Tuscan"— there are few cypresses, vineyards, or olive groves—but it is a fascinating area combining the cultures of mountain and sea.

The foods, of course, reflect this. If the Lunigiana still offers an authentic country cuisine based on wild herbs, mushrooms, chestnuts, and other "land" ingredients, Versilia's beach resorts boast some of the region's best fish restaurants. New discoveries in the area include a talented young chef at Carrara and a fine young winemaker at Massa.

AZIENDA PROMOZIONE TURISTICA
LUNGOMARE VESPUCCI, 24
54037 MARINA DI MASSA, MASSA
0585 240063, FAX 0585 869015
WEB SITE www.turismo.toscana.it

VIALE CARDUCCI, 10
55049 VIAREGGIO, LUCCA
0584 962233, FAX 0584 47336

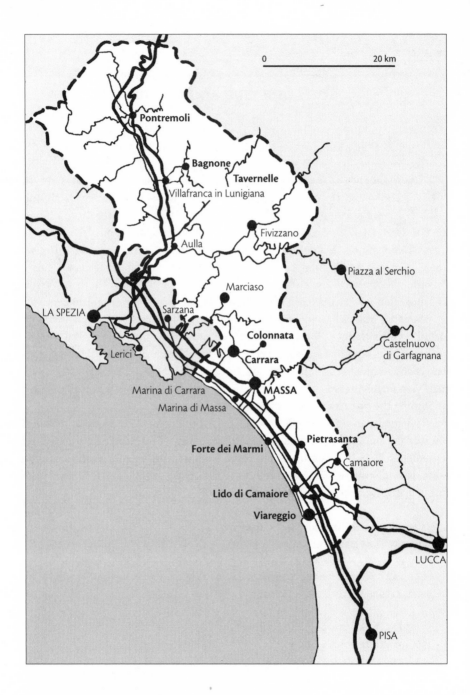

Boldface type indicates towns that are included in this chapter.

Bagnone

I FONDI
RESTAURANT

BORGO DELLA REPUBBLICA, 26 BAGNONE MASSA
TELEPHONE 0187 429086

OPEN Lunch and dinner **CLOSED** Tuesday; January **CREDIT CARDS** Visa, MC
ENGLISH SPOKEN Yes **RESERVATIONS** Recommended **PRICE** $$
DIRECTIONS On Bagnone's main street

I Fondi are "the depths" of a fifteenth-century building in this Apennine hillside village. Enter the restaurant down a tunnel staircase that seems carved out of the rock. Its dining rooms and terrace overlook Bagnone's namesake (the word means "large bath"): a cascading river with waterfalls. The food is country fare cooked by Anna Bruno. Seasonal antipasti include local *salumi* and savory vegetables. The choice of *primi* is good; and *testaroli*, pastalike pancakes with garlic and basil pesto, are specialties (this area borders with Liguria, where pesto originates). Tagliatelle are homemade and substantial. Duck is baked, sausages are grilled—this is unpretentious home cooking with, unusually, a good choice of vegetable *contorni* (side dishes). The local specialty, *bomba di riso,* rice with pigeon sauce, can be ordered in advance. If you don't want dessert, end with a piece of fine Parmigiano Reggiano; it is made just on the other side of the mountain.

Carrara

DROGHERIA RIACCI
GROCERY STORE

VIA ROSSELLI, 1 54033 CARRARA MASSA
TELEPHONE 0585 71936
WEB SITE www.anticadrogheria.com

OPEN 7:00–13:15, 16:30–20:00 **CLOSED** Wednesday afternoon, Sunday **CREDIT CARDS** None
ENGLISH SPOKEN No **DIRECTIONS** In the town center

This general grocery store, or *drogheria,* still has its Liberty-style (Italian for art nouveau) interior, unchanged since the early 1900s. The walls are lined with carved wood and glass cabinets with handsome iron detailing. The long marble counter had a zinc bar for serving liqueurs (a *drogheria's* license enabled it to sell spirits), but now it holds an espresso machine. *Drogherie* once carried exotic spices and products like Turchetino—a bluish powder rinse added to the water, when washing whites, for a fresh blue sparkle (when ash was used instead of soap for washing clothes)—and black dye, for women having to attend a funeral who had no black dress. Times have changed, and sadly, shops like this have all but disappeared.

The shop now also organizes Liberty architectural tours of Carrara.

NINAN   VIA LORENZO BARTOLINI, 3 54033 CARRARA MASSA
RESTAURANT   TELEPHONE/FAX 0585 74741
                                        E-MAIL ninan@tiscalinet.it

OPEN Lunch and dinner   **CLOSED** Sunday in winter; Sunday lunch in summer
CREDIT CARDS Visa, MC, Amex   **ENGLISH SPOKEN** Yes   **RESERVATIONS** Necessary
PRICE $$$$ **DIRECTIONS** In the town center

It is always heartening to discover the work of a talented young chef, especially one who has the courage to open a restaurant off the beaten track. Marco Garfagnini has put Carrara firmly on the gastronomic map (Colonnata got there first), making the town a must now for gourmets as well as sculptors.

Chef Garfagnini, who was thirty in 2001, started working when he was fourteen. He traveled and cooked in France and Britain before coming back to his roots—the small restaurant's dining room was once his grandmother's parlor.

Garfagnini has a clean palate and clear ideas about what he is cooking. He also has the technical skills to put them in practice. His *menu degustazione* (which must be taken by the whole table) offers very good value and is a fine way to sample the range of his cooking; an à la carte menu also exists.

In spring, dinner started with a sautéed butterflied shrimp served simply with raw tomato sauce bound with delicate olive oil. The area's star ingredient, *lardo di Colonnata* (see p 33), was brilliantly used in the antipasto: strips of fresh sole were wrapped around a tiny "core" of dried tomato, then wrapped themselves in strips of the sliced *lardo*. These rounds were quickly browned under a hot broiler, leaving the fish perfectly cooked and the fragrant *lardo* translucent and crisped in places. They came served on a velvety sauce of cauliflower, dotted with chervil.

Crunchy potato gnocchi were just that: the soft dumplings were given a golden crust and topped with thin slices of pungent *pecorino di fossa*, peeled baby fava beans, and cubes of oven-dried tomato for a touch of sweetness. Again, a well-balanced yet unusual combination. Pigeon breasts were seared and served with an onion "brulée"—a soft pudding of caramelized onions with a browned sugar top. The demiglaze was lightly flavored with licorice, adding a note of spice to the aftertaste. Dessert too was masterful, and fun. The "variations on milk" were three: *gelato di latte*, baked milk custard (without egg), and a deeper-toned cooked milk pastry whose flavor was reminiscent of *dulce de leche*. All was arranged with artistry on the plate.

The wine list offers a good variety of wines and prices. There are six tables in the room, with the kitchen upstairs; the service, like everything else at Ninan, is careful and bright.

Also

BAR GELATERIA TOGNOZZI   VIA ROMA, 1. 0585 72850

This ice-cream parlor definitely has some of the best gelati in the area: not sickly or cloying, but deeply flavorful with a good clean texture. The less-common fruit flavors, like the tangy blood orange when it is in season, are fresh tasting and creamy, and there is an interesting selection of nut flavors: almond, pinoli, and walnut, as well as the ubiquitous hazelnut.

DA OMETTO
RESTAURANT

VIA MARTIRI DEL LAVORO BEDIZZANO 54033 CARRARA MASSA
TELEPHONE 0585 768211

OPEN Lunch and dinner   **CLOSED** Some Sundays in summer   **CREDIT CARDS** None
ENGLISH SPOKEN No   **FEATURES** Summer terrace   **RESERVATIONS** Recommended in summer
PRICE $ **DIRECTIONS** From Carrara go toward Colonnata; after 3 kms, Da Ometto will be on the right before Bedizzano

The sign outside this trattoria reads: *Da Ometto tutto è perfetto* (everything is perfect at the "little man's"). Perched breathtakingly high in Carrara's marble mountains, this was until recently a "circolo ARCI e ANPI"—a recreational bar for members of the workers' and Italian partisan associations. Before dinner the dining room was filled with quarry workers and aging partisans, smoking, drinking, and playing cards. Now it has been transformed into a *trattoria casalinga*—a country trattoria serving genuine home cooking.

If the Ometto is in a welcoming mood, you will have an unpretentious but very good dinner. The cook does justice to the local specialties: her excellent *pasta e fagioli* is an herbed bean soup with homemade *tagliolini* noodles; the popular tripe is well stewed in a piquant tomato sauce. There are mountain *salumi*, rabbit, and seasonal game. Wines are local. In summer you eat outside at monolithic marble tables on the breezy terrace, amid the high quarries.

Colonnata

VENANZIO
RESTAURANT

PIAZZA PALESTRO, 3 COLONNATA 54030 CARRARA MASSA
TELEPHONE/FAX 0585 758062

OPEN Lunch and dinner   **CLOSED** Thursday; Sunday evening; December 20 to January 20
CREDIT CARDS Visa, MC   **DIRECT SALE** *Lardo* may be bought from Alimentari Cattani, Piazza Palestro, 2   **ENGLISH SPOKEN** A little   **RESERVATIONS** Necessary   **PRICE** $$$–$$$$
DIRECTIONS Colonnata is signposted from Carrara (7 kms); park in the car park on the left upon entering Colonnata and walk up the stairs to the square and restaurant

Driving from Carrara to Colonnata is exciting: the road winds steeply up through the imposing, cavernous quarries that for centuries have given the world its finest marble. Even Michelangelo got his stone here. It is overwhelming to think of the human labor that has gone into taming these monumental mountains. The tiny stone village of Colonnata is tucked into this dramatic landscape. Its only restaurant is now synonymous with a special food: *lardo di Colonnata*, salt-cured pork fat from the animal's back.

"Our *lardo* is as old as the quarries," explained Venanzio Vannucci, who brought Colonnata's *lardo* into the gastronomic spotlight. "For a thousand years this village has conserved slabs of *lardo* in *conche*, troughs or bowls carved in marble. Recipes for the *salamoia*—curing salt, herbs, and spices—are generations old." Using this *salamoia* for six months in the marble results in a pure white, aromatic *salume*— nothing like its yellowed, rancid, and tough air-dried counterpart.

Venanzio's is exquisite. My February lunch began with pieces of hot bread topped with fine, ribbonlike slices of *lardo*, with only a tiny streak of pink meat within the white. A sprig of fresh rosemary lay on the piping hot plate; its warmed, aromatic perfume hit me first. The heat of the bread, the light, buttery softness of the *lardo*, its delicate yet exotic fragrance and perfectly balanced seasonings were unexpected and extraordinary. An unusual carpaccio followed: a fillet of Chianina beef was marinated in the *lardo's salamoia* for three days, then sliced paper thin. The tender coral meat, whose delicate flavor just hinted at the spices and herbs it had been kept with, came surrounded by *mentuccia*—a vibrant wild mint. These pure foods had the clarity of birdsong.

A freshly made omelette was filled with just-picked sprigs of fragrant *vignalba*, a wild clematis, and topped with slivered gray truffle. The truffle's heady perfume complemented the herb's sweet bitterness. A sensual, brilliant dish. Tender ravioli with a light meat stuffing came in a fresh tomato and basil sauce. Sliced *tagliata* of beef arrived on a searingly hot plate and cooked as I watched, with an intense sauce of soy and truffle. A frozen chocolate dessert was decorated with flowers Venanzio had gathered himself. There are wonderful wines (Sergio Manetti's ladies smiled down from his Pergole Torte labels) and a relaxed atmosphere in this small room, where quarry workers eat alongside foreign visitors. After lunch Venanzio showed me his garden. I left with my hands full of wild herbs and violets.

Forte dei Marmi

LORENZO
RESTAURANT

VIA CARDUCCI, 61 55042 FORTE DEI MARMI LUCCA
TELEPHONE 0584 874030, 89671   FAX 0584 874030

OPEN Lunch and dinner; dinner only in July and August
CLOSED Monday in winter; December–January   **CREDIT CARDS** Visa, MC, Amex
ENGLISH SPOKEN Yes   **RESERVATIONS** Necessary   **PRICE** $$$$–$$$$$
DIRECTIONS Via Carducci runs parallel to the sea, a few blocks inland, by Piazza Marconi

---

Lorenzo's is a great restaurant—the kind you enjoy immediately and look forward to returning to. It has all the right elements: unbelievably fresh ingredients (especially fish) cooked deliciously yet simply, a lively atmosphere that is elegant but not stuffy, an award-winning wine list, and an owner-host with a rare talent for his calling.

"I choose and buy my fish every day," explained the charming Lorenzo Viani, who personally visits local fishermen and Viareggio's auction in his quest for the freshest seafood. "A fish has twenty-four virtues—but loses one with each hour that passes."

The *cernia di fondale* (stone bass), *gallinella,* and *capone* (both in the gurnard family) do not lose many of theirs before becoming a tartare of deep-water fish. This meltingly soft, cool patty of ground raw fish is subtly enhanced with lemon, herbs, fruity olive oil, and tomato. The *fritto di mare* is the best I have ever had. The fish seem Lilliputian: tiny *rossetti* (transparent goby) the size of minnows, colorless despite their Italian name; slender shrimp no longer than a bay leaf, so tender you eat them whole; miniature *calamaretti* (squid), fine-skinned and delicate. They are dipped into a light batter and quickly fried, a far cry from mundane deep-frying.

Natura di totanini al forno is equally unusual: small flying squid (Alan Davidson explains in *Mediterranean Seafood* that they do not fly, but propel themselves out of the water) are baked whole, partially gutted, with just their own liquids to stew in. If at first they are a bit disconcerting—the transparent "quill" is still inside the sac—they have remarkable intensity of flavor. Sautéed red mullet topped with tomato, celery, and raw fava beans is fresh, light, and Mediterranean.

Lorenzo's best-loved pasta dish is *bavettine sul pesce,* thin linguini with seafood. Its secret is that the pasta is cooked along with the fish—shrimp, squid, *calamaretti*—with water added gradually as for risotto. The result is more fish than pasta, which has good biting texture and a depth of flavor boiled pasta rarely attains. At Lorenzo's shellfish are alive until they are prepared, either raw or cooked simply so as not to lose their character. Fish are lightly baked, poached, or grilled over a wood fire with Mediterranean aromatics. A parallel "land" menu also exists. "It is important to eat well," asserted Lorenzo, "but just as important to feel well afterward."

Lorenzo and a cousin have recently taken over the oldest bar in Forte: Bar Roma (Via Mazzini, 2), in the town's central square. Stop in for a drink or a light meal.

Also

GASTRONOMIA "DEI PARMIGIANI"   VIA MAZZINI, 1/B. 0584 89496

Forte dei Marmi is one of the coast's fanciest resorts. If you are planning an elegant picnic on the beach, stock up at this *gastronomia.* It offers Italy's top cheeses—including truffle-scented *crutìn* and rare pit-matured *formaggio di fossa*—salumi (prosciutti from Parma, San Daniele, and Tuscany), prepared rice salads, pasta dishes, cooked vegetables, wines . . . everything you'll need for your epicurean feast.

MAGAZZINI DEL FORTE   VIA CARDUCCI, 19. 0584 89542

The stylish displays at this housewares store are arranged by ex–fashion buyers Raoul and Amanda Doni. The Magazzini once sold fittings for sailboats and fishermen; now it carries everything from fine linens to designer kitchen gadgets, cookbooks to cutlery, tapestry wools to tabletop objects.

Lido di Camaiore

GASTRONOMIA VIALE COLOMBO, 444 55043 LIDO DI CAMAIORE LUCCA
ENOTECA GIANNONI TELEPHONE 0584 617332   FAX 0584 981791
SPECIALTY FOODS: DELICATESSEN

OPEN 7:30–13:30, 16:30–20:00 in winter; till 20:30 in summer   **CLOSED** Wednesday afternoon, Sunday in winter, Sunday afternoon in summer; October   **CREDIT CARDS** Visa, MC, Amex **ENGLISH SPOKEN** A little   **DIRECTIONS** Viale Colombo is the main road along the coast, running parallel to the sea

---

I haven't given awards in this book, but I would give one to this handsome gourmet shop, located unexpectedly on a busy road near the coast. It would not be out of place on the world's fanciest shopping streets. The big, high-ceilinged room is lined with attractive wood-and-glass cases displaying beautiful foods.

A long counter features selected Italian cheeses and a few international stars. So alongside fresh and smoked *bufala mozzarella* delivered from Campania, or Tuscan pecorini of varying ages, are Stilton and chèvre. *Salumi* are excellent: the brothers Giuliano and Sauro Giannoni mature selected prosciutto hams near Parma for up to two years, far longer than usual. There is also wonderful *lardo di Colonnata,* which is cured in marble containers (see p 33).

The Giannonis also cook vegetables, pasta, sauces, main courses, desserts, and pastries of a very high standard, which are sold to take out. Individual "soufflés" are made of artichoke hearts or spinach; the pesto is of fresh basil; the apple tarts are as good as they look. The brothers' passion for fine foods also extends to wines; they feature the top Tuscans and import French wines and Champagne *crus*. A really great store.

Massa

ALIMENTARI CECCARELLI PIAZZA GUGLIELMI, 9 (LA CONCA) 54100 MASSA
SPECIALTY FOODS: TELEPHONE 0585 42094
SALT COD & STOCKFISH

OPEN 8:00–13:00, 17:30–21:00 in summer; 8:00–13:00, 16:00–20:00 in winter   **CLOSED** Wednesday afternoon, Sunday   **CREDIT CARDS** None   **ENGLISH SPOKEN** A little   **DIRECTIONS** In the town center, near Piazza degli Aranci

---

At Massa, Ceccarelli's has been synonymous with *baccalà* and *stoccafisso* since the 1930s, when Dante Ceccarelli began importing the cured North Sea fish, which was first brought to Italy by the Vikings. Once a staple in households where women had the time to devote to its preparation, the well-flavored fish is now competing with its frozen counterparts. Ceccarelli offers free local recipes to stimulate interest in this popular Italian food: deep-fried in *fritelle* or stewed in a spicy tomato sauce, *in umido*.

Baccalà is cod fished in winter (from mid-January onward, when the fish is oiliest). It is cleaned aboard ship, processed on land in brine with 20 percent salt for five days, dried for twelve hours, then layered with more salt. It must be soaked, preferably under running water, for at least twenty-four hours before cooking. *Baccalà* is sold in different grades; the finest comes from Norway, Iceland, and the Faeroe Islands. *Stoccafisso,* or stockfish, is also cod, but air-dried, not salted, in the Arctic for sixty days at an optimal outdoor temperature of 0° or 1°c. When properly dried, the fish should have almost no odor. Stockfish must be soaked for forty-eight hours before cooking.

The store, now run by Marilisa Ceccarelli and her husband, Antonio, has elegant marble baths with wrought-iron animal's head spouts for soaking the fish, which can be bought *bagnato,* ready to cook. The shop's recent renovation has retained the feel of an old-fashioned store. Other products include selected local *salumi* and cheeses, Tuscan olive oils, grains, chickpea flour for *farinata,* and mortars and pestles made of Carrara marble.

DROGHERIA "GLI SVIZZERI"
SPECIALTY FOODS

VIA CAIROLI, 53 54100 MASSA
TELEPHONE 0585 43092

OPEN 7:00–13:00, 17:00–20:00 in summer; 7:00–13:00, 16:00–19:30 in winter   **CLOSED** Wednesday afternoon, Sunday   **CREDIT CARDS** None   **ENGLISH SPOKEN** None   **DIRECTIONS** In the town center, near Piazza degli Aranci

---

"Gli Svizzeri" is one of Massa's oldest stores, named for the original Swiss proprietors who came to the Lunigiana in the 1850s. It changed from a *speziale,* or spice shop (the pharmacies of that time), to a *liquoreria* at the end of the 1880s, before becoming a *drogheria* in the 1920s. *Drogherie* were general grocery stores stocking everything, including products not easily found: oriental spices, medicinal teas, imported extracts, and tinctures.

The Belatti family's shop remains a "colonial" treasure trove, selling China Yerba tea and Argentinian maté, whole Indian spices, sacks of aduki beans and basmati rice (hard to come by in Italy), flavored extracts for home-blending triple sec or vermouth, loose candied fruits for making *mostarda,* imported North Sea herring, and local *lardo di Colonnata* displayed in carved marble troughs. There is even a small bar at one end of the counter where you can stand for a coffee and let your mind wander to spice routes and camel trains.

CIMA
WINE, RESTAURANT

VIA DEL FAGIANO, 1 SAN LORENZO 54100 MASSA
TELEPHONE/FAX 0585 830835
E-MAIL cima.candia@iol.it

OPEN Lunch and dinner   **CLOSED** Monday in winter   **CREDIT CARDS** Visa, MC, Amex
DIRECT SALE Yes   **ENGLISH SPOKEN** A little   **RESERVATIONS** Recommended   **PRICE** $$
OTHER Panoramic terrace for summer dining   **DIRECTIONS** From the Massa exit of the *auto-strada*, head toward Massa *centro*. At the Aurelia traffic lights, turn left. After 500 meters, go right on Via Romagnano; go straight and follow signs to Cima

Underneath his family's unpretentious country trattoria, Aurelio Cima has created a large *cantina* for making his wines. What started as a way of producing wine for the restaurant has become a full-time endeavor for the young man, who recently began working with Matura, a group of some of Italy's most talented winemaking consultants.

"This is an area whose wines were known mainly to the locals," admitted Aurelio, "but the white Vermentino grape has long produced fine wines here. Many people had heard of the Candia wines, but few had ever tasted them. I decided to stretch the local repertoire a bit by making serious red wines as well, and so far, the results have been very positive."

The winery now has 20 hectares (49 acres) of vineyards, some of which rise steeply above the restaurant. "Here in these hills, it takes painstaking manual work to tend the vines," Aurelio explained. "But as we are very close to the sea, the salty breezes intensify the flavor of the grapes."

Cima produces a fine Candia dei Colli Apuani DOC, of 90 percent Vermentino, with 10 percent of Albarola, a traditional local grape, added to it. There is also a wine of pure Vermentino fermented in *barriques*. His reds are Montervo, of pure Merlot coming from fifty-year-old vines, which is aged for sixteen months in *barriques*, and Romalba, of 85 percent Sangiovese and 15 percent Massaretta—another local grape variety—also aged in small barrels.

I enjoyed the Candia wine, with its floral nose, hints of tropical fruit, and balanced acidity. I also enjoyed my dinner at Cima's restaurant, of *bruschetta*, local prosciutto, and meats grilled over a big wood fire.

Also

IL PANE   VIA MURA NORD, 8

Massa's best bakery makes assorted unsalted Tuscan breads and focaccia—made in a wood oven and brushed with a little oil before baking. Excellent focaccia is topped with soft cooked onions subtly tasting of vinegar. Alfio Morandi sells an aromatic *torta d'erbi*, brought in from Villafranca in Lunigiana. *Torta di riso*, Massa's favorite Easter dessert, is made to order.

Pietrasanta

L'ENOTECA MARCUCCI
WINE BAR, RESTAURANT

VIA GARIBALDI, 40 55045 PIETRASANTA LUCCA
TELEPHONE/FAX 0584 791962

OPEN Wine bar 10:00–13:00, 17:00–1:00 A.M. ; dinner 20:00–24:00   **CLOSED** Monday in winter
CREDIT CARDS Visa, MC   **DIRECT SALE** Yes   **ENGLISH SPOKEN** A little
RESERVATIONS Always recommended   **PRICE** $$ **DIRECTIONS** In the town center

Pietrasanta (holy stone) is a sculptor's haven: near Carrara's monolithic marble quarries, it is bursting with artisanal *botteghe*, or well-equipped workshops where sculptors may carve the stone. Sculptures adorn every public space, making it a nice cultural outing for anyone interested in three-dimensional art.

The *enoteca* opened in 1988. A friend described its style as *chic povero*—poor chic. It is a great space: a high-vaulted room lined with tall shelves of wine bottles, like stacks in a library, with whites on the right, reds on the left. Long stone-topped tables are used for tasting by day, dinner by night. There are Italian and international wines, including Tuscany's stars and a good range of the best local producers. The young Marcucci brothers are enthusiastic and knowledgeable. Wines may be bought to take out or drunk at the *enoteca*.

For dinner (the only meal served), the Marcucci parents do the cooking. The menu is easygoing and the prices are reasonable. There are hearty soups and pastas and some less usual starters: herrings with steamed potatoes, small peppers stuffed with anchovies (a Piemontese specialty), and a "salad" of boiled meat with capers and olives. Main courses feature meats, including duck and ostrich (*struzzo*), grilled over wood embers (*alla brace*), and seasoned with herbs grown by Signor Marcucci. Vegetable dishes are interesting, and desserts homemade. The kitchen is open late, but reservations are necessary at this "in" spot.

Pontremoli

SALUMERIA ANGELLA
MEAT: SALUMI

VIA GARIBALDI, 11 54027 PONTREMOLI MASSA
TELEPHONE 0187 830161

OPEN 8:00–12:45, 16:00–19:30   **CLOSED** Wednesday afternoon   **CREDIT CARDS** None
ENGLISH SPOKEN No   **DIRECTIONS** The shop is on the corner of Via della Bietola, near the Duomo

Armando Angella is one of Tuscany's finest *salumieri*, if not its most senior. The business was begun in the 1850s by his grandfather. After more than forty years of work, this sprightly artisan is still passionate about his art. In his small workshop he personally "transforms" over two hundred quality local pigs per year. The *salumi* mature in tiny cellars beneath the quaint shop, which has recently been taken over by Tiziana Bertocchi.

Spalla cotta con l'ossa, or cooked cured shoulder on the bone, is Angella's specialty. An unusual halfway house between boiled ham and *prosciutto crudo,* the pork shoulder is salted and hung for four months before being simmered in several changes of fresh water for five to six hours to draw off some of the salt. It is a deep dusky pink, darker than normal boiled ham, and retains the marked flavor of its cure. Sliced off the bone by hand, it is eaten with peas or mashed potatoes in sweet counterpoint to its salt. Angella's other specialties include Lunigiana *mortadella nostrana,* a spiced salami bearing no resemblance to its large Bolognese cousin; *tartaruga,* a cured and wrapped *culatello* (rump); and *lardello,* a lean salami to which only 5 percent white fat, salt, and peppercorns are added.

When I first met him, Signor Angella was pessimistic about finding an apprentice able to maintain his high standards. European Union laws are hard on small *artigiani* who have made excellent products for decades without knife sterilizers or walk-in refrigerators. To have had to buy them now or be faced with closure has been demoralizing for the independent-minded Signor Angella. "I will keep going as long as I can," he confided, "and hopefully I'll find a way to keep my family's artistry alive." With Ms. Bertocchi's help, it seems he has succeeded.

IL FUNGO
PRODUCE: MUSHROOMS

VIA 1 MAGGIO, 14 54027 PONTREMOLI MASSA
TELEPHONE 0187 832574   FAX 0187 830189
WEB SITE www.ilfungopontremoli.it

OPEN 7:30–12:30, 16:00–19:30   **CLOSED** Wednesday afternoon, Sunday   **ENGLISH SPOKEN** No
DIRECTIONS On the town's southern outskirts, southwest of the river

---

Being an early bird is the best way to find mushrooms, assuming you know where to look. It also guarantees you get them before anybody else does. The *contadini,* or peasants, living around Pontremoli are rewarded in cash for their early-morning searches, and Il Fungo gets the freshest supply of the wood's harvest. The prized porcini (*Boletus edulis*) grow under the sweet chestnut trees, but other varieties include chanterelles, *galletti,* and *Volvaria volvacea.*

The Giumellis trade in the offerings of the woods and fields: mushrooms are sold fresh, sun-dried, and *sott'olio*—under oil. The porcini season begins in June, then tails off until September and October, but preserved mushrooms are usually available. The attractive store sells produce all year, including wild salad greens popular in Tuscany and wild strawberries, blueberries, and raspberries.

DA BUSSÉ
RESTAURANT

PIAZZA DUOMO, 31 54027 PONTREMOLI MASSA
TELEPHONE 0187 831371

OPEN Lunch Saturday–Thursday, dinner Saturday and Sunday   **CLOSED** Friday; July
CREDIT CARDS None   **ENGLISH SPOKEN** A little   **RESERVATIONS** Recommended on weekends
PRICE $$–$$$ **DIRECTIONS** Near the Duomo

When Da Bussé opened in 1930, Pontremoli was a popular stopping point on the CISA, the main road cutting through the mountains from north to south. The family-run trattoria became known for its unpretentious Pontremolese cuisine and for the intimacy of its dining rooms—small interconnecting parlors on the ground floor of a house.

Despite the modern *autostrada,* which now bypasses Pontremoli completely, things haven't changed much. Da Bussé does a brisk lunch trade, and you may find yourself sitting near local lawyers or councilmen who have been coming here for years. The mercurial Signora Antonietta knows them all, and keeps up a steady banter as she flashes in and out of the rooms bearing the fruits of the kitchen's labors.

Local *testaroli,* pancakelike pasta rectangles served with *pinoli*-less pesto, are aromatic but oily; eat them for lunch or as a half portion. Vegetable tarts reflect the local passion for wild greens: in spring, *erbadella* has polenta-flour pastry and a quichelike filling of scallions and potatoes, with a note of anise from the wild fennel. *Secondi* often include stewed rabbit, boiled veal, or meatball-stuffed *involtini:* meat rolls in light tomato sauce, served in a terra-cotta dish.

Nut tarts are classic desserts, as is the Sunday *torta al mascarpone.* In season, *frutti di bosco,* wild berries from the local woods, are exquisite.

LA TRATTORIA "DEL GIARDINO" DA BACCIOTTINI
RESTAURANT

VIA RICCI ARMANI, 13
54027 PONTREMOLI MASSA
TELEPHONE 0187 830120

OPEN Lunch and dinner   **CLOSED** Monday   **CREDIT CARDS** None   **ENGLISH SPOKEN** A little
RESERVATIONS Recommended   **PRICE** $$$ **DIRECTIONS** On the town's central street

Bacciottini's restaurant is one of Pontremoli's best known; begun by the present owner's parents, it specializes in traditional Lunigiana foods. After Signor Bacciottini died, his son Rafaelo reopened with his young wife, Clara, who has a fine repertoire of local recipes. The trattoria occupies a large vaulted room reached by a passageway from the town's main street. The atmosphere is informal but friendly.

Clara is a natural cook, especially with vegetable-based dishes. The area's famous *testaroli*—flat rectangles of a pancakelike pasta cooked on cast-iron *testi,* or molds—are here served with an easily digestible light herb pesto infused with garlic. Stockfish and salt cod are regular features on the menu, in the local tradition. Stockfish cooked with Mediterranean eggplant, capers, olives, and yellow peppers is delicious, offering a sweet contrast to the intense fish. Spring *minestre* (soups) and *torte* (savory tarts) use wild herbs. *Erbadella* features wild fennel; *torta d'erbi* contains beet and other greens, potatoes, and onions in a light crust. Autumn wild mushrooms are served many ways, including deep-fried. Meats here tend to be cooked simply: grilled, fried, or stewed.

Also

**PASTICCERIA AICHTA
"DEGLI SVIZZERI"**   PIAZZA DELLA REPUBBLICA, 21. 0187 830160

If you are in the mood for a sweet treat, stop in here, at the town's best dessert bakery and bar. Good local pastries include *baci di dama*, chocolate-filled cookie sandwiches, and *Amor*, crisp wafers or butter cookies with a thick *crema* filling.

Tavernelle

VILLA VALENTINA COOKING SCHOOL   0187 425003   www.villavalentina.com

Popular Italian-British cookbook writer Valentina Harris has taken over a villa in a tiny mountain village in the unspoiled hills above Aulla near where she was born. She gives hands-on cooking classes in English during the course of a fun week that includes a trip over the mountain to Parma to see cheese and ham makers and other visits. See another Tuscany, and learn a lot of great recipes.

Viareggio

ROMANO   **VIA MAZZINI, 120 55049 VIAREGGIO LUCCA**
RESTAURANT   TELEPHONE/FAX 0584 31382

OPEN Lunch and dinner   **CLOSED** Monday; January   **CREDIT CARDS** Visa, MC, Amex
ENGLISH SPOKEN Yes   **RESERVATIONS** Recommended   **PRICE** $$$$$
DIRECTIONS Via Mazzini runs perpendicular to the sea from Piazza Mazzini

---

"When we opened here, over thirty years ago," recounted Romano Franceschini, "I was twenty-two years old and my wife, Franca, was sixteen. Then lunch cost 1.000 lire [less than a dollar]." Today, Romano is famous for his fine fish cookery. The current restaurant, on a busy street near the market, is comfortable, well appointed, and newly redecorated. Romano's wife and children all work there. The food is distinctly Mediterranean and includes some meat. There is an extensive wine list.

My spring lunch began with *dentice* (dentex, a fish in the porgy family) served with tangy fresh tomato sauce, puréed green radicchio, and fine homemade mayonnaise. *Insalata di mare*—tender squid, shrimp, crayfish, and sliced octopus tossed with oil and herbs—was accompanied by Tuscan *fagioli* (white beans) and good olive oil. A striped, silver-skinned fillet of *ombrina* (ombrine) on a bed of julienned carrots and zucchini was flavored with balsamic vinegar and chives. Olives and capers added sharper accents. Giant mussels were garnished simply with lemon.

The *calamaretti ripieni* were excellent: miniature squid stuffed with finely ground vegetables and bread crumbs. *Spannocchi* (the local word for *mazzancolle*, large shrimp) came with an unusual piquant warm honey sauce and fried artichoke slices that were cold and crunchy. The squid reappeared in a *zuppa*, an herbed broth with fresh tomato; toasted Tuscan bread and fruity oil completed this rustic dish. In *bavette con scampi*, pasta was rich with shrimp in a light tomato and herb sauce—a classic Riviera dish. Fish are fried, poached, or grilled. Desserts include sorbets, mousses, and Viareggio's characteristic seasonal carnival pastries.

Also

LA BOTTEGA DI MAMMA RÒ   VIA FRATTI, 284. 0584 31192

"Humble materials in tasteful contexts" is this store's subtitle. Its bright, earthy objects fit well with today's notions of country style. A wide range of glazed terracotta objects includes bowls and vases, plates and cook pots; the colors are pretty, though I wish more were made without logos. There are rough-weave cotton fabrics, chunky colored glasses, kitchen utensils, and chopping boards—all reasonably priced. This store belongs to a Lucca-based franchising network with branches in the United States.

CHAPTER 2

Lucca and the Garfagnana

*L*ucca is one of Tuscany's most fascinating towns. An independent city-state until the nineteenth century, Lucca's wealth and power were based on commerce. Historic walls enclose an active center of medieval streets, Romanesque churches, and stately palazzi. Lucca's rich silk merchants and noble families summered in villas built in the gentle hills around the town. These villas, often baroque with formal gardens, are surrounded by olive groves. The area is known for its mild, almost sweet, extra-virgin olive oil.

To Lucca's north the hills steepen as the River Serchio traces a course between the Apuan Alps and the Apennines, forming an area known as the Garfagnana. Here the summers are cool and breezy, amid forests of pine, beech, and chestnut. Stone houses cluster in villages surrounded by mountain pastures for sheep and goats.

The cooking of the Garfagnana is hearty, with thick soups of *farro*—the locally cultivated spelt wheat—chestnut flour, and pulses. There is game and mutton, sheep's cheese and wild mushrooms. If this mountain fare represents *la cucina povera*, Lucca's classic dishes reflect the city's wealth: *torta di erbe* is a Renaissance vegetable pie studded with pine nuts and raisins, fragrant with spices only the rich could afford.

AZIENDA PROMOZIONE TURISTICA
PIAZZA SANTA MARIA, 43
55100 LUCCA
0583 491205, FAX 0583 469964
WEB SITE www.turismo.toscana.it

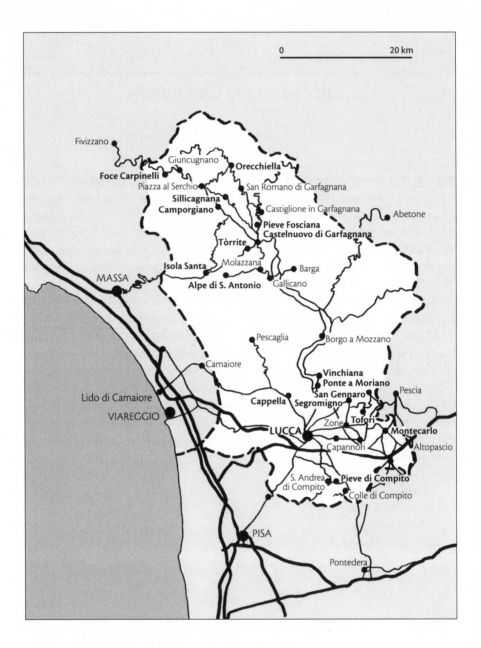

Boldface type indicates towns that are included in this chapter.

Alpe di S. Antonio

LA BETULLA
RESTAURANT

VIA PERITANO SOTTO, 3 55020 MOLAZZANA
TELEPHONE/FAX 0583 760052   E-MAIL roavaio@tin.it

OPEN Lunch and dinner   **CLOSED** Monday; March   **CREDIT CARDS** None
ENGLISH SPOKEN A little   **RESERVATIONS** Always recommended, necessary on weekends
PRICE $$ **DIRECTIONS** From Castelnuovo follow signs for Monte Perpoli and Molazzana, then
Alpe di S. Antonio. At the top of the mountain, signs lead to the restaurant

Nestled near the mountaintop, this unpretentious restaurant has a curious history. In 1987 Stefano Bresciani and his sister, Lia, decided to open a restaurant in their village. No suitable buildings were available, and construction was impossible. By chance they learned that prefabricated buildings once used to house earthquake victims were to be sold off. "Large houses were going for a song," recounted Stefano. "You just had to go and get them. We paid less than five dollars for ours." They dismantled it, trucked it to Tuscany and up the mountain, reassembled it—and their restaurant was born. On a clear day the views are spectacular as you drive up the winding roads to the village.

In autumn a cheery fire burns in the fireplace. Unusual homemade antipasti include local *"grifoni"* mushrooms preserved in oil, looking like pale coral; *pomodori acerbi*, pickled green-gold tomatoes; *baccalà sott'olio*, deep-fried salt cod put "under oil"; sliced herbed tongue; and home-cured *salumi*. Primi are hearty: flat pasta sheets sauced with light meat *ragù;* and fresh ricotta and spinach ravioli. *Sformato di cavolfiore* is a savory cauliflower bake.

Rosticciana coi rapini are roast pork ribs served over stewed turnip greens. Veal slices come topped with juicy chunks of porcini. Sheep's cheeses are made by the family, who also grow much of the restaurant's produce. Up on the mountain the atmosphere is informal—after meals, the long wooden tables are used for card games or conversations to while away the mountain evenings.

Camporgiano

MULIN DEL RANCONE
RESTAURANT, BAR

55036 CAMPORGIANO
TELEPHONE/FAX 0583 618670   WEBSITE www.garfprod.it

OPEN Restaurant for lunch and dinner; bar 8:00–24:00   **CLOSED** January and February
CREDIT CARDS Visa, MC   **DIRECT SALE** Yes—shop for specialty foods   **ENGLISH SPOKEN** Yes
FEATURES Eight rooms; mountain refuge; camping; horses; river swimming
RESERVATIONS Recommended   **PRICE** $$ including wine   **DIRECTIONS** The mill can be
reached from both sides of the Serchio River, from Camporgiano or from San Romano; there are signs

Mulin del Rancone is a hub of Garfagnanan activity. Down by the river the rural stone buildings of the former mill house myriad activities: besides a lively restaurant there is a bar, a shop selling local specialty foods, rooms to rent, horses to ride, river pools to swim in . . . the list is endless.

The restaurant offers a chance to taste genuine Garfagnanan cuisine. Mixed antipasti include excellent homemade *sott'olii* and *sott'aceti*, vegetables preserved in oil or vinegar; well-seasoned local *salumi;* and savory tarts and *crostini*. In the

ABOUT FARRO

Farro is the Italian name for one of the world's oldest grains, *Triticum dicoccum.* Its earliest citings date to 6000 B.C.; it was cultivated in Syria and Palestine and by the ancient Egyptians, who used it for soups and rudimentary breads. It eventually spread to other Mediterranean countries, and by the third millennium B.C. it was known as *oliria,* for its pure white flour. The Greeks brought it to Italy. In the Roman Empire, *farro* symbolized honor and glory; it was awarded to heroes. Pliny called it *primus antiquis latio cibus,* "the primary food of Ancient Rome."

Farro is a whole grain rich in fiber and starches, wonderful in soups or stews. Boiled and cooled it forms the basis of salads, replacing rice or other grains. Ground into flour it goes into pasta and bread, alone or with other flours. Some desserts are even made with it.

In English *farro* is often called "spelt wheat," though that is not completely accurate: spelt is *Triticum spelta,* not *Triticum dicoccum.* The *farro* kernel is protected by a thin, dark outer skin that may be polished away to facilitate cooking or grinding. It is now cultivated in only several hundred hectares in Italy, of which one hundred are in the Garfagnana. The plant thrives in poor soils at altitudes of 350 to 1,000 meters (1,000 to 3,200 feet). Most Garfagnana *farro* is organic. A consortium has been formed to safeguard and market the grain.

WHAT TO LOOK FOR

Ideal *farro* grains are an elongated oval, split along one side into two parts. If they have been polished (*brillato*), the color will be mottled, the tan outer skin partially rubbed away to reveal the bright white interior. *Farro* of this type needs no presoaking, though it may be rinsed briefly in warm water before cooking. Unpolished grain needs presoaking and longer cooking. Poor-quality spelt has no floury interior: it is all dark without the white, needs long cooking, and lacks the plump starchiness of fine *farro.* Break a kernel in half crosswise. If it is white inside, it is *farro;* if the outer husk seems empty and dark, it is grain of little culinary interest.

earthy *zuppa di funghi,* sliced porcini mushrooms float in a flavorful broth over a slice of dark country bread. Tortellini are made of whole wheat and *farro* flour, filled with meat and served in broth. Mulin del Rancone has been active in the rebirth of *farro* as one of the area's most important ingredients (see previous page).

Gabriele Bertucci explained why the Garfagnana has a large repertoire of *primi* (first courses) such as soups and pastas, corn polenta, chestnut-flour polenta, and *farro.* "Up here in the mountains the people were very poor," he recounted, "and winters were cold. These simple foods were calorific and kept them warm. Meats were harder to come by." Meat is no longer scarce, but main courses here reflect their humble origins: rabbit is stewed with bitter olives, chicken is fried, and pies are made of vegetables.

Pastries are baked in-house by Enzo Pedreschi, the area's best-loved *pasticciere.* He makes biscuits with chestnut, corn, or *farro* flours. The menu at the mill changes daily, depending on the offerings of the fields and woods and the whims of the charming cooks.

Cappella

TERRE DEL SILLABO
WINE

PONTE DEL GIGLIO 55060 CAPPELLA
TELEPHONE 0583 394487   FAX 0583 395800
E-MAIL clara.giampi@lunet.it

OPEN Sales and visits by appointment only   **CREDIT CARDS** None   **DIRECT SALE** Yes
ENGLISH SPOKEN Yes   **DIRECTIONS** Terre del Sillabo is on the main Lucca-Camaiore road, about 8 kms from Lucca

---

Terre del Sillabo is the new name of the winery that until 2001 was called Le Murelle—a family-run winery that has gained recognition for its modern-style white wines. "When my grandfather bought the property in 1929 as an investment," explained Giampi Moretti, the young man now running the winery, "it was still cultivated under the *mezzadria,* or sharecropping, system. The land was terraced for growing grains, olives, and grapes."

This area has always produced some wine, because before the 1861 unification of Italy, wine could not easily be imported from outside the independent republic of Lucca. "Each state had its own customs point and was tied to its own traditions," said Moretti. "And tradition often leads to stagnation." Since there was steady local demand for unbottled wines, nobody bothered to improve them. Moretti emphasized that Buonamico (see p 58) was the first winery to make any big changes in the area.

When his grandfather died in 1984, Moretti took over. His first task was to oversee the harvest, and he watched in horror as grapes both ripe and rotten were thrown into decaying wooden barrels. "The grapes were squashed semimanually," he recalled, "and it all began to boil away down there. I was appalled. 'Can it be that in this day and age we are still making wine like this?' I asked myself."

He took courses and met a few key people who encouraged him to start from scratch. "From Silvano Formigli, who was responsible for launching Ama [see p 186], I learned there could be nothing accidental about it. Changes had to be programmed and prepared." He did experimental planting to decide which grapes would do best. The answer was clearly whites, so in 1990 he began planting Chardonnay and Sauvignon. "We decided to go for quality, and there was no risk with these internationally popular varieties," he said.

The first bottled vintage was 1993, with immediately encouraging results. The well-balanced Chardonnay, which spends some time in *barriques*, has good structure and a pleasant taste of honey. "Our terrain seems to be giving the grapes enough acidity to be able to benefit from a little aging," Moretti explained. The fine Sauvignon is not matured in wood. There is now also a *cru* of each of these varietals.

Recently Moretti engaged the help of winemaker Alberto Antonini, of Matura, and they are planning to expand the winery's terrain and range of wines. "I felt it was time to try another red, so we are now making Niffo, of Cabernet with a bit of Cabernet Franc, Sangiovese and Colorino," he said. "And soon we will be coming out with a Merlot wine too—it will be a new adventure."

Castelnuovo di Garfagnana

CASEIFICIO BERTAGNI   VIA PROVINCIALE, 9 PONTARDETO 55036 PIEVE FOSCIANO
CHEESE   TELEPHONE 0583 62723   FAX 0583 62846
                                                  E-MAIL caseifbertagni@mclink.it

---

OPEN 8:00–12:00, 15:00–19:30   **CLOSED** Never   **CREDIT CARDS** None   **DIRECT SALE** Yes
ENGLISH SPOKEN A little   **DIRECTIONS** From Castelnuovo go toward San Romano; after about 2 kms, the *caseificio* is signposted on the left

---

This small cheese factory makes cheeses of sheep's, cow's, and goat's milk using local and other Tuscan milk. "My grandfather had his own herd, my father made cheeses, and I followed on from him," explained the soft-spoken young Verano Bertagni. "Though we don't have our own herds anymore."

A range of cheeses is sold in the small shop beside the house, including 100 percent sheep pecorini, mixed sheep's- and cow's-milk cheeses, and fresh cow's-milk *caciotta*. The well-matured pecorino called Tuada, which means "aging cellar" in the local dialect, has a hard grayish surface and a close inner texture with small air bubbles. Its flavor is piquant, almost spicy, with a strong character of sheep's milk. The *semi-stagionato*, aged for sixty days, has a golden-yellow exterior and paler interior—compact and smooth, with a faint sharpness to its taste. Palareto is a creamy, soft *caprino*, or goat's cheese.

OSTERIA VECCHIO MULINO
WINE BAR, SPECIALTY FOODS

VIA VITTORIO EMANUELE, 12
55032 CASTELNUOVO DI GARFAGNANA
TELEPHONE 0583 62192   FAX 0583 65063
WEB SITE www.ilvecchiomulino.com

OPEN 7:30–20:00   **CLOSED** Sunday in winter; holidays variable   **CREDIT CARDS** Visa, MC
DIRECT SALE Yes   **ENGLISH SPOKEN** Yes   **DIRECTIONS** In the town center

Andrea Bertucci is a guiding force of Garfagnana gastronomy. A large, jovial young man with the personable character of a natural host, he has for years been an active promoter of the traditional foods of this distinctive mountain region. His small but lively wine bar is one of the key addresses in the area: nobody travels up or down the mountain valley without stopping in for a glass of wine, a sandwich, or a chat.

His sandwich stuffers are legendary, beginning with the humongous Bologna mortadella (the real bologna), which occupies center stage on its specially built trestle. This he hand-slices to accompany crisp local focaccia or the excellent potato bread made at Tòrrite (see p 65). There are great cheeses, Italian and French, and Andrea's personal pick of Tuscan *salumi*.

Wines are sold by the glass or bottle. The wine list is eclectic: hard-to-find local labels stand beside their better-known Tuscan cousins. Wine tastings and courses are enthusiastically organized by the tireless Andrea. This is a good place to buy the Garfagnana's foods: *farro* wheat, chestnut flour, mushrooms under oil or dried, mountain honey, and local olive oil.

Recent additions to the shop include non–genetically modified ground corn for use in baking or polenta, called Ottofile; the sausages and *biroldo*—a kind of local headcheese that has been singled out by Slow Food as endangered—are made by hand by local butchers Nuttini and Regalati.

Also

CAFFÈ ARIOSTO
PIAZZA UMBERTO I, 2. 0583 62647

If you are hankering for an American-style cocktail, this bar is for you. Walter Borelli is an expert at all the classics, and he even has concocted a few brightly colored specials of his own. Many are fruit-based, with or without alcohol. On Friday and Saturday nights the bar jumps with prediscotheque action, but during the day it functions like every other Italian bar, serving coffee, drinks, snacks, and sandwiches.

Foce Carpinelli

AZIENDA AGRICOLA GABRIELE DAVINI   VIA STATALE, 60 55030 CARPINELLI
FARM PRODUCE   TELEPHONE 0583 611239, 611044

OPEN 8:00–13:00, 15:00–20:00   **CLOSED** Never   **CREDIT CARDS** None   **DIRECT SALE** Yes
ENGLISH SPOKEN A little   **DIRECTIONS** On the main road between Castelnuovo di Garfagnana
and Aulla, 27 kms from Castelnuovo, 30 kms from Aulla

This wonderful farm sells all its own produce: fresh vegetables and fruits, home-made preserves, cheeses, *salumi*, and fresh meats. It is a family-run business, as Gabriele Davini explained: "We do everything ourselves, from rearing the animals to butchering and preparing the meats. We grow grain, grind flour, and bake breads in our wood-burning oven. We have done this all our lives, trying to keep it all on a human scale, our scale." He added with a chuckle, "Our dream is to be completely self-sufficient, and I guess we have come close."

At 840 meters high, the farm overlooks the surrounding mountains and valleys. There are vegetable patches, chicken coops, cow stables, orchards—the classic vision of a real working farm. In autumn the farm shop is fragrant with locally gathered dried mushrooms. Many varieties—with local names such as *grifoni*, *famigliole*, and *galletti*—are preserved in oil. Signora Luciana explained that sixty-eight varieties of chestnuts grow in the Garfagnana woods. Wooden boxes, or "safes," as they are known in dialect, store the farm's flours: chestnut, corn, wheat, and *farro*. There are baskets of flat little pink-red apples, *mela casciana* or *rosina*, that last through winter if kept in straw. Despite their irregular shapes, their perfume is exceptionally fragrant. The Davinis' daughter makes beautiful fruit jellies and the best wild blueberry jam I've tasted.

Of the pork *salumi*, a favorite is the *mortadella nostrale*, or *mondiola*, whose ends are tied around a bay leaf. The deep pink shoulder meat is lean, tender, and well seasoned. It is matured for three months, hanging near a warm fireplace to dry out.

Isola Santa

DA GIACCÒ   VIA DI VALDARNI, 2 55030 ISOLA SANTA
RESTAURANT, BAR   TELEPHONE 0583 667048

OPEN Restaurant for lunch and dinner; bar all day for snacks   **CLOSED** Tuesday; for dinner in
winter if there are no bookings; two weeks in November   **CREDIT CARDS** Visa, MC
ENGLISH SPOKEN Yes   **FEATURES** Outdoor terrace   **RESERVATIONS** For dinner, necessary
in winter   **PRICE** $$ **DIRECTIONS** From Castelnuovo di Garfagnana go toward Arni and
Pietrasanta; after 13 kms, the restaurant is on the left

Isola Santa, the holy island, is a tiny village of gray stone buildings and roofs now perched at the edge of a lake formed by one of the area's many hydroelectric dams. When the valley was flooded the village was abandoned: its population fell to two. Despite this exodus, its restaurant has remained.

Gabriele Mazzei took it over in 1994. "I wanted to serve real local food, as I remembered it from my grandmothers," the soft-spoken chef explained. "Our cuisine used ingredients grown in the mountain fields or foraged from the woods. Simple but wholesome food, without pretensions." Gabriele is re-creating this culinary atmosphere. He serves mountain cheeses, game and country meats, and wild mushrooms and greens.

An autumn lunch in the cozy dining room began with antipasti that included *fettunta*, fragrant toasted bread rubbed with garlic and drizzled with olive oil; truffle-scented coarse-grained pork salame; and corn-yellow grilled polenta with sharp goat's cheese. Homemade tagliatelle were nicely elastic, sauced with woodsy wild mushrooms *in bianco* (no tomato). Soft stone-ground polenta was dressed with melted butter and truffle shavings.

Gabriele explained that the milk of cows grazed in mountain pastures produces more flavorful cheeses and meat than that of cows from lower altitudes. Chops of young goat and lamb came sizzling hot, grilled over a chestnut-wood fire, their flavor intense without being gamy, accompanied by thick slices of deep-fried porcini. For dessert there are home-baked tarts of ricotta or of the sweet walnuts that were once pressed for oil in this region.

Lucca

FORNO AMEDEO GIUSTI   **VIA SANTA LUCIA, 18/20 55100 LUCCA**
BREAD   **TELEPHONE 0583 496285**

OPEN Summer: 8:00–13:00, 16:45–19:45; winter: 8:00–13:00, 16:30–19:30
CLOSED Sunday; Wednesday afternoon in winter; Saturday afternoon in summer; July
CREDIT CARDS None   **ENGLISH SPOKEN** Yes   **DIRECTIONS** Near the Duomo

---

You can buy a slice of this bakery's delicious focaccia right from the street through the shop's sliding window. At *merenda* time (mid-morning or afternoon break) schoolchildren line up with their small change to buy a slice. In addition to the usual salted and olive-oiled version, Giusti makes focaccia olive studded, topped with onions, and unusually sweet with sugar and raisins. Baked fresh every two hours, it is so crisp, crunchy, and warm, you'll end up eating it as you walk home. So buy a little extra, or try some of the bakery's sixty types of bread.

CIOCCOLATERIA CANIPAROLI
CHOCOLATE

VIA SAN PAOLINO, 96 55100 LUCCA
TELEPHONE 0583 53456

OPEN Summer: 9:00–13:00, 16:00–20:00; winter: 9:00–13:00, 15:30–20:00   **CLOSED** Monday in summer; Sunday afternoon and Monday in winter; August   **CREDIT CARDS** None
ENGLISH SPOKEN Yes   **DIRECTIONS** On the street between the Duomo and Piazzale Verdi

A must for chocolate lovers, this austere, stylish little shop opened in 1994 and makes the town's best chocolates. Young chocolate maker and pastry chef Piero Caniparoli trained in France, Belgium, and Switzerland before coming home to set up shop. Using primarily Belgian *couverture*, with 55 to 70 percent cocoa solids, he specializes in filled chocolates, with a nice range of centers.

His ganache fillings are delicate and meltingly creamy: the truffles have an intense richness of flavor; an unusual *fondente al tè* is unmistakably perfumed with Earl Grey. "I aim for chocolates with clear, decisive flavors," Caniparoli explained. A range of milk and white chocolates complements the dark.

Don't expect to find them in June or July, however. In the summer months, Italians switch their passion for chocolates (it's too hot to make them) to cakes and *semifreddi*, frozen desserts. In winter, the shop's cake range is limited to a few delicious but decadent creations.

MARIA PACINI FAZZI
COOKBOOK PUBLISHER

PIAZZA SAN ROMANO, 16
CASELLA POSTALE 173 55100 LUCCA
TELEPHONE 0583 55530   FAX 0583 418245

OPEN Not open to the public   **DIRECT SALE** All of Lucca's bookstores carry the books, as do many others in Tuscany   **MAIL ORDER** Yes   **ENGLISH SPOKEN** Yes

Being a cookbook collector, I spotted Maria Pacini Fazzi's little colored paperback cookbooks as soon as I moved to Italy. They present unusual, genuine local recipes, nicely printed and illustrated; they are not expensive, and several have been translated into English. Maria Pacini Fazzi started publishing thirty years ago. Her subjects include gastronomy, folk culture, philosophy, local history, literature, and Lucchese guides.

"I have always been fascinated by this area's culture," she confirmed. "Our cookery books research authentic recipes from historical documents, and from the people who still carry on these traditions."

English-language titles include *Traditional Recipes of Lucchesian Farmers, Traditional Recipes from Florence,* and *Cooking with Olive Oil,* plus numerous guides to Lucca's culture and countryside. The Italian selection is much wider.

"A people is judged by its food," she observed. "It all depends how you look at what is around you. *La cucina povera* is only poor when made by poor people. Here many people were rich with refined tastes and were able to turn this simple cuisine into something of quality."

PASTICCERIA TADDEUCCI
PASTRY

PIAZZA SAN MICHELE, 34 55100 LUCCA
TELEPHONE 0583 494933

OPEN Summer: 8:00–20:00; winter: 8:00–13:00, 15:00–20:00   **CLOSED** Thursday; ten days in summer
CREDIT CARDS None   **ENGLISH SPOKEN** A little   **DIRECTIONS** In the town's central square

Right behind Lucca's Duomo is Taddeucci's bakery, a Lucchese cornerstone since 1881, when the present owner's great-grandfather founded it. The beautiful wood-paneled and mosaic-tiled shop offers a piece of Lucca as it once was, as well as two of its great pastry specialties.

The most famous is the *buccellato*. Traditionally sold in a round ring (but also baked in a long loaf), this antique sweet yeast bread is flavored with aniseed and golden raisins. Its hard chestnut-brown crust is brushed with sugar syrup before baking. A card suggests how to stuff, toast, top, fry, or steep your *buccellato! Torta di erbe* is a tasty, sweet, spiced vegetable pie, its speckled green filling studded with pine nuts and raisins. It calls for beet greens and parsley, eggs, sugar, spices, and pepper.

Other pastries include seasonal *fave dei morti:* almond-paste confections shaped like fava beans for All Saints' Day. Taddeucci also makes *panforte* and *cantucci* biscuits—good presents to take home.

BUCA DI SANT'ANTONIO
RESTAURANT

VIA DELLA CERVIA, 1/3 55100 LUCCA
TELEPHONE 0583 55881 FAX 0583 312199
E-MAIL la.buca@lunet.it

OPEN Lunch and dinner   **CLOSED** Sunday evening, Monday   **CREDIT CARDS** Visa, MC, Amex
ENGLISH SPOKEN Yes   **RESERVATIONS** Recommended   **PRICE** $$$–$$$$
DIRECTIONS Near the Duomo

This is Lucca's oldest and best-known restaurant, originating in 1782 as an inn. Located close to the Duomo, it is used to dealing with foreigners. The attractive dining room is well appointed, with wooden beams hung with copper pots and walls adorned with spare architectural prints. The service is fairly formal, professional, and fast. Sample the Lucchesia's culinary specialties here: vegetable and grain (especially *farro*) soups, tarts and pastas, wild mushrooms, and grilled meats and game.

Zuppa di farro alla Garfagnina, a substantial soup, features locally grown *farro* (p 48) in a vegetable and bean base with ham and cinnamon; it is very good. *Tortina di funghi,* a puff pastry tartlet, has a salty filling of ricotta and porcini mushrooms. Its flavor is delicately earthy, though my pastry was not quite cooked through. *Tordelli Lucchesi,* handmade pasta cushions, are stuffed with pork, beef, sausage, beet greens, and borage and seasoned with nutmeg. Main courses include T-bone steaks (*la Fiorentina*) grilled over a wood fire; split one between two. Seasonal porcini mushrooms are stewed, fried, or baked in paper, *al cartoccio.*

The restaurant has interesting desserts. Stewed fruit is a mixture of pear, apple, and semidried grapes. Lucca's special *torta di erbe* is surprisingly green, with a sweetly spiced beet-green filling reminiscent of pumpkin pie. Chef Giuliano Pacini said "you would need a book" to list all its ingredients.

DA GIULIO IN PELLERIA   VIA DELLE CONCE, 45 PIAZZA SAN DONATO 55100 LUCCA
RESTAURANT   TELEPHONE/FAX 0583 55948

OPEN Lunch and dinner; third Sunday of each month for the antiques market
CLOSED Sunday and Monday; one week in August   **CREDIT CARDS** Visa, MC, Amex
ENGLISH SPOKEN Yes   **RESERVATIONS** Recommended   **PRICE** $$
DIRECTIONS In the town center, near the San Donato gate in the city wall

---

This large bustling restaurant serves wholesome food at wholesome prices, and it is always packed with locals, students, and travelers. The service is fast, with the cheery atmosphere special to big, busy restaurants.

Try one of Lucca's rustic soups, of *farro* or beans, or *ribollita*—mixed pulses and vegetables soaked up with bread. These are well-cooked, substantial dishes. The *farro*, spelt wheat, in vegetable broth with lentils and potatoes is rich and peppery. A warming dish of loose yellow corn polenta comes in broth with vegetables. The Lucchese's characteristically sweet olive oil is brought separately. Pastas can be ordered as a *tris*—a sampling of three.

Winter main courses are fish or meat based. (Summer features more seafood and salads.) Stockfish topped with stewed sweet onions, and beet greens cooked with squid are served with soft-centered fried polenta. Meats are roasted or stewed with olives. Many are quite salty, as is customary in Tuscany. Desserts include creamy tiramisù, Vin Santo with *cantucci* biscuits, or Lucca's *torta di erbe*— spiced vegetable dessert tart. There are Chianti flasks on each table (pay for what you drink), plus selected Lucchese and Tuscan wines.

ANTICA BOTTEGA DI PROSPERO   VIA SANTA LUCIA, 13 55100 LUCCA
SPECIALTY FOODS: PULSES, SEEDS & GRAINS   TELEPHONE 0583 91198 (HOME NUMBER)

OPEN 8:00–13:00, 16:00–19:30   **CLOSED** Sunday; Wednesday afternoon in winter; Saturday afternoon in summer   **CREDIT CARDS** None   **ENGLISH SPOKEN** A little   **DIRECTIONS** Near the Duomo

---

This old-fashioned shop started out so long ago (it has been in the Marcucci family for more than three hundred years) it has ended up selling the oddest assortment of dried goods—everything from lentils to daffodil bulbs. It is a great source of edible legumes and grains, rices and dried herbs. Sacks of beans, seeds, flours, and nuts line one side of the simple, stylish shop. Goods are sold by weight, scooped out and measured by the friendly staff. Cooking hints are exchanged freely with people waiting to be served. There are pink marbled *borlotti* beans, white *cannellini*, and the rarer *Sorana* and *zolfino* varieties (see pp 76 and 372): more expensive but worth trying to see just how tender and delicate beans can be. Those with vegetable gardens will find seeds for red radicchio, arugula, fennel, and wild field chicory.

Also

FERRAMENTA BARZANTI   VIA SAN PAOLINO, 88

This hardware store stocks a few hard-to-find kitchen items, such as the shallow copper rounds for baking *castagnaccio*, chickpea flour for *farinata*, and the pierced pans used to roast chestnuts over a fire.

IL TRIFOGLIO   VIA ELISA, 31. 0583 493122

This good-size health food store sells organic produce and dried goods, organic dairy products, and tofu, which is hard to find in Italy. It also carries natural cosmetics, macrobiotic ingredients, and freshly baked whole-grain breads.

Montecarlo

ANTICO RISTORANTE FORASSIEPI   VIA DELLA CONTEA, 1 55015 MONTECARLO
RESTAURANT   TELEPHONE 0583 229475   FAX 0583 229476

OPEN Lunch and dinner   **CLOSED** Tuesday, Wednesday lunch   **CREDIT CARDS** Visa, MC
ENGLISH SPOKEN Yes   **FEATURES** Outdoor terrace for summer dining
RESERVATIONS Recommended   **PRICE** $$$–$$$$ **DIRECTIONS** The restaurant is outside the
Porta Nuova gate, east of the town

Valdo Verreschi's recently opened restaurant is just outside Montecarlo, surrounded by olive groves and vineyards. Its fabulous wide outdoor terrace commands a panoramic view over the extensive Val d'Arno. In summer it's a real pleasure to sit over a leisurely lunch or dinner there, cooled by the breeze. Inside, the large stone building has been completely refurbished; it was once an oil mill.

The menu offers seasonal, local dishes cooked with a bit of modern flair. In early spring, polenta comes topped with an earthy sauce of porcini mushrooms; zucchini flowers are stuffed with ricotta; assorted cured meats are of game. Risotto features the great asparagus of nearby Pescia, and pasta comes dressed with a wild boar sauce; local free-range chicken is stewed with olives. Desserts are well made by Sophie Verreschi, who is French. The nicely selected wine list features Tuscan wines, with a spotlight on the best from the local wineries.

FATTORIA DEL BUONAMICO
WINE

VIA PROVINCIALE DI MONTECARLO, 43
55015 MONTECARLO
TELEPHONE/FAX 0583 22038

OPEN Monday–Friday 8:30–12:30, 14:00–19:00; Saturday 8:30–12:30; Saturday afternoon and Sunday by appointment; tastings and cellar visits by appointment   **CLOSED** Sunday
CREDIT CARDS Visa, MC   **DIRECT SALE** Yes   **ENGLISH SPOKEN** Yes
DIRECTIONS From Montecarlo, go toward Altopascio; the Fattoria is on the left after 1 km

---

A trip to the hill town of Montecarlo, with its tiny wooden 1790s theater, should include a visit to its wine producers. The area's wines have been noted for more than a thousand years; its white wines were popular during the Renaissance. In the 1850s, French grape varieties were introduced here by Giulio Magnani; they are now included in Montecarlo Bianco, granted DOC status in 1969.

Fattoria del Buonamico, with its personable director, Vasco Grassi, recently enlarged its modern *cantine* with the sophisticated equipment required for good white wines. The estate has 24 hectares (60 acres) of vineyards. Its white Montecarlo DOC is a blend of 50 percent Trebbiano grapes, with white and gray Pinots, Sauvignon, Sémillon, and Roussanne making up the rest. Vasario, of selected Pinot Bianco grapes, is fermented in small oak *barriques*.

The Fattoria's best red wine is a modern-style *vino da tavola* called Cercatoia Rosso, made only in very good years. Of selected grapes—40 percent Sangiovese, with Syrah, Cabernet Sauvignon and Merlot—it is a full-bodied wine aged in *barriques*. Il Fortino, of Syrah, has also been well received by Italian critics.

A new addition to the list is the late-harvest meditation wine, Oro di Re. This sweet wine—whose name means "the king's gold"—is as delicious with pâté and with cheese as it is by itself.

TRATTORIA "DA BAFFO"
WINE, RESTAURANT

FUSO CARMIGNANI VIA DELLA TINAIA, 7
55015 MONTECARLO
TELEPHONE 0583 22381

OPEN Restaurant May–September for dinner only; winery by appointment   **CLOSED** Monday
CREDIT CARDS None   **DIRECT SALE** Yes   **ENGLISH SPOKEN** A little   **FEATURES** Outdoor dining garden   **RESERVATIONS** Suggested   **PRICE** $$ including wine   **OTHER** A few rooms to rent   **DIRECTIONS** From Fattoria del Buonamico go toward Montecarlo. Turn left onto Via Cercatoia Alta. Turn left on the unpaved road marked Via Tinaia to sign for Fuso Carmignani

---

Gino Carmignani is an eccentric character. He and his parents live on a country farm, make wine, and in summer run a small rustic trattoria serving three home-cooked dishes each evening. "My philosophy has been to bring the world into my back garden," he asserted. "It's the opposite of traveling. People come from all over to eat with us or to buy my wines, especially For Duke."

A major jazz fan and keen winemaker, Gino dedicated his pure Sangiovese wine to Duke Ellington. Believing that great wines are made in the vineyard rather than the cellar, he has invested heavily in intensive plantings.

"I'll never use technology to make wines," he added. "We are the last of the artisans. I vinify in wood, using what I call my 'acoustic' method." Whatever that is, he has earned himself a following—and an evening spent eating and drinking under the Carmignani's medlar tree will never be dull.

Orecchiella

LA GREPPIA
RESTAURANT

ORECCHIELLA 55038 SAN ROMANO
TELEPHONE/FAX 0583 619018
E-MAIL ristorantelagreppia@tin.it

OPEN Lunch and dinner   **CLOSED** Tuesday in winter   **CREDIT CARDS** Visa, MC, Amex
ENGLISH SPOKEN A little   **RESERVATIONS** Always recommended   **PRICE** $$
DIRECTIONS From Castelnuovo, follow signs to Corfino (via Castiglione). The restaurant is signposted from there, about 7 kms from Corfino

This restaurant is high in the Garfagnana mountains, beside a large nature reserve. The views are expansive. In summer you eat in the garden, with space for children to play. Phone before going up: the restaurant sometimes closes for private functions.

Talented owner-chef Mariano Rapaioli makes rustic local fare with a refined touch. *Manafregoli con panna* is a thick soup of chestnut flour, sweet yet smoky from the chestnuts' drying, with liquid cream on top. An individual quiche is given a decisive, salty flavor by *prosciutto Toscano* in fine, well-baked pastry. *Zuppa di farro* is deliciously aromatic: a fine purée of beans is the base for a soup containing plumped *farro*, local spelt wheat grains, whole beans, and herbs. In autumn, mushrooms rather than meat may star as a main course, arriving in a puffed cushion of silver foil—*al cartoccio*. This seals in all the flavor; the thickly sliced mushrooms stew in their juices with oil, garlic, and wild herbs. Other specialties are grilled meats and game. Desserts are elaborate and well made. The restaurant is nicely appointed without being too formal, as befits a mountain refuge.

Pieve di Compito

FRANTOIO SOCIALE
DEL COMPITESE
OLIVE MILL

VIA DEL TIGLIO, 609 55065 PIEVE DI COMPITO
TELEPHONE/FAX 0583 907898
E-MAIL info@coopfrantoiocompitese.it

OPEN Shop 10:00–12:30, 15:00–18:30; mill November and December   **CLOSED** Sunday
CREDIT CARDS None   **DIRECT SALE** Yes   **ENGLISH SPOKEN** A little
DIRECTIONS The *frantoio* is set back from the SS 439 Bientina to Lucca road, between San Leonardo in Treponzio and Colle di Compito

This large *frantoio*, or olive-oil mill, is housed in a modern building with light-green trim clearly visible from the main road. It was built in 1994 by a cooperative of olive growers in the Compitese area. During the season (November and December), growers bring their olives to be milled. Some oil is left to be sold in the mill's large shop, which is also set up for tastings. Other artisan-made products include pasta, organic honey, and local beans. Visitors are welcome.

This *frantoio* operates using the modern stainless-steel "continuous cycle" system, generally agreed to be more hygienic and versatile than the old-fashioned method. The olives, in airy crates, are brought in as soon as possible after picking. They are weighed, washed, and ground between grooved stone cylinders.The pulp is gently heated (indirectly) to 30°–35°C (86°–95°F) and churned before being spun in a centrifuge with some added water; the oil and water mixture are then separated from the ground pits and pulp (*sansa*). In the final procedure, the oil and water are spun in a cold vertical centrifuge, separating the vegetal waters from the finished oil. Filtering is optional.

Pieve Fosciana

MOLINO ERCOLANO REGOLI
FLOUR MILL

MOLINO DI SOTTO 55036 PIEVE FOSCIANA
TELEPHONE 0583 666095

OPEN 8:15–12:30, 15:00–19:00   **CLOSED** Wednesday afternoon, Sunday   **CREDIT CARDS** None
DIRECT SALE Yes   **ENGLISH SPOKEN** No   **DIRECTIONS** Ask anyone in Pieve Fosciana; everyone knows the miller and can point the way

---

Every so often you step into a building and have the sensation of stepping out of time present and into time past. It is a moving experience—but also a little sad. For all the progress that is being made, so much is still being lost, and the hard-won experience of our ancestors is slipping away.

"There used to be many water-powered mills in this area," recalled Ercolano Regoli, the miller. "Each little stream had its own. In those days chestnuts were the staple food. Now our mill is the last one remaining. Since my wife and I have no children, I expect this tradition will end when we retire."

When I was there, in early November, the chestnuts were still in the smoke-houses, not yet ready for milling. But the great pairs of horizontal stone wheels were turning, each in their private cubicle. In one, bright yellow corn was being ground for polenta; in another, white-centered *farro* grains were yielding a flecked flour. The soft-spoken miller moved from one to the other, turning hand wheels to adjust the force of the sluices. The narrow room was alive with the hum of rushing water and spinning stones and filled with a clean, wholesome smell. "When the chestnut season starts we'll work twenty-four hours a day," he confided. "There's quite an art to grinding them: unless they are completely hard and dry, their paste clogs between the stones and burns with the friction. The water is important—we also have electricity here—but water power is slower, it heats less, so the flour remains sweet, not bitter." At the beginning of each season the massive stones are slid apart, their grooves cleaned out, and if necessary, recarved.

The Regoli mill supplies local bakeries with flour. Wheat flours of various grades are for sale, as well as *farro*, chestnut, and yellow corn flours—in large or small quantities. Visitors are welcome, but only a few at a time. The centuries-old building wasn't built with modern tourism in mind.

Ponte a Moriano

LA MORA
RESTAURANT

VIA SESTO DI MORIANO, 1748 55029 PONTE A MORIANO
TELEPHONE 0583 406402   FAX 0583 406135

OPEN Lunch and dinner   **CLOSED** Wednesday; October 10–30   **CREDIT CARDS** Visa, MC, Amex
ENGLISH SPOKEN Yes   **FEATURES** Garden terrace   **RESERVATIONS** Necessary for dinner
PRICE $$$–$$$$ **DIRECTIONS** At Ponte a Moriano cross the bridge toward Sesto di Moriano; the restaurant is signposted

La Mora is an easy drive from Lucca up the valley of the Serchio. It is one of the area's finest restaurants and worth the detour for its genuine Lucchese cuisine. With its two fixed-price tasting menus—regional or seasonal—and an à la carte selection, it is good value for the money. The tasting menus provide seven dishes, plus desserts. If you are planning one special meal in the area, you won't be disappointed here.

The main dining room is an inside-outside kind of space—a large glassed-in cube situated in a verdant garden that backs enigmatically onto a train line. In summer there is a trellis-covered patio. The restaurant is owned and run by Sauro Brunicardi. A tall, distinguished man, he explains the menu and takes the orders. A sommelier serves the wines from a fine selection in all price ranges; they are also sold at retail in the restaurant's shop. The service is gracious and efficient.

Antipasti include a coral unmolded *budino,* or custard, of red peppers with a light Gruyère-flavored béchamel and a vegetable-stuffed puff pastry with a light herb sauce. A pure cool salad of plump *farro* grains is tossed with outstandingly fruity Lucchese olive oil (characteristically sweet), finely minced fresh green olives, and tiny tomato chunks; its success is entirely a result of the fine local ingredients.

The inspired *pan di fagiano,* literally pheasant "bread," is adapted from Pellegrino Artusi's *La scienza in cucina e l'arte di mangiar bene* (Science in the kitchen and the art of eating well), his classic cookbook of 1891. A scoop of the warm *pan*— finely minced pheasant, its juices beaten into a stiff béchamel—is served on a little toast with a tangy salad of grated carrots, green tomatoes, and red radicchio.

Of the *primi,* ricotta and spinach-filled ravioli with a fresh marjoram sauce of are light and aromatic. The fine pasta is still cranked by hand by the elderly Signora Brunicardi. *Risotto sulla pernice,* a creamy partridge risotto, is enriched with pieces of meat and the bird's pan juices. Autumnal main courses in Tuscany often feature game. A hearty stew of wild boar is set off by sweet and sour green olives and served with fried polenta wedges. Delicious desserts end the meal.

San Gennaro

FATTORIA DI FUBBIANO	55010 SAN GENNARO
OLIVE OIL, WINE	TELEPHONE 0583 978011 FAX 0583 978344

OPEN Visits and tastings by appointment only   **CLOSED** Saturday and Sunday
CREDIT CARDS Visa, MC   **DIRECT SALE** Yes   **ENGLISH SPOKEN** Yes
OTHER Vacation houses available   **DIRECTIONS** From the main SS 435, follow the yellow signs from either Lappato or Gragnano

---

Lucca is better known for its oil than for its wine. While the nearby town of Montecarlo is noted for its whites, the Colline Lucchesi are associated with a Chianti-like red that gained early DOC status in 1968.

Anyone interested in how the old-fashioned *governo Toscano* works should visit this estate in autumn. In this largely outmoded winemaking technique, selected grapes are picked before the main harvest, hung indoors on racks to dry for several weeks, and then added into the newly fermented wine to induce a secondary fermentation. "By mid-November the dried grapes are ready to use," explained Sauro Corsini, the farm's longtime manager. "They are destalked and stirred into the new wine, in a ratio of 4 kgs [8.8 lbs] of grapes to 100 liters [26.6 gallons] of wine. The *governo* makes the wine ready to drink sooner. It is costly and difficult, but it can add perfumes to the wine if aromatic grapes are used." The fermentation is slow, lasting until mid-February. When the wine is decanted, a thick layer of sediment remains.

The Fattoria, with a beautiful eighteenth-century villa at its nucleus, now belongs to Giampiero de Andreis, a Milanese medical publisher. He and his wife are enthusiastically restoring the estate, modernizing the winemaking, and producing good olive oil.

Segromigno Monte

FATTORIA MANSI BERNARDINI   VIA DI VALGIANO, 34 55018 SEGROMIGNO MONTE
OLIVE OIL   TELEPHONE 0583 921721   FAX 0583 929701
E-MAIL fmbsas@tin.it

OPEN 8:30–17:30   **CLOSED** Saturday and Sunday   **CREDIT CARDS** None
DIRECT SALE Yes, by appointment   **MAIL ORDER** Possible for large orders
ENGLISH SPOKEN Yes   **OTHER** Vacation houses for rent   **DIRECTIONS** From Segromigno's old church, go west past Bar Puccini for 200 meters. At T-junction turn right, go over a small hill, then turn right again; the Fattoria is after about 500 meters. Or ask at Bar Puccini

---

Lucca's grand and historic country villas are famous. Many make fine olive oil, as the hills are well suited for it, positioned between the sea and the mountains. The Mansi Bernardini estate is no exception. Its olive groves are among the best tended I have seen, with rows of healthy young plants growing out of a perfect green lawn. "We keep grass in our olive groves partly for aesthetic reasons," explained Marcello Salom, the estate's owner, "and partly because the European Community gives incentives for banning weed-killers. It certainly looks nicer this way."

The estate has modernized its olive-picking techniques. High handheld "combs" driven by compressed air coax the olives from the trees, dropping them into nets stretched below. Very few trees are worked at a time, so the olives are milled as quickly as possible at the nearby *frantoio*.

Lucca's oil is considered among Tuscany's best. Its sweetness places it between the lighter Ligurian oils and the more intense, fiery oils from farther south. I was lucky to sample Salom's oil freshly milled. A bright yellow-green (oils lose some of this vividness after a few months), it has a clear, fresh perfume of freshly cut grass, a sweet fruity taste, and only a light pepperiness in the finish.

Sillicagnana

ANGELA PIERONI   VIA PROVINCIALE PER SILLICAGNANA 55038 SILLICAGNANA
HONEY   TELEPHONE 0583 62944

OPEN Saturday and Sunday, or by appointment   **CREDIT CARDS** None   **DIRECT SALE** Yes
ENGLISH SPOKEN A little   **DIRECTIONS** Look for the sign on main road between Sillicagnana and San Romano

---

Angela Pieroni makes honey because she loves bees. "I was a housewife, but I had always been fascinated by bees," the vivacious Angela told me. "The hardest part was convincing my husband to help me—he was afraid of the bees at first. But I won him over." They started in 1983, using positioned hives (unlike the "nomadic" system, in which hives are moved to flowering areas). Angela produces a prize-winning pure acacia honey containing more than 90 percent of that flower's nectar.

The acacia is in bloom for fifteen to twenty days; when the blossoms fade, the hives are emptied.

"With acacia it is easy to tell," she confided. "No other honey is as clear or as light in color." Hers is a pale watery yellow, with the consistency of thick corn syrup and a remarkably subtle taste, not overly sweet, with a wonderfully delicate sensation of flowers. By contrast, *castagne* (chestnut) is much more forceful, deep in color and in taste. Other varieties include *erica* (broom) and *mille fiori*—literally, a thousand flowers.

Also

GARFAGNANA COOP   VIA PROVINCIALE, 9. 0583 613242

This cooperative was formed in 1994 to reclaim the increasing number of abandoned fields in the Garfagnana. "Well-cultivated land in our grandparents' day was now overgrown with weeds," explained Lorenzo Satti. "So we planted spelt wheat, *farro*, the Garfagnana's special grain." They registered with AIAB, the Italian organic growers' association. Other products they sell use wild fruits and berries, mushrooms, and chestnuts from the woods. The cooperative's *farro* and fruits can be bought in Castelnuovo.

Tofori

FATTORIA VILLA MAIONCHI   55010 TOFORI
OLIVE OIL, WINE   TELEPHONE 0583 978194   FAX 0583 978345
                                          E-MAIL info@fattoriamaionchi.it

OPEN Sales: summer 8:00–12:00, 14:30–18:30; winter 8:00–12:00, 13:30–17:30; cellar visits and tastings by appointment only   CLOSED Sunday   CREDIT CARDS Visa, MC   DIRECT SALE Yes   ENGLISH SPOKEN Yes   OTHER Weekly rentals available   DIRECTIONS Tofori is not on the Touring Club map, but it is located off the SS 435 between San Gennaro and Zone. The Fattoria is well signposted in the area

The seventeenth-century Villa Maionchi has everything: frescoed interiors, great views of Lucca's plain, a formal garden, landmarked farm buildings, wonderful olive oil, underground wine cellars—even a ghost. "He's called the Colonel," volunteered Maria Pia Maionchi. "And after I experienced him for myself I named our grappa after him!" Maria Pia's husband, who looks as if he stepped out of a Renaissance painting, smiled and shrugged.

The farm produces a range of wines from 11 hectares (27 acres) of vineyards, improving now with a winemaker. The unusual Rubino di Selvata is of pure Muscat of Hamburg grapes. Collegrosso is a Sangiovese, while Toforino is a fragrant white of Vermentino and Malvasia.

Their olive oil is wonderful, made of hand-picked olives stone ground in an old-fashioned *frantoio* at San Gennaro and extracted in a stacked "castle" press. The oil, which is sold in half-liter bottles, is fresh and fruity, with a delicacy and sweetness that is special to Lucca's hills. The family is active in promoting tourism in the area and offers various kinds of visits and tastings.

Tòrrite

PANIFICIO RENATA GINESTRI
BREAD

VIA DEL BAGNO, 3
TÒRRITE 55032 CASTELNUOVO DI GARFAGNANA
TELEPHONE 0583 62613

OPEN 7:00–13:00, 15:00–19:00   **CLOSED** Wednesday afternoon, Sunday; June or July
CREDIT CARDS None   **ENGLISH SPOKEN** A little   **DIRECTIONS** The shop is at the far end of
Tòrrite, coming from Castelnuovo, by the river, off the main road

Renata Ginestri makes one of Tuscany's best breads. Known as *pane scuro, pane rustico,* or *pane di patate,* it is a dense, moist bread with a nicely chewy nut-brown crust. The loaves are round or oval, and as you cut into them the aroma is like old-fashioned sourdough. It is made in two versions: with white "O" flour or with deeper-toned stone-ground grain.

"This type of bread was typical here," Signora Renata explained from behind her flour-dusted counter, "but we are the only ones still baking it in the traditional way. The secret of its moistness is in the mashed potato that is added to the flour, giving the bread its faint sweetness and keeping it fresh for days. It requires long rising using natural yeasts." Her focaccia and *pasimata,* the local Easter bread, are also excellent.

Vinchiana

FRANTOIO BIANCHI
OLIVE MILL

55050 VINCHIANA
TELEPHONE 0583 965276

OPEN Mid-November to mid-January; sales by appointment   **CREDIT CARDS** None
DIRECT SALE Yes   **ENGLISH SPOKEN** No   **DIRECTIONS** From Ponte a Moriano, go straight
toward the Garfagnana. Just after the sign into Vinchiana, turn right on the small road immediately past
the small bridge on the right, at a curve. The *frantoio* is on the left after the road curves to the right

This small, private *frantoio* processes some of the area's best olives. It operates traditional-style *macine* (stone wheels) for grinding. After washing, the olives are ground to a pulp; the paste is churned as it is heated slightly and indirectly before being spun in a centrifuge to separate the oil and vegetable water from the mass. A final spin separates the oil from the water. You can visit the *frantoio* during the season. If you phone ahead, it is also possible to buy oil directly.

CHAPTER 3

Pistoia and Mount Abetone

*P*istoia is one of Tuscany's better-kept secrets. Its walled center, with the handsome medieval *piazza del Duomo* at its heart, is lovely—yet it is less visited than Arezzo or Pisa. I like its human scale: you can walk comfortably from one side of town to the other. Beside the Duomo are interesting narrow streets, with the small marketplace, known as La Sala, selling foods of all kinds.

Pistoia is set against the Apennines, the mountain range that divides Tuscany from the north of Italy. Its highest mountain resort, on Mount Abetone (1,388 meters/4,555 feet), is popular for winter skiing. It is reached by a curvy road that was built in 1777 to link the territories of the grand dukes of Tuscany and Modena. In summer and autumn the majestic forests are full of wild berries, mushrooms, and chestnuts; the area's most typical cuisine makes use of these "spontaneous" foods.

Anyone interested in spa towns should visit Montecatini Terme, a rather grand late-nineteenth-century town built to accommodate those who "took the waters." The mineral salt–rich water's effects are (rapidly) purgative. To compensate, the town offers a host of biscuit, pastry, candy, and ice-cream shops, restaurants, and wine bars.

AZIENDA PROMOZIONE TURISTICA
PIAZZA DUOMO, 4
51100 PISTOIA
TELEPHONE 0573 21622
FAX 0573 34327
E-MAIL apt12pistoia@tin.it

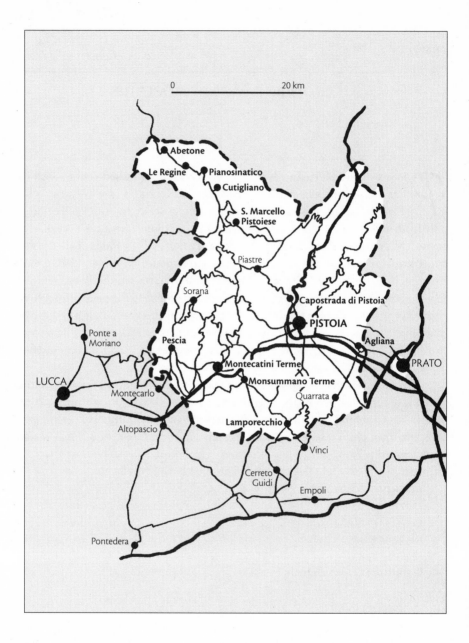

Boldface type indicates towns that are included in this chapter.

Abetone

IL CHICCO
PASTRY

VIA BRENNERO, 494 51021 ABETONE
TELEPHONE 0573 606869

OPEN 7:00–20:00   **CLOSED** Tuesday; May, June, and October   **CREDIT CARDS** None
ENGLISH SPOKEN A little   **DIRECTIONS** The shop is on the lower level of Via Brennero
in the center of town

This *pasticceria* is the young skiers' favorite. In winter, *bomboloni*, deep-fried pastry balls, are filled with jam, chocolate, or custard and served piping hot. In summer, the *gelato al cartoccio* is served with a fragrant hot fruit sauce.

Agliana

ROBERTO CATINARI
ARTE DEL CIOCCOLATO
CHOCOLATE

VIA PROVINCIALE, 378 51031 AGLIANA
TELEPHONE 0574 718506

OPEN 8:00–13:00, 15:30–19:30   **CLOSED** Sunday; Monday in summer; Monday morning in
winter; August   **CREDIT CARDS** None   **ENGLISH SPOKEN** A little
DIRECTIONS The shop is on the main provincial Pistoia–Prato road at Agliana

Roberto Catinari is one of Tuscany's leading chocolate *maestri*. With his long gray beard and twinkling eyes, he might have stepped out of the chocolate factory in a child's fairy tale. Trained in Switzerland, he started his own business in Italy in 1974. He currently makes more than one hundred different *cioccolatini*, filled chocolates.

Catinari also specializes in liqueur- and wine-filled chocolates, including Vin Santo and Chianti Classico. As you bite into them the sugar crystal lining gives way to a warm, heady fullness that complements the dark chocolate casing. Just be sure to bite on them once they are completely in your mouth—not before!

Catinari starts with high-quality *couverture* chocolate from Belgium, Switzerland, or France, with a cocoa-solids content of up to 85 percent. He blends this with cocoa solids from the Ivory Coast or Ecuador for his finest bitter chocolate. Milk chocolate comes from Lindt in Switzerland. Fine Piemontese hazelnut paste is used in his *gianduja*.

I particularly liked Catinari's *torta di Bardalone*—a dense, rich chocolate paste with an almost smoky depth to it, studded with almonds, hazelnuts, and tangy candied orange and citron peel. This tribute to *panforte* comes in discs of 500 grams, wrapped in crisp red cellophane.

At Eastertime, sculpted eggs can be commissioned to enclose a surprise gift of the customer's choosing. The shop is inhabited by endearing chocolate animals and unlikely cocoa-covered "rusty" tools.

MACELLERIA SALUMIFICIO MARINI
MEAT: SALUMI

VIA SELVA, 313 FERRUCCIA 51030 AGLIANA
TELEPHONE/FAX 0574 718119

OPEN 8:00–13:00; also Friday 16:30–20:00 in summer; Friday and Saturday 16:30–19:30 in winter
CLOSED Sunday; two weeks in August   **CREDIT CARDS** Visa, MC   **MAIL ORDER** Yes
ENGLISH SPOKEN A little   **DIRECTIONS** From the Prato Ovest exit on the A11 *autostrada*, go toward Quarrata and Ferruccia 3 kms, then follow signs

Marini's is the quintessential butcher's shop: spotlessly clean, odorless, with walls of cheerful red and white tiles, and handsome marble counters. *Salumi* are hand-made: "There must be a separate room for each stage of the curing procedure," explained Adriano Marini, "with designated temperature and humidity levels. The freshly butchered meat goes in one end and travels through them as it is 'transformed'—cut, salted, spiced, and dried."

Using local country pigs, the Marini family produces many regional specialties. The refined prosciutto is aged for twelve months; a deep salmon pink, it is only a hint saltier than its Parma cousin. The coarse-grained, fennel-scented *finocchiona* is made of lean shoulder meat and fat from the jowl. It is eaten very fresh. Many of Marini's *salumi* are available vacuum-packed for easy transportation. The fresh meat counter showcases excellent beef, corn-fed free-range Comet chickens (*pollo nostrale*), and tender milk-fed lamb.

Marini supplies some of Tuscany's best restaurants, whose owners like to come personally to select their goods and to visit the affable family. It is not unusual to find them there, late in the afternoon, sampling *salumi* with a glass of good wine. Adriano's brother, Claudio Marini, has a butcher's shop at Via Statale, 317 at Olmi, with the same hours.

ENOTECA CARLO LAVURI
WINE STORE, SPECIALTY FOODS

VIA PROVINCIALE 154/G SPEDALINO 51031 AGLIANA
TELEPHONE 0574 751366, 751125   FAX 0574 751366
E-MAIL calavuri@tin.it

OPEN 8:30–13:00, 15:30–20:00   **CLOSED** Sunday; two weeks in August
CREDIT CARDS Visa, MC, Amex   **MAIL ORDER** Yes   **ENGLISH SPOKEN** Yes
DIRECTIONS Take Via Provinciale, the main road from Pistoia toward Prato. The shop is on the outskirts of Spedalino, before you reach Agliana. It is on the ground floor of a modern building, set back from the road, on the right

"You need to educate your vineyard as you would a child," declared Carlo Lavuri, this wine store's friendly owner. "Things are changing fast in Tuscan wines. The natural conditions were always there, but we are now making the most of their potential—and tasting the results."

Lavuri's excitement for his subject is contagious. The modern, clean-lined shop is stocked with several hundred labels, most of them Italian, many Tuscan. Tastings are held regularly; Lavuri is happy to discuss and recommend wines from the best big and small producers. There is a fine selection of Tuscan estate-bottled olive oils, and many hard-to-find specialty foods, including the authentic *aceto balsamico tradizionale di Modena*—costly vinegar, but worth every penny. The shop also serves excellent coffee.

Also

GELATERIA BAR ANISARE   VIA ROMA, 93. 0574 718490

This small *gelateria* makes very fine fresh-fruit ices and gelati. It is open late and has tables out on the shady sidewalk in summer.

Capostrada di Pistoia

GASTRONOMIA CAPECCHI   VIA DALMAZIA, 445 51033 CAPOSTRADA DI PISTOIA
SPECIALTY FOODS: DELICATESSEN   TELEPHONE 0573 400208
E-MAIL capecchisnc@freemail.it

OPEN 7:00–13:30, 16:30–20:00   **CLOSED** Sunday; Saturday afternoon in summer; Wednesday afternoon in winter; August   **CREDIT CARDS** None   **ENGLISH SPOKEN** A little
DIRECTIONS From the northwest corner of the town of Pistoia, take Via Dalmazia (SS 66) north toward Abetone and Bologna for 3.5 kms until it crosses SS 64 at Capostrada; the shop is at that junction

---

This gastronomic treasure trove has been run by the Capecchi family since 1908. They make their own bread, cakes, and ready-to-eat dishes and sell many of Tuscany's finest artisan-made foods.

Of the founder's grandchildren, Piero is the baker, and Stefano and Cinzia make the prepared foods. Classic Tuscan breads include a rustic *focaccia all'olio di oliva,* baked on oven bricks, and excellent *cantucci* biscuits using a nineteenth-century recipe. The prepared foods change daily but always include *primi*—hearty soups or pastas—and a range of *secondi,* from stewed *baccalà* (salt cod) to baked chickpeas or beans.

The display cases contain yellow bags of Martelli's excellent pasta (p 129), pasta sauces from Grosseto, Florentine oils, goat cheeses from Ville di Corsano (p 301), ash-cured Pienza pecorini, *lardo* from Colonnata (p 33), great *salumi* from nearby Marini (p 70), and much more.

Cutigliano

DA FAGIOLINO
RESTAURANT

VIA CAREGA, 1 51024 CUTIGLIANO
TELEPHONE 0573 68014

OPEN Lunch and dinner   **CLOSED** Tuesday evening and Wednesday in winter; November
CREDIT CARDS Amex, DC   **ENGLISH SPOKEN** Yes   **RESERVATIONS** Recommended
PRICE $$–$$$ **DIRECTIONS** In the village center

Da Fagiolino has been a keystone of local mountain fare for more than fifty years. This is a good place for a rustic country lunch after a hike in the woods. Specializing in seasonal wild mushrooms, chestnuts, and game, the menu also offers freshwater fish from nearby streams. As antipasti, the selection of *salumi di selvaggina* may include cured wild boar or venison, and the *crostini di funghi porcini* are flavorful and hearty. Porcini appear again in soups, risotti, polenta, or pasta sauces, and they come deep-fried. Main courses include roast lamb, rabbit, and goat. The experienced waitresses are friendly and efficient, the tablecloths perfectly pressed, and the glassed-in terrace offers views of the neighboring hills.

Also

LATTERIA TIZIANA PAGLIAI

VIA PACIONI, 17. 0573 68280

This small store stocks the Pistoiese Apennines' best offerings: exceptional sheep's-milk ricotta and pecorini made near the shop by Anita Fini or Giovanni Ricci, local honeys and wild berry jams, dried herbs, flavored oils, and pasta sauces.

Lamporecchio

OLEIFICIO COOPERATIVO MONTALBANO
OLIVE MILL

VIA GIUGNANO, 135
51030 LAMPORECCHIO
TELEPHONE 0573 803210/1   FAX 0573 800175

OPEN 8:00–12:00, 14:00–18:00   **CLOSED** Saturday afternoon, Sunday   **CREDIT CARDS** None
DIRECT SALE Yes   **MAIL ORDER** Yes   **ENGLISH SPOKEN** A little   **FEATURES** Guided tours
and tastings by appointment   **OTHER** The cooperative's other mill is in Via Beneventi,
Vinci tel/fax 0571 56247   **DIRECTIONS** The *frantoio* is just outside Lamporecchio on the road
toward Larciano and Montecatini Terme

This is the modernized *frantoio*, or olive mill, of a large cooperative with 1,850 members (*partitari*), who are offered a choice between the traditional grinding stone and modern temperature-controlled centrifuge systems. The stainless-steel machinery is easily cleaned and therefore more hygienic; temperatures for each phase may also be controlled. Batches are always analyzed and tested before being bottled or blended.

Under the name Montalbano Agricola Alimentare Toscana, the cooperative sells several grades of extra-virgin oil, extracted from 100 percent Tuscan olives with an acidity level below 0.5 percent. The cooperative runs another *frantoio* in the town of Vinci. Both have shops selling their members' oils and may be visited.

Le Regine

L'ERBOLAIO   **VIA BRENNERO, 112 CECHETTO 51021 ABETONE**
SPECIALTY FOODS: FRUIT PRODUCTS   **TELEPHONE 0573 60514**

OPEN 9:00–13:00, 14:00–17:00 (later in August)   **CLOSED** Never   **CREDIT CARDS** None
MAIL ORDER Yes   **ENGLISH SPOKEN** No   **DIRECTIONS** The shop is on SS 12 from San Marcello Pistoiese to Abetone, at Cechetto, on the right as you go up

This enterprising cooperative was formed in 1980 to process the wild berries growing in the magnificent mountain woods. About thirty people, mostly women, pick the wild raspberries, blueberries, and blackberries. They also gather mushrooms. Strawberries come from a local grower.

"The competition is fierce," one woman explained. "You have to get up at the crack of dawn and walk for miles to find the best fruit, or your neighbor will beat you to it."

The fruit is pesticide free; no artificial colorants or preservatives are used. The jams contain fruit and sugar in equal parts. I liked some better than others: the blueberry *confettura* is very good, with tiny whole berries in a delicately flavored jelly; the dark red *fragola* jam is sweeter and contains nice whole fruits; the puréed blackberry jam is overcooked and oversweet. *Bibita al lampone* is an intensely fruity, crimson raspberry drink. It is highly concentrated but would be refreshing diluted with water or soda.

L'Erbolaio makes an unsweetened extract of blueberries. The local *mirtilli* (*Vaccinium myrtillus*) are smaller and more flavorful than their domestic counterparts. They apparently have curative powers: this pasteurized extract is a tonic for the eyesight and circulation, taken by the spoonful. The shop also provides gastronomic souvenirs of gift packages and miniatures.

IL BAGGIOLO   **VIA BRENNERO, 355 LE REGINE 51020 ABETONE**
SPECIALTY FOODS: FRUIT PRODUCTS   **TELEPHONE 0573 606644**

OPEN 9:00–13:00, 14:30–18:30   **CLOSED** Wednesday   **CREDIT CARDS** None
MAIL ORDER Yes   **ENGLISH SPOKEN** A little   **DIRECTIONS** The shop is on SS 12 from San Marcello Pistoiese to Abetone, about 3.5 kms before Abetone, on the left going up

Like l'Erbolaio (see preceding entry), this little shop features products made from wild berries. Specializing in fruit-flavored grappas, liqueurs, and jams, they also carry a handful of other local products: honey, pecorino, fruit biscuits, and hand-made soaps. For those who enjoy novelty items, fruit alcohols in decorative bottles come in a rainbow of colors and flavors—raspberry, blueberry, rose petal, rue, and walnut.

Monsummano Terme

**SLITTI CAFFÈ
E CIOCCOLATO**
CHOCOLATE, COFFEE, BAR

VIA FRANCESCA SUD, 240 51015 MONSUMMANO TERME
TELEPHONE/FAX 0572 640240
WEB SITE www.slitti.it

OPEN 7:00–13:00, 15:00–20:00   **CLOSED** Sunday; August 10–20   **CREDIT CARDS** None
MAIL ORDER Yes   **ENGLISH SPOKEN** Yes   **DIRECTIONS** From the Montecatini exit of
A11 *autostrada,* go to Monsummano Terme, then toward Fucecchio. Slitti is 1 km out of the center of Monsummano

Take one step into this elegant marble shop and you will be overwhelmed by the aroma of fresh coffee and chocolate. The Slitti family has made its name selling select coffees, with a penchant for 100 percent pure Arabica (which naturally contains about 50 percent less caffeine than other coffees). In 1988 the talented young Andrea Slitti devoted himself to another, complementary, passion: chocolate. In 1994 he won first prize for artistic presentation at the Grand Prix International de la Chocolaterie in Paris, and he has since collected a wall full of other prizes.

Slitti's chocolate creations are a delight to the senses: beautifully presented, their heady perfume precedes a rich taste experience. Slitti starts from a bitter paste of 70 percent Central American and 30 percent African cocoa, making *ciocco-latini,* nut-centered *dragees,* imaginative Easter eggs, bitter chocolate bars (the bitterest has 100 percent cocoa solids), and his signature bittersweet coffee spoons. A cluster of cocoa-dusted "rusty" tools pays homage to the local *maestro,* Roberto Catinari (p 69).

Grani d'Arabica, chocolate-covered coffee beans, are excellent. Bite down through the shiny bittersweet chocolate to a barely resistant Arabica bean, custom-toasted to be tender and aromatic. *Slittosa,* a glossy hazelnut-cocoa spread, is Slitti's refined answer to the Italian staple Nutella. Lattenero, a recent line of superior milk-chocolate bars, is graded by percentages of cocoa solids.

Andrea Slitti is charming and enthusiastic; a perfectionist who loves his work. His family's newly enlarged shop merits a detour, whether to sample the hand-made chocolates, to admire the imaginative Christmas or Easter "themes" or the giant hand-painted ceramic coffee jars made by the Taccini brothers (see p 121) with the history of coffee woven into the *"raffaelesco"* decoration, or just to enjoy a fragrant *caffè* at the bar.

Montecatini Terme

PASTICCERIA BARGILLI
PASTRY

VIALE GROCCO, 2 51016 MONTECATINI TERME
TELEPHONE/FAX 0572 79459
WEB SITE www.italyquality.com

OPEN 8:00–13:00, 15:30–20:00   **CLOSED** Monday in winter; January   **CREDIT CARDS** None
MAIL ORDER Yes   **ENGLISH SPOKEN** A little
DIRECTIONS The shop is just off Viale Verdi, in the town center

Le cialde are Montecatini's most popular souvenir. The sweet, crunchy biscuits are a favorite antidote to the purgative effects of Montecatini's waters. Bargilli's has been making them since 1936, when Paolo Bargilli's father bought the business. "*Era una cosa empirica*. It was a matter of trial and error," explains Paolo. "Over time we modified and refined the *cialde* to arrive at the present biscuit."

Cialde are made by sandwiching crushed almonds and sugar between two host-thin wafer disks. They contain only sugar, flour, milk, eggs, and top-quality almonds from Puglia. The result is a brittle golden disk like a medallion, just an eighth-inch thick. The wafer batter is press-molded as it cooks and heated again to bind it with the filling.

PASTICCERIA DESIDERI
PASTRY

VIA GORIZIA, 5 (PIAZZETTA BICCHIERAI)
51016 MONTECATINI TERME
TELEPHONE 0572 71088

OPEN 8:30–13:00, 16:00–20:00   **CLOSED** Monday in winter; February   **CREDIT CARDS** None
MAIL ORDER Yes   **ENGLISH SPOKEN** No   **DIRECTIONS** In the town center

Montecatini is famous for two kinds of biscuits, *brigidini* and *cialde*. And two *pasticcerie* in town stand out as making the best: Desideri and Bargilli.

Stefano Desideri's grandfather was making *brigidini* (also claimed by the nearby town of Lamporecchio as their specialty) before 1900, and by 1918 he had won prizes with them at international fairs. Crisp, wavy wafers delicately flavored with anise, the classic *brigidini* are baked for only a few seconds and are light as air. They contain sugar, eggs, flour, and extract of aniseed. Once made by hand, they are now made on machines designed by Signor Desideri that are so secret he did not want me to see them. If kept in airtight containers, the fragile biscuits last for several months; they are traditionally served with ice-cream or soft fruit desserts. Desideri also makes a very good version of the *cialde* (see above), sold loose or in attractive tins with art nouveau decorations.

FAGIOLI DI SORANA—TUSCANY'S FINEST BEANS

Tuscany is famous for its *fagioli* (beans), and its most celebrated are the pearly white *fagioli di Sorana*. These flat, oval, shiny beans are remarkably thin skinned, and they have long been a favorite delicacy of the rich and famous who visit Montecatini Terme, just a few kilometers from the village for which they are named. They are thought to be descended from the *bianco di Spagna*, a larger, white, Spanish bean.

Valdo Verreschi, cook (see p 57) and author of a book on the beans, explained: "The origins of our bean are shrouded in mystery. Legend has it that, centuries ago, a caravan of pilgrims was passing along this valley on its way to Rome, when a big storm broke out. A sack split, and the beans were scattered and washed up along the small River Pescia. Its silty bed proved a perfect breeding ground for the beans, which rot in heavier soils." Indeed, to this day, the *fagioli* are watered using small irrigation canals of river water, *le gore.*

Sorana is a tiny village set high up above the river valley, and today only a handful of country people still grow the beans. They are cultivated in grooves (*solchi*) and trained up high poles. The small beans are partially dried while still on the plant; the pods are then removed.

"Once, these beans were considered a *brutto legume*—the poorest of poor foods," Verreschi went on. "Today, they satisfy the most refined palates." The traditional way to cook them is in a wine flask: the *fiasco* is filled partway with beans and water and seasoned with oil, sage, and salt. The bottle is loosely corked and placed beside wood embers for at least three hours.

ENOTECA GIOVANNI
RESTAURANT

VIA GARIBALDI 25/27 51016 MONTECATINI TERME
TELEPHONE 0572 73080   FAX 0572 71695

OPEN Lunch and dinner   **CLOSED** Monday; two weeks in August
CREDIT CARDS Visa, MC, Amex   **ENGLISH SPOKEN** Yes   **FEATURES** Outdoor dining terrace open on summer evenings   **RESERVATIONS** Recommended   **PRICE** $$$–$$$$
DIRECTIONS In the town center

Giovanni Rotti has been a restaurateur since 1984. His Enoteca comprises a high-class restaurant with creative cooking on one side and a less formal *enoteca* serving hearty Tuscan food on the other. The elegant restaurant has a modern feel, with a large wall of wines as the primary decoration. Giovanni is a true wine expert and enthusiast, and both sides of his restaurant draw on the 12,000 great wines he has in his cellar. The rustic *enoteca* has wooden tables, with hams and sausages on display. This is a good place to taste artisan cheeses or have a plate of pasta with your wine.

In the restaurant, antipasti range from raw fish to a delicate Parmesan soufflé. In eary spring, tiny *calamaretti* were served in a subtle broth with fresh arugula and cherry tomatoes. A few of the first *funghi porcini* were at their best simply sautéed. A fillet of red mullet worked well in a tangy (and pretty) blood-orange sauce. Pigeon breast was seared and fanned on the plate, delicately flavored with rosemary. Desserts are accomplished. The friendly service at Giovanni's is professional—as is everything in this successful, old-school restaurant.

Also

PASTICCERIA GIOVANNINI   CORSO MATTEOTTI, 4. 0572 79848

This great sixties-style bar is the place in town for a great coffee, fine pastry, or *cioccolatino*—a filled chocolate. Signor Giovannini is one of the area's *maestri* at making beautiful chocolates.

Pescia

RISTORANTE CECCO   VIA FORTI, 96/98 51017 PESCIA
RESTAURANT   TELEPHONE 0572 477955

OPEN Lunch and dinner   **CLOSED** Monday; two weeks in January; July
CREDIT CARDS Visa, MC, Amex   **ENGLISH SPOKEN** A little   **FEATURES** Outdoor terrace
RESERVATIONS Recommended on weekends   **PRICE** $$$ **DIRECTIONS** In the town center; the
restaurant can be entered from the riverfront or from Piazza Mazzini

---

Cecco is a wonderful place to sample Pistoia's gastronomic specialties. The menu always includes a few hard-to-find dishes and features locally grown produce such as Pescia's renowned jumbo green asparagus. The attractive dining room has a high vaulted stone ceiling with unadorned ocher walls, and the service is great: the waiters have worked here for years and are proud of the food they serve.

Antipasti include tasty *salumi*, chicken liver *crostini*, and the exceptional *fagioli di Sorana*, fine-skinned local beans topped here with salty shavings of *bottarga di tonno*—sun-dried tuna roe.

Cecco is famous for cooking mushrooms; in early summer, fresh porcini begin to appear in soups and pasta dishes, alone, or with meats. Homemade potato-herb gnocchi (*della casa*) are delicious, topped with sliced raw porcini, shaved Parmesan, melted butter, and wild marjoram. In autumn rare *ovoli* (*Amanita caesarea*) are gathered in woods nearby and served raw or with spaghetti. Winter is truffle season.

Cecco's *pollastrino al mattone* is popular: half a local chicken is seasoned, weighted with bricks to flatten it, and cooked on a griddle, resulting in a crisp browned exterior and moist lean meat. Cecco's *fritto misto* of deep-fried mixed meats and vegetables is prepared in a feather-light, crunchy batter—the finest I encountered. More adventurous diners should try the local specialty, *cioncia alla Pesciatina:* diced beef muzzle in an aromatic tomato sauce.

Desserts are nicely presented: mixed wild berries (*frutti di bosco*) come in a little tart with a mascarpone filling or are stewed with sweetened white wine and spooned hot over ice-cream. The wine list is almost exclusively Tuscan.

Pianosinatico

SILVIO LA STORIA A TAVOLA   VIA BRENNERO, 181/183 51020 PIANOSINATICO
RESTAURANT   TELEPHONE 0573 629204, 629274
E-MAIL ircvan@tin.it

OPEN Lunch and dinner   **CLOSED** Tuesday; a week in spring; two weeks in October
CREDIT CARDS Visa, MC, Amex   **ENGLISH SPOKEN** Yes   **RESERVATIONS** Recommended, especially on weekends   **PRICE** $$$ **DIRECTIONS** The restaurant is between Cutigliano and Abetone, in the village of Pianosinatico

---

Eating at Silvio's merits a detour. After a steep but scenic drive up the mountain, you reach the small restaurant in the sleepy village of Pianosinatico.

Inside, in the little dining room to the right past the bar, a nice mix of local workers and visiting food lovers eat at the restaurant's few tables. The service is informal but attentive: the waiter announces each dish with pride. Silvio often comes in from the kitchen, jovial in his tall chef's hat, to confer with the customers who have traveled to eat there.

A culinary historian, self-taught cook, and former professor of medieval history, Silvio Zanni ran a wine bar in Prato, a restaurant in Paris, and a trattoria on this mountain before opening this restaurant with his partner, Andrea Vannucci, in 1992. Working only with seasonal ingredients, Silvio offers an affordable *menu degustazione* of five different vegetable-based *primi* each day, followed by simple meat *secondi* for those who want them. The menu changes daily and offers an interesting choice of dishes *à la carte*. A wine connoisseur, Silvio suggests wines to accompany each dish, but there is also an excellent *carta dei vini*.

An early summer *primi* menu consisted of *passato di piselli e porcini,* a warm puréed soup of sweet fresh peas and porcini, which had a woodsy undertone from the mushrooms; handmade *ricotta tortelli,* tangy from the local sheep's cheese and set off by a salty vegetable broth and a sprig of sage; spaghetti with red onions, a deceptively simple combination of sweet and sharp tastes and textures; *gnocchi al tartufo,* fresh potato gnocchi with some resistance to the bite, coated with a creamy sauce and slivers of pungent black truffle; and *farfalle con bietole e basilico,* pasta bows stained pink by sweet fresh beets with a peppery counterpoint in the basil leaves. Each vegetable's flavor is experienced fully, married to the pasta shape that suits it best.

Silvio and Andrea have sought out great artisan-made ingredients, such as *lardo di Colonnata* (see page 33) and the aromatic raw-milk pecorini of the Pistoiese Mountains, which now are included in Slow Food's Ark of protected foods.

The subtitle of the restaurant, *la storia a tavola*, means "history at the table," and Silvio often exploits his culinary knowledge by incorporating recipes and food combinations from past eras of Italian cooking.

Pistoia

CONFETTERIA CORSINI

PIAZZA SAN FRANCESCO D'ASSISI, 43 51100 PISTOIA

CANDY

TELEPHONE 0573 20138

OPEN 8:00–13:00, 16:00–19:00   **CLOSED** Sunday; Saturday afternoon in summer; two weeks in August   **CREDIT CARDS** None   **MAIL ORDER** Yes   **ENGLISH SPOKEN** Yes **DIRECTIONS** The piazza is in the northwest corner of the town, within the old walls

---

No Italian baptism, christening, or marriage would be complete without *confetti*, hard white candies that are tied into tulle bundles and given away to commemorate the occasion or thrown like rice at newlyweds for good luck. This custom has very old roots: *confetti* were first brought to Venice around 1100 by traders from the Far East. During carnival, noble families threw *confetti* from their palace windows to the populace below. Good *confetti* did not shatter on impact.

Pistoia's *confetti* are unusual. Instead of a smooth almond shape, they have a bumpy surface, like pieces of knobbly white coral. Corsini offers *confetti a riccio* with various "souls": the hard candy exterior contains a firm core of chocolate, nuts, candied fruit, or aniseed. The coating procedure takes more than ten hours and is a well-kept trade secret. These and other chocolate confections are available from the unfussy shop by loose weight or in gift boxes, and they may be custom ordered.

The Corsini's expertise is well known: the shop was commissioned to re-create sixteenth-century blue *confetti* for the film *Casanova*. The old-fashioned laboratory and shop still houses fascinating early candy-making machinery.

Also

Pistoia, a beautiful little city, has at its heart (near the Duomo) a square called La Sala. Six mornings a week, a food market is held here; there are also a number of permanent food stores in the buildings that surround the square.

San Marcello Pistoiese

S.A.M.   PIAZZA CINI, 10 51028 SAN MARCELLO PISTOIESE
SPECIALTY FOODS   TELEPHONE/FAX 0573 630535

OPEN 7:30–13:00, 16:30–19:00   **CLOSED** Sunday in winter; Wednesday afternoon
CREDIT CARDS None   **ENGLISH SPOKEN** A little   **DIRECTIONS** The shop is in the
village's main square

This small supermarket stocks all the staples, but it is worth visiting for its selected artisan foods. S.A.M. stands for Società Agricola Montana, a cooperative of mountain farmers and shepherds. Fresh cheeses are exceptional, especially the pecorini and the fine-textured, fragrant sheep's ricotta. There are mountain *salumi*, local vegetables, and mushrooms and berries from the surrounding woods, plus great honeys, pasta, and herb teas.

Also

GELATERIA BAR TERRAZZA   VIA GAVINANA, 7A. 0573 630150

This ice-cream parlor and bar is on the bridge in the town center. It has a large outdoor terrace and makes fresh gelati using seasonal fruits.

CHAPTER 4

Firenze (Florence), Prato, and Their Provinces

*T*he great Renaissance city of Firenze (Florence) should need no introduction: it is the cultural heart of Tuscany, admired by everyone who visits it. From a food and wine lover's point of view, the city and its surrounding provinces have much to offer.

Despite mass tourism, Firenze has maintained the integrity of its food markets and grocery shops—few tourists do much cooking. There are still market stalls selling homegrown produce from the Tuscan countryside and hand-picked *erbe* (wild herbs), for adding a bitter note to salads and vegetable dishes. The city still has several *fiaschetterie*, although many have disappeared; these unpretentious wine bars took their name from the straw-covered Chianti *fiasco* and offer a glass of wine and a *panino* of locally cured salty ham or pecorino cheese.

Of course, there are also grand and fine restaurants for tasting the region's best foods and wines. Some of these great wines are produced within the province of Firenze: Chianti Rùfina is a small but excellent wine zone only a short distance to the city's east; Carmignano is another to its west. Chianti Classico, some of which is also within this province, has its own chapter (p 183).

The hills above Pontassieve contain an exceptional organic bakery; Prato is renowned for its great *biscotti*, and for a prize-winning pastry chef; fine extra-virgin olive oil is produced all around the area. Firenze is a wonderful starting point for exploring the foods and wines of Tuscany's varied countryside.

AZIENDA PROMOZIONE TURISTICA
VIA CAVOUR, 1R
50129 FIRENZE
055 290832/3, FAX 055 2760383
WEB SITE www.provincia.firenze.it

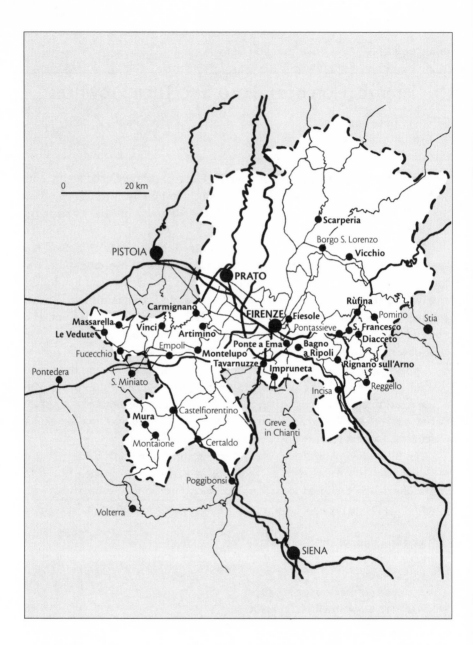

Boldface type indicates towns that are included in this chapter.

Artimino

DA DELFINA
RESTAURANT

ARTIMINO 50042 CARMIGNANO FIRENZE
TELEPHONE 055 8718119, 8718074   FAX 055 8718175

OPEN Lunch and dinner   **CLOSED** Sunday for dinner; Monday; August   **CREDIT CARDS** None
ENGLISH SPOKEN Yes   **FEATURES** Outdoor terrace   **RESERVATIONS** Necessary
PRICE $$$ **DIRECTIONS** The restaurant is at the entrance to Artimino, before the villa

Da Delfina's summer terrace overlooks the beautiful Medicean villa Artimino and its vineyards. The restaurant offers some of the most wonderful and authentic food in Tuscany. "There is an increasing demand for a return to the simple rustic dishes of our past," explained Carlo Cioni, the restaurant's owner. "We have always tried to keep these peasant dishes alive." Ingredients and produce are local or wild, gathered in the woods and fields.

When I arrived in early spring, the elderly Signora Delfina was hunched over the kitchen table, painstakingly cleaning freshly picked wild herbs. Lunch began with a bright green *sformato di rapa*—unmolded rape soufflé. It was soft and light and came with a sage-scented purée of beans. I tasted crisp fried *malva* (mallow) leaves, a *crostino* of strong liver, polenta topped with cheese, and a *Parmigiano* of eggplant and herbs. But the most unusual, most exceptional dish was a Florentine Renaissance recipe of baby goats' tongues cooked in *agro dolce*—a sweet and sour sauce with pine nuts and raisins. The meat was tender and delicate, the sauce complex and intriguing. I can think of no other restaurant that would have proposed such a dish, nor pulled it off with such artistry.

Homemade *taglierini* are thin noodles dressed with an egg sauce of wild asparagus tips. Delfina's *ribollita* is recooked in a frying pan: the substantial vegetable and herb soup thickened with bread is browned at the edges and drizzled with fragrant green oil. A stew of veal and potatoes is ocher, the potatoes a reddish orange. Young lamb chops are grilled over a wood fire, topped with bay leaves, and accompanied by white beans that had been fried or roasted—they are crunchy as soft nuts.

Dessert was a light cream mousse and a slice of *ghirighio*, a thin cake of chestnut flour studded with pine nuts and rosemary that was the finest I have had. A thoughtfully selected Tuscan wine list completes this feast of the senses.

ARTIMINO
WINE

VIALE PAPA GIOVANNI XXIII, 1 50040 CARMIGNANO FIRENZE
TELEPHONE 055 8751424   FAX 055 8751480

OPEN Visits by appointment only   **CLOSED** Weekends   **DIRECT SALE** Artimino's wines are available from shops in the village of Artimino: Via Cinque Martiri, 3   **ENGLISH SPOKEN** Yes
OTHER Hotel, restaurant, convention center   **DIRECTIONS** The villa is at the top of the hill, clearly visible; the *cantina* is below the town

Artimino is called the "Villa of the Hundred Chimneys," and indeed, the late-sixteenth-century Medicean villa is adorned with a vast collection of them. The villa, whose interior is not open to the public, is part of a large estate: 730 hectares (1,800 acres), of which 80 (197) are vineyards. The villa is rather grand and impersonal, but worth seeing—and it offers great views.

The winery recently invested in modern cellars at the bottom of the hill. "These *cantine* may not be very poetic—we have enough poetry up on the hill—but better wines are certainly made this way," affirmed Giuseppe Poggi, Artimino's director. Artimino's first vintage using the new equipment was 1993, and the recent wines are already showing improvement. The most important wine is Carmignano DOCG Riserva Medicea, which is made only in great years. It contains 65 percent Sangiovese, with 15 percent each of Cabernet and Canaiolo, the remainder divided between other red grapes. It spends two years in wood. Other wines include the reasonably priced Barco Reale (Carmignano's "younger brother"), and Carmignano's unique rosé, Vin Ruspo. See also Carmignano, p 85.

Bagno a Ripoli

CENTANNI
RESTAURANT

VIA DI CENTANNI, 7 50012 BAGNO A RIPOLI FIRENZE
TELEPHONE 055 630122   FAX 055 6510445

OPEN Lunch and dinner   **CLOSED** Saturday for lunch, Sunday; August   **CREDIT CARDS** Visa, MC, Amex   **ENGLISH SPOKEN** Yes   **FEATURES** Summer terrace   **RESERVATIONS** Necessary during summer and on weekends   **PRICE** $$$ **OTHER** Apartments available for holiday rentals   **DIRECTIONS** Centanni is clearly signposted from Bagno a Ripoli; look for the yellow signs

---

Silvana Bianchi is a lovely woman who started her restaurant more than thirty years ago. Centanni is situated in the hills outside Firenze amid silvery-green olive groves. A large dining room has tall picture windows. Signora Bianchi sees to the flowers and plans the daily menu. Everything, from the bread sticks to the pasta, is handmade by local women who work in the kitchen; if you arrive early for lunch, you can watch them fill the ravioli.

Cappelletti di piccione are pasta ovals stuffed with subtly flavored minced pigeon. Spinach and ricotta ravioli, of the same fine pasta, are topped with a savory meat sauce. There are also several fresh country soups.

Centanni's signature main course is not particularly Tuscan. *Pollo Centanni* is a breaded chicken breast topped with porcini mushrooms, prosciutto, and cheese. There are grilled steaks and chops, assorted fried meats, and a good range of vegetable dishes. Desserts, too, are homemade. I sampled a rich pineapple upside-down cake and a warm apple tart that was thankfully not too sweet. The well-priced wine list is highly informative; there is a good group of Tuscans and drinkable house wines.

Carmignano

**TENUTA DI
CAPEZZANA**
WINE, OLIVE OIL

VIA CAPEZZANA, 100 SEANO 50040 CARMIGNANO FIRENZE
TELEPHONE 055 8706005, 8706091   FAX 055 8706673
WEB SITE www.capezzana.it

OPEN 8:30–12:30, 14:30–18:30; *cantina* visits and tastings by appointment only
CLOSED Saturday and Sunday   **CREDIT CARDS** Visa, Amex   **DIRECT SALE** Yes
ENGLISH SPOKEN Yes   **OTHER** Holiday apartments for rent; cooking courses for professionals
DIRECTIONS From the Prato Ovest exit on A11 *autostrada*, go toward Seano and Carmignano; the
winery is signposted from there

Located in the hills between Firenze and Prato, Tenuta di Capezzana is synonymous with one of Tuscany's smallest but most distinguished wine denominations,
Carmignano DOCG. "Carmignano's history is fascinating: wine was made here by
the Etruscans," recounted Ugo Contini Bonacossi. "And in 1396 Ser Lapo Mazzei
[p 196], a notary, documented paying a high sum for it." The Medicis were also
fond of Carmignano's wines, and in a 1716 decree they delimited the boundaries of
its production area. "Under Fascism, estates were pressured to produce quantity
rather than quality," Contini Bonacossi continued. "And even in the fifties and sixties our wines were lumped in with the surrounding Chianti producers. The unique
qualities of Carmignano's wines were being lost in the shuffle." After a long, almost
single-handed battle, Contini Bonacossi was able to reestablish an autonomy for
his area's wines, gaining DOC status in 1975 and DOCG in 1990. This was also the
first Tuscan denomination to allow what the locals called "the French grape"—
Cabernet—in the blend of Carmignano Rosso DOCG. Cabernet has been planted
here since the time of Caterina de' Medici, who brought it from France.

Carmignano is a well-structured, well-balanced red wine made in "normal"
and reserve versions. Barco Reale has the same grape varieties but is made to drink
young, as its tannins are not bitter. Contini Bonacossi described it as "never too
young, never too old." Ghiaie della Furba is Capezzana's acclaimed super-Tuscan of
70 percent Cabernet and 30 percent Merlot. Other wines include Vin Ruspo—
Carmignano's particular rosé—Chianti Montalbano, and Vin Santo.

Capezzana is itself a beautiful villa built for one of the Medici daughters. It
has a maze of underground cellars, a *vinsantaia*, courtyards of lemon trees, and
a fine *orciaia*—the room in which the large terra-cotta urns of olive oil were
stored. The lovely Contini Bonacossi family welcomes interested visitors by
prior arrangement.

FATTORIA IL POGGIOLO
WINE

VIA PISTOIESE, 90 50042 CARMIGNANO FIRENZE
TELEPHONE 055 8711242   FAX 055 8711252
WEB SITE www.ilpoggiolo.it

OPEN 8:00–12:00, 13:00–17:00; tastings and visits by appointment   **CLOSED** Saturday and Sunday (unless by appointment)   **CREDIT CARDS** None   **DIRECT SALE** Yes   **ENGLISH SPOKEN** Yes
DIRECTIONS The winery is on the road between Carmignano and Seano, 1 km from Carmignano

---

Giovanni Cianchi Baldazzi has one of Carmignano's larger estates, with over 30 hectares (74 acres) of vineyards and 14 hectares (72 acres) of olive groves. Traditional methods are used for producing Carmignano DOCG. Giovanni's son, Giuseppe, is the estate's young *enotecnico*—wine technician.

Giuseppe told the story of Vin Ruspo, a rosé made from the same grapes as Carmignano's red wine. In the days of sharecropping, the peasants used to secretly draw off a couple of demijohns of must while the grapes were being transported from the vineyards to the landowner's farm. This must was left to ferment, and the resulting wine, of a light ruby color, was called Vin Ruspo. It was traditionally drunk during the corn harvest. Vin Ruspo now forms part of the Carmignano DOC's list of wines.

Diacceto

FORNO A LEGNA "LA TORRE"
BREAD

VIA SANTONI, 3 DIACCETO 50060 PELAGO FIRENZE
TELEPHONE 055 8326635

OPEN Monday, Wednesday, Friday 8:00–20:00; Thursday, Saturday 8:00–14:00
CLOSED Tuesday; Sunday   **CREDIT CARDS** None   **DIRECT SALE** Yes; see also La Raccolta in Firenze, p 91   **ENGLISH SPOKEN** Yes   **DIRECTIONS** From Pontassieve take SS 70 for the Consuma and Bibbiena. Via Santoni runs parallel to the main road through Diacceto. There are signs for the bakery in the village

---

In my opinion, Stefano Borselli makes the best bread in Tuscany. This remarkable young man left a career in electronics to join a Gandhian-style pacifist group in the 1980s, and he became increasingly interested in the organic and "alternative" movements.

"I thought it over," he explained simply, "and decided that the best, most useful thing I could do for my community was to bake bread. In the old days bread was the fundamental basis of everyday life. Now it has been reduced to the role of a *soprammobile*—a decorative ornament—in our society. But I believe that this can change." In 1985 he started baking, and in 1989 he opened this wonderful bakery, high on a hill to the east of Firenze. Specialist artisans built his large wood-burning oven—free of lead and iron. Borselli, who is helped by his parents and wife, studied different enzymes and their effects on flours to develop three types of natural yeasts.

The first, for use with high-fiber whole-grain flours, is made of water and rye flour. *Pane Toscano,* Tuscan unsalted bread, requires a less acid starter made from water, rye, and wheat flours. The third type of yeast, used only for sweet dough, is made from fresh fruit soaked in water for a week, until it ferments. His *pasticceria* is given very long raising times (up to twenty-four hours) in order to sterilize the acids in the doughs. These yeasts also give the baked products an extended shelf life. All his flours and other ingredients are certified organic. Many of the flours are stone ground.

I sampled several of Borselli's breads—and was knocked out by them. His large round of unsalted Tuscan bread, weighing 1 kg (2.2 lbs), has a crunchy golden crust and the flavor of fresh grain; it is perfect for Tuscany's famous bread soups. The bakery also produces an interesting range of whole wheat and complex breads. One compact loaf was topped with sesame seeds and packed with olives, sweet peppers, herbs, and seeds. *Pane di S. Egidio* is delicious, a cross between a fruitcake and a savory bread, thick with figs, almonds, raisins, chopped nuts (including some wonderfully fresh walnuts), and a pinch of *peperoncino*—hot chili pepper. Borselli also makes breads for special and allergic diets. Anyone making the trip to visit this talented young baker will not be disappointed.

Fiesole

TRATTORIA TULLIO   ONTIGNANO, 48 50014 FIESOLE FIRENZE
RESTAURANT   TELEPHONE 055 697354

OPEN Lunch and dinner   **CLOSED** Wednesday   **CREDIT CARDS** Visa, MC, Amex
ENGLISH SPOKEN Yes   **FEATURES** Terrace dining room   **RESERVATIONS** Necessary weekends and summer for terrace dining room   **PRICE** $$ **DIRECTIONS** Go up through Fiesole and after 2 km pass Au Petit Bois. Take the next right toward Montebeni; the restaurant is signposted from there

From Fiesole the trip to this restaurant is a picturesque drive through pine woods and olive groves. This country trattoria has a panoramic dining room; in summer its many windows are opened. As is often the case in restaurants popular with Italians, the simplest dishes are the best. A modest slice of Tuscan bread toasted over an open fire, rubbed with garlic, and topped with hot *cannellini* beans, fruity olive oil, and pepper is delicious. Tagliatelle with meat sauce or thick vegetable soup makes a good first course.

Fritto misto—deep-fried meats and vegetables—is a trattoria favorite. Tullio's is good: in spring a light crispy batter encases sliced red onion, eggplant, and tender artichokes, as well as chunks of rabbit, chicken, and lamb. Other meats are grilled over wood embers, *alla brace.* Desserts are homemade, the house wines unpretentious, and the service is experienced but not formal.

VILLA SAN MICHELE
HOTEL RESTAURANT

VIA DOCCIA, 4 50014 FIESOLE FIRENZE
TELEPHONE 055 5678200   FAX 055 5678250
E-MAIL reservations@villasanmichele.net

OPEN Lunch and dinner   CLOSED In winter   CREDIT CARDS Visa, MC, Amex
ENGLISH SPOKEN Yes   RESERVATIONS Recommended   PRICE $$$$-$$$$$
DIRECTIONS The hotel is on the road between Firenze and Fiesole, at the entrance to Fiesole

Villa San Michele is one of Firenze's most exclusive—and expensive—hotels. If you can't splurge for a room but still want to enjoy its luxurious villa atmosphere, great service, and spectacular views, drive up and treat yourself to lunch or dinner there. In warm weather, the dining room is out on *la Loggia*, a romantic covered terrace overlooking Firenze and its hills, with a bar for predinner *aperitivi*. The menu offers refined Tuscan and other Mediterranean dishes; the wine list is extensive. A fixed-price three- or four-course tasting menu is available, in addition to the à la carte selections.

Firenze

FIRENZE–FLORENCE

In the city of Firenze (Florence), street addresses are numbered with two systems simultaneously—one for domestic buildings (black numbers), the other for businesses (red, or *rosso*), which have an "R" after them.

IL FORNAIO GALLI
BREAD

VIA MATTEO PALMIERI, 24R VIA FAENZA, 39R
VIA GUICCIARDINI, 3 50122 FIRENZE
TELEPHONE 055 2480336   FAX 055 2479705

OPEN 7:30–14:00, 17:00–19:45   CLOSED Wednesday afternoon in winter, Saturday afternoon
in summer   CREDIT CARDS None   ENGLISH SPOKEN A little

This bakery, with its warm wood interior, produces and sells an extensive range of regional Italian breads at three locations, including the Cantinetta dei Verrazzano (see next entry). The Galli family makes great Tuscan classics: large rounds of unsalted *pane sciocco* use selected flours and natural yeasts. The choice of flat breads, *schiacciata*, is impressive. The plain has a good crisp crust, baked until golden brown, but my favorite is the whole-wheat variety: the thin bread is bran flecked, its crunchy crust sprinkled with coarse sea salt and drizzled with fruity olive oil. It is great with cheese or by itself and is best eaten fresh. They bake it in big slabs and cut off and weigh as much as you want. *Pasqualina* tarts are stuffed with green, creamy spinach filling or savory ham and cheese. Pizzas, also sold by weight, are topped with delicate potato and rosemary or traditional tomato. *Pan di romarino* is a glazed bread roll between sweet and salty, whose airy dough is laced with aromatic rosemary and raisins.

Desserts include biscuits, tarts, and *schiacciata alla Fiorentina*, a layer of moist orange-flavored cake dusted with powdered sugar. It is sold plain or split and filled with whipped cream or vanilla or chocolate custard. I was impressed by the patient serving staff, who took time with tourists asking for just a handful of *grissini* or one bread roll.

CANTINETTA DEI VERRAZZANO	**VIA DEI TAVOLINI, 18/20R 50100 FIRENZE**
BREAD, WINE, COFFEE SHOP, SALUMI	TELEPHONE 055 268590; WINERY 055 854243
	FAX 055 295189 WEB SITE www.verrazzano.com

OPEN 8:00–21:00   **CLOSED** Sunday   **CREDIT CARDS** Visa, MC, Amex   **DIRECT SALE** Yes
ENGLISH SPOKEN Yes   **RESERVATIONS** None accepted   **DIRECTIONS** Off Via dei Calzaiuoli

The Cantinetta puts four expert producers of foods and wine under one roof—and it works. A nicely styled ground-floor position between the Duomo and the Ponte Vecchio gives each partner a sales point within the whole.

Savor an excellent *caffè* or centrifuged fruit juice at the Piansa coffee counter (p 90), choose from Il Fornaio Galli's delicious breads (see preceding entry), or sit and eat a piece of cake or freshly baked focaccia—I love the one stuffed with peas—made regularly in the wood oven.

The adjacent room features Falorni of Greve's *salumi* (p 199) and the fine wines of Chianti's Castello di Verrazzano. From 3 P.M. until closing there is service at the tables for snacks or wines. The "Specialità Verrazzano" is a beautiful plate of open-faced sandwiches on special Galli breads (the spiced *pandivino* is reminiscent of French *pain d'épices*). Falorni toppings include peppered wild boar sausage, coarse-grained *finocchiona* with fennel seeds, *soppressata* (head cheese) flavored with lemon peel, and pecorino and pear.

If you don't have time to visit the Verrazzano Castello at Greve, you can sample the wines here or buy them to take with you. In addition to the Chianti Classico and its powerful Riserva, there are two pure Sangiovese super-Tuscan wines to try: award-winning Sassello and Bottiglia Particolare (which has a bit of Cabernet Sauvignon added to it). New Yorkers will be interested to note that the Castello was the birthplace of explorer Giovanni da Verrazzano—namesake of the Verrazzano Narrows Bridge.

CAFFELLATTE
CAFÉ

VIA DEGLI ALFANI, 39R 50121 FIRENZE
TELEPHONE 055 2478878

OPEN 9:00–24:00   **CLOSED** Sunday   **CREDIT CARDS** None
ENGLISH SPOKEN Yes   **DIRECTIONS** Off Via della Pergola

Six little tables, a bunch of wildflowers in a jar, a handsome old marble counter—Caffellatte is an easygoing place to have a coffee while you read the paper or to sit over tea with a friend. In what was once a butcher's shop and then later a *latteria* (dairy), Eleonora and her mother, Vanna Casati, offer a peaceful, welcoming respite from the pressures of city life.

There are organic teas to choose from, and Arabica coffee from Nicaragua sold by the CTM cooperative, bypassing the multinationals and their markup. The women make good desserts: carrot and almond or apple cake, Tarte Bretonne (a kind of baked custard), and some sugarless and other special-diet cakes. The *caffellatte* comes in large bowls and is great for breakfast with toast and jam.

CAFFETTERIA PIANSA
CAFÉ

BORGO PINTI, 18R 50121 FIRENZE
TELEPHONE 055 2342362

OPEN 7:30–2:00 A.M.   **CLOSED** Sunday; August   **CREDIT CARDS** None
ENGLISH SPOKEN Yes   **DIRECTIONS** Off Via di Mezzo

This handsome *caffetteria* is a good inner-city outlet for Pietro Staderini's Piansa coffee (see next entry). You can buy selected coffees by weight, including Piansa's pure Arabica blend, the Magnificent Ten. The large bar serves coffee, tea, and drinks all day, plus sandwiches, salads, pastries, *primi*, and snacks that may be eaten at the tables.

DROGHERIA PIANSA
COFFEE, COFFEEHOUSE

VIALE EUROPA, 126/128R 50126 FIRENZE
TELEPHONE 055 6532117, 6531987   FAX 055 645774
E-MAIL torrefazione@caffepiansa.com

OPEN 8:00–13:00, 16:00–20:00   **CLOSED** Sunday, Wednesday afternoon in winter, Saturday afternoon in summer; holidays in summer   **CREDIT CARDS** None   **ENGLISH SPOKEN** Yes
DIRECTIONS Viale Europa is south of the Arno, southeast of central Firenze, near Badia a Ripoli and the Firenze Sud *autostrada* entrance

Piansa is the city of Firenze's leading coffee roaster, with outlets all over the city. This is its "home" base and southern Firenze's favorite coffee bar. The double-fronted store has a long counter serving Piansa coffees, drinks, great sandwiches, and pastries. There are also a few tables. The other storefront carries Piansa's extensive range of coffees, roasted by Pietro Staderini in nearby Ponte a Ema; they are sold as beans or ground to order. The shop also stocks teas, candies, and assorted specialty foods.

Piansa's most popular blend is the Magnificent Ten, *I Magnifici Dieci*, blended from ten pure Arabica coffees, including Jamaica Blue Mountain, Hawaii Kona Kay, Santo Domingo Barahona, and Ethiopia Mocca Yrga. These and other premium coffees, including decaffeinated, are also sold singly. Piansa is one of the food artisans participating in the Cantinetta dei Verrazzano (see p 89) and has a café in Borgo Pinti, 18R.

ASSOCIAZIONE CULTURALE "LA RACCOLTA"
HEALTH FOODS

VIA LEOPARDI, 10 (DOWNSTAIRS) 50121 FIRENZE
TELEPHONE/FAX 055 2479068

OPEN 10:00–14:00, 16:00–19:30   **CLOSED** Monday morning, Saturday afternoon, Sunday
CREDIT CARDS None   **ENGLISH SPOKEN** Yes   **OTHER** Courses and seminars
DIRECTIONS Via Leopardi is one block north of Piazza Beccaria. La Raccolta is in the cellar of a residential building. Go in main entrance and down stairs on left

---

The sure measure of a health food store is the freshness of its organic produce. In Italy, where the concept of eating chemical-free foods is, sadly, still little known, it is a struggle for those promoting the organic cause. Sometimes the produce, necessarily more expensive than its treated counterparts, looks too worn out to buy. Not so the range of fresh fruits and vegetables on display at this cheerful shop, in the bowels of a residential palazzo not far from the Sant'Ambrogio market. The constant turnover permits daily deliveries of certified organic foods from Tuscany and beyond.

It was a pleasure to discover that La Raccolta sells my favorite Tuscan organic breads, from Forno "La Torre" (p 86), I Pulitini and Montegemoli, near Pisa. La Raccolta (which means the harvest or gathering), began in the late 1980s. It features selected dairy foods, herbal remedies from Aboca (p 339), a huge range of pastas, bottled vegetables, grains, pulses, seeds and all the other standard health food products. Great for macrobiotics and everyone who cares about the quality of the foods they eat.

DE HERBORE
HERBAL PRODUCTS

VIA DEL PROCONSOLO, 43R 50122 FIRENZE
TELEPHONE 055 211706   FAX 055 683207

OPEN 9:00–13:00, 15:30–19:30   **CLOSED** Monday morning, Sunday; one week in August
CREDIT CARDS Visa, MC   **ENGLISH SPOKEN** Yes   **DIRECTIONS** Near the Bargello

---

Health foods, natural cosmetics, bouquets of silk flowers, dried herbs, vitamins, macrobiotic ingredients, soaps, potpourri . . . De Herbore has all this and more. Spectacularly set in a grandiose hall on the ground floor of Palazzo Pazzi, the shop is the brainchild of two brothers, Doctors Luciano and Arnaldo Tanganelli, erstwhile owners of a pharmaceutical company.

"Nowadays the only thing that brings me joy is to help people heal themselves from the problems our modern society is subjecting us to," Luciano Tanganelli confided. "All the unnatural hormones and additives in our foods, the pollution,

---

FIRENZE'S ORGANIC PRODUCE MARKETS

La Fierucola is a large organic fair held twice yearly, in September and December, in Piazza della Santissima Annunziata. La Fierucolina is a smaller organic market held on the third Sunday of each month in Piazza Santo Spirito.

FIRENZE'S FOOD MARKETS

Central Firenze has two major permanent food markets: San Lorenzo and Sant'Ambrogio. Both are in covered buildings but spill out into the surrounding streets. They are great to visit—and for shopping. Most produce is sold by the *kilo* (2.2 lbs) or *etto* (100 grams, or 3.5 ounces).

MERCATO CENTRALE

Monday–Saturday 7:00–14:00, Saturday 16:00–19:00

The Mercato Centrale, or San Lorenzo market, is in a large nineteenth-century cast-iron building. It houses hundreds of food stalls of all types, some selling ready-cooked foods to take away. Upstairs the market continues with more stalls, including some of the most interesting salad and herb sellers. Baroni Alimentari (stall 278–280) carries the exceptional coffee of Le Piantagioni del Caffè (see p 119–120). Nerbone (tel: 055 219949), established in 1872, is a Florentine favorite and the best place to try *trippa* (tripe), *lampredotto* (chitterlings), and other specialties. The stall has a few tables and a take-out business; it is run by the son of Loriano Stagi, who owns the Vecchia Bettola restaurant (p 104). Perini (tel: 055 2398306) has a spectacular prepared food and grocery stall; it sells bread baked in a wood oven, and it also caters.

For a real slice of Italian life, the area around the market is fun to explore. Via Sant'Antonio has a number of cut-price food and wine stores, some of which

the stress—they're no good for us." Dr. Tanganelli mixes individual "cocktails" of curative herbs or can suggest some of the many remedies his shop is stocked with.

Even if you are feeling perfectly healthy, the shop, with its extravagant displays, is fun to explore: the sweetly scented lotions and potions make great presents. So treat yourself.

---

are old-fashioned and interesting. There is still a *friggitore* at number 50R selling deep-fried doughnuts.

In Via del Melarancio, the China Foodstores stock some international foods. Back on the other side of the marketplace, at Via Panicale, 16R, Afro Market (tel: 055 2382694) is the place to go if you have a yen for pounded yam, green bananas, or African spices. Indian and other Far Eastern foods can be found nearby in Piazza Santa Maria Novella, 21/22R, at Asiamasala. This nice shop is run by the owners of India, the Indian restaurant at Fiesole in Via Gramsci, 43A (tel: 055 599900).

MERCATO DI SANT'AMBROGIO
Monday–Saturday 7:00–14:00

This market is a smaller, more intimate affair. As well as indoor stalls covering the entire gastronomic spectrum, there are outside stalls grouped around the sides of the building—with small vendors coming in from the countryside to sell their homegrown produce. Look for the little bunches of *erbi di campo*—hand-picked wild field greens to cook or to use in salads.

Across the street from Cibrèo (see p 98–99), at Via de' Macci, 117R, the Pescheria Silvestri sells wonderfully fresh fish and will even give cooking suggestions to those who can muster a little Italian.

The hardware store Mesticheria-Casalinghi Mazzanti, in Borgo La Croce, 101R (tel: 055 2480663), has a second entrance a few doors down from Cibrèo (Via del Verrocchio). It stocks lots of inexpensive items: wooden spoons of all shapes and sizes, terra-cotta cooking pots, olive-wood cheese graters, chopping boards, oil tins with spouts, rustic spatterware pottery, and more. It is fun to browse in if you are in the neighborhood.

OFFICINA PROFUMO-FARMACEUTICA
DI SANTA MARIA NOVELLA
HERBAL PRODUCTS

VIA DELLA SCALA, 16 50123 FIRENZE
TELEPHONE 055 216276; FOR ORDERS 055 4368315
FAX 055 288658; FOR ORDERS 055 4222432
E-MAIL officina@smnovella.com

OPEN 9:30–19:30; Sunday in summer 10:30–18:30   **CLOSED** Sunday in winter
CREDIT CARDS Visa, MC, Amex   **ENGLISH SPOKEN** Yes
DIRECTIONS Near Santa Maria Novella

The Officina is an extraordinary antique pharmacy founded by Dominican friars in 1542. Inside is a timeless world devoted to the senses. The fragrance of rarified perfumes strikes you first, then the strains of meditational early music; the eye is charmed by the beauty of the interiors, with their painted tiles, frescoes, sculptures, and furnishings. Rare honeys, herbal teas, and *elisirs* are sold here, as well as an extensive range of natural preparations and skin-care products. Some of them seem right out of an eighteenth-century romance novel: lavender salts to prevent fainting spells, rhubarb elixir to aid the digestion, mint spirit to clean the breath. Exotic perfumes, extracts, and essences are derived from violet and verbena, acacia and amber, hay and pomegranate. There are soaps and creams, oils, astringents, and ointments. There is even something called Armenia Paper "to be burnt to scent the air." All in all, a hedonist's haven.

FIRENZE'S TRIPE SELLERS

Tripe is a popular Florentine food, and it is served in many ways. Boiled tripe was traditionally sold by vendors from stands and carts, a few of which remain in central locations, selling *la trippa* warm as a filling for crunchy rolls. They include Palmino Pinzauti, Via dei Cimatori; and Luciano Piani, Piazza Sant'Ambrogio.

MACELLERIA VIGNOLI
MEAT: BUTCHER

PIAZZA SAN PIER MAGGIORE, 1R; VIA ROMANA, 131R;
VIA GASPERI, 19R; VIA PISANA, 359 50122 FIRENZE
TELEPHONE 055 2480436

OPEN 8:30–13:15, 17:00–20:00   **CLOSED** Wednesday afternoon, Sunday
CREDIT CARDS None   **ENGLISH SPOKEN** A little

Vignoli owns several butcher's shops in the city. In addition to its range of beef (including Chianina) and pork, it specializes in game (including wild boar) and poultry: free-range chicken and pigeon, duck and guinea fowl. Some meats are sold ready to cook—*involtini,* or meat rolls, stuffed with mortadella or sage leaves, and stuffed chicken.

As for the *salumi,* Spartacco, the friendly manager of the store, told me that cured shoulder of pork (*la spalla*) was more "typical" than prosciutto in Tuscany. Vignoli's is locally produced, as are the sausages, *finocchiona,* and *soppressata*—head cheese.

DOLCI & DOLCEZZE
PASTRY

PIAZZA BECCARIA, 8R 50121 FIRENZE
TELEPHONE 055 2345458   FAX 055 2346698
E-MAIL dolciedolcezze@dada.it

OPEN Tuesday–Saturday 8:30–20:30; Sunday 8:30–13:00, 16:00–20:00   **CLOSED** Monday
CREDIT CARDS None   **ENGLISH SPOKEN** A little   **DIRECTIONS** The piazza is at Porta alla Croce

This pastry shop sells some of Firenze's finest and most decadent cakes. Giulio Corti was a portrait photographer who loved making desserts; his wife, Ilaria, worked in an office. They started baking cakes for friends, then just for restaurants, and they finally opened this elegant shop in 1991. The dessert counter is complemented by a small range of savory baked goods and a stand-up bar for Piansa coffee or a glass of dessert wine.

"We never had a formal *pasticciere's* training," explained Ilaria, "and that has left us free to invent our own range." The buttery pastry tarts come with various custard-cream fillings, including deep chocolate, chocolate flavored with orange zest, *gianduja* (chocolate and hazelnut), and fresh orange and raspberry in summer. There are apple or orange pies (on Saturday), rice puddings, and a good range of cakes. A provocative cake declares, "I am the best chocolate cake in the world"—try one and judge for yourself!

I DOLCI DI PATRIZIO COSI
PASTRY, BAR

BORGO DEGLI ALBRIZI, 15R 50122 FIRENZE
TELEPHONE 055 2480367

OPEN 7:00–13:00, 15:30–20:00   **CLOSED** Sunday   **CREDIT CARDS** None
ENGLISH SPOKEN No   **DIRECTIONS** Near the Via Verdi post office

Walk into this pretty shop in the morning and you'll find it full of Florentines on their way to work or on their mid-morning break, standing up to eat a *pasta* (here it means pastry, not noodles) with a cappuccino chaser. In the afternoon, it's the same story, different crowd: a steady flow of admirers enjoying Patrizio Cosi's freshly baked croissants and doughnuts, apple tarts and raisin twists, rice *budini* or custard-filled *bignoline* (bite-size *choux* pastries), plus some savories for those not in the mood for something sweet. The shop recently expanded, and there are a few tables for those in less of a hurry.

CANTINETTA ANTINORI
RESTAURANT, WINE BAR

PALAZZO ANTINORI PIAZZA ANTINORI, 3 50123 FIRENZE
TELEPHONE 055 292234; WINERY INFORMATION 055 23595
FAX 055 2359877   WEB SITE www.antinori.it

OPEN Lunch and dinner   **CLOSED** Saturday, Sunday; August   **CREDIT CARDS** Visa, MC, Amex
DIRECT SALE Yes, for small quantities of wine or oil   **ENGLISH SPOKEN** A little
RESERVATIONS Recommended   **PRICE** $$$–$$$$ **OTHER** Visits to the wineries are not currently possible, but watch the Web site for changes in this policy   **DIRECTIONS** On Via Tornabuoni

A high-vaulted room on the ground floor of the fifteenth-century Palazzo Antinori is the setting for this noble Florentine family's wine bar and restaurant. According to its genial host, Gianfranco Stoppa, the landed gentry in Firenze formerly sold produce and wines from their estates directly to the public from a small window of the palazzo.

What began in the 1950s as a simple place to drink the Antinoris' wines has become a sophisticated restaurant that belies its rustic-style interior. A large dark wood bar and wooden tables with white linen place mats (useful for seeing the color of the wines) are the setting for an elegant menu and a list of the family's exceptional wines.

Wine lovers can sample the current release wines by the bottle or glass—a rare opportunity to compare Marchese Piero Antinori's groundbreaking super-Tuscan Solaia (of 80 percent Cabernet Sauvignon with 20 percent Sangiovese) with its stablemate Tignanello (the same grape varieties in the opposite proportions), or the big *barrique*-aged Cervaro, of Chardonnay and Grechetto, produced in the family's Umbrian estate Castello della Sala. The extensive list includes Ornellaia and Poggio alle Gazze from brother Lodovico Antinori's estate at Bolgheri (see p 149–150). You can sample wines at the bar without ordering food.

As for the menu, it is traditional Tuscan (where else, if not here?) prepared with attention and style. When I visited in February, mixed *crostini* included one toast topped with *cavolo nero*, the sweet Tuscan winter cabbage. *Salmone chiodato* (salmon home-cured in salt, sugar, and cloves) was more delicately aromatic than smoked salmon. A plate of fettuccine was dressed in a green sauce of finely puréed herbs: rosemary, sage, and parsley. *Baccalà*, an Italian Friday special, was unusually mild and tender, cooked with tomatoes and served with chickpeas. Chicken drumsticks were stewed with a savory sauce of chopped black olives and onions and came with mashed potatoes—a perfect dish to accompany the decisive red wines. Interesting salad combinations offered modern accents: radicchio and pecorino cheese were served with thinly sliced baby artichokes, as were poached shrimp and crayfish. Much of the produce comes from the Antinori estates, some of the largest holdings in Tuscany.

Dessert was highlighted by the aromatic late-harvest meditation wine Muffato della Sala, also made in Umbria. It is a wine to savor and sip, and it produced a remarkable taste contrast with a slice of warmed *castagnaccio,* the chestnut-flour cake flavored with rosemary and pine nuts, here topped and tempered by a paper-thin layer of ricotta.

BECCOFINO
RESTAURANT, WINE BAR

PIAZZA DEGLI SCARLATTI, 1R
(LUNGARNO GUICCIARDINI) 50125 FIRENZE
TELEPHONE 055 290076   FAX 055 2728312
E-MAIL baldovino.beccofino@inwind.it

OPEN Winter: lunch Saturday–Sunday; dinner Tuesday–Sunday. Summer: lunch and dinner Tuesday–Sunday   **CLOSED** Monday   **CREDIT CARDS** Visa, MC   **ENGLISH SPOKEN** Yes
RESERVATIONS Necessary for dinner   **PRICE** $$–$$$$
DIRECTIONS On the south side of the Arno between the S.Trinità and Carraia bridges

This large restaurant, with its international, modern feel, comprises three spaces: a restaurant, a wine bar with wines by the glass and a light meal menu, and an outdoor terrace. Not all are open at all times, but the main restaurant is open only for dinner (and for Sunday lunch in summer). The terrace operates as wine bar during the day and as restaurant in the evening.

The partners in this enterprise are Filippo Mazzei, winemaker from Fonterutoli (see p 196–197); David Gardner, who runs other restaurants in Firenze; and chef Francesco Berardinelli, from Rendola (see p 364–365). Together they have created a modern-style environment that is as popular with American tourists as it is with Florentine trendies. Beccofino is a good place to see and be seen.

Berardinelli is a fine chef from the Aretino looking to expand his image. At lunch there are composed salads, sliced meats and carpaccio, and daily pasta and risottos. The evening menu is more complex and more ambitious, served with a postmodern chef's flair. In early summer, a spicy soup of escarole and octopus, or tagliatelle with chickpeas and shrimp tails, are good starters, while Argentinian beef comes with a pesto of capers and raisins. The wine list has been assembled by people who know about wine, so you'll find all the Tuscan stars, as well as up-and-coming Sicilians such as COS—and, intelligently, grape varieties are given whenever possible.

OSTERIA DELLE BELLE DONNE
RESTAURANT

VIA DELLE BELLE DONNE, 16R 50123 FIRENZE
TELEPHONE 055 2382609

OPEN Lunch and dinner   **CLOSED** Saturday, Sunday; holidays in summer   **CREDIT CARDS** None
ENGLISH SPOKEN Yes   **RESERVATIONS** Recommended for dinner   **PRICE** $$
DIRECTIONS Behind Palazzo Antinori

This colorful restaurant's small interior is dominated by an enormous fruit, vegetable, and flower arrangement reminiscent of an Arcimboldi painting. Simple tables are topped with hand-painted tiles, butcher-paper place mats, and decorated plates; seating is on stools. The daily menu is written on a blackboard. Soups, salads, and pastas are unpretentious and affordable. The place is informal and usually packed, so get there early.

CAFFÈ CONCERTO
RESTAURANT

LUNGARNO COLOMBO, 7 50136 FIRENZE
TELEPHONE 055 677377   FAX 055 676493
E-MAIL caffeconcerto@tiscalinet.it

OPEN Lunch and dinner   **CLOSED** Sunday; three weeks in August   **CREDIT CARDS** Visa, MC
ENGLISH SPOKEN Yes   **RESERVATIONS** Necessary   **PRICE** $$$$
DIRECTIONS In the city center on the road, north of the river, that leads east out of Firenze

Few restaurants are as romantic at night as Caffè Concerto. Its big windows overlook the river Arno, but the mood remains introspective, with spotlights above each table and an abundance of leafy plants dominating the chiaroscuro.

Gabriele Tarchiani has created a lovely environment for enjoying fine food and great wines. His is an ambitious menu that stretches from Tuscan classics, such as the wholesome *farro* soup, or the fillet of Chianina beef sauced with celery and red wine, to more imaginative dishes using seasonal produce and artisan cheeses and meats. Tarchiani is well versed in French cuisine, and some of this technique comes through in the cooking.

In spring a terrine of artichokes was balanced by a sauce of shallots and potato. Thinly sliced raw scallops were composed in an abstract design with green cress dressing, dotted with red beet and black squid-ink highlights. A loose *risotto rosso* paired rare red rice with chopped shrimp and zucchini flowers. Turbot was served in a potato sauce that bordered on soup, white on white, with crunchy fried onions as accents. A lemon dessert crêpe was classically French. The wine list reflects Tarchiani's extensive, exuberant knowledge of wine.

IL CIBRÈO
RESTAURANT

VIA DE' MACCI, 118R 50122 FIRENZE
TELEPHONE 055 2341100   FAX 055 244966
E-MAIL cibreo.fi@tin.it

OPEN Lunch and dinner   **CLOSED** Sunday, Monday; August, one week in January
CREDIT CARDS Visa, MC, Amex   **DIRECT SALE** Selected specialty foods on sale at restaurant during meal times   **ENGLISH SPOKEN** Yes   **RESERVATIONS** Necessary at restaurant; none accepted at trattoria   **PRICE** $$$$ restaurant; $$ trattoria
DIRECTIONS Near Sant'Ambrogio market

Located amid the hustle and bustle of the Sant'Ambrogio market square, Cibrèo is Firenze's most compelling restaurant. Fabio Picchi has enriched the whole neighborhood with his three-in-one: one kitchen positioned between two storefronts supplies both an elegant, fully serviced restaurant on one side and a casual trattoria on the other. Across the street is the charming Cibrèo Caffè, where diners may order snacks and a few dishes. At mealtimes, waiters scurry back and forth through the traffic, carrying plates of food. At the restaurant and trattoria the food is the same (though the restaurant's menu gives more choices); the trattoria offers no trimmings, but its prices are half those of the restaurant. Note that Cibrèo serves no pasta. (Fabio Picchi said: "It's easy to make, and we all eat it at home anyway. So what's the point?")

My February lunch in the restaurant began with some wonderful antipasti: thin slices of Cibrèo's deliciously moist potato bread came topped with melted *robiola* cheese and jewel-like slivers of *mostarda,* the piquant candied fruit that made the cheese seem sweet. *Sformato di ricotta* was a subtle mousse with just a hint of the milky curds' sharpness; Picchi's three-liver *crostino* topping was as light as a cloud, with none of the bitterness this dish often has. A refreshing tomato aspic was excellent: scented with basil and garlic, it was served chilled with a spoonful of the new season's oil. A room temperature "salad" of marinated tripe was spiced with crisp red onion and parsley.

Picchi's yellow pepper soup has become a classic: pure in taste and color, it exemplifies the restaurant's refined rustic style. A potato *sformato* ("unmolded") was creamy and delicately flavored, served with a *ragù* of white meats and enriched with butter and Parmesan.

I tried two main courses, a Swiss-style meat loaf of veal and ricotta, which was nicely herbed and served with a fine tomato sauce, and another of the restaurant's signature dishes, *calamari in inzimino*. This is the Cibrèo dish that struck me most. A traditional peasant recipe that, Picchi explained, has its origins in Turkey, it seemed to me primordial, deep, and dramatic. Dark-red-stained squid is stewed with chard and spinach greens cooked down to resemble seaweed. The strong, memorable dish is highly spiced with hot chili.

For dessert there are cakes, tarts of bitter orange, summer berries, or cheese. Or try the rich *meringata con castagne*—meringue with chestnuts. The fine wine list includes Tuscany's best, as well as excellent after-dinner spirits. Whatever your budget, this is a must for interested food and wine lovers.

DEI FAGIOLI   CORSO DEI TINTORI, 47R 50122 FIRENZE
RESTAURANT   TELEPHONE 055 244285

OPEN Lunch and dinner   **CLOSED** Sunday, Saturday in summer; August   **CREDIT CARDS** None
ENGLISH SPOKEN Yes   **RESERVATIONS** Recommended for dinner   **PRICE** $$
DIRECTIONS From the Uffizi, take Via dei Neri to Corso dei Tintori

---

This centrally located trattoria is run by the extended Zucchini family. The father has cooked here for thirty years, creating the kind of friendly, uncomplicated place you are always happy to come back to. The cuisine is decidedly Tuscan; the empha-sis is on the simple, home-cooked dishes the region is famous for. So sample *crostini tipici* (canapés topped with chopped chicken livers), *ribollita* (bread-thickened veg-etable soup), or *pappa al pomodoro* (summer tomato and bread soup).

Main courses include classic *bollito misto* (assorted boiled meats served with an intense parsley sauce), *baccalà* with chickpeas (a Friday special), or the Fiorentina—T-bone steak grilled over a wood fire. As a side dish, try a plate of *fagioli* beans or chickpeas drizzled with new oil. The wine list is short but adequate. To finish the meal, order one of the make fine homemade jam *crostate* (tarts), for which Signora Zucchini uses her grandmother's recipe

FIRENZE'S FIASCHETTERIE

These unpretentious wine bars got their name from the flasks (*fiaschi*) Chianti was traditionally bottled in. They range from small stand-up shops selling un-bottled wines and sandwiches to slightly larger bars with a few tables serving drinkable wines and a few simple dishes. They are centrally located, atmos-pheric, and very reasonably priced. Here are some of the best among many: Fani, Via degli Alfani, 70R; La Fiaschetteria, Via dei Neri, 17R; Vecchio Vinaio, Via dei Neri, 65R; and Antica Mescita San Niccolò, Via San Niccolò, 60R.

IL GUSCIO
RESTAURANT

VIA DELL'ORTO, 49 50124 FIRENZE
TELEPHONE 055 224421
E-MAIL fgozzini@tiscali.it

OPEN For dinner only   **CLOSED** Lunch; Sunday and Monday in winter; Saturday and Sunday in June and July; August   **CREDIT CARDS** Visa, MC, Amex   **ENGLISH SPOKEN** Yes
RESERVATIONS Necessary   **PRICE** $$$ **DIRECTIONS** In San Frediano, on the south side of the Arno near Santa Carmine

---

Il Guscio is one of Firenze's most popular restaurants—with the Florentines. The food in this relaxed but ever busy trattoria is cooked by three generations of women in the Gozzini family.

"That's why it tastes like real food," exclaims Francesco Gozzini as he brings the dessert. "It is!" The flavors are authentically Florentine, with a seasonal menu that sounds so good it's hard to choose. In late spring I started with a delicate *tortino*—like a mousse—of ricotta and Parmesan accompanied by a subtle truffle sauce, which formed part of the mixed antipasti of the house. A rustic soup fol-lowed, of fresh white beans and spring porcini mushrooms topped with chunks of Tuscan bread and fruity olive oil: a poem of simplicity. *Bavettine*, or linguine, were served with a real fisherman's sauce of pounded *gallinella,* celery, tomato, and parsley, with just a hint of hot *peperoncino.* The main course was spectacular: a sizzling pan (*padella*) of mixed Mediterranean fish and shellfish dressed with garlic and herbs, with a thick slice of toast to mop up the juices; it made me feel I was eating at the seaside. The menu stretches to meats and vegetables, all cooked with a satisfying style. The large wine list will please wine enthusiasts, as it contains some unusual finds, and it is sorted by price. Save room for desserts, and don't forget to book well in advance. The two rooms plus a few tables outside are always packed.

IL LATINI   VIA DEI PALCHETTI, 6R 50122 FIRENZE
RESTAURANT   TELEPHONE 055 210916   FAX 055 289794

OPEN Lunch and dinner   **CLOSED** Monday; two weeks in August
CREDIT CARDS Visa, MC, Amex   **ENGLISH SPOKEN** Yes   **RESERVATIONS** Recommended
for groups   **PRICE** $$$ **DIRECTIONS** Off Via della Vigna Nuova

"Ninety percent of our customers love us to death," exclaimed Giovanni Latini, one of Il Latini's family of owners. "The rest are just not wild about this type of atmosphere." The ever packed restaurant has an age-old, inimitable style: the large sprawling dining room is filled with refectory tables that hold at least eight. Diners are seated wherever there is a space and often find themselves in conversation with their neighbors (which is part of the charm of the place). There is a mad mixture of stuff around, including prosciutto hams hanging from the ceilings, bottles of the Latinis' wines, and flasks of Chianti. The half-paneled walls are thick with photographs of literary figures. The family offers an annual literary award to writers whose lives have been dedicated to their art; the prize consists of a convivial dinner at the restaurant and a prosciutto.

The menu is Tuscan-in-a-hurry: the hearty soups are simple but good, pasta dishes arrive in seconds and tend to be soft, and there are hand-cut *salumi,* ready-cooked roast meats, and stews. So go for the fun of it.

TRATTORIA MARIO   VIA ROSINA, 2R 50122 FIRENZE
RESTAURANT   TELEPHONE 055 218550
                                          WEB SITE www.trattoriamario.com

OPEN Lunch only   **CLOSED** Sunday; August   **CREDIT CARDS** None
ENGLISH SPOKEN A little   **RESERVATIONS** None accepted   **PRICE** $
DIRECTIONS Beside the Mercato Centrale

Located a few steps from the San Lorenzo market, this is a genuine Florentine gem—if you get there early enough to secure a table. The kitchen takes up half of the tiny dining room, and the tables are a crush, but the food and jolly atmosphere are worth it. A few *primi* are prepared each day: simple soups, such as the wonderfully warming chickpea and rice, and a couple of pastas. Then there are steaks, roasts, *baccalà* (salt cod), and *bollito* (boiled meats). *Contorni*, side dishes, include boiled vegetables to eat with a little good olive oil. You can have a glass of wine at the table or at the minuscule bar (open all day) by the front door after your meal.

LE MOSSACCE
RESTAURANT

VIA DEL PROCONSOLO, 55R 50122 FIRENZE
TELEPHONE 055 294361

OPEN Lunch and dinner   **CLOSED** Saturday, Sunday; August   **CREDIT CARDS** Visa, MC, Amex
ENGLISH SPOKEN Yes   **RESERVATIONS** None accepted   **PRICE** $$
DIRECTIONS One block south of the Duomo

Le Mossacce is a popular trattoria in central Firenze with fair prices. Squeeze in past the narrow entrance to the dining rooms, which are crammed with regulars and tourists at peak hours. There is always a warm atmosphere and quick turnover.

The menu features Tuscany's unpretentious signature recipes: *la ribollita* (thick bread and vegetable soup), *pasta e fagioli* (white bean soup with pasta), and minestrone. Main courses include *spezzatino* (stew), *arista* (roast pork), *trippa* (tripe), and the celebrated Tuscan T-bone, *la Fiorentina*. There are several vegetable side dishes to choose from, a few desserts, and basic wines.

ENOTECA PANE E VINO
RESTAURANT

VIA SAN NICCOLÒ, 70R 50125 FIRENZE
TELEPHONE 055 2476956   FAX 055 4211009
E-MAIL paneevino@yahoo.it

OPEN Dinner   **CLOSED** Lunch; Sunday; August 7–21   **CREDIT CARDS** Visa, MC, Amex
ENGLISH SPOKEN Yes   **RESERVATIONS** Recommended   **PRICE** $$–$$$
DIRECTIONS On the south side of the Arno, near Ponte alle Grazie

The brothers Pierazzuoli opened Italy's first wine bar in 1979. "Right from the start we wanted to serve Italy's greatest wines in big Riedel glasses, even if it was on yellow butcher's paper mats," recounts Gilberto. Now, more than twenty years later, Pane e Vino has grown into a truly Florentine institution. "We have helped to educate our young clients, and they have remained loyal to our search for the best—and often undiscovered—wines around," says Ubaldo. They are enthusiastic hosts and are happy to make suggestions about what to drink. In the meantime, the kitchen has grown and improved to complement this exceptional culture of wine.

In spring, I tasted Barbara Zattoni's "flan" of pecorino. It was as soft as egg custard, baked like a yellow cheesecake and served with a bright green, coarse purée of fresh fava beans. Potato-filled *tortelli* were set off by a meat sauce flavored with dried mushrooms. Assorted raw-milk cheeses featured sheep's milk pecorini, while selected blue cheeses were served with bitter *corbezzolo* honey. Pane e Vino, in its two modest rooms decorated only with bottles, offers good value for the money and a stimulating environment in which to learn more about wine.

ENOTECA PINCHIORRI
RESTAURANT

VIA GHIBELLINA, 87 50122 FIRENZE

TELEPHONE 055 242777, 242757   FAX 055 244983

OPEN Lunch and dinner   **CLOSED** Sunday, Monday, and Tuesday for lunch; August
CREDIT CARDS All   **DIRECT SALE** Wines are not for sale except in the restaurant
ENGLISH SPOKEN Yes   **FEATURES** Summer garden dining   **RESERVATIONS** Necessary
PRICE Lunch $$$$$, Dinner $$$$$$ **DIRECTIONS** Near Teatro Verdi

---

Few places create a sense of occasion as well as grand restaurants, which are necessarily formal, polished, and larger than life—anything less and we might be disappointed. The Enoteca Pinchiorri fits readily into this category, offering world-class wines, refined cuisine, and over-the-top service. So if you are in the mood to go out for a really special meal with all the attendant pomp and circumstance, reserve a table here.

The restaurant is on the ground floor of Palazzo Ciofi-Iacometti. The well-lit rooms are high and vaulted, the colors clear pastels, and the materials heavy linen, silver, and fine crystal (more than seventy styles). In February, an enormous vase of white lilies and glossy-leaved magnolia branches mirrored the volume of an imposing Murano chandelier. An army of slim waiters (including one just for water) caters to the customers' every need.

Giorgio Pinchiorri has a world-famous cellar, with tens of thousands of bottles of great wines. So, to complement its catalogues of Italian, French, and other wines, the list offers several set-price wine "combinations." The expert wine staff is happy to share its knowledge and offer advice.

As for the food, in addition to an à la carte menu, diners are offered two *degustazione* (tasting) menus: "Menu Toscano," traditional Tuscan recipes revisited, or "Menu del Giorno," creative seasonal dishes (served as a surprise). I chose the former.

Chef Annie Féolde's *pappa al pomodoro* was unlike any other. Three spoonfuls of warm spicy tomato-bread paste arranged in a row (like rosy quenelles) were topped with wafer-thin round *schiacciatine*—hot salted biscuits fragrant with olive oil. Their cold green basil sauce tasted purer than pesto. It was all delicious; if you closed your eyes, you had the essence of the humble recipe done with a pinch of humor, culture, and refinement. Steamed fillets of red mullet (shiny side up) on a pale celeriac purée looked like an abstract painting with colorful accents: fried basil, parsley, and tomato skin.

A soup of spelt wheat (*farro*) was "garnished" with jumbo shrimp roasted with stark leaves of bay. Livornese *cacciucco* was here a silk-smooth coral sauce of fish stock and tomato, with chunks of clam and lobster, sea bass and bream. Narrow *pinci*—eggless noodles—floated in this deeply flavored sauce. Tortelloni had mashed potato fillings and an intense dry sauce of dried porcini, tomato *concassé*, and thyme. Smoky-sweet *necci* (chestnut-flour pancakes) were stacked with fine ricotta, toasted *pinoli*, and rosemary. Seared duck breast came with soft stewed fennel and sharp black olives.

These technically proficient, sophisticated dishes never lose sight of the taste of their *cucina povera* origins. "I always try to come back to the purity and simplicity of the ingredients," Féolde explained. Pure and simple they may be, but at its best this food impresses for the clarity of its flavors, the lightness of its touch, and the style of its presentation.

ALLA VECCHIA BETTOLA   VIALE ARIOSTO, 32/34R SAN FREDIANO 50100 FIRENZE
RESTAURANT   TELEPHONE 055 224158

OPEN Lunch and dinner   **CLOSED** Sunday, Monday; three weeks in August
CREDIT CARDS None   **ENGLISH SPOKEN** Yes   **RESERVATIONS** Recommended
PRICE $$ **OTHER** The house wine is included in the cover charge
DIRECTIONS The restaurant is south of the Arno, by Piazza Tasso

---

"I come from a long line of Florentine street food sellers," Loriano Stagi explained proudly as he added a place for me at his table. "My grandmother was well known here in the *rione* [quarter] of San Frediano for selling *capi roti* [broken heads]—the good parts cut from bruised oranges."

Loriano opened here in 1979 with his wife, Carla Zetti. They wanted to re-create the kind of unpretentious eating house once common in Firenze, the *bettole*. Its interior of tiled walls, marble-topped tables, and wooden stools is embellished with compositions of fruit and flowers, hanging salami and prosciutti. An old-fashioned iron stove heats the room in winter. The menu, written on ocher butcher's paper, changes daily. "It depends what's fresh in the market," recounted the amiable Carla. "Our cuisine is based on the simple foods of *la cucina povera*: hearty bread soups, pasta, fried or roasted meats, tripe, and other organ meats."

I sampled a series of dishes, all well flavored and delicious: *crostini* toasts topped with a delicate paste of *milze* (spleen), anchovies, and capers; baked artichokes stuffed with home-cured pancetta and herbs; *penne alla bettola*, a spicy pasta with tomatoes, hot pepper, and vodka; cauliflower cooked with tomatoes and fennel seeds; fagioli beans drizzled with fruity olive oil. *Lampredotto* (chitterlings), "cooked in the manner of tripe," was sliced and stewed until tender. The restaurant serves fine T-bone steak—*la Fiorentina*. The salumi have been carefully selected: you can sample the genuine *prosciutto Toscano* cured by Belsedere (p 299–300).

One of the couple's sons runs the famous Nerbone stall inside the San Lorenzo (Mercato Centrale) food market, which specializes in filled rolls. It's a great place for a snack when browsing through the market (p 92).

ZIBIBBO
RESTAURANT

VIA DI TERZOLLINA, 3R 50129 FIRENZE
TELEPHONE 055 433383   FAX 055 4289070

OPEN Lunch and dinner   **CLOSED** Sunday; August   **CREDIT CARDS** Visa, MC, Amex
ENGLISH SPOKEN Yes   **RESERVATIONS** Recommended   **PRICE** $$$
DIRECTIONS Careggi is at the northern edge of the city, a short taxi ride from the center, or take bus 14c from Santa Maria Novella to the end of the line at Piazza dei Careggi. The restaurant is a few doors away from the bus stop, with the former tobacconist's "T" sign visible outside

Benedetta Vatali is an expert on the Florentine restaurant scene: she was married to Fabio Picchi for many years and helped create their famous restaurant, Cibrèo (see p 98). In 1999 she started one of her own.

"I wanted to move out of the most touristic part of town," she said, "and open an unfussy place people would enjoy, with home-cooked, simple foods." Zibibbo, named for the sweet muscat grape used in Sicilian winemaking, is just that: an airy, colorful, relaxed restaurant that serves uncomplicated but flavorful food with a clear Mediterranean feel.

Vatali's female chefs work well with vegetables and with dishes from the *cucina povera:* cold octopus salad; lentil soup enriched with rice; handmade noodles with duck sauce; spaghetti dressed with garlic, tiny clams, and mussels; "sweet and sour" swordfish topped with capers, raisins, tomatoes, and onions; a salad of mixed field greens. The wine list is well chosen, and well priced. After the meal, have a coffee at the little stand-up bar on the way out, just as the regulars do.

LEOPOLDO PROCACCI
SPECIALTY FOODS: TRUFFLE SANDWICHES

VIA TORNABUONI, 64R 50100 FIRENZE
TELEPHONE 055 211656

OPEN 10:30–20:30   **CLOSED** Sunday, Monday; August   **CREDIT CARDS** Visa, MC, Amex
DIRECT SALE Yes   **ENGLISH SPOKEN** Yes   **DIRECTIONS** Near Palazzo Strozzi

This wonderfully old-fashioned shop is a must for epicures. At its heart, a quaint glass case contains the *panini tartufati,* truffle-scented sandwiches, that have made it justly famous. Eat a couple standing at the bar as you sip a glass of *spumante* for a suggestively grand-tour experience.

After 111 years in the same family, the shop has now been taken over by the Antinoris (see p 96), who have changed it as little as possible. "We still use only the finest local truffles," explained manager Walter, "like the white *Tuber magnatum pico.* They are found in the winter months around San Miniato and San Giovanni d'Asso."

The shop's elegant wall cabinets house fancy foods and wines, and the sandwich range has been increased to include Brie and salmon, but the quintessential Procacci delights are those genteel little rolls with their earthy, fragrant paste.

DINO BARTOLINI
TABLE CRAFTS: KITCHENWARES

VIA DEI SERVI, 30R 50122 FIRENZE
TELEPHONE 055 211895   FAX 055 264281
WEB SITE www.dinobartolini.it

OPEN 9:00–12:30, 15:30–19:00   **CLOSED** Monday morning and Saturday afternoon in summer; Monday in winter; three weeks in August   **CREDIT CARDS** Visa, MC   **MAIL ORDER** Yes **ENGLISH SPOKEN** Yes   **DIRECTIONS** Via dei Servi runs northeast from the Duomo

---

This is one of the best kitchen supply shops in Firenze, if not in Tuscany. They carry a lot of everything, from pasta pots to Alessi's copper pans, cheese graters to *mezzaluna* (half-moon) choppers, espresso pots to prosciutto stands, gelato scoops to oil cruets. There are departments for fine china, crystal glassware (including Riedel sommelier wine glasses), chef's knives, baking pans . . . and much more. They even stock cork stoppers in all shapes and sizes—so measure your topless jars or bottles before you go. Bartolini holds its annual three-week sale beginning at the end of January—a winter's treat!

HEMINGWAY
TEA ROOM, CHOCOLATE, BAR

PIAZZA PIATTELLINA, 9R 50124 FIRENZE
TELEPHONE/FAX 055 284781
WEB SITE www.hemingway.fi.lyork

OPEN Winter: Tuesday–Saturday 16:30–1:00 A.M.; Sunday 11:30–20:00. Summer: Tuesday–Friday "Hemingway by night" midnight–7:00 A.M.   **CLOSED** Monday in winter; Saturday–Monday in summer   **CREDIT CARDS** Visa, MC   **DIRECT SALE** Yes   **ENGLISH SPOKEN** Yes **RESERVATIONS** Recommended for meals   **PRICE** $–$$
DIRECTIONS On the south side of the Arno, near Piazza del Carmine

---

It's hard to know what category to put Hemingway into—it offers so many things: a tearoom that also does brunch; a rendezvous for chocoholics that stays open all night in summer; a relaxed spot to have great cake, but also salads and fine artisan cheeses . . . Monica Meschini and Emma Mantovani run a lively, free-form meeting place on the south side of the Arno that started with a passion for chocolate and just kept growing. They make the best hot chocolates I've ever tasted and sell chocolates from many of Tuscany's *maestri,* including de Bondt (p 135–136), Mannori (p 113), and Slitti (p 74)—they even run a chocolate association. They carry ice-creams made by the award-winning *maestro* of Sansepolcro, Ghignoni (see p 370).

Buffet salads and cold snacks are available at brunch on Sunday, as well as all night in summer. There are a few wines, plus imported beers in summer. All in all, a fun place to hang out!

MARCHESI DE'FRESCOBALDI
WINE

VIA SANTO SPIRITO, 11 50125 FIRENZE
TELEPHONE 055 27141   FAX 055 280205, 211527
WEB SITE www.frescobaldi.it

DIRECT SALE No   **ENGLISH SPOKEN** Yes

The Frescobaldi head office is in Firenze, and appointments may be made at the above numbers to visit the family's Tuscan wineries. (For visiting information and groups, speak with Cristina Rinaldi.) Or see Rùfina (p 114) for the Castello di Nipozzano and Pomino estates; Montalcino (p 313–314) for the Castelgiocondo estate. For Laudemio oil, see p 117.

ENOTECA BOCCADAMA
WINE BAR

PIAZZA SANTA CROCE, 25R 50121 FIRENZE
TELEPHONE 055 243640
FAX 055 241932 (specify Boccadama on the cover sheet)

OPEN 8:30–1:00 A.M.   **CLOSED** Monday in winter; Saturday evening in summer
CREDIT CARDS Visa, MC, Amex   **ENGLISH SPOKEN** Yes   **PRICE** $–$$

Andrea Poli ran one of Firenze's finest wine stores before he joined Ornella Barsottelli in an ambitious new venture: to create a great wine bar in one of the city's most touristic piazzas. Here you will find fabulous cheeses and *salumi* made by the real artisans of Tuscany and beyond; soups and pastas at mealtimes; salads, meats, and vegetable dishes (with a bigger choice at dinnertime); and a huge selection of exceptional wines by the glass or bottle—in all price ranges. You can also taste the great coffees produced by Le Piantagioni del Caffè (see p 119). There are even a few tables out in the piazza to sit at while you admire the beauty of one of architecture's greatest façades.

Also

PASTICCERIA ROBIGLIO

VIA DEI SERVI, 112R. 055 214501;
AND VIA DE' TOSINGHI, 11R

Robiglio is a Florentine institution favored by the city's well to do. Pastries can be eaten at the bar with a coffee or bought in a *vassoio* (tray). There is also a good range of savory snacks.

CAFFÈ RIVOIRE

PIAZZA DELLA SIGNORIA, 5R. 055 214412

After an exhilarating (but exhausting) visit to the Uffizi, unwind in the old-worldliness of the Rivoire tearooms. The cakes and pastries are fresh and good, and the *cioccolata con panna*—Italian-style hot chocolate with whipped cream—is sinfully rich. You won't need dinner afterward!

UN PUNTO MACROBIOTICO   VIA DEI PILASTRI, 10R. 055 2346975

The successful macrobiotic restaurant from Arezzo and Sansepolcro (see pp 342 and 366) has recently opened a restaurant and shop in Firenze.

ENOTECA FUORIPORTA   VIA MONTE ALLE CROCI, 10R. 055 2342483
CLOSED SUNDAY

This wine bar is firmly established as one of Firenze's best. It has a list of more than six hundred wines, with many by the glass, and offers simple but good light meals to go with them. In summer the tables spread out onto the steep little street, which you can take to San Miniato sul Monte, one of Tuscany's most beautiful churches.

Impruneta

FATTORIA LA QUERCE   VIA IMPRUNETANA PER TAVARNUZZE, 41
OLIVE OIL, WINE   50023 IMPRUNETA
TELEPHONE/FAX 055 2011380

OPEN 10:00–13:00, 15:00–19:00; wine visits and tastings by appointment only
CREDIT CARDS Visa, MC, Amex   DIRECT SALE Yes   ENGLISH SPOKEN Yes
DIRECTIONS From Impruneta go toward Tavarnuzze; the farm is on the left after 1,200 meters

---

Massimo Marchi's estate produces wine and olive oil. La Querce, a modern-style red of 90 percent Sangiovese and 10 percent Colorino, is aged in *barriques*. Chianti Colli Fiorentini La Torretta is also primarily of Sangiovese grapes, with some Canaiolo added; it is a wine to drink young and comes out after one year. There is also a traditional Chianti, which still includes some white grapes with the red. The wines are now being made by the estate's young manager, Marco Ferretti, in collaboration with the winemaker Alberto Antonini.

The estate is also known for its extra-virgin olive oil, which has been voted one of Tuscany's twenty best oils. Marchi prefers the traditional stone-grinding system. "When used properly, it makes the oil less bitter," explained Ferretti. "Tuscan oil can initially be difficult for foreigners to appreciate, with its strong, decisive flavors, artichoke bitterness, and peppery finish. But given time, it grows on you."

MARIO MARIANI   VIA CAPPELLO, 29 50023 IMPRUNETA
TABLE CRAFTS: POTTERY   TELEPHONE 055 2011950

OPEN 8:00–12:00, 14:00–19:00   CLOSED Saturday, Sunday, except by appointment
CREDIT CARDS None   ENGLISH SPOKEN A little   DIRECTIONS From Impruneta's central square, go down toward Ferrone until the road to Ferrone turns left. Go straight toward Vanni; after 200 meters Mariani's gate is on the left

---

"What you need to make these pots are fire, earth, water, and elbow grease!" exclaimed the vivacious Mario Mariani. His human-size terra-cotta urns are indeed handmade from local clay and fired in a wood-burning kiln as big as a room. To see the kiln loaded with mountains of logs, ready to be lit, is a spectacle. Urns may not be easy to carry home (Mariani produces some smaller objects), but anyone interested in original artisan crafts should see these. They even adorn the presidential palace in Rome.

Le Vedute

LE VEDUTE
RESTAURANT

VIA ROMANA LUCCHESE, 121 50050 FUCECCHIO
TELEPHONE 0571 297498   FAX 0571 297201

OPEN Lunch and dinner   **CLOSED** Monday; August   **CREDIT CARDS** Visa, MC, Amex
ENGLISH SPOKEN A little   **FEATURES** Summer terrace   **RESERVATIONS** Recommended
on weekends and for terrace   **PRICE** $$$$ **DIRECTIONS** On main road from Fucecchio
to Altopascio

The ample menu in this well-groomed restaurant is divided between "land" and "sea" and changes daily. This is a family-run restaurant with professional service and a certain style; the spacious indoor rooms are comfortable, with a vine-covered terrace for summer meals. Many customers are tannery managers from nearby Santa Croce.

My autumn meal celebrated wild mushrooms and truffles. From a piping-hot dish came a startling, intense perfume: white truffle shavings were scattered onto sizzling stewed leeks—the earthy aroma was remarkable. Warm butterflied shrimp came with arugula and sliced yellow-gilled *ovoli*, delicate wood mushrooms that resemble eggs before they open.

Straccetti all'aragosta, a "sea" pasta, had irregular "rags" of vivid green pasta tossed in a coral lobster sauce; the fine-flavored fish married well to its light cream binding. Other *primi* included risotto blackened by squid ink, linguine with shellfish, and tagliatelle with mixed mushrooms.

As main courses, mushrooms came grilled, fried, stuffed—alone or with veal, lamb chops, or stewed kidneys and potatoes. Fish and shellfish were paired with olives and capers, steamed vegetables, or rosemary and oil. Some were cooked *in cartoccio*—packets of foil to seal in the cooking juices. A well-stocked dessert trolley was irresistible. The wine list had a good selection of Tuscans and a fair selection of prices.

Massarella

IL CACCIATORE
RESTAURANT

VIA DELLE CERBAIE, 36/38 MASSARELLA 50054 FUCECCHIO
TELEPHONE 0571 296238

OPEN Lunch and dinner   **CLOSED** Tuesday   **CREDIT CARDS** Visa, MC
ENGLISH SPOKEN A little   **RESERVATIONS** Recommended on weekends
PRICE $$ **DIRECTIONS** Massarella can be reached from the Montecatini-Fucecchio road

This is a classic Tuscan-style trattoria serving local specialties, including home-made pastas and soups, such as the thick vegetable and bread *ribollita*. Main courses feature meats and game grilled on the big wood barbecue, *alla brace*. In autumn and winter there is wild boar, hare, and local duck cooked simply but well, and there is a nice choice of Tuscan wines and local oils.

Montelupo Fiorentino

ND DOLFI
TABLE CRAFTS: POTTERY

VIA TOSCO ROMAGNOLA NORD, 8 50056 MONTELUPO FIORENTINO
TELEPHONE 0571 910116, 51264   FAX 0571 910116
E-MAIL nd.dolfi@iol.it

OPEN 9:00–20:00   **CLOSED** Monday   **CREDIT CARDS** Visa, MC, Amex   **DIRECT SALE** Yes
MAIL ORDER Yes   **ENGLISH SPOKEN** No   **DIRECTIONS** From Montelupo take the SS 67 toward
Firenze; the pottery is on the left after 3 kms

This artisan pottery has been in the Dolfi family for three generations, but there has been a tradition of fine hand-painted ceramics at Montelupo since 1500. In the nineteenth century, local clay pits were rediscovered; the town now boasts a ceramics museum. Many historic designs use only blue and white, but more recent Montelupo motifs—such as courtiers with daggers—are featured on a distinctive yellow background.

Some of the deeper colors used on decorative plates, tiles, and vases contain lead, but all plates destined for the table are guaranteed to be lead free. In addition to classical medieval and Renaissance patterns, the Dolfis' handsome showroom features colorful modern designs painted on tiles, urns, candlesticks, platters, and wall ornaments.

Also

LA BOTTEGA DELL'ARTE FIORENTINA   CORSO GARIBALDI, 72. 0571 911044

In the small central piazza of Montelupo, this pottery shop sells the traditional large creamy platters with curlicued handles that are special to Montelupo, and which make great serving dishes for a buffet dinner.

Mura

CASA MASI
TRATTORIA TOSCANA
RESTAURANT

SAN BENEDETTO MURA 50050 MONTAIONE
TELEPHONE 0571 677170   FAX 0571 677042
E-MAIL casamasi@nautilo.it

OPEN Lunch and dinner   **CLOSED** Monday   **CREDIT CARDS** Visa, MC
ENGLISH SPOKEN Yes   **RESERVATIONS** Recommended for dinner   **PRICE** $$
OTHER Fifteen apartments available for summer rental   **DIRECTIONS** From Mura, go down
toward San Miniato; after 2 kms, turn left just before the small bridge and follow the unpaved road
to the restaurant

Casa Masi is in a large stone barn in a shady garden. Alessandro Masi and his wife, Luciana, have adorned the walls nicely with baskets, old cutting boards, wooden tools, and other collectibles. There is a lively, convivial atmosphere.

The food is good country fare, *alla Toscana*. "We want to bring back the flavors of foods we knew as children," explained the attractive Luciana. "Some of these recipes were my grandmother's—and they are wonderful." The menu marks "old Tuscan" recipes with an asterisk.

Autumn antipasti included artisan-made *salumi*, mixed *crostini*, *salame* with fresh figs, and fried polenta wedges topped with stewed leeks and sausage. *N'cavolata nera* was a rustic soup of finely chopped vegetables, beans, and Tuscan black winter cabbage. Another satisfying soup featured chickpeas and beet greens. *Gnuddi* of spinach and ricotta were little green dumplings nicely flavored with sage.

Stewed rabbit was tender, as was guinea fowl cooked with Vin Santo and served with onions and field mushrooms, in earthy contrast to the sweet sauce. Pecorino was grilled and served hot with aromatic truffle oil. Desserts were well made and showed some northern influence in their finesse. A tart of thinly sliced apples was served with a lustrous crème anglaise. A rich chocolate tart had good depth of flavor and a fudgelike consistency. The wines are local, the service is friendly, the place fun.

Ponte a Ema

CASA EDITRICE "IL FIORE"
BOOK PUBLISHER

VIA B. FORTINI, 124/1 50125 PONTE A EMA
TELEPHONE 055 643288   FAX 055 641554
WEB SITE www.casaeditriceilfiore.it

DIRECT SALE No   **MAIL ORDER** Yes   **ENGLISH SPOKEN** Yes

Aldo Capobianco's independent publishing house, Il Fiore, has produced some authoritative books on Tuscan gastronomy. The biggest and most complex is *Vino e Olio in Toscana—Wine and Oil in Tuscany.* The comprehensive book includes essays by experts and a comprehensive list, zone by zone, of Tuscany's key wineries. One label from each estate is reproduced in color.

Other books include historical and cultural treatises on Firenze and Tuscany. *Carmignano: L'Arte del Vino* is a fascinating book in Italian on this small but historic wine-producing area near Firenze. Il Fiore's books may be ordered directly from the publisher or through bookstores in Firenze.

Prato

BISCOTTIFICIO ANTONIO MATTEI
PASTRY

VIA RICASOLI, 20 50047 PRATO
TELEPHONE 0574 25756   FAX 0574 36650
WEB SITE www.antoniomattei.it

OPEN 8:00–13:00, 15:30–19:30 in winter; 8:00–13:00, 16:00–20:00 in summer
CLOSED Sunday afternoon and Monday in winter; Sunday and Monday in summer
CREDIT CARDS None   **MAIL ORDER** Yes   **ENGLISH SPOKEN** Yes
DIRECTIONS Near Piazza San Francesco

Seekers of the true *cantucci* should make a pilgrimage to Prato, home of the original *biscotti di Prato*—better known (everywhere but in Prato) as *cantucci.* Near the imperial castle is the marvelous old bakery that first created these almond-studded biscuits; with Vin Santo they are the quintessential ending to a Tuscan meal. The bakery's store is handsome: a large, lofty room with a marble counter displays cobalt-blue biscuit packages printed with gold. A glass case contains cookies, cakes, and Antinori Vin Santi and wines (the companies have a mutual admiration society).

The bakery was founded in 1858 by Antonio Mattei. Today the crunchy *biscotti* (meaning twice-cooked) are made according to his original recipe, using the same ingredients. "Only the finest almonds, freshest eggs, sugar, and flour are used," explained one of the founder's granddaughters. "Thirty years ago some procedures were mechanized, so biscuits that were once hand-sliced are now cut by machine." But that is the only thing that has changed.

Mattei produces a few other baked goods: *brutti ma buoni* (ugly but good) are chunky, coarse-grained macaroons with a rich nut flavor; *il filone candito* is a low cake of brioche-type pastry dotted with liqueur-soaked cherries and covered with crunchy marzipan; and *la Mantovana* is a moist yellow cake topped with almonds and powdered sugar.

As I entered the shop, my eye was drawn to the unusual window displays of old handwritten postcards from the 1950s and 1960s. The senders were given a multiple-choice question: Were the cookies bad, good, or excellent (*ottimi*)? You can guess the responses: *ottimi, ottimi, ottimi!*

PASTICCERIA LUCA MANNORI
PASTRY, CHOCOLATE

VIA LAZZERINI, 2 (CORNER OF VIA POMERIA)
59100 PRATO FIRENZE
TELEPHONE/FAX 0574 21628   WEB SITE www.mannoriluca.com

OPEN Monday, Wednesday–Saturday 7:00–20:00; Sunday 7:00–13:30, 15:30–20:00
CLOSED Tuesday   **CREDIT CARDS** Visa, MC   **DIRECT SALE** Yes   **ENGLISH SPOKEN** Yes
DIRECTIONS The *pasticceria* is across the street from Prato's hospital

This small but elegant coffee shop is home to one of Italy's most brilliant pastry chefs, Luca Mannori. This remarkable young man has competed with the very best French *patissiers*—and won! Yet he is not as famous as he deserves to be in his native Tuscany. He is thinking of opening a shop in Firenze, and let's hope he does, so many more people will become fans of his extraordinary products.

Everything in the shop is prepared from the finest, freshest ingredients and is beautifully displayed: cakes and other baked goods, chocolates, *gelati*, fruit pastes, even jams and jellies.

The cakes are works of art and come in large sizes as well as scaled-down single portions. In 1997 Mannori won the World Pastrymaking Championship in Lyon with a cake called "The Seven Veils," a layered chocolate and hazelnut confection that is still being made.

"You can spend months perfecting the recipe for one of these very complex cakes," admitted the friendly Mannori. "But people now expect me to surprise them with new creations, so we have to do it."

I love his deeply flavored chocolate and raspberry ice-cream, a combination that is repeated in his unusual chocolate and raspberry jam, and again as a fruit jelly and chocolate square. "Raspberries go well with chocolate because of their acidity," he explained. Dark chocolates are formed into elaborately decorated Easter eggs or filled with subtle tea-scented ganaches—even with Chianti Classico wine!

There is a stand-up bar for coffee and a few tables where you can sit over a cup of rare tea as you indulge in some of the world's most sophisticated desserts. So plan a detour to Prato.

GASTRONOMIA ENOTECA BARNI
SPECIALTY FOODS: DELICATESSEN,
WINE BAR, RESTAURANT

VIA FERRUCCI, 24 50047 PRATO
TELEPHONE 0574 33835, 607845 ENOTECA
FAX 0574 607845   WEB SITE www.enobarni.it

OPEN Shop 7:00–14:00, 16:30–20:30; restaurant Monday lunch only, Tuesday–Friday lunch and dinner, Saturday dinner only   **CLOSED** Sunday. Shop: Wednesday afternoon in winter, Saturday afternoon in summer; August   **CREDIT CARDS** Visa, MC, Amex   **ENGLISH SPOKEN** Yes
RESERVATIONS For dinner at restaurant   **PRICE** $$$ for dinner   **DIRECTIONS** In the town center

This double-fronted shop is a delicatessen on one side and a wine bar and restaurant on the other. The shop, in the same family for sixty years, began as a flour mill and bakery. The *gastronomia* sells fine cheeses, *salumi*, breads baked in its wood oven, pastries, oils, and preserves, but it is also known for its freshly cooked foods. There are pasta specials and rustic vegetable soups to start. Main courses include tripe, roasted pig's liver, roasted meats, and *baccalà alla Livornese* (salt cod) on Fridays.

Go in the other door for the *enoteca*. Here, well-selected wines may be bought to go, or drunk at the bar by the glass or bottle. At lunchtime the back rooms serve as a *tavola calda* restaurant with ready prepared dishes; at night they function as a full restaurant with a full menu.

Rignano sull'Arno

FATTORIA IL POGGIO
OLIVE OIL: ORGANIC

IL POGGIO, 60 50067 RIGNANO SULL'ARNO
TELEPHONE 055 8348346   FAX 055 8348562
WEB SITE www.poggiotrelune.com

OPEN Always, but best to phone first   **CLOSED** Never   **CREDIT CARDS** None
DIRECT SALE Yes   **ENGLISH SPOKEN** Yes   **OTHER** Holiday apartments available
DIRECTIONS From Rignano, go toward Incisa. After 1.5 km turn right toward Troghi. The farm is on the right after another 1.5 km

Enrico Brambilla and his wife run a biodynamic farm (under the auspices of Demeter; see page 224 for more on biodynamic farming), producing organic olive oil, grape juice, and grains. When they took over the farm, chemical pesticides and fertilizers were still being used. "The land was ruined," explained Enrico. "So we joined the Set Aside European Union program and left the land alone for five years, as a kind of purge." Having no animals to produce manure, they buy organic manures and use biodynamic and homeopathic preparations to accelerate growth and improve the soil's fertility.

Their extra-virgin oil is obtained in a traditional stone mill at low temperatures. It can be bought from the farm. In summer they grow their own organic vegetables, which visitors can purchase when available.

Rùfina

OSTERIA LA CASELLINA
RESTAURANT

VIA COLOGNESE, 28 MONTEBONELLO
50065 PONTASSIEVE FIRENZE
TELEPHONE 055 8397580   FAX 055 8396213
E-MAIL casellina@centroin.it

OPEN For dinner; lunch also Saturday and Sunday   **CLOSED** Monday in summer; Monday and Tuesday in winter   **CREDIT CARDS** Visa, MC   **ENGLISH SPOKEN** Yes
FEATURES Summer terrace   **RESERVATIONS** Recommended   **PRICE** $$
DIRECTIONS From Pontassieve, go to Rùfina. In the center of Rùfina, follow signs to the Osteria: turn left from Rùfina, cross a train track, then the river; turn left to the Osteria

is an active supporter of the area's best artisan food and wine
ers, and his unpretentious country restaurant uses them to
of the partners in Rùfina's Wine Museum wine bar (see p 118).
on a pretty flower-filled terrace, with views of vineyards. In
ing room is warm and cheerful. The cooking here is uncompli-
e interesting local dishes at affordable prices.

NA	SS 67 50065 PONTASSIEVE
	TELEPHONE 055 8369848 FAX 055 8316840

:oo; visits, sales, and tastings by appointment only
r CARDS None   **DIRECT SALE** Yes; also from farm shop "Torracino"
ISH SPOKEN Yes   **DIRECTIONS** Selvapiana is east off the main road
ind Rùfina

__eadily been gaining recognition as one of Tuscany's most
interesting, albeit smaller, wine-producing zones, primarily thanks to Francesco
Giuntini of Selvapiana. His long-standing belief in the area's potential, his considerable personal charm, and his fine wines have convinced the wine world of
Rùfina's quality. He now also makes wine for Fattoria di Petrognano at Pomino:
the tiny Pomino DOC is above Rùfina and comprises two producers, the other
being Marchesi de' Frescobaldi (see next entry). Pomino wines are characterized
by their French grape varietals, planted there in the last century. Cabernet and
Merlot form part of the Pomino Rosso blend with Sangiovese; Chardonnay goes
into the white.

Working with his adopted children and winemaker Franco Bernabei, Giuntini
produces classic Sangiovese-based wines that conform to Chianti specifications—
without the optional white grapes. From 50 hectares (123 acres) of vineyards, they
produce Chianti Rùfina DOCG and *crus* Vigneto Bucerchiale (of pure Sangiovese)
and Fornace (of Sangiovese with 10 percent Merlot and Cabernet). These are well-
structured, warm, and elegant wines that only improve with age.

Selvapiana also makes a great Vin Santo. "We pick the Malvasia and Trebbiano
grapes for it at the end of September, when they are very ripe and sweet," said
Federico Masseti, Giuntini's adopted son. "The grapes are left to dry for a long
time, till March, and then the must is put into small *caratelli* of new oak, because
we have found that this keeps the wine's perfumes cleaner." The wine spends five
years in these barrels. A project for a new, modern *cantina* is also in the works.

I was impressed by the atmosphere of culture at Selvapiana, a handsome
seventeenth-century villa with a formal garden. Giuntini and Masseti offer a complete and generous education to interested visitors, showing them the vineyards
and explaining the winemaking process; tastings are guided also. Because many
winery visitors are not experts, this openness encourages further interest. It is no

wonder that Rùfina's winemaking is rapidly improving, for many smaller estates have seen this magnanimity and are now following suit. Giuntini's dream of a wine museum in Rùfina has also finally been realized (see p 118).

MARCHESI DE'FRESCOBALDI
WINE

CASTELLO DI NIPOZZANO
SS 70 DELLA CONSUMA 50060 PELAGO
TELEPHONE NIPOZZANO 055 8311325;
POMINO 055 8318810;
FOR GROUP APPOINTMENTS,
CALL CRISTINA RINALDI 055 27141
FAX 055 280205

OPEN Monday–Saturday and one Sunday per month 9:00–12:00, 14:00–18:00; guided tastings by appointment only   **CLOSED** Three Sundays a month   **CREDIT CARDS** None
DIRECT SALE Yes, from Nipozzano   **ENGLISH SPOKEN** At Nipozzano   **DIRECTIONS** Nipozzano is signposted off the SS 70 west of Diacceto

---

"When you write the word Rùfina," urged Marchese Ferdinando Frescobaldi, "please put the accent on the *u*." For Rùfina denotes the area northeast of Firenze where this noble family has some of its biggest estates. The Frescobaldis' motto, "castles and vineyards since 1300," suggests how central a role this family has played in Tuscan winemaking. The present-day directors of the company are three brothers, Vittorio, Ferdinando, and Leonardo; they have been responsible for bringing the family's traditional-style wineries up to date.

On a sunny winter's day I visited two important estates with Ferdinando Frescobaldi: Nipozzano and Pomino. The large holdings—Nipozzano has 180 hectares (445 acres) of vineyards, Pomino has 100 (247)—are beautifully positioned in the foothills of the Apennines. "Being on high ground [between 350 and 700 meters/1150 and 2300 feet], our vines experience greater extremes of temperature than those lower down," he explained. "But the wines are more perfumed and *fruttato*."

The estates' *cantine*, dating back to the fifteenth century, epitomize the recent changes to Tuscany's wineries: rows of small *barriques* now stand in cellars built to accommodate enormous wooden *botti*. Many Frescobaldi wines reflect this marriage of the traditional with the new.

The Pomino estate, cradled high on a south-facing slope of Mount Pomino, has produced wines for centuries. Chardonnay, the primary grape in the white Pomino Il Benefizio DOC, was first planted there in the 1850s; the vast Benefizio vineyard, 23 hectares (57 acres) at 700 meters, was replanted with selected Chardonnay clones in the 1980s, when the *barriques* were introduced. The elegant modern-style wine is fermented and aged in these small oak casks; it has a full perfumed bouquet, with a fine balance between fruit and wood. Other Pomino DOC wines include Pomino Rosso, the nonreserve Pomino Bianco, and Vin Santo.

The nearby eleventh-century Castle of Nipozzano produces Chianti Rùfina DOC wines Castello di Nipozzano Riserva, and Montesodi from a single vineyard of Sangioveto grapes; they are both elegant, drinkable wines of good structure. Like these, Mormoreto, a Cabernet Sauvignon *cru*, is aged mainly in *barriques*.

See also Castelgiocondo at Montalcino (p 313) and Laudemio (below) for their extra-virgin olive oil.

LAUDEMIO: A NOBLE OIL

"Laudemio is both the definition of a territory and a philosophical concept," explained Marchese Ferdinando Frescobaldi, one of its creators. "Laudemio denotes the hills of central Tuscany; extra-virgin olive oil bearing this name above the producer's is guaranteed to come from olives of this area. A group of producers set up guidelines for the oil: each estate makes oil under its own label but adheres to common principles.

"Every stage, from the growing of the plants to the picking and pressing of the olives, is rigorously controlled. A deadline of December 15 has been set for the picking—to exclude overmature olives. Olives must be picked from the trees, not be so ripe as to fall to the ground. The extraction must be at low temperatures, by whichever process is preferred.

"A special bottle was designed for Laudemio extra-virgin oils. I hope other geographical areas will follow suit—only then can customers be assured of what they are buying."

Other members of the Laudemio group include Marchesi Antinori, Riccardo Falchini, and Fattoria di Bossi. As with fine wines, the quality and taste vary with each producer and *terroir* of production; Laudemio's prices, however, are consistently high.

For further information, contact Bona Frescobaldi or Dr. Piero Tesi, 055 2336565, Consorzio Olivicoltori della Toscana Centrale.

AZIENDA AGRICOLA COLOGNOLE
WINE

VIA DEL PALAGIO, 15 50068 COLOGNOLE RÙFINA FIRENZE
TELEPHONE 055 8319870   FAX 055 8319605
E-MAIL colognol@centroin.it

OPEN Sunday to Friday 10:00–12:00, 14:00–18:00   CLOSED Saturday   CREDIT CARDS Visa, MC
DIRECT SALE Yes   ENGLISH SPOKEN Yes   OTHER Six apartments for holiday rental
DIRECTIONS From Rùfina, take the SS 67 toward Dicomano; turn left toward Colognole and follow
signs up to the winery

This large winery commands exceptional views of the Sieve River valley and is housed in what was once a fortified medieval tower that was key to Firenze's defense against attack from the north. Gabriella Spalletti Trivelli inherited it from her family and decided to keep the country house and make wine there. She is a member of the Donne del Vino (Women of Wine) organization, which is composed of women who are active in the wine world, and now works with her sons to improve the wines and olive oil produced on the estate. "Our vineyards are quite high up," she explained, "so the wines may not have big structure, but at their best they are *profumati* and elegant."

VILLA POGGIO REALE
WINE BAR,
WINE MUSEUM

VIALE DUCA DELLA VITTORIA, 7 50068 RÙFINA FIRENZE
TELEPHONE/FAX 055 8395078   FAX 055 8396213
WEB SITE www.comunerufina.fi.it

OPEN 11:00–19:00, later on weekends   CLOSED Monday   CREDIT CARDS Visa, MC, Amex
DIRECT SALE Yes   ENGLISH SPOKEN Yes   PRICE $ DIRECTIONS In the town center

In a handsome villa historians say was designed by Michelangelo, the Comune di Rùfina has sponsored the creation of what is Tuscany's first wine museum–cum–wine store, featuring the wines of Rùfina and Pomino. The wine bar is managed by two local restaurateurs from Osteria La Casellina (see p 114) and from the spectacular Villa Pittiana hotel, which is situated in an antique villa at Donnini-Reggello (055 860397, fax 055 860326). The *enoteca* offers a great selection of local cheeses, *salumi*, and other light snacks to accompany the wines—which are sold by the glass or bottle. The museum has long been a dream of Francesco Giuntini of Selvapiana's (see p 115), and much of the collection of winemaking tools, memorabilia, and documentation has been donated by him. Future projects include a restaurant.

PULITI "GRANDI VINI"
WINE STORE

VIALE DUCA DELLA VITTORIA, 15 50065 RÙFINA
TELEPHONE 055 8397081, 8397251   FAX 055 8397081
WEB SITE www.icot.it/pulitisilvano

OPEN 9:00–13:00, 15:30–20:00   CLOSED Wednesday afternoon, Sunday   CREDIT CARDS Visa
ENGLISH SPOKENn No   DIRECTIONS On the main road through Rùfina

You would be forgiven for not immediately understanding that this store sells many of Italy's greatest wines: the front part sells loose candies and *bomboniere* (candy souvenirs), while the "stacks" are at the back—industrial shelving holding an amazing range of 974 wines and 76 types of whiskey. This is a no-frills wine store with a lower than usual markup.

Silvano and Fernanda Puliti run a cheerful business. "It started back in the sixties, when our customers began asking for bottled wines," explained Silvano as he tied a pink bow onto a candy dish. "Before that it was mostly *sfuso*—unbottled. I became increasingly interested in quality wines, and now you could say I was hooked!" His list includes all the hardest to find wines.

On Saturday, which is market day in Rùfina, wine tastings are held regularly for interested buyers—but everyone is welcome. The Pulitis stock the fine local Rùfina and Pomino wines and selected Tuscan and other Italian wines. Extra-virgin olive oils complete the range. "I only sell good wines," he declared simply. "And I'm glad young people around here are now more serious about wine. They are the future, and they'll be a lot better prepared than we were."

San Francesco

GELATERIA SOTTANI
VIA FORLIVESE, 93. 055 8368092

This *gelateria* is on the SS 67 between Firenze and Rùfina, north of Pontassieve. Giancarlo Sottani specializes in fruit gelati, with exotic summer flavors such as papaya, pineapple, watermelon, and pomegranate. He favors natural dyes like beets rather than artificial ones. The *creme* range includes a fine *nocciola* made with pure crushed hazelnuts, *castagne* (chestnut), and a group of invented flavors with fanciful titles.

Scarperia

LE PIANTAGIONI DEL CAFFÈ
COFFEE

VIALE KENNEDY, 172/C 50038 SCARPERIA FIRENZE
TELEPHONE 055 846734   FAX 055 8468826
WEB SITE www.lepiantagionidelcaffe.com

OPEN 9:00–18:00   **CLOSED** Saturday and Sunday   **CREDIT CARDS** No   **DIRECT SALE** Yes
ENGLISH SPOKEN Yes   **DIRECTIONS** From Borgo San Lorenzo, go west to S. Piero a Sieve, then north toward Scarperia; 200 meters after the ERG gas station (2.5 kms before arriving at Scarperia), turn left at the left-handed curve, and follow the signs

---

Tasting the coffees of this company came as a revelation to me: the variety of pure, clean aromas available from the diverse coffees it produces is astounding. This is coffee drinking at the highest level, backed up with descriptions of each plantation and the coffee's characteristics and best uses. Each variety is grown with natural cultivation methods in countries as diverse as Guatemala, India, Ethiopia, and Bolivia. What singles them out are their distinctive perfumes and tastes.

The coffees are available in selected stores in Tuscany (including Enoteca Boccadama in Firenze, see p 107) and beyond. Contact the Piantagioni offices for further information and outlets.

Tavarnuzze

MACELLERIA TOGNACCINI   VIA DELLA REPUBBLICA, 17. 055 2374544

This small, family-run butcher's shop has a good range of fresh meats and home-cured *salumi*. *Arista salata sull'asse* is a specialty: boned pork fillet cured on a wooden board; it makes a lean meat to eat, thinly sliced, as an antipasto.

Vicchio

IL FORTETO   SS 551 50039 VICCHIO
CHEESE, MEAT, PRODUCE   TELEPHONE/FAX 055 8448183
                                          WEB SITE www.forteto.it

---

OPEN Tuesday–Friday 8:30–13:00, 15:30–19:30; Saturday–Sunday 8:00–20:00
CLOSED Monday–Thursday in July   **CREDIT CARDS** Visa, MC   **ENGLISH SPOKEN** Yes
DIRECTIONS From Dicomano, take the SS 551 toward Vicchio. Il Forteto is on the main road after 4 kms, on the right

---

Il Forteto is a cooperative of cheese makers, cattle breeders, and vegetable growers. Since 1977 it has expanded to include a modern supermarket featuring the members' products. Its specialties are sheep's and cow's cheeses and beef of the acclaimed Chianina breed. Farm produce is also available.

Cheeses are made from Tuscan milk: fresh creamy ricotta; pecorini, fresh and matured; even a cow's-milk mozzarella. I particularly like the Riserva del Casaro, a crumbly, well-flavored pecorino matured for six months with an olive-oiled crust.

Il Forteto is a leading Tuscan producer of Chianina beef. The pale-colored animals with large dark eyes were once used primarily for farm work. "The politics of beef-raising has changed," explained Mauro Vannucchi, responsible for the farm's Chianina. "Ten years ago they were practically extinct." In recent years demand for their meat has increased: the best *bistecche alla Fiorentina*, or T-bone steaks, call for them. The meat has less fat and more protein than other beef, and the pure-breed animals are raised and butchered under strict controls of the European Union and the breeders' consortium. In Italy, the use of hormones is forbidden by law, and all meat is rigorously tested.

At Il Forteto the animals are raised in large barns, spending some of their lives outdoors (a rarity in Italy). They are fed only hay and grain produced on the farm. Its mountainous show bull and cows may be visited just a few steps from the store.

LA CASA DEL PROSCIUTTO
RESTAURANT, DELICATESSEN

VIA PONTE A VICCHIO, 1 50039 VICCHIO
TELEPHONE 055 844031

OPEN Bar and shop 8:00–15:00, 17:00–19:30 (till 20:00 in summer); trattoria for lunch only
CLOSED Monday; Tuesday afternoon; holidays in July and January   CREDIT CARDS Visa, MC
ENGLISH SPOKEN No   RESERVATIONS Recommended, especially on weekends   PRICE $
DIRECTIONS From the SS 551 at Vicchio, go toward Ponte a Vicchio; the restaurant is across the narrow bridge

This little trattoria-delicatessen-bar is atmospheric, with hams hanging from the ceiling. The loyal clientele stands at the counter for coffee or a sandwich and glass of wine. Lunchers can sit in the dining room, choosing from a menu of moderately priced rustic country dishes.

The "ham house," on the site of an inn dating back to 1400, is named for its fine home-cured prosciutti and other *salumi*—everything from a fennel-seed-studded *finocchiona* to the head cheese, *biroldo* or *soppressata*, that is so popular in Tuscany. Worth sampling are its excellent farm-produced pecorini and ricotta cheeses, made by a local woman from Santa Agata. The cheeses and cured meats may be bought to take away or in sandwiches.

Vinci

FRATELLI TACCINI
STUDIO D ARTE
TABLECRAFTS: POTTERY

STRADA PROVINCIALE DI MERCATALE, 252
50059 VINCI FIRENZE
TELEPHONE 0571 508081   FAX 0571 501962
WEB SITE www.taccini.it

OPEN 9:00–19:00 Monday–Friday; 9:00–13:00, 16:00–19:00 Saturday; 16:30–19:00 Sunday in winter
CLOSED Saturday afternoon and Sunday in July and August   CREDIT CARDS Visa, MC, Amex
DIRECT SALE Yes   ENGLISH SPOKEN Yes   OTHER Custom-designed ceramics may be ordered
DIRECTIONS From Vinci take the road toward Empoli; the shop is on the right after 9 kms, next to IP gas station

"We are children of the Renaissance," said Alessandro Taccini. "Our family has been producing fine hand-painted ceramics for centuries here on the banks of the river Arno ever since the era of the Medicis." For it was the ruling Medici families in the fifteenth and sixteenth centuries who first brought majolica glazes from Spain to Florence and began a ceramics tradition that continues today. "It is said that for certain Medici banquets, dinner services numbering hundreds of pieces were specially decorated to be used only once."

The three Taccini brothers, with their father and sons, have created an extra-ordinary workshop outside of Vinci (Leonardo's birthplace) that resembles the artists' *botteghe* Leonardo and Michelangelo must have worked in. Here, in an atmosphere of peace and concentration, you can find Fulvio delicately painting traditional curlicued motifs on a museum-quality platter, Vittorio putting the finishing touches on a large clay sculpture, and Alessandro preparing a set of col-orfully decorated dishes that would look great on even the most elegant of tables.

"Nowadays, everyone wants to work at top speed, but we have another tradi-tion," explained Alessandro. "If you look carefully at our plates and vases, you can recognize our family's personal language in the markings and decorations we use."

"Yes," replied Fulvio as he mixed a bit more glaze. "You could say that we work with our emotions, our creativity and ideas."

In their large showroom, each piece is more beautiful than the last. I love the large ceremonial platters, which would enhance any wall; the elaborately painted jugs, with their beaklike spouts; and the graphically drawn "Spanish Guard" plates. I have one hanging on my dining room wall—it is an authentic Tuscan treasure. You can see fine recent examples of their work at Slitti's chocolate shop in Mon-summano Terme (see p 74).

CHAPTER 5

Pisa and Its Hills

*P*isa's Piazza dei Miracoli—Place of Miracles—seems aptly named and is one of the world's most spectacular plazas. The beautiful square contains not only the famous Leaning Tower, but also the white marble Romanesque Duomo and its Baptistery. Pisa was once a strategic seaport, positioned at the mouth of the river Arno. By the sixteenth century, however, the river had silted up, and Livorno had become the area's most important harbor.

Pisa is lovely to walk in, with the river Arno weaving a picturesque course through its center. It contains great foods, a charming marketplace, and interesting restaurants. Beyond the Arno's valley, the Pisan hills, *le Colline Pisane,* are some of Tuscany's most unspoiled. Small rural villages are surrounded by patchwork fields of olives, vineyards, and crops. Farther inland is Volterra, one of the Etruscan civilization's most important cities. It is a remarkable place, positioned high on a flat hilltop. It is famous also for alabaster—the translucent white stone worked then as now by skilled artisans. To the Arno's north is Vicopisano, where Brunelleschi's brilliantly conceived fortress has recently been restored; it is visitable on weekends and is well worth seeing.

The province of Pisa contains a handful of top food producers and winemakers—including the creator of fabulous handmade chocolates, one of Italy's oldest pasta factories, and a producer of organic sheep's cheeses.

AZIENDA PROMOZIONE TURISTICA
VIA CAMEO, 2 (NEAR PIAZZA DEI MIRACOLI)
56126 PISA
TELEPHONE 050 560464
FAX 050 40903
WEB SITE www.pisa.turismo.toscana.it

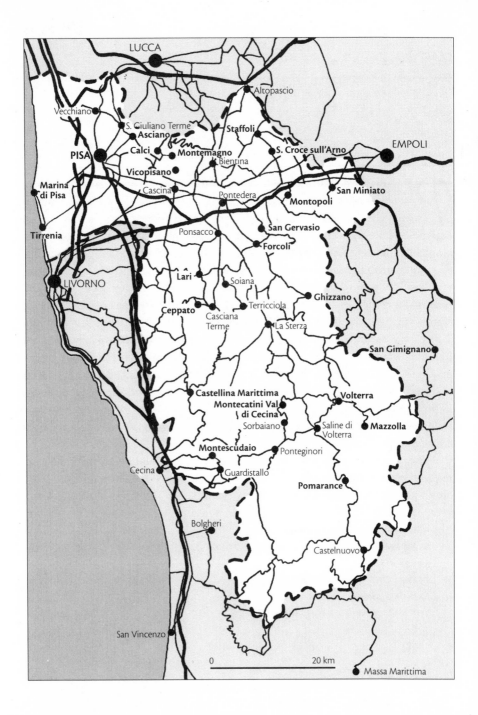

Boldface type indicates towns that are included in this chapter.

Asciano

FATTORIA DI ASCIANO
OLIVE OIL

VILLA SCERNI VIA TRIESTE, 8
56010 ASCIANO PISANO
TELEPHONE/FAX 02 76025678, 050 855924
E-MAIL radev@libero.it

OPEN Sales all year, by phone appointment only   **CREDIT CARDS** None   **DIRECT SALE** Yes
ENGLISH SPOKEN A little   **OTHER** The villa is available for functions   **DIRECTIONS** Facing the
church in Asciano, Villa Scerni is the large villa to its left; ring the bell on the right

For anyone living in the Mediterranean, olive oil is as elemental as water or wine. It gives an unmistakable character to the flavors of the area's cuisines and to its landscapes. The hills just north of Pisa look down over what was once an extensive marsh. Asciano is a distinguished sixteenth-century villa, and it produces one of the area's finest—and my favorite—olive oils.

"Centuries ago, our villa and its lands formed part of the Medici hunting grounds," explained Tea Raggi, who makes prize-winning oil from more than 9,000 olive trees on her family's estate. "But even then, the hills were planted to olives—at the Medicis' request."

Her olive groves do seem a part of history: narrow lanes curve steeply up between dry-stone-walled terraces planted with gnarled old trees that look like sculptures. "These hills are sheltered from the north winds," she said, as we climbed to see the view, "so our trees survived the terrible freeze of 1985 that killed most of Tuscany's century-old olive trees." The steep terraced groves are inaccessible to tractors, but Marchesa Angelica Raggi de Marini Scerni and her daughter have found a picturesque solution for keeping the grass down and the land fertilized: they have enlisted the help of a troop of horses. The animals roam the olive groves and do a fine job of organic recycling.

I watched their oil being made: the hand-picked olives are ground to a paste at Asciano's private mill by huge granite stones. The paste is then spun in a modern machine that separates the oil from its vegetable water.

"The olive is a fruit, and at its best, olive oil is the juice of this fruit," Tea explains. "We must treat it with delicacy to safeguard its freshness and flavors."

The Fattoria's stone grinding mill and old-fashioned press may be visited in November and December, when the hand-gathered olives are being processed. At other times, oil may be bought directly from the farm manager (by appointment only). It is sold bottled or unbottled (*sfuso*). The rich, golden oil is a cross between light Ligurian oil and the intense, *piccante* oils of Tuscany's hills, with some of the sweetness and fragrance characteristic of Lucchese oils.

Calci

AZIENDA AGRICOLA IL COLLETTO
OLIVE OIL

PAR DI ROTA 56010 CALCI
TELEPHONE 050 938320
E-MAIL marcochiletti@libero.it

OPEN By appointment only   **CREDIT CARDS** None   **DIRECT SALE** Yes
ENGLISH SPOKEN Yes   **DIRECTIONS** The small farm is difficult to find; Marco Chiletti will meet clients in Calci and lead the way

The groves of this organic olive oil producer are high on a hillside above the sea. A narrow winding road climbs up through steep walled terraces of olive trees. Marco Chiletti hand-picks his olives early in the season, taking each batch quickly to be milled in a "continuous cycle" *frantoio* nearby. He believes that the future belongs to these hygienic modern steel systems.

"When my oil is fresh, it's so green it hurts your eyes!" exclaimed Chiletti, the farm's young owner and oil expert, who has produced a CD-ROM about oil making. His fine Olio del Par di Rota is fiery and full of character, with a nice bitterness and decisive "pepperiness" to it. It is also sold from his wife's restaurant at Monte-magno Calci (see p 132).

"The biggest problem facing olive growers at low altitudes is the olive fly, *dacus oleae*," he explained. "It is more prevalent in humid areas near the sea. We have developed a complicated defense system that does not rely on chemicals." The critical period is from July to October. By setting traps to attract the males and taking samples from many trees, Chiletti can monitor the fly's behavior. Insect predators and bitter herb solutions sprayed on the trees help ward off attack. Chiletti is also now experimenting with biodynamic and homeopathic treatments for the olive trees.

Castellina Marittima

CASTELLO DEL TERRICCIO
WINE

VIA BAGNOLI LE BADIE 56040 CASTELLINA MARITTIMA
TELEPHONE 050 699709   FAX 050 699789
WEB SITE www.terriccio.it

OPEN Visits by appointment only   **DIRECT SALE** No, but wines are available at Bolgheri
ENGLISH SPOKEN Yes   **DIRECTIONS** Leave the Aurelia SS 1 at the Vada exit; turn right toward Cecina; after 150 meters, turn left into Terriccio's gates

"What makes this part of the country unique is its luminosity," explained Gian Annibale Rossi di Medelana as we sat on his terrace looking out over the hills that slope down to the sea. "The longer I live here, and the better I know these wines, the more convinced I am that this luminosity, this reflected warmth from sea, sun, and sky, can be felt in the wines."

"These wines" caused quite a stir in the wine world in the 1990s by repeatedly winning the highest accolades from critics internationally. And this from a coastal zone that until recently was considered to have no vocation for winemaking. Of course Bolgheri is close by, just a dozen kilometers to the south.

"Both Piero Antinori and Niccolò Incisa were instrumental in encouraging me to start making wines," Rossi de Medelana said. "I went to Bordeaux in the late 1980s to learn about their methods, and in 1988 I planted the first serious vineyards to Cabernet Sauvignon and Merlot." The result was Lupicaia, a powerful, well-structured *barrique*-aged blend that is now considered one of Italy's top wines. It is made in collaboration with Carlo Ferrini, one of Tuscany's most able enologists. The estate's second wine is Tassinaia, also of Cabernet and Merlot, but now with some Sangiovese added. It is a very drinkable warm wine that reflects the terrain on which it was produced.

"People say they can taste a hint of mint and eucalyptus in my wines," he said, "and that makes sense, for some of the vineyards are bordered by huge eucalyptus trees. But the other 'ingredient' here is the mineral-rich soil we have. Indeed, the Etruscans mined iron and copper on this land, and these elements, still present in the earth, are transmitted to the wines."

The beautiful estate is large, with 1,700 hectares (4,200 acres) of land, of which 24 (60) are planted to vines. Show-jumping horses are bred here, and organic cereal crops such as *farro* are grown in the rolling fields. Terriccio also produces three white wines, as well as a fine organic olive oil milled in its own *frantoio*.

Ceppato

LA FRATTINA
RESTAURANT

VIA PISANA, 22 CEPPATO 56034 CASCIANA TERME
TELEPHONE 0587 649233   FAX 0587 979046
E-MAIL scalzi2@interfree.it

OPEN Monday, Wednesday–Saturday dinner only; Sunday lunch and dinner   CLOSED Tuesday; variable winter holidays   CREDIT CARDS Visa, MC   ENGLISH SPOKEN Yes
RESERVATIONS Recommended   PRICE $$$, including house wine   DIRECTIONS From Casciana Terme, follow signs for Ceppato; look for the fork-and-knife restaurant symbol

---

This friendly *osteria* is in a minuscule village in the Pisan hills. In hot weather you eat out on the shaded terrace; in winter the warm dining room has a log fireplace. In this family-run restaurant, the home-cooked dishes change daily. If there is a written menu, I never saw it. The all-inclusive price fluctuates with the cost of ingredients, but it always includes house wine and is a good value. Lino and Elisabetta serve two *primi* and two *secondi* daily, depending on the season. Mixed antipasti precede them, and a simple dessert ends the meal. Despite this system, the kitchen was flexible enough to accommodate a vegetarian without advance warning.

Our mid-September Sunday lunch began with assorted *crostini* canapés, local *salumi*—including well-flavored *prosciutto Toscano*—onion frittata (Italian omelette), and crunchy deep-fried bread dough. Pasta dressed with pumpkin and yellow pepper sauce followed a rustic dish of *pappardelle con la lepre*, wide ribbon noodles with hare. Tender roast pheasant was served with hot grapes and a creamy sauce of mascarpone. Rabbit was stewed with small olives and herbs. A refreshing plate of sliced peaches sprinkled with lime rounded the meal off nicely.

Forcoli

SAVITAR   STRADA COMUNALE PALAIESE, 34 53060 PALAIA
SPECIALTY FOODS: TRUFFLE PRODUCTS   TELEPHONE 0587 629339   FAX 0587 629739
E-MAIL savitar@savitar.it

OPEN 9:00–13:00, 15:30–19:00   CLOSED Saturday afternoon, Sunday   CREDIT CARDS Visa, MC
ENGLISH SPOKEN Yes   DIRECTIONS From Forcoli, take the road up toward San Gervasio and the restaurant Belvedere. Turn left at the T-junction; Savitar is immediately on the right

This artisan company prepares foods using truffles, including the highly prized white San Miniato truffle, *Tuber magnatum pico*. In this area the truffles, a type of fungus, are routed out from under trees by specially trained dogs that have been weaned on them. The white variety, to which San Miniato dedicates an annual fair (p 141), is found in late autumn and winter.

Savitar's unique truffle-scented honey offers an unusual taste sensation: sweet from the honey and earthy, almost pungent from the truffle. They sell it in tiny jars (as with all truffle products, a little goes a long way), and it makes an affordable present for adventurous food lovers. Other truffle-flavored products include pâté, anchovy paste, pasta, cheese spreads, pecorino cheese, truffle butters, pastes, and oils. Fresh truffles last only a few days, but these products preserve the truffle sensations long enough to get them home! The small shop's staff is friendly, knowledgeable, and happy to explain more about this exquisite (and expensive) wild food.

Ghizzano

TENUTA DI GHIZZANO   GHIZZANO 56030 GHIZZANO DI PECCIOLI
WINE   TELEPHONE 0587 630096   FAX 0587 630162
WEB SITE www.tenutadighizzano.com

OPEN Visits by appointment only   CLOSED Mid-August   CREDIT CARDS Visa, MC
DIRECT SALE Yes   ENGLISH SPOKEN Yes   OTHER Six apartments for holiday rentals
DIRECTIONS From Pontedera, go south to Forcoli, then toward Peccioli; Ghizzano is signposted from there

Ghizzano is a beautiful place: a fifteenth-century villa crowns this small medieval village, with a symmetrical box-hedged *giardino all'Italiana* laid out before it. From its tower you can see the estate's 350 hectares (865 acres) of property all around it, with the vineyards in neat rows, and Volterra high on the horizon. "Wines are linked to a territory," said Ginevra Venerosi Pesciolini, the attractive young woman who now runs the estate. "This land has been in my family since 1300, and it's important to me to communicate its character in my wines."

Ginevra recently took over from her father, Pierfrancesco, who was the first to believe in the potential of Ghizzano's wines. She now works with the experienced winemaker Carlo Ferrini. "I have been lucky, she said. "It's hard for anyone to do this alone, but friends such as Piermario Meletti Cavallari (see p 155) have been very supportive."

The estate's acclaimed wines are now reflecting recent investments in the vineyards and cellars. The most important are the powerful Nambrot, of pure Merlot aged knowingly in *barriques;* the well-balanced and elegant Veneroso, of Sangiovese, Cabernet Sauvignon, and Merlot; and Chianti delle Colline Pisane, which is one of the best Chiantis produced in the Pisan hills. Vin Santo and extra-virgin olive oil complete Ghizzano's fine portfolio.

Lari

MARTELLI FRATELLI ARTIGIANI PASTAI	**VIA SAN MARTINO, 3 56035 LARI**
PASTA	TELEPHONE 0587 684238 FAX 0587 684384
	WEB SITE www.famigliamartelli.it

OPEN 8:00–12:30, 14:30–19:00, but best to phone first   **CLOSED** Wednesday, Sunday
DIRECT SALE No, but shops in Lari sell the pasta   **ENGLISH SPOKEN** Yes
DIRECTIONS The factory is at the top of the village, below the castle

Martelli's pasta is some of Italy's finest, and its sun-yellow packages are the best harbingers its friendly makers could have. A visit to their tiny factory is a memorable event—especially on Tuesday or Friday, when spaghetti is being made. It is a thrill to see it "raining" down in long hairlike strands from quaint 1960s machinery. "We are the opposite of the big pasta companies," laughed Mario Martelli, one of two brothers who, with their wives and children, run the business. "They are afraid of industrial espionage. But we love showing visitors how our pasta is made—it says so on our packages."

The Martellis use only top-quality Canadian durum wheat. The flour is mixed with cool water—as opposed to industry's hot water—which maintains its fresh wheat flavor, though it lowers yields. "Our pasta is still made in the traditional way," Mario's brother, Dino, explained enthusiastically. "We don't overcompress it when forcing it through the bronze dies, so its surface is not too smooth." The pasta is dried slowly (at 30°C/86°F) in wooden drying cupboards for up to two days. It is packed by hand. The pasta comes in just four shapes: spaghetti, spaghettini, penne, and maccheroni. Its texture is softer, more elastic, and more porous than that of its industrial counterparts. The Martellis advise using a greater quantity of water than usual when cooking it.

Everything in both the village and the 1870 factory is on a reassuringly human scale, and it takes only two steps to reach the family's dining room. "The big industries may have a point," Mario concluded, as he twirled his fork in a steaming bowl of spaghetti. "After all, they produce as much pasta in eight hours as we make in a year! *Buon appetito!*"

Marina di Pisa

GASTRONOMIA MANZI
SPECIALTY FOODS: DELICATESSEN

VIA MAIORCA, 43/45 56013 MARINA DI PISA
TELEPHONE/FAX 050 36647
WEB SITE www.manzifood.com

OPEN Summer: 7:30–14:30, 17:00–21:00; winter: 8:00–13:30, 16:30–19:30
CLOSED Sunday afternoon and Wednesday in winter   CREDIT CARDS Visa, MC, Amex
ENGLISH SPOKEN Yes   DIRECTIONS On the main road as you enter Marina di Pisa from Pisa

---

This excellent *gastronomia* is the Italian equivalent to a deli, selling a range of specialty foods: fruit and vegetable preserves, pasta (Martelli's), honey, olive oil, and wine. Fresh foods include cheese, homemade *salumi*, and breads. Cooked dishes to take out change daily: soups or pastas, roast meats, seafood, and freshly made pasta sauces. The multitalented Manzis also bake cookies. Their unusual *cantucci* are excellent: rich and soft, with the consistency of macaroons, and enriched with honey and sweet almonds from Puglia. All in all, a great place for foods to take home or to eat on the beach.

Across the street, the family's *gelateria* makes delicious ice creams, too.

Mazzolla

VIVAIO VENZANO
PLANT NURSERY: HERBS

MAZZOLLA 56048 VOLTERRA
TELEPHONE/FAX 0588 39095
WEB SITE www.florealia.com/venzano.asp

OPEN Thursday–Sunday from mid-February to mid-December   CLOSED Monday–Wednesday
CREDIT CARDS None   ENGLISH SPOKEN Yes   OTHER Will design gardens for private clients
DIRECTIONS From Volterra, go toward Colle Val d'Elsa and Siena. After 4 kms turn off toward Mazzolla and follow signs to Venzano

---

The Mediterranean garden has long held a fascination for northern Europeans and Americans. The vivid colors and exotic perfumes of jasmine, bougainvillea, lemon, hibiscus, and lavender trigger memories of warm nights by the sea, of physical and spiritual well-being, of Baudelaire's (or Matisse's) *luxe, calme, et volupté.*

Creating a garden in the hot arid land, however, is not always easy. Water in rural Tuscany is often scarce; the earth is poor, rocky, and intractable. Donald Leevers and Lindsay Megarrity, in their extraordinary nursery at Venzano, concentrate on scented and herbal plants (more than twelve hundred species), many of which survive quite readily in this habitat. Donald Leevers described a mixed border they have created using only indigenous flowering plants: "These wild Mediterranean plants—rosemaries, *Romneya, Cistus,* and lavender—require no watering, yet provide color and interest almost all year."

Venzano is a place of almost mystical allure. Set high above Volterra's round hills, it was built around a natural spring in a grotto existing since Roman times. It feels like an oasis: the crumbling thirteenth-century monastery buildings are set among terraced, walled gardens of simplicity and beauty. Fragrant plants are everywhere. Many culinary herbs are for sale, including thyme, savory, aliums, and *Balsamita major.* There is even the autumn-flowering crocus, *Crocus sativus,* whose precious stigma are saffron.

Montecatini Val di Cecina

FATTORIA SORBAIANO
WINE

VIA PROVINCIALE TRE COMUNI
56040 MONTECATINI VAL DI CECINA
TELEPHONE 0588 30243   FAX 0588 31842
E-MAIL fattoriasorbaiano@libero.it

OPEN 9:00–12:00, 14:00–17:00; *cantina* visits by appointment only   **CLOSED** Saturday afternoon, Sunday   **CREDIT CARDS** Visa, MC   **DIRECT SALE** Yes   **ENGLISH SPOKEN** Yes
OTHER Sixteen apartments available for short rentals   **DIRECTIONS** From Montecatini Val di Cecina, go toward Ponteginori. After 1 km turn right to Sorbaiano. Turn left down a hedged road, passing the villa to reach the winery

This large farm commands spectacular views across the wide Cecina River valley to Volterra. Sorbaiano is one of the area's up-and-coming wineries. The estate has 16 hectares (40 acres) of vineyards under the Montescudaio DOC. The Picciolini family has worked with one of Tuscany's top winemakers, Vittorio Fiore, to improve wines.

Five wines and Vin Santo are made: Rosso delle Miniere is a full-bodied red of primarily Sangiovese grapes; it is aged for one year in *barriques,* small oak casks, and is improved by further cellaring. Lucestraia, of selected Trebbiano and Vermentino grapes, also spends time in small wood barrels. Pian del Conte is a wine of pure Sangiovese that is not aged in *barriques:* it is a fruity wine to drink young. The red and white Montescudaio DOC are very affordable—this winery offers good value for your money.

Montemagno Calci

TRATTORIA DI MONTEMAGNO
RESTAURANT

PIAZZA VITTORIA VENETO, 2
56010 MONTEMAGNO CALCI
TELEPHONE 050 936245

OPEN Dinner only; Sunday lunch only in winter   **CLOSED** Monday; Sunday dinner in winter
CREDIT CARDS None   **ENGLISH SPOKEN** A little   **FEATURES** Outdoor summer dining
RESERVATIONS Necessary in summer and on weekends   **PRICE** $
DIRECTIONS The village is 1 km beyond the Certosa di Pisa. Park in the car park to the left just before entering Montemagno (signed with a P); walk up through the village to the square

Montemagno is beyond Pisa's Certosa, a seventeenth-century Carthusian monastery with a splendid façade. The center of this tiny village is a tiny square; the trattoria's outdoor tables nearly fill it. This relaxed restaurant is a favorite with Pisa University students. The food is fresh, appetizing, and very affordable. A set-price menu includes antipasto, *primo, secondo,* side dish, and dessert, with water, service, and cover charge thrown in. Wine and other beverages are extra. The daily choice of first and main courses is written on a blackboard. There are two owners: Mariella and Laila (Mariella is married to the organic oil producer Marco Chiletti at Calci, p 126). They have earned a loyal following with their delicious home cooking, and the restaurant has recently expanded within the piazza.

Autumn mixed *antipasti* included onion frittata; *crostini* of *peperonata,* stewed peppers, and basil-cheese paste; a salad of *nervetti,* boned calf's trotters; and fragrant herbed olives. Lasagne layered with pesto, string beans, and béchamel was unusual and good; a rustic soup of mixed legumes and grains was satisfying, drizzled with the owners' fiery oil. Main courses were roast pork with vegetables, stuffed cabbage leaves, and *piccante* tender squid stewed with beet greens—the most interesting of the three.

One homemade dessert complemented artisan gelati from Lucca: a well-filled strudel of pears and *amaretti.* The house wines were Vernaccia and Chianti.

Montescudaio

FATTORIA POGGIO GAGLIARDO
WINE, OLIVE OIL

POGGIO GAGLIARDO 56040 MONTESCUDAIO
TELEPHONE 0586 630661, 630775
FAX 0586 685960
WEB SITE www.poggiogagliardo.com

OPEN 8:30–12:30, 15:00–19:00; group visits and tastings by appointment   **CLOSED** Sunday
CREDIT CARDS None   **DIRECT SALE** Yes   **ENGLISH SPOKEN** A little
OTHER Summer apartments available for rent   **DIRECTIONS** From Cecina, go toward Guardistallo; go under the *superstrada,* and after 200 meters turn right toward *zona artigianale,* with many company names signposted. The farm is at the end of that road, past the warehouses

Poggio Gagliardo is in the low rolling hills just inland from the coast. This is a real working farm, the farmyard a hive of activity: crops are cultivated and barns filled with beautiful Chianina cattle. Once bred here for beef, they now are used for showing. Visitors are welcome to see them.

When Walter Surbone bought the farm in 1968, it was run down. He came from Piemonte's Monferrato, a winemaking center, and developed the farm's energies in that direction. "We spent years flattening the earth to create these large, even vineyards," he explained as we toured them. "I was interested in engineering a system of underground irrigation, and we now have over 22 kilometers (14 miles) of pipeline buried under our 50 hectares (123 acres) of vineyards." The estate's wines are improving steadily. Grape yields have been reduced and sophisticated equipment installed for the vinification, such as the white wines' soft presses.

Poggio Gagliardo falls within the Montescudaio DOC established in 1977; Walter Surbone is president of its consortium of thirty-four producers. His estate's wines include the economical *podere* line, Montescudaio DOC Rosso and Bianco, and top-of-the-line *barrique*-aged white Vigna Lontana and red Rovo. Of Sangiovese with some Colorino and Malvasia Nera, Rovo is a concentrated, well-structured, modern-style wine admired by Italian critics. A new quality wine, conceived by his son Andrea, who has recently taken over the winemaking at the estate, has now joined it: Gobbo ai Pianacci is a Montescudaio Rosso DOC of Cabernet Sauvignon and Merlot.

An extra-virgin olive oil is also available. The friendly farm is well organized for tastings, group visits, and sales.

Also

LOGICA TRE   VIA DELLA LIBERTÀ, 25. 0586 655355

This small shop in Montescudaio's center sells a good selection of Montescudaio DOC wines, plus organic oils, honeys, and preserves.

Montopoli in Val d'Arno

QUATTRO GIGLI   PIAZZA MICHELE, 2 56020 MONTOPOLI IN VAL D'ARNO
RESTAURANT   TELEPHONE 0571 466940, 466878   FAX 0571 466879
                                          WEB SITE www.quattrogigli.it

---

OPEN Lunch and dinner   **CLOSED** Monday; holidays variable   **CREDIT CARDS** Visa, MC, Amex
ENGLISH SPOKEN Yes   **FEATURES** Summer terrace   **RESERVATIONS** Recommended, especially
on weekends   **PRICE** $$–$$$ **OTHER** Quattro Gigli is a three-star hotel
DIRECTIONS In the village center

Anyone interested in the history of Tuscan food will appreciate this attractive restaurant. Its seasonal menus include recipes from the fifteenth to the eighteenth centuries. Many seem remarkably modern. "We have always loved adapting recipes from old cookbooks," confided Fulvia Puccioni, the talented chef. "They readily fit into today's fresh, flavorful cuisine: combinations like chicken with pomegranate or perch with orange sound new, but are not!"

Fulvia and her husband, Luigi Bacchini, have also created a complex personal style in the restaurant's look, layering warm colors, decorative paintings, and unusual traditional Montopoli ceramics (see next entry). A romantic summer terrace with nice views is adorned with flowering vines and painted flowerpots.

Our late summer lunch began with *antipasto fantasia*. A beige-toned salad of raw field mushrooms, pine nuts, and pecorino had a wonderfully woodsy flavor; *sformato di carote* was a coral pudding of carrot; saffron-yellow *crostini* toasts were topped with egg-yolk paste; well-salted *prosciutto Toscano* was perfectly paired with fresh fig purée. For *maccheroncini di pane*, a rustic fourteenth-century *primo*, day-old bread was soaked in broth, squeezed, mixed with flour and oil, and formed into pasta strips. They were boiled and served with fragrant oil, fresh herbs, and pecorino. Fifteenth-century "gnocchi" of pecorino and egg were dense little corn-yellow dumplings with a fresh cheese flavor, their sauce of herbs and finely ground walnuts. Main courses included loin of pork with honey and walnuts, cod with fresh tomatoes, and boned guinea fowl with prunes (from the sixteenth century).

For dessert there was Vin Santo with *cantucci* cookies, ice-cream-filled meringue with chocolate sauce, or fresh fruit *bavarese*. The wine list is extensive, the service efficient but personalized.

TERRE DI MONTOPOLI   PIAZZA MICHELE, 10 56020 MONTOPOLI IN VAL D'ARNO
TABLE CRAFTS: POTTERY   TELEPHONE 0571 466940   FAX 0571 466879

OPEN The Quattro Gigli staff will open the shop by request   **CREDIT CARDS** Visa, MC, Amex
ENGLISH SPOKEN Yes   **DIRECTIONS** Across the street from the Quattro Gigli hotel

---

This small artisan pottery shop is run by the owners of the Quattro Gigli hotel (see preceding entry). They hope to keep Montopoli's antique ceramics tradition alive, as long as the one remaining craftsman is willing to continue.

Gino Fossetti is very old now, but he still works hard, decorating beautiful plates and vases in this village's style. Plates are made of local red and white clays on a potter's wheel and dried before being decorated. Fassetti's designs date to the fourteenth century, when Montopoli boasted five pottery workshops.

Very old stencils, *spolveri*, are used to mark out the designs. A central motif—a stylized peacock, heraldic figure, or flower—is surrounded by an elaborate decorative border in a graphic, semigeometric style. There are two stages to the decoration: the outlines are traced with a shallow groove, and the plates fired for the first time. Colored glazes are then applied in the warm earth tones that characterize Montopoli's ceramics, and the plates are fired a second time.

Pisa

DE BONDT
CHOCOLATE

VIA TURATI, 22 (CORTE SAN DOMENICO) 56100 PISA
TELEPHONE 050 501896   FAX 050 506302
E-MAIL debondt@tiscalinet.it

OPEN 10:00–13:00, 16:00–20:00   **CLOSED** Monday; Sunday afternoon   **CREDIT CARDS** Visa, MC
ENGLISH SPOKEN Yes   **DIRECTIONS** The Corte may also be reached from Corso Italia, 131

Paul de Bondt and Cecilia Iacobelli are an interesting young couple. He, a brilliant chocolate maker, and she, a designer, got together and opened a shop to showcase the talents of each. "Our idea was to make chocolates of very high quality," explained Cecilia, "and to display them in an unusual way." They have amply succeeded in both. As far as the aesthetics go, the chocolates are presented in a spare, clean-lined environment softened by Cecilia's lovely still-life arrangements; they are sold in attractive geometric boxes. Even the chocolate bars with nuts or candied fruits are beautifully styled.

Paul de Bondt is Dutch. After training as a pastry chef in Holland, he dedicated himself to chocolate. "I was looking for a simplicity, a purity of taste and texture," he explained. "Molded and filled chocolates are never very fine, as the outer chocolate casing is always thick, thus interfering with the sensation of the filling."

De Bondt's hand-dipped coverings are almost imperceptibly thin—with just enough chocolate to protect the fillings and allow them to be handled. The chocolates, nearly all with chocolate-based ganache fillings, are deliciously rich and clean flavored. Each offers a unique taste experience, with a balance of sweet and bitter, soft and hard, to complement the subtle fillings: lemon, tea, chestnut honey, nut. The coffee-scented ganache is so finely flavored you sense the coffee rather than taste it, without its usual acidity. "Each filling has its own character," continued Paul, "and I try to match it with its covering—I work with eight dark chocolates from France and Belgium, so there is a lot of scope."

De Bondt makes a personal range of milk and dark chocolate bars with different percentages of cocoa solids in them, as well as two aromatic single-variety crus. Custom cakes and chocolates may be ordered; chocolate novelty shapes make affordable presents.

Paul and Cecilia have also been active in the promotion of the culture of chocolate within Italy: they helped to launch and organize the annual Eurochocolate fair in Perugia, Umbria. If you are a chocolate lover and in Pisa anytime but summer, when the chocolates are not made, don't miss out on these—they are the finest Tuscany has to offer.

L'ALTRA ROBA	PIAZZA DELLE VETTOVAGLIE, 3 56100 PISA
HEALTH FOODS	TELEPHONE/FAX 050 598987

OPEN 8:00–13:00, 16:00–20:00 (17:00–20:00 in summer)   **CLOSED** Wednesday afternoon, Sunday
CREDIT CARDS None   **ENGLISH SPOKEN** Yes   **DIRECTIONS** From Lungarno Pacinotti, take Via Vigna to the market

Piazza Vettovaglie is Pisa's central food market. Just north of the river, it is an old porticoed square with stalls in the center and permanent shops around the edge. One of these is L'Altra Roba—literally, "the other stuff." The narrow shop is crammed full of loose and packaged rices, legumes, and grains. Its owner, Berto Tessieri, told me he had "all the pulses you can find in Italy." I counted eighteen types of dried bean, including *pavoni*, a large speckled variety resembling birds' eggs, and the expensive, tender-skinned *fagioli di Sorana* (p 76). Interesting mixes, such as rice and orange lentils, need only twenty minutes' cooking. Many products are organic, either fresh or bottled: pasta sauces, honeys, olive oils, and fruit preserves. There are also seasonal fresh fruits and vegetables. I am grateful to Berto for introducing me to the Santarella family's wonderful organic breads (p 164). I first tasted them in his shop and consider them among Tuscany's best.

PASTICCERIA FEDERICO SALZA	BORGO STRETTO, 46 56100 PISA
PASTRY, BAR	TELEPHONE 050 580244 FAX 050 580310
	WEB SITE www.salza.it

OPEN 8:00–20:30   **CLOSED** Monday   **CREDIT CARDS** None   **ENGLISH SPOKEN** Yes
RESERVATIONS Not usually necessary for the lunchroom   **DIRECTIONS** Borgo Stretto runs north from Ponte di Mezzo

The Salza family has run Pisa's finest bar and *pasticceria* since the 1920s. "My family came from Turin," explained Silvio Salza. "This is our eighth generation in the trade. It passes from father to son, from Silvio to Federico, and back to Silvio again. Ours is a family of male children, and we always use the same names."

The double-fronted shop on one of Pisa's principal streets is instantly inviting, with a delicious aroma of freshly roasted coffee, pastries, and chocolate. On the right a long display counter of cakes and chocolates features excellent *pasticceria mignon*, bite-size pastries to eat there or buy by the trayful. The pastry, custards, and glazes are refined in flavor and execution. Salza makes soft *panforte*, a spicy rich confection studded with fruit and nuts. Even the chocolates (often disappointing in *pasticcerie*) are of good quality.

On the other side is the large bar and sandwich counter, serving more than forty types of sandwiches, savory tarts, and snacks to eat at the bar or take away. At lunchtime hot sandwiches and pasta are available; a waiter-served luncheonette is in the back. The company also runs a large catering facility. Signor Salza, a spruce gentleman of the old school, is a perfectionist; he believes great service and quality are imperative, whether he is preparing a society wedding banquet or one of his delicious cappuccini.

OSTERIA DEI CAVALIERI
RESTAURANT

VIA SAN FREDIANO, 16 56100 PISA
TELEPHONE 050 580858   FAX 050 581259
WEB SITE www.toscana.net/pisa/odc/

OPEN Lunch and dinner   **CLOSED** Saturday lunch, Sunday; August
CREDIT CARDS Visa, MC, Amex   **ENGLISH SPOKEN** No, but there is an English menu
RESERVATIONS Suggested for dinner   **PRICE** $$
DIRECTIONS Off Piazza dei Cavalieri, north of the Arno

This *osteria* (between a trattoria and a ristorante), in the university section of town, is a nice place for a simple lunch or dinner. The atmosphere is relaxed, children are welcome, and the menu offers ample choices, from soups and pastas to vegetable plates and meats. There are reasonably priced one-dish specials like osso buco (veal shanks with risotto), or mixed grilled fish with pasta. The house wines are drinkable, and there is a good list for anyone feeling more ambitious.

I liked the deep ocher soup of pumpkin with added ground almonds for texture and the mixed grilled vegetables—zucchini, eggplant, and peppers—with grilled *scamorza* cheese. The desserts look good; a frozen cream pudding, *semifreddo al zabaglione*, has a light citrus flavor and crunchy praline.

Also

MELANI   CORSO ITALIA, 44. 050 502323

This large kitchen supply shop stocks everything from pots and pans to decorative glassware and china. Its collection of designer tableware and kitchen accessories includes Alessi. Wine lovers will find tasting glasses by Bremer and Villeroy decanters.

COLTELLERIA FONTANA   CORSO ITALIA, 124. 050 41369

I have always been fascinated by shops specializing in knives—a key tool for anyone who likes to cook. This recent shop has a great range. It also stocks the typically Italian equipment that's fun to bring home: ravioli cutters—both the trays used with a small rolling pin and the individual wooden-handle type—Parmesan wedges for splitting chunks of the cheese, fluted pasta wheels, meat pounders, nut crackers, and more.

CAGLIOSTRO   VIA DEL CASTELLETTO, 26/30. 050 575413

This spacious restaurant and wine bar serves lunch, dinner, and drinks. The decor is striking and eclectic, and the cooking is imaginative—with a great list of cheeses to match its fine wines.

RISTORANTE SERGIO   VIA AURELIA SS 1, KM 338 (MADONNA DELL'ACQUA)
050 894068; FAX 050 894932
WEB SITE www.ristorantesergio.com

Sergio's was a key restaurant in Pisa until it moved out of town; now it has moved back to the city's northern outskirts—to the Park Hotel California. It operates two dining rooms: an affordable brasserie open daily, and a more refined restaurant serving regional and international recipes and fine wines. It is closed Monday. In summer, eat out in the garden.

Pomarance

MACELLERIA MARIS FROSALI   PIAZZA DE LARDEREL, 28 56045 POMARANCE
MEAT   TELEPHONE 0588 64611

OPEN 8:00–13:00, 17:00–20:00   **CLOSED** Wednesday afternoon, Sunday, early August
CREDIT CARDS None   **ENGLISH SPOKEN** No   **DIRECTIONS** In the village center

This old-style marble butcher's shop is a guaranteed source of Chianina beef—the best Tuscan breed (many place it among the world's best). Maris Frosali belongs to the 5R association, which controls Italy's five top beef breeds, of which Chianina and Maremmana are special to Tuscany.

Chianina beef is firm-fleshed and has a layer of pure white fat around it. With its high-protein, low-fat content, it is the beef of choice for the famous *Fiorentina*, the wood-grilled Tuscan T-bone steak, which now comes from younger animals. Anyone interested in seeing the beautiful animals on their farms may ask the butcher for a 5R leaflet, which lists them. The shop has a full range of other meats, including locally bred pigeons.

San Gervasio

AZIENDA AGRICOLA　　　　**SAN GERVASIO DI PALAIA 56025 PONTEDERA**
SAN GERVASIO　　　　　　TELEPHONE 0587 483360　　FAX 0587 484361
WINE, GAME　　　　　　　　　WEB SITE www.sangervasio.com

OPEN 8:00–12:00, 14:00–20:00; tastings by appointment or Wednesday 17:00–18:00
CLOSED Sunday　**CREDIT CARDS** Visa, MC　**DIRECT SALE** Yes　**ENGLISH SPOKEN** Yes
FEATURES Folklore museum　**OTHER** Holiday apartments available　**DIRECTIONS** From Forcoli,
go up the hill toward San Gervasio and the restaurant Belvedere. Turn left at the T-junction at the top
of hill; San Gervasio is on left after 1.3 kms

San Gervasio is a self-contained medieval *borgo*, or village, originally belonging to the bishops of Lucca. Its circular-structured castle was the site of many battles between Pisans and Florentines. The Tommasini family from Pontedera have run San Gervasio since 1964. Two sons, Luca and Claudio, have turned it into an organic farm and, with the talented enologist Luca D'Attoma, have seriously improved the wines.

The estate has 11 hectares (28 acres) of vineyards. A new wine, I Renai, is of pure Merlot aged in *barriques;* this is a well-structured wine whose influence is clearly down the coast at Bolgheri. Small French casks are also used for aging A Sirio, of 100 percent Sangiovese, and the white table wine Marna, of 65 percent Trebbiano, 25 percent Chardonnay, and 10 percent Sauvignon. San Gervasio also makes a wonderful Vin Santo: Recinaio is of Trebbiano, with 20 percent of the unusual San Colombano grapes added to it.

San Gervasio's Museum of Rural Work and Customs features old farm tools. The farm also has a large hunting reserve; pheasant and other game birds are raised. It is possible to order game birds, wild boar, and hare for the table. The *borgo* is surrounded by olive groves, whose olives are milled at a modern-style *frantoio* nearby. Here, too, the owners are switching to organic methods of cultivation.

A final note: San Gervasio's restaurant, Al Belvedere (tel: 0587 628232), is located on the road toward Forcoli and is independently managed. It is a pleasant place; the food is well cooked. It also rents mountain bikes.

San Miniato

MACELLERIA SERGIO FALASCHI　　**VIA AUGUSTO CONTI, 18/20 56027 SAN MINIATO**
MEAT　　　　　　　　　　　　　　TELEPHONE/FAX 0571 43190
　　　　　　　　　　　　　　　　　WEB SITE www.sergiofalaschi.it

OPEN 7:00–13:00, 16:30–20:00; plus Sunday in November for truffle fair
CLOSED Sunday, Wednesday afternoon; July　**CREDIT CARDS** Visa, MC
ENGLISH SPOKEN A little　**DIRECTIONS** In the center of town, near Piazza del Popolo

This well-stocked butcher's shop sells fresh meats, homemade *salumi* (cured meats and sausages), and a range of sauces for pasta or *crostini* toasts. Sergio Falaschi, following his father and grandfather, makes a special salt-cured shoulder, *spalla,* and a well-seasoned *prosciutto Toscano.* There are spicy sausages scented with truffles or hot pepper, blood sausage studded with pine nuts and raisins (*mallegato alla Sanminiatese*) and head cheese (*soppressata*). A new line of *salumi* is being made with pork meat from the prized Cinta Senese breed.

The fresh meats include sought-after Chianina beef, which should be hung for fifteen to twenty days. It is recognizable by its fine pure-white fat and firm-fleshed red meat. Ready-to-cook meats include boned rabbit scented with truffle for a quick dinner solution.

IL CANTUCCIO DI FEDERIGO
PASTRY

VIA P. MAIOLI, 67 56027 SAN MINIATO
TELEPHONE 0571 418344
E-MAIL gazzarrini@easyclick.it

OPEN 8:00–13:00, 15:00–20:00   **CLOSED** Sunday afternoon; August   **CREDIT CARDS** Visa, MC
ENGLISH SPOKEN Yes   **DIRECTIONS** The bakery is within the old town walls

---

Rino Gazzarrini is a master baker (and inventor) of desserts, cakes, and biscuits. With his son Paolo, he runs a wonderful pastry shop at the edge of the old town that is worth a detour: some of the cakes were among the best I have tasted in Tuscany.

Gazzarrini specializes in sweet yeast breads, such as Christmas *panettone* and Easter *colomba.* Usually produced only in traditional flavors, Gazzarrini has stretched the repertoire. His rich, buttery *colomba* (Easter dove) comes flavored with coffee, chocolate, or lemon, or made with whole-wheat flour, scented with *moscato* wine, or studded with candied exotic fruits—there is no limit. And they are truly delicious. *Colomba al caffè* is enriched with bitter coffee and studded with rare coffee-flavored semisweet French chocolate chips. Rino Gazzarrini called it one of his "little masterpieces."

"*Panettone* is considered a Milanese specialty," he admitted, "but why should they be the only ones to have it?" He tried his hand at it, praying for guidance, and the result was a light, buttery, airy confection that is quite irresistible. Gazzarrini explained that the dough for *panettone* was *parecchio gentile,* pretty fine, and that part of the secret of its high raised dome was to let it cool—or "put it to sleep"— upside-down.

His son Paolo has a passion for fine wines; some are available from the bakery. He has also reinvented one of the area's sacred cows, the *brigidino.* This crunchy, wafer-thin, anise-scented biscuit originated near Montecatini Terme. It can be good (see p 75), but all too often it is sold at fairs and is oversweet and artificially flavored. Not so the Gazzarrinis'! Paolo makes *brigidino* in ten flavors, including one with real anise seeds and a deep dark chocolate one studded with fine crumbs of orange peel (my favorite). They are sold in cellophane bags to keep out the damp. A great selection of cakes and tarts (sold whole or cut in half), pastries, petits fours, and cookies are on sale from the tiny shop—at very reasonable prices.

SAN MINIATO'S TRUFFLE FAIR

Each November the town of San Miniato celebrates the season's local harvest of the *Tuber magnatum pico*, or white truffle, by hosting Tuscany's most important truffle fair—la Fiera del Tartufo—which takes place over a weekend. It is great fun to visit. The place goes truffle-mad: at the top of the lovely medieval hill town are stalls selling the precious fungus; local restaurants feature truffle-based menus; the Association of Truffle Hunters (L'Associazione Tartufai Sanminiatese; Tel: 0571 418251) organizes various events; and best of all, there is a truffle-hunting contest for specially trained truffle dogs.

If it is not too cold a day, the truffle hunt is wonderful to watch, in a peculiarly uneventful sort of way. A group of overexcited dogs, with human trainers, are let, one at a time, into a confined area in which several small truffles have been buried (usually the children's playground). The object is to sniff out the hidden truffles in the allotted five minutes. This sounds easier than it is. When I watched, the first dog did very well and found them all, but the remaining dogs seemed more interested in the scent of the preceding dogs than in the buried treasure—much to the frustration of their owners. The prize . . . a large truffle!

Also

ENOTECA "SPIRITO DI VINO"   PIAZZA DEL POPOLO, 19. 0571 401059

This is a small wine shop specializing in Tuscan wines, with an emphasis on less well known producers from the Colline Pisane. There are wines from other Italian regions and a nice group of *passiti*—dessert wines made from partially dried grapes—that Benedetto Squicciarini (of the nearby winery Tenuta di Cusignano) has chosen with Carlo Gazzarrini.

Santa Croce sull'Arno

PASTICCERIA OTTAVIO SCARSELLI   VIA DI PELLE, 1. 0571 30659

Santa Croce is Tuscany's leather-tanning center. This large *pasticceria* and bar is a favorite of the tannery workers, who come for cups of Scarselli's home-roasted coffee. The assortment of pastries includes one that is special to the town: *amaretti di Santa Croce*. Shaped like little pyramids, these are mounds of ground sweet and bitter Sicilian almonds, sugar, and egg white, baked until golden brown on top but still nicely chewy in the center. They stand on tiny squares of hostlike rice paper. The town dedicates an annual *sagra*, or festival, to them in late autumn.

Staffoli

DA BEPPE   VIA LIVORNESE, 35/37 56020 STAFFOLI
RESTAURANT   TELEPHONE 0571 37002   FAX 0571 37385

OPEN Lunch and dinner   **CLOSED** Sunday evening, Monday; two weeks in August
CREDIT CARDS Visa, MC, Amex   **ENGLISH SPOKEN** A little   **RESERVATIONS** Recommended
for dinner   **PRICE** $$$$–$$$$$ **DIRECTIONS** On the main street through Staffoli

---

In his restaurant, Luca Cristiani experiments with ambitious combinations of ingredients and flavors. Like all experiments, some are wildly successful, others are less so. The setting, too, is curiously unsettled. Mint-green waxed walls are set off by (jar with?) pink frilled curtains that border on kitsch. A mixed collection of oil paintings adorns the walls. There are vaulted brick ceilings; tables with differently hued pink tablecloths and greenish underskirts, and unusual fan-tined forks.

For our meal, superb handmade rolls preceded the *grande antipasto di pesce*, which was served on a very, very large charger and consisted of nine fish-based hors d'oeuvres. Other options included a warm salad of oranges with river shrimp, baby squid with porcini mushrooms, stuffed cuttlefish with saffron, and several land-based choices. For *primo*, a spinach leaf was stuffed with barley, celery, and pieces of white fish. A dish of rice was stained black by squid ink and contained minuscule white squid tentacles, mussels, and tomato chunks. My companion liked it because it was sweetish and barely tasted of squid ink. I couldn't help wondering if that wasn't what it was missing.

An adult cuttlefish stewed with beet greens and some tomato had a strong presence of garlic, but it lacked the fiery impact this rustic dish often has. A large fillet of sea bass was beautifully topped with row upon row of perfect porcini slices and drizzled with garlicky green oil. The pastry chef, who may also be the bread maker, did an excellent job baking the desserts. Luca Cristiani is an enthusiastic man who has worked under some of Italy's most prestigious chefs. He came back from his travels to take over this popular trattoria from his father, Beppe, and has given it his own personal stamp.

Tirrenia

DANTE E IVANA
RESTAURANT

VIALE DEL TIRRENO, 207/C 56018 TIRRENIA
TELEPHONE/FAX 050 32549

OPEN Monday–Saturday lunch and dinner; in August, nightly for dinner only   **CLOSED** Sunday; lunch in August; January   **CREDIT CARDS** Visa, MC, Amex   **ENGLISH SPOKEN** Yes   **RESERVATIONS** Recommended for dinner   **PRICE** $$$$ **DIRECTIONS** Viale del Tirreno runs parallel to Tirrenia's sea front, separated from the beach by a pine wood

---

This well-known fish restaurant has a tranquil modern interior with soft diffused light. The varied menu offers fish and shellfish from the Tyrrhenian Sea as well as other varieties from farther afield. The ingredients that accompany and enhance them are Mediterranean: tomatoes, *cannellini* beans, zucchini flowers, herbs, wine, and most important, extra-virgin olive oil. The restaurant uses a sweet and fruity oil from nearby Buti, which stars in many of the dishes. Dante Grassi, who runs the restaurant with his wife, Ivana Lucchesi, is an experienced restaurateur and sommelier. His extensive wine list leans toward whites and supplies information on producers and grape varieties.

My *antipasto carpaccio* of raw sea bass came on a sizzlingly hot plate, topped with arugula and peppery olive oil. A beautiful green-ribbed zucchini flower was stuffed and steamed with a compact mousse of *aragosta*—the clawless spiny lobster; it, too, was accompanied by the golden-green oil. Spaghetti was offered with clams, shellfish, or lobster (priced accordingly).

A specialty from nearby Lucca were *tacconi*—egg pasta handkerchiefs richly sauced with chunks of shrimp, tomato, and arugula. *Bavettine*, like thin linguine, were great with flaked *triglie*, red mullet, sweet cherry tomatoes, parsley, and oil. Red mullet is popular along this coastline; its firm flesh and full flavor stand up well to Mediterranean aromatics.

Main courses included fresh scampi, large shrimp tossed into a colorful, crunchy salad of carrot, fennel, and radish. Here, too, the oil played its part. Chunks of filleted *orata* (gilt-head bream), were sautéed with meaty porcini mushrooms. Fish were available simply steamed or grilled. A refreshing sorbet of muscat wine and pink grapefruit finished the meal.

Vicopisano

This lovely small medieval *borgo* is characterized by its many towers. The top one is part of the Rocca di Brunelleschi, a brilliantly ingenious military fortress designed by the great Renaissance architect in 1434. It was recently restored and is well worth a visit; it is open on weekends, with excellent guides provided by the Comune (Comune telephone 050 79654; guide telephone 050 551285). If you go, stop in at Taverna degli Olivi (tel 050 799938) for a typically Tuscan meal on a terrace overlooking Vicopisano and its valley.

Volterra

VOLTERRA'S ALABASTER

Volterra has been a center for alabaster since the Etruscans carved it for their funerary urns a thousand years before Christ. Visit the town's extraordinary Etruscan Museum to see these. The beautiful, at times translucent, stone is found all around the area in both surface and underground mines. More than fifty varieties are known, ranging from marblelike veined dark stone to the better-known powdery-white version, which looks like cloudy glass.

The town is full of artisan and semi-industrial boutiques selling alabaster objects in shapes from the sublime to the ridiculous. Seeing so many all together may be a bit overwhelming, but some of the simpler objects, such as the wide shallow bowls, have a purity of line and substance that makes it worth the effort of taking them home.

Note that alabaster must not come into contact with water, which erodes it, or direct heat, which consumes it.

SOCIETÀ COOPERATIVA ARTIERI ALABASTRO
ALABASTER

SHOP PIAZZA DEI PRIORI, 5 VOLTERRA 56048 PISA
TELEPHONE SHOP 0588 87590, OFFICE 0588 86135
FAX 0588 86224
WEB SITE www.italbusiness.it/volterrasalabaster

OPEN Daily: summer 9:00–20:00; winter 9:00–18:00 **CLOSED** Never **CREDIT CARDS** Visa, MC, Amex **DIRECT SALE** Yes **ENGLISH SPOKEN** Yes **OTHER** Workshop visits by appointment **DIRECTIONS** In the town center

Renaissance sculptors favored alabaster for its radiance and translucency, as did the ancient Etruscans, who lived in Tuscany before the Romans. The Etruscans built their greatest cities on hilltops high enough to bring them closer to their gods. Volterra is my favorite of these cities. It rises up above a "moonscape" of rounded, treeless hills in one of Tuscany's most evocative landscapes.

Around Volterra, many Etruscan funerary sculptures have been found—endearing portraits of smiling men and women reclining peacefully on one elbow—carved in alabaster, which is itself strangely lunar in quality.

"Alabaster is not a stone, but a mineral—hydrated calcium sulphate," explained Giovanni Nerei, who runs the hundred-year-old alabaster artisans' cooperative in the town. "It is found buried like large white eggs in the Volterran hills." These bright white "drops" measure a meter or more across.

Today, sixty master carvers still work in the town, continuing their unique artistic traditions creating lovely objects to adorn the finest tables—hand-carved candlesticks, ornamental bowls, urns, and centerpieces.

"Alabaster's only enemy is water," Nerei advised. "So be sure never to use it for foods or liquids. Wipe it occasionally with a little clear oil and it will last for at least another millennium!"

AZIENDA AGRICOLA LISCHETO **56048 VOLTERRA**
CHEESE: ORGANIC TELEPHONE/FAX 0588 30403
E-MAIL lischeto@libero.it

OPEN 8:00–12:30, 14:30–19:00 **CLOSED** Never **CREDIT CARDS** Visa, MC, Amex
DIRECT SALE Yes **ENGLISH SPOKEN** Yes **OTHER** Holiday apartments available
DIRECTIONS From Volterra, go toward Pontedera and Montecatini Val di Cecina. The farm is signposted after about 7 kms. Follow the unpaved road to the end

---

Giovanni Cannas's farm is situated in a remarkable position. Perched on top of one of the pure, treeless round hills that characterize this part of the country, its stone buildings look across a strange "moonscape" to the town of Volterra. It is a moving sight. Giovanni's father, a Sardinian shepherd, took over this land in the 1960s. "There was nothing here then, just some ruined buildings in an abandoned landscape," recounted Giovanni. "My father brought a few sheep and put in thirty years of work to turn it into a thousand-head herd."

When Giovanni decided to make cheese, his father was against it. But Giovanni convinced him both to make the cheeses and to convert the farm to an organic one. "That was my dream," he confided. "And this land lent itself well. It is very poor terrain, so we sow it with clover and sulla [*Hedysarum coronarium*], a flowering leguminous plant. The sheep like it and it makes their milk very sweet. We are now the biggest organic cheesemaker in Tuscany—even if we are very small."

From pasteurized sheep's milk, Cannas makes mild, sweet, aromatic ricotta, *ravaggiolo* (a fresh single-curd cheese), and a range of pecorini. The small round *tomino*, a bright white fresh cheese, has a more compact consistency. Lightly salted, it is delicious sprinkled with good olive oil and pepper. The orange-rind pecorino is matured for two months and has a delicate tang to it. *Pecorino stagionato* is aged for six months. It has a natural brown crust, a smooth consistency, and a decisive, unmistakable flavor of sheep's milk. A "super-Tuscan" pecorino is aged in *barriques* full of *vinacce,* the wine-soaked grape residues left over from the wine-making process.

A new line of raw-milk pecorini from the Balze Volterrane has recently been successful. The farm has a small shop for selling its cheeses, organic olive oil (made from olives grown in Bibbona), and honey.

PASTICCERIA MIGLIORINI
PASTRY

VIA GRAMSCI, 21 56048 VOLTERRA
TELEPHONE 0588 86446   FAX 0588 86946
E-MAIL migliorini@sirt.pisa.it

OPEN 7:30–13:00, 16:00–20:00   CLOSED Sunday afternoon, Tuesday; holidays in July and January
CREDIT CARDS None   ENGLISH SPOKEN A little   DIRECTIONS Off Piazza XX Settembre

This lovely pastry shop makes a fine variation on *panforte.* Torta Etruria is a dense, spiced honey confection studded with chopped toasted almonds and candied orange peel; it is topped with a nice layer of dark chocolate. Other unusual pastries include the *pane del pescatore* (fisherman's bread), a short-crust pastry enriched with almonds and nuts. The *pasticceria* produces a full range of cookies, dough-nuts, cakes, and *semifreddi*—frozen desserts.

RISTORANTE SACCO FIORENTINO
RESTAURANT

PIAZZA XX SETTEMBRE, 18 56048 VOLTERRA
TELEPHONE/FAX 0588 88537

OPEN Lunch and dinner   CLOSED Wednesday; January–February
CREDIT CARDS Visa, MC, Amex   ENGLISH SPOKEN A little   RESERVATIONS Recommended
in summer   PRICE $$ DIRECTIONS In the town center, near the museum

This restaurant offers a traditional menu enriched with local dishes and artisan-made *salumi* and cheeses. There are good *primi*—pastas and soups—and *secondi,* such as chicken, rabbit, and grilled meats. You can choose to have just a light meal or more, with or without wine. The wine list is strictly Tuscan, with more than a hundred wines of varying prices.

CHAPTER 6

Livorno and Its Coast

*T*he great Medicean port of Livorno was heavily bombed during World War II. Today little remains of the town's once grand center or fine palazzi. A pleasant but rather anonymous postwar district has replaced it. Despite this, I found Livorno interesting; in 1593, Ferdinand I declared it a free port and an open city, one in which people of all religions were free to worship, and it has retained something of that atmosphere of acceptance and interchange. Its great sea dish, *cacciucco,* a mixed-fish stew, is well worth experiencing.

Livorno's shore, stretching south along the Tyrrhenian Sea as far as Piombino, is known as the Coast of the Etruscans. This early Italian civilization existed here from 900 to 600 B.C., founding many towns and leaving a legacy of seaports, roads, and irrigation. Today the area is celebrated for the fine wines of Montescudaio, Val di Cornia, and Bolgheri (including Sassicaia, the legendary first "super-Tuscan"). World-class vineyards now cover hills that until recently were considered unsuitable for vine growing. Olive oil, too, is increasingly being improved as better methods of cultivation and processing are practiced. The flat coastal strip is used for agriculture, producing wonderful tomatoes, tiny artichokes, fava beans, and fruit, and there is an amazing variety of local fish to be found in its markets and restaurants.

AZIENDA PROMOZIONE TURISTICA
PIAZZA CAVOUR, 6
57126 LIVORNO
0586 898111, FAX 0586 896173
WEB SITE www.livorno.turismo.toscana.it

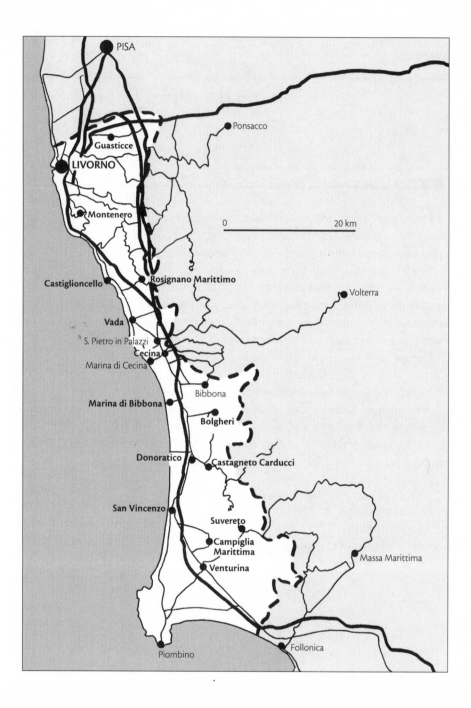

Boldface type indicates towns that are included in this chapter.

Bolgheri

LE MACCHIOLE
WINE

LE CONTESSINE VIA BOLGHERESE, 189 57020 BOLGHERI
TELEPHONE 0565 766092 FAX 0565 763240

OPEN Visits by appointment only; no tastings **DIRECT SALE** No, but the wines are available from the *enoteche* at Bolgheri and Castagneto Carducci **ENGLISH SPOKEN** No **DIRECTIONS** On the road between Bolgheri and Castagneto Carducci

Compared to his neighbors Ornellaia and San Guido, Eugenio Campolmi's winery may seem small, but it has provided him with big results. "I was considered the black sheep of my family," confided the tall, broad-shouldered young man. "They had run a business for seven generations, but I had my heart set on making wine." He bought the property in 1983, and in 1984 began planting the vineyards. He now works 23 hectares (57 acres) of vineyards.

Campolmi's prize wine is his Paleo Rosso, a big, *barrique*-aged red wine in the new Bolgheri style of 90 percent Cabernet Sauvignon with 10 percent Sangiovese. "Its first year was 1989—a terrible year. I wasn't sure what to call my wine. I looked out at the rainy vineyards high with weeds and said in our local jargon: '*Che paleo che c'è quest'anno* [what high grass there is this year].' And there was the name: I wanted a short, decisive, masculine-sounding name."

The earliest vintages of Paleo had higher percentages of Sangiovese. "The Sangiovese was added because it takes the edge off the green sharpness of the Cabernet, making it rounder, mellower," Campolmi explained. Even so, this is a wine with big tannins that benefits from being cellared before drinking. After letting it age in the small casks for eighteen to twenty-four months, Campolmi fines it in the bottle for eighteen months before selling it.

Working with the talented winemaker Luca D'Attoma, Campolmi has brought his wines up to be competitive with those of his famous neighbors. What was the secret, I asked?

"A lot has changed here in the last twenty years," replied D'Attoma. "Italians used to think that great wines were made in the cellars, but that has changed. They recognize that the vital work is done in the vineyards. And no matter what a winemaker says, the real 'soul' of each winery is its owner."

TENUTA DELL'ORNELLAIA
WINE

VIA BOLGHERESE 57020 BOLGHERI
TELEPHONE 0565 71811 FAX 0565 718230
WEB SITE www.ornellaia.it

OPEN Visits by prior written request only **DIRECT SALE** No, but Ornellaia's wines are sold in all the local wine shops, subject to availability **ENGLISH SPOKEN** Yes **DIRECTIONS** On the road between Bolgheri and Castagneto Carducci

Since its first vintage in 1985, Ornellaia has been esteemed by the international wine circuit. Its wines are modern in style and have been particularly appreciated by Americans. Ornellaia's proprietor, Marchese Lodovico Antinori, studied and lived in California, and the estate's original consultant was André Tchelistcheff, the "father" of California's wine industry. Another key consultant was Michel Rolland, one of Bordeaux's leading winemakers.

Thanks to the example set by Ornellaia's neighbor, San Guido—whose Cabernet, Sassicaia, started the so-called Tuscan wine revolution—the winemaking potential of Bolgheri was recognized. Antinori also determined to produce quality French-style wines in a coastal area previously considered unsuitable for such an enterprise.

Large investments followed. The estate's 135 hectares (333 acres) of vineyards were planted with select clones of popular international grape varieties: the Cabernets Sauvignon and Franc, Merlot, and Sauvignon Blanc. Consultants Tibor Gal from Hungary and Danny Schuster from New Zealand were called in to oversee the *cantina* and vineyards. (Gal has recently been replaced by Thomas Duroux.) The ultramodern cellar was designed by the Florentine architect Farinelli, who was visibly inspired by the Renaissance architect Bernardo Buontalenti: the cellar's half-buried pentagonal structure recalls the Medicis' fortresses.

Ornellaia's award-winning, powerful reds are Masseto, of pure Merlot, and Ornellaia, a Bordeaux-style blend of Cabernet Sauvignon, Merlot, and Cabernet Franc—described by critic Daniel Thomases as "silky and feminine" compared to the masculinity of Sassicaia (see next entry). Now a second, junior, wine is being made from the Ornellaia vineyards: Le Serre Nuove costs about half the price of Ornellaia, though it is without any Cabernet Franc. Le Volte is of 40 percent Cabernet, with 30 percent each Sangiovese and Merlot. Poggio alle Gazze is the estate's most popular white: of Sauvignon Blanc matured without wood, it is a fragrant, balanced wine that has earned its loyal following.

TENUTA SAN GUIDO	**CAPANNE, 27 57020 BOLGHERI**
WINE	TELEPHONE 0565 762003 FAX 0565 762017
	WEB SITE www.sassicaia.com

OPEN Visits by prior written request only   DIRECT SALE No, but Sassicaia is sold in the wine shops of Bolgheri; sales are normally limited to two bottles per person   ENGLISH SPOKEN Yes
DIRECTIONS On the road from the SS 1 to Bolgheri

Visiting the home of Tuscany's most famous wine is a great experience. I was pleased to discover how unpretentious, how normal, a home it is. Tenuta San Guido is, first and foremost, a working farm—albeit an exceptional one. Wine (and they make just one) is just one of its activities. Its grand old buildings, historic cypress avenue, and stately villa are imposing, but thankfully free of hype, hoopla, and PR persons. However, to visit you must write in advance to make an appointment.

Marchese Niccolò Incisa della Rocchetta, an unassuming, intelligent man with lively, attentive eyes, believes in meeting personally with journalists. The contact is direct—who better than he can explain his legendary wine, Sassicaia?

"When it all started there was no intention to sell this wine," he began as we sat in his small private office. "Sassicaia was the product of my father's passion. He was a man of culture and refinement—perhaps more so than other Tuscan landowners of his generation. He wanted to make wines of quality. This was back in 1944."

At that time most Tuscan wines were sold unbottled, or exported *en masse*, like Chianti. Marchese Mario Incisa took the radical step of planting Cabernets Sauvignon and Franc, of drastically reducing grape yields, and of following vinification principles common in France.

"My father saw it as an adventure, a challenge," Incisa recalled. "To make a good red wine in an area with a terrible reputation. I like to think that Sassicaia was born from his hardheadedness—he was determined to prove his point." He paused to smile. "I think we can safely say he succeeded."

For almost twenty years Mario Incisa considered the wine an experiment. It was never drunk outside of family circles. "In the late 1960s," his son continued, "his experiment turned into something more important." Mario Incisa decided to sell Sassicaia, but he was unsure if it would age well. It would be sold through Marchese Piero Antinori, whose winemaker was Giacomo Tachis.

"Antinori was very impressed by Sassicaia's original *impronto,* or stamp, but felt we needed help in handling its vinification and in making it more consistent. He suggested Tachis could advise us on that." A long and fruitful collaboration ensued between Tuscany's most brilliant enologist and the Incisa della Rocchetta family. Sassicaia immediately won admirers internationally; it was favorably compared to the greatest Bordeaux, despite having no official status at home beyond that of a mere *vino da tavola,* or table wine. The super-Tuscan generation had begun.

"If there is one thing that really pleases me," said Niccolò Incisa, "it is to see the way in which Italian winemaking has changed since then. Sassicaia and its success triggered a revolution from Piedmont to Sicily—one that continues today."

After an assiduous grape selection in the estate's 50 hectares (123 acres) of vineyards, Sassicaia's vinification takes place in stainless-steel vats. It is matured for twenty-four months in French *barriques* before being united in one giant vat prior to bottling. This ensures that all the wine from a vintage is the same—an important fact, given that more than one hundred thousand bottles are now produced annually. It then spends six months in the bottle before being sold. Niccolò Incisa recommends ideally cellaring the wine for several years before drinking, in order to fully savor its complexity and elegance.

"Sassicaia is always liked by the people who drink it," he affirmed. "The most important thing is that it should be appreciated by normal wine lovers, not just by specialists and critics."

As this book went to press, it seemed likely that San Guido would be coming out with a second wine in the near future—not a "junior" Sassicaia, but a wine of a completely different style.

ENOTECA TOGNONI	STRADA GIULIA, 6 AND 4 57020 BOLGHERI
WINE STORE, SPECIALTY FOODS	TELEPHONE/FAX 0565 762001

OPEN 8:00–23:00 in summer; 8:00–19:00 in winter   **CLOSED** Wednesday in winter; November
CREDIT CARDS Visa, MC   **DIRECT SALE** Yes   **ENGLISH SPOKEN** A little
DIRECTIONS On the main street of the village

Fabio Tognoni and his wife, Paola, run adjacent stores in Bolgheri. One specializes in wines, the other offers specialty foods—oils, local cheeses, preserved vegetables, *salumi*, pasta sauces—and snacks, which can be eaten there or bought to go. At the *enoteca*, almost all the wines of Bolgheri and Castagneto Carducci may be tasted before being bought, with the exception of Sassicaia and Ornellaia.

Campiglia Marittima

IL CAPPELLAIO PAZZO	VIA DI SAN VINCENZO 57021 CAMPIGLIA MARITTIMA
RESTAURANT	TELEPHONE 0565 838358

OPEN Lunch and dinner   **CLOSED** Tuesday in winter; February, part of November
CREDIT CARDS Visa, MC, Amex   **ENGLISH SPOKEN** Yes   **FEATURES** Summer garden dining
RESERVATIONS Recommended   **PRICE** $$$–$$$$ **OTHER** The farmhouse has six guest rooms
DIRECTIONS Take the San Vincenzo Sud exit from the *superstrada* (SS 1); go toward Campiglia Marittima. The restaurant is on the left; look for signs

The "Mad Hatter" is a farmhouse restaurant in a pastoral setting between hills and sea. In summer you eat outside in the garden; in winter, in the large dining room, whose mad collection of hats is colorful and welcoming. Denni Bruci is a well-traveled young man with fresh ideas about food. He and his mother, Michela, prepare a creative, eclectic cuisine based on local ingredients combined imaginatively. Their food is fragrant with herbs, spices, and truffles.

For *primi*, a round toast is topped with plump mussels and shrimp blanketed in a savory zabaglione stained yellow with saffron. A deep-fried rice-paper roll contains shrimp, basil, and shredded greens. A slice of lightly smoked sturgeon is served warm, garnished with grated zucchini and sage. *Linguine con astice* comes studded with chunks of tender lobster and fresh tomato. Green vegetable risotto is scented with earthy San Miniato truffles.

For *secondi*, rabbit is boned, braised with rosemary, and served with a wonderfully delicate purée of garlic. Sea bass is grilled simply over wood embers. Desserts, too, are uncomplicated yet finely flavored: pears are poached in white wine and served with a deep chocolate sauce and toasted pine nuts; apples are stewed and married to a sweet and sharp raspberry *aspretto*. There is a well-selected wine list featuring many of the area's great wines.

Castagneto Carducci

CAMARCANDA
WINE

VIA GUADO AL MELO SANTA TERESA
57022 CASTAGNETO CARDUCCI
TELEPHONE/FAX 0565 763809

OPEN Visits only by prior written appointment   **DIRECT SALE** No, but wines are available from
Bolgheri wine shops   **ENGLISH SPOKEN** Yes

Angelo Gaja, the great Piedmontese wine producer, has launched into a second Tuscan wine adventure, in Bolgheri, after first buying an estate in Montalcino for making Brunello (see p 321–322). What draws him to Tuscany?

"Tuscany is not so far from Piedmont, and just like Piedmont it has a great vocation for making red wines," he said as we walked briskly through his handsome new vinification cellar in Bolgheri. "My goal here is to make wines that reflect the soul, the earth, and the colors of Tuscany."

If in Montalcino he is dealing with the vicissitudes of Sangiovese, a grape that is known to be difficult to work well with, in Bolgheri his two wines will be from blends of Cabernet and Merlot.

"Compared to Piedmont or Montalcino, it seems much easier to work here by the coast," he said. "Both the climate and the lay of the land make it more favorable. I chose these grape types after seeing San Giudo's successful results with Cabernet, and Ornellaia's with Merlot. My wines will combine the two."

"The recent effect of Americanization has changed many of our ideas about ourselves, and our wines. Up until then we Europeans thought we were the kings of the world, but we have had to rethink this. The Americans have created what I call 'wines of sun and light,' which are exuberant and powerful and have less to do with the *terroir*. I feel we must be humble and prepared to change our attitudes: after all, why shouldn't we use those grape varieties too? All great wines have equal dignity."

In Bolgheri, Gaja is working with winemaker Guido Rivella, with whom he collaborates so brilliantly at Barbaresco. The cellar was just being completed as I visited it, an imposing, sculptural construction nestled in a landscape of olive groves and vineyards. It combines technology with style within a framework of elemental materials: bronze, copper, varnished rusted steel, local stone, black basalt. The *barricaia* is impressive, with row upon row of small wooden barrels.

"My wines here will be called Camarcanda and Magari," he explained, and he smiled. For *magàri* is a word of many meanings in Italian: "of course!" "and how!" "you bet!" but also "if only" and "no such luck!"

"Whenever possible I have given my wines names with an ironic undercurrent to them! Magari will be a wine to drink young. It will spend some time in wood, but I don't want the *barriques* to be evident in it. Camarcanda will be the bigger wine, more structured for longer cellar aging. Merlot maintains a good level of acidity here, which will help keep the wines fresh-tasting as they age.

"I hope to make elegant wines in Bolgheri, wines that are pleasant to drink even when they are young," asserted Gaja. "I do not want to make international-style wines, but wines that will reflect the south of Tuscany, its *terroir*—and its sun."

GRATTAMACCO
PODERE SANTA MARIA
OLIVE OIL

GRATTAMACCO 57022 CASTAGNETO CARDUCCI
TELEPHONE/FAX 0565 763933
E-MAIL trainiagri@infol.it

OPEN By appointment only   **CREDIT CARDS** None   **DIRECT SALE** Yes
ENGLISH SPOKEN Yes   **OTHER** Two apartments available for holiday rentals
DIRECTIONS Take the road from Bolgheri to Castagneto Carducci. After about 5 kms turn left at sign for *ristorante*. After 300 meters, turn left on dirt road. The farm is after about 1 km, by an enormous oak tree. Or follow the directions for Grattamacco (next entry) and after the modern *cantina* follow the dirt road down to the next farm

---

Podere Santa Maria once formed part of the Grattamacco estate. Claudio Traini came with the Meletti Cavallaris from Bergamo when they bought it in the late 1970s (see next entry). The farms later divided. Traini makes one of the area's most delicious olive oils. It is produced organically from the *podere*'s fifteen hundred trees, some of which are more than five hundred years old. "We were lucky here in 1985," Claudio Traini explained. "Being close to the sea, when the big freeze came, our trees were barely affected.

"When we first arrived the olive groves had been abandoned," Traini continued. "If olive trees are not pruned regularly, they send up suckers from the roots, which eventually overpower the main trunk. We studied and experimented with different cultivation techniques."

New plants may be grown in either of two forms: *monocono* (a single trunk growing upright that lends itself to mechanized harvesting) or *cespuglio* (a wider bush with three or four leading trunks, best for hand-picking or steep terrains). Traini favors the latter system, as his trees grow on sloping ground.

"Pure extra-virgin oil, being a natural product, is different every year. It's like wine; some vintages are less good due to climatic conditions. Only industrial oils can guarantee consistency, but that is because they are chemically adjusted."

Traini's oil is very fruity, with a fabulous full perfume and a light but pleasant bitterness. When I held a blind taste test with friends of a group of Tuscan oils, Traini's won.

GRATTAMACCO
WINE, OLIVE OIL

PODERE GRATTAMACCO 57022 CASTAGNETO CARDUCCI
TELEPHONE 0565 763840   FAX 0565 763217
WEB SITE www.grattamacco.com

OPEN 9:00–12:00, 15:00–18:00, prior appointment recommended; group tastings possible by prior arrangement   **CLOSED** Saturday, Sunday   **CREDIT CARDS** No   **DIRECT SALE** Yes, subject to availability   **ENGLISH SPOKEN** Yes   **OTHER** Apartments available for holiday rentals
DIRECTIONS From Donoratico, go through Castagneto Carducci. About 2 kms after the village, follow yellow signs to restaurant Il Cacciatore. Follow the road from there to the right, to the *cantina* building, a modern construction. Or follow directions for last entry, and after passing Podere Santa Maria, continue straight to the modern *cantina*

Piermario and Paola Meletti Cavallari produce some of Bolgheri's most interesting wines. Their estate, in the hills between Castagneto and Bolgheri, includes 10 hectares (25 acres) of vineyards and more than one thousand olive trees. The couple is from Bergamo, in northern Italy. When Piermario decided to change his life and leave Milan, he first opened a wine store.

"I met some of the smaller wine producers," he recounted, "and I began to think it would be more interesting to be producing wine than selling it." The couple bought Grattamacco and set about planting vineyards. That was more than twenty-five years ago, when the Bolgheri winemaking "revolution" had just begun.

"I have tried to apply my intelligence to this work," he explained as we visited their new aging cellar. A large oval room with a striking night-blue ceiling appears to have been scooped out of the hillside: cut-out "windows" along its smooth circumference reveal bare earth and stones. "This is as natural an environment as possible for the wine's maturation," Piermario explained enthusiastically. "Here it can breathe." It was raining that day, and water trickled freely down the "open" earth walls and away.

"We have everything to thank Mario Incisa for," he remarked. "Without his intuition about making great red wines, we would all still be making whites, no doubt lost in obscurity. He was an unforgettable man."

Piermario has maintained the practice of fermenting his red wine in open-topped wood barrels. (San Guido's Sassicaia was originally made this way, but later switched to closed stainless steel as market demand increased.) "This is by far the most organic system," Piermario said of the open barrels. "They need space, but the wood offers the wine a natural insulation, resulting in softer tannins."

Natural is a word Meletti Cavallari likes: just as he has eliminated chemical fertilizers and reduced fungicides in the vineyard, his new cellar minimizes the use of pumps and filters. "I love the idea of letting the wine move under its own weight. Being small," he concluded, "we are free to make the wines we like, without having to adapt to the market's demands."

"It's true," added his wife. "People have always enjoyed our wines. They are intense yet elegant, but very drinkable." Grattamacco Rosso (of 60 percent Cabernet, 25 percent Merlot and 15 percent Sangiovese) is indeed an elegant wine, and one that benefits from a few extra years' cellaring; Grattamacco Bianco (of pure Vermentino) is a clean, balanced wine with great character. Only 20 percent of this wine is aged in wood. Both wines are now Bolgheri DOCs and are available as long as stocks last. The couple also produces excellent extra-virgin olive oil.

MICHELE SATTA
WINE

VIGNA AL CAVALIERE 57020 CASTEGNETO CARDUCCI
TELEPHONE/FAX 0565 773041
E-MAIL satta@infol.it

OPEN Visits, tastings, and sales by previous appointment only　**CREDIT CARDS** Visa, MC
DIRECT SALE Subject to availability　**ENGLISH SPOKEN** A little
DIRECTIONS From Castagneto, take SS 329 toward Donoratico; then take Via dell' Accattapane; the *cantina* is on the left after 100 meters

---

"Wine comes from the land, not the sky!" exclaimed Michele Satta enthusiastically as he showed me his newly planted vineyards. Satta was trained as an agronomist, and he loves the hands-on work of the land. "Even when the work is the most tiring or difficult," he continued simply, "I find it irresistible. For me, it is not a dream of country life that holds me here, but a physical, concrete attachment to this earth, these plants."

Michele Satta came to winemaking in Bolgheri by chance. He was vacationing when he met a local landowner looking for an assistant. "I was only twenty years old, but I couldn't wait to 'put my hands in the dough,' as we say. I worked for him while I finished my degree. I loved the job but wanted to be my own boss."

He rented a few acres of vineyards, enough to make a serious start at winemaking. In 1988 came the next step: with winemaker Attilio Pagli, he decided to invest in vineyards to supplement those he rented. At present the winery comprises 25 hectares (62 acres). A new *cantina* has just been finished, with room for sales and tastings.

Satta is a warm, open man who readily communicates his excitement for his work and its fruit. His wines, too, have a wonderful warmth to them. Cavaliere, named for the single vineyard the grapes are picked from, is made of pure Sangiovese.

"This is a *cru* from a low, flat vineyard," he explained. "Here in Castagneto the *terroir* is unique: the ground is rich in minerals, the position very luminous and hot. The vines develop impetuously, precociously, even violently, and this enormous burst of energy makes the wines elegant and less 'tired' than the local wines traditionally have been."

Satta's other "table wine" is Piastraia, a blend of equal parts of Sangiovese, Merlot, Cabernet Sauvignon, and Syrah. This, too, is an intense, fruit-rich wine with a lively quality. Satta's wines are well structured but drinkable, with balanced tannins. Diambra, his affordable "simple" red wine, is fresh and fruity and made to be drunk young. La Costa di Giulia is a white wine made primarily from the Vermentino grapes that have long been associated with this part of the Mediterranean coast, with 30 percent Sauvignon added. Other wines are the Bolgheri DOCs Bianco and Rosato. Satta has also been experimenting with Viognier and some other Mediterranean varietals, such as Fiano and Falanghina, for new wines of the future.

ENOTECA IL BORGO	**VIA VITTORIO EMANUELE, 25/27**
WINE STORE	**57020 CASTAGNETO CARDUCCI**
	TELEPHONE/FAX 0565 766006

OPEN 10:00–12:00, 17:30–23:00   **CLOSED** Monday; November–Christmas, January–Easter
CREDIT CARDS Visa, MC   **DIRECT SALE** Yes   **ENGLISH SPOKEN** Yes
DIRECTIONS In the town center

Pasquino Malenotti runs one of the best wine stores in the area. It features a large selection of Tuscans, with special emphasis on the great local wines and on Chianti. Wines may be bought by the glass at the stand-up bar, along with grappa and Vin Santi. The store holds tastings and caters to groups. Snacks are available, as well as a selection of local oils. Across the street is a modest trattoria, Da Ugo (same phone), which is run by the *enoteca*'s owners. I found its wine list of a higher caliber than its food. It does, however, have a fabulous view.

Castiglioncello

DAI DAI	**VIA DEL SORRISO, 16 57012 CASTIGLIONCELLO**
FROZEN DESSERTS	**TELEPHONE 0586 752754 FAX 0586 751653**

OPEN Café: June, July, August 21:30–till late in the evening; winter Friday–Saturday 21:30 till late, Sunday: 15:30–20:00   **CLOSED** Café: Monday–Thursday in winter; office: Saturday and Sunday
CREDIT CARDS None   **DIRECT SALE** Yes, from the office, Monday–Friday 8:30–17:30 for large orders   **ENGLISH SPOKEN** A little   **FEATURES** Café's terraced garden overlooks the sea
RESERVATIONS None accepted   **DIRECTIONS** From Castiglioncello take the SS 1 Aurelia toward Livorno. Just beyond the village there is a small turn on the right, signposted; go up to the top of the hill

How many ice-cream companies are named for the call of a cart driver to his mule? How many can claim to dip all their frozen bonbons by hand? Or boast of having Oliviero Toscani as their photographer? I certainly can't think of another. In the world of frozen desserts, Dai Dai is unique.

"Last year we broke fifty-seven thousand eggs here," the company's spirited owner, Antonio Bartoletti, volunteered. "Every ingredient we use, from the Maremman cream to the Pisan pine nuts, is fresh and authentic—no artificial anything!"

The mule and cart story may seem apocryphal, but it's true—*"Dai! Dai!"* is the Italian equivalent of "Giddy up!" In the 1920s a Sicilian hawker drove his cart along the local beach, selling ice creams as he cajoled his mule; the phrase stuck. Sixty years later Bartoletti bought the recipe for his *cassatina,* and Dai Dai was born.

"We started with one product," he said, "and then added only a few more. The ice-cream industry is very, very tough to crack into. The big companies can squeeze the little guys out by refusing them space in the freezers they place in almost every bar and restaurant. The only way to survive is not to compete—to make a limited range of artisan products in a different category."

Dai Dai makes *semifreddi,* not gelati. *Semifreddi* are desserts frozen after they have been made, whereas gelati, or ice creams, are frozen as they are being made. One of Bertoletti's most popular items is the *bocconcino,* a bite-size chilled cream custard square, hand-dipped in chocolate and then frozen. It retains the crystalline structure of frozen but unbeaten whipped cream.

Dai Dai sells its geometric-shaped desserts to many restaurants and in its lovely café, perched high on the hill overlooking the Mediterranean. The range includes *pezzi duri* (hard pieces), triangles of fresh fruit sorbets made with mineral water; *tartufini,* rich chocolate truffles; *mattonella,* a *semifreddo* cream studded with pine nuts; and the original *cassatina,* individually wrapped slices of frozen cream hand-covered with a thin layer of bittersweet Pernigotti chocolate.

Cecina

MEDITERRANEA BELFIORE— FAMIGLIA CIARLO
PRESERVED VEGETABLES

VIA GUERRAZZI LA CINQUANTINA
SAN PIETRO IN PALAZZI 57023 CECINA
TELEPHONE 0586 620555   FAX 0586 622363

OPEN 9:00–12:00, 15:00–19:00   **CLOSED** Sunday   **CREDIT CARDS** None   **DIRECT SALE** Yes; also available at Casa Belfiore, Via Turati, 11 Cecina   **ENGLISH SPOKEN** Yes   **DIRECTIONS** Exit from SS 1 *superstrada* at S. Pietro in Palazzi (just north of Cecina). Go toward Cecina Mare on Via Guerrazzi. After about 2 kms, follow green sign to Famiglia Ciarlo along an unpaved road

---

This farm, located on flat land near the sea, produces wonderful bottled vegetables, sauces, and preserves. The Ciarlo family began processing tomatoes in 1974, especially for *passata*—a purée of fresh, lightly cooked tomatoes—which forms the basis of many sauces.

"My father took advantage of this area's exceptional tomatoes," explained Emiliana, one of the three Ciarlo daughters. "He cultivated and bottled them. We only work hand-picked mature tomatoes: human pickers are able to select ripe, healthy tomatoes—machines are not." The Ciarlos make fresh-tasting ready-made tomato sauces and bottle tomatoes for organic producers such as La Selva (p 242).

Other fine products include seasonal vegetables preserved in olive oil (peppers, sun-dried tomatoes, red onions); olive, red pepper, or tuna *creme* (purées to put on pasta or *crostini*); roasted vegetables (artichoke hearts, eggplant, peppers) in olive oil; and a fresh pesto that needs refrigeration but is packed with cheese and fresh basil. All are available from the farm shop.

Donoratico

L'OASI TOSCANA
SPECIALTY FOODS: HEALTH FOODS

VIA AURELIA 1/F 57024 DONORATICO
TELEPHONE 0565 773010   FAX 0565 773729

OPEN Summer: 9:00–13:00, 16:30–20:00; winter: 9:00–12:30, 16:00–19:00   CLOSED Sunday
CREDIT CARDS Visa, MC   ENGLISH SPOKEN A little   OTHER Another shop is in Livorno
on Via S. Gallo, 3/5/7   DIRECTIONS On the SS 1 Aurelia just north of Donoratico, set back slightly
from the main road

This modern health food store is one of the biggest and best I have found in Italy. It carries a wide selection of organic and other natural products from Tuscany, elsewhere in Italy, and beyond, as well as locally grown organic produce. There are counters of cheeses and dairy products and selections of organic olive oils and wines. There are also nonorganic wines from the three local DOC areas: Montescudaio, Bolgheri, and Val di Cornia.

Of the food producers, many are written about in this book. There is also a large *erboristeria* section, selling herbal treatments, cosmetics, and remedies, plus books, natural clothing and more . . . A great store!

Also

COAGRI

VIA CASONE UGOLINO, 2. 0565 775488

This fine oil-making cooperative has a modern-style olive press (*frantoio*), which mills olives grown by its members. Some of its oil is organic.

Guasticce

OSTERIA DEL CONTADINO
RESTAURANT

VIA D. STURZO, 69 57010 GUASTICCE
TELEPHONE 0586 984697 FAX 0586 983963

OPEN Lunch and dinner   CLOSED Saturday for lunch; Sunday; August   CREDIT CARDS Visa,
MC, Amex   ENGLISH SPOKEN Yes   RESERVATIONS Recommended   PRICE $$$
DIRECTIONS Guasticce is on the main road (SS 555) from Livorno going east. Or get off the Li-Pi-Fi
(SGC) at Collesalvetti and follow signs to Guasticce. Via Sturzo is the main road through the village

This cheery restaurant is full of local color. Hams, flasks, dried peppers, and garlic hang from the ceiling; pitchers are filled with flowers; and tables are laden with cheeses, *salumi*, and breads. But don't be misled by the rustic appearance—this is no tourist trap but a rare chance to taste Tuscany's authentic country foods. Bruno Gastaldìn, its host and creator, is himself a character. An expansive, bearded fellow with a fine sense of humor, he is very knowledgeable about the foods and customs of the country.

"My restaurant celebrates the simple dishes that were once staples on farmers' tables," he explained. "It is getting harder to find good artisan-produced ingredients, but you can sample them here." With his talented family, Gastaldìn offers a menu that follows the seasons, as produce is mostly homegrown.

My autumn dinner began in the well-stocked wine room with an *aperitivo* and a chunk of well-matured Parmesan. A selection of antipasti included a salad of raw porcini mushrooms and flaked Parmesan; frittata of egg, leek, and garlic; *sformato di funghi,* a tender custard of wild *chiodini* mushrooms; small wild boar *salamino;* butter-soft *lardo* wrapped around a fragrant Italia grape; toasted polenta topped with chopped chicken and rabbit livers; and a slice of ash-matured (by Gastaldìn) *prosciutto Toscano,* moist and not too salty. All in all, a true panoply of decisive flavors.

Primi were equally abundant and well cooked. Noodles are handmade with eggs from the family's free-range chickens—and you can taste the difference. *Zuppa di farro* was the color of red clay from the puréed beans and had plumped grains of spelt wheat in it. The *gnocchetti al tartufo* were exceptional: these small dumplings are made from baked, not boiled, potatoes and are soft without being gummy. They came dressed with aromatic truffle-butter and sprinkled with truffle flakes.

Main courses feature meats cooked *alla brace,* over a wood fire. There was delicious black Maremman lamb (whose flavor is more gamy than American or British lamb) grilled with garlic and rosemary; a tender pork loin slightly smoky from the embers; and medallions of pork stewed with truffle-scented white beans. Even the cheese was given an added sparkle: Amiata pecorino was matured in a barrel of ash, then heated quickly and served with two tiny fried quail's eggs. There are homemade cakes and Dai Dai ice creams (p 157) for anyone who still has room. All in all, a gastronomic feast for the hungry that merits a detour.

Livorno

MERCATO CENTRALE	**SCALI SAFFI VIA BUONTALENTI 57126 LIVORNO**
FOOD MARKET	TELEPHONE 0586 892188

OPEN Monday to Friday 5:00–14:00; Saturday 5:00–19:30   **CLOSED** Sunday
DIRECTIONS The landmark building is in the town center

Livorno's large covered food market, with more than 180 stalls, is well worth a visit. The historic 1895 building (identical to Firenze's Mercato Centrale) is home to vendors of fish, meat, fresh produce, grains, bread, dairy products—just about everything one could imagine to eat. The atmosphere is lively, and colorful characters abound. The market activities spill out into the surrounding streets, including Piazza delle Erbe, where fresh vegetables are sold.

When I scouted the area in early autumn, I found an old woman selling tiny skinned frogs on skewers and live crabs; a boy with a cardboard box full of bunches of scented-geranium leaves and of thyme; mounds of porcini and orange-yellow *ovoli* mushrooms; a cart laden with shiny *castagne* (sweet chestnuts), persimmons, pomegranates, fresh walnuts, and *giuggiole* (jujube berries); bundles of spindly cardoons; and bunches of saffron-colored zucchini flowers.

PASTICCERIA IL GIGLIO
PASTRY

VIA ERNESTO ROSSI, 25 57123 LIVORNO
TELEPHONE 0586 899369

OPEN Tuesday–Saturday 7:00–14:00,16:00–21:00; Sunday 7:00–14:00, 18:00–21:00
CLOSED Monday; mid-July to mid-August   **CREDIT CARDS** None   **DIRECT SALE** Yes
ENGLISH SPOKEN A little   **DIRECTIONS** Off Via Ricasoli, in the town center

This small *pasticceria* makes some unusual Livornese specialties in addition to a wide range of pastries. *Roschette* are bite-size rings of dough that are baked and salted. The classic version uses plain flour, but I liked the pale yellow variety made with granular corn flour. They are deliciously crunchy and go well with a glass of wine.

Between Lent and Easter Vinicio Pinelli makes the *schiacciata Livornese*, a complex sweet Easter bread that requires three separate risings. It is flavored with rose water and anise seeds and contains a lot of eggs. Another local dessert pastry is the *torta di ricotta e cioccolato:* a short-crust pastry case filled with chocolate custard and sweetened sheep's ricotta.

RISTORANTE ANTICO BORGO
RESTAURANT

VIA DON QUILICI, 10 57123 LIVORNO
TELEPHONE 0586 839308

OPEN Lunch and dinner   **CLOSED** Tuesday; September   **CREDIT CARDS** Visa, MC, Amex
ENGLISH SPOKEN Yes   **RESERVATIONS** Recommended for dinner and Sunday lunch
PRICE $$–$$$ **DIRECTIONS** At the corner of Via della Vecchia Casina, in the town center

In this unpretentious, moderately priced restaurant you can sample some of Livorno's favorite recipes. As in all great ports, the culinary tradition is sea-based, with many local Mediterranean fishes starring in simple but appetizing dishes once cooked by fishermen's wives. What you find here depends on the day's catch.

Tamara Taddei and her son Massimiliano prepare *cacciucco*, the celebrated Livornese multifish soup that is a meal in itself, usually by advance order only. But I was able to try *triglie alla Livornese*, the town's special way of cooking red mullet (in an aromatic tomato sauce). I also had a plate of mixed smoked fish that included swordfish, salmon, and tuna. Shellfish were served steamed with big wedges of lemon. The popular *fritto misto* was fried in a light batter and, in autumn, comprised shrimp, calamari, and little fishes.

For *primo* there was *riso nero*, black stained from squid ink, with its characteristic intense sea flavor, and spaghetti with clams tossed in oil and garlic. Main courses are dominated by whatever seafood is to be found fresh in the market, though some meats are also served. The wine list offers choices in various price ranges.

DA GAGARI	**VIA DEL CARDINALE, 23 57126 LIVORNO**
SNACK BAR	TELEPHONE 0586 884086

OPEN Summer: 8:00–12:30, 17:00–21:00; winter: 8:00–21:00   **CLOSED** Sunday; July
CREDIT CARDS None   **DIRECT SALE** Yes   **ENGLISH SPOKEN** No
DIRECTIONS Across the street from the covered Mercato Centrale

Every great city has its favorite popular foods, and Livorno is no exception. *La torta* is Livorno's answer to a slice of pizza or a hot dog, and Da Gagari is the place to get it. The tiny shop is always crammed full of locals waiting patiently for the latest panful to be pulled, bubbling hot, out of the deep wood-burning oven. Signora Fiorella, a Botero figure with a jolly disposition, stands at the ready.

"*Cinque e cinque!*" calls the first person in line. "Five and five" is local jargon for a wedge of chickpea flour pancake sandwiched between a slice of split focaccia. Fiorella slices off a piece of the thin, ocher-colored *torta*, sprinkles it with pepper, and wraps it in the bread. The cost? About the same as a cup of coffee and a doughnut. "In the old days," she explained as she waited for the next batch to cook, "it was called by this name because you would ask for five *soldi*'s worth of pancake and five *soldi*'s worth of bread. The prices changed, but somehow the name stuck!"

Moroccan chickpea flour is mixed with water, peanut oil, and salt and left to rest for a couple of hours in winter—less in summer—or it may *prendere forte*, or ferment. It is poured into a vast, round, shallow, tin-lined copper pan and baked for about fifteen minutes. The resulting cake is crunchy on the outside and still just creamy on the inside—a bit like eating a dense purée.

Fiorella's husband, whose name is Salvatore Chiappa but who is known locally as "Gagari" (he was nicknamed after Gagarin, the Russian astronaut), has been making the *torta* in this shop for more than thirty-six years. When I visited, he was stacking the next lot of branches neatly underneath the oven as Fiorella watched approvingly. "*Si, così si fa bella figura!*" "Yes," she asserted, "that's the way to create a good impression!"

CANTINA NARDI
WINE BAR

VIA CAMBINI, 6/8 57123 LIVORNO
TELEPHONE/FAX 0586 808006

OPEN 8:30–20:30   CLOSED Sunday; part of August   CREDIT CARDS Visa, MC, Amex
DIRECT SALE Yes   ENGLISH SPOKEN No   RESERVATIONS Recommended for lunch
PRICE $ DIRECTIONS In the town center, off Via Marradi

Two rooms lined with wine bottles, a few tables inside, a few more in the garden: the Cantina Nardi has been a fixture in Livorno for more than thirty years. This is a fine place for an easygoing lunch—a plate of local food with a glass of Tuscan wine (among others from farther afield). Nadio Nardi has a vast assortment of wines for sale by the bottle or glass. There is also a little marble bar for those who prefer to stand for an *aperitivo* with hors d'oeuvres.

The menu changes daily, but there are always a few *primi* and *secondi:* baked polenta with cheese, pasta with homemade sauces, salt cod (*baccalà*), tripe, egg frittata with vegetables, or the humble boiled beef "redone" with onions. It is open all day for wine or snacks, so drop in anytime.

ENOTECA DOC
WINE BAR

VIA GOLDONI, 40/44 57126 LIVORNO
TELEPHONE/FAX 0586 887583

OPEN 12:00–15:00, 20:00–3:00 A.M.   CLOSED Monday   CREDIT CARDS Visa, MC, Amex
DIRECT SALE Yes   ENGLISH SPOKEN Yes   RESERVATIONS Necessary for dinner
DIRECTIONS Off Via Mayer, in the town center

This is Livorno's trendiest wine bar, with all that the word implies. It has an extensive international and Italian wine list and an impressive showcase displaying the bottles. A big, modern-style bar serves wines by the glass and American-style cocktails. A few tables are scattered around for meals and snacks from an eclectic menu. This is a good after-dinner spot if you are feeling hip (and long on attitude).

Also

CIBO PER LA PACE

CORSO AMEDEO, 69. 0586 893591
ciboperlapace@li.technet.it

The name of the centrally located Cibo per la Pace means "food for peace," and it is a fine health food store and restaurant. Open daily for lunch, Saturday for dinner, closed Sunday.

V.A.D.

VIA DI FRANCO, 38. 0586 884106.
www.vadsnc@interfree.it

A stone's throw from the covered food market, this shop is full of big wheels of Parmesan cheese. Bruno Simonini sells aged and young Parmesan as well as a small range of more typically Tuscan *pecorini*.

ORGANIC BREADS

Pasticceria Angela. Via delle Cateratte, 96. Livorno. 0586 829994.

Angelo and Maria Santarella (who used to be known as I Pulitini) make some of the most wonderful organic breads in Tuscany. They used to make them at their tiny farm, but they now work from this larger bakery, which is not open to the public. Their bread can be found in many shops throughout Tuscany, including those listed below. Phone ahead to find out other sellers' names. You can also special-order breads and biscuits for people with food intolerances or allergies (to wheat, dairy, and sugar).

The Santarellas are registered organic bakers, and they use only certified organic flours—many stone-ground—and purified water. Their breads are characterized by fresh ingredients and natural yeasts.

"It was difficult for us to adjust to the association's organic requirements," confided soft-spoken Signora Maria. "But we would never go back—people feel so much better when they eat chemical-free products. It is really healing. That is what keeps us going."

From a wide range of flours, including wheat, *farro*, quinoa, kamut, and amaranth, the bakers produce white-flour breads: unsalted *pane sciocco*, plain or with walnuts; olive oil *schiacciata*, plain or with vegetables or olives; and unusual "health" breads. I liked the *farro* loaf. Oil-free, it is made from spelt-wheat flour, natural yeasts, and water—without salt. With a thin crust, its café-au-lait-colored dough has small air holes, a slight yeasty sourness, and a pronounced fragrance of fields. The thin *farro* crackers are also good, topped with sesame seeds and baked in rectangular slabs.

I Pulitini's breads may be found at L'Altra Roba, Pisa (see p 136); Cibo per la Pace, Livorno (see p 163); and L'Oasi Toscana, Donoratico (see p 159).

Marina di Bibbona

RISTORANTE LA PINETA   VIA DEI CAVALLEGGERI NORD, 27. 0586 600016
CLOSED MONDAY. PRICE $$$$

This well-heeled restaurant is right on the beach, with a scenic outdoor terrace to eat on in hot weather. It serves fine local seafood accompanied by a serious wine list. It's very popular, but not very big, so book well ahead.

Montenero

MONTALLEGRO
BAR, RESTAURANT

PIAZZA DEL SANTUARIO DI MONTENERO, 3 57128 MONTENERO
TELEPHONE 0586 579030
E-MAIL montallegro@tin.it

OPEN Restaurant: lunch all year, dinner also May–September   **CLOSED** Tuesday in winter;
November   **CREDIT CARDS** None   **ENGLISH SPOKEN** Yes   **FEATURES** Panoramic terrace
PRICE Lunch $; dinner $$–$$$ **OTHER** Montallegro is also a hotel
DIRECTIONS In Montenero's main square, beside the sanctuary

Anyone who is fascinated, as I am, by ex-voto paintings will be keen to visit
the Sanctuary of Montenero, where a truly exceptional collection exists. Dedi-
cated to the Virgin Mary, whose image was said to have appeared to a shepherd
in 1345 at the site of the sanctuary, these naïf paintings offer thanks for and tes-
timony to the miracles of everyday life of the past 250 years. For example, if a
young man survived after falling badly from his horse, an ex-voto was painted of
the accident in honor of his recovery. Touching scenes of disasters at sea, on land,
and at home are depicted in remarkable ways, often by unschooled painters; they
offer a window onto the world as it once was.

The sanctuary attracts thousands of pilgrims each year, and after visiting it,
many find their way to this large restaurant and bar for sustenance. It, too, is
something of a reminder of times past: meals are served in a ballroom that has
barely changed since 1929. The Orlandi family, the original owners of this hotel
and restaurant, are a welcoming bunch. In addition to a full-service bar that is
open almost all the time, they offer a set-price "pilgrim's lunch" and, in summer,
an à la carte dinner menu. The outdoor terrace offers romantic views of Livorno
and its coast.

Rosignano Marittimo

LA GATTABUIA
RESTAURANT

VIA GRAMSCI, 32 57016 ROSIGNANO MARITTIMO
TELEPHONE 0586 799760
WEB SITE www.gattabuia.it

OPEN Lunch and dinner   **CLOSED** Tuesday except July and August; Sunday lunch in summer
CREDIT CARDS Visa, MC, Amex   **ENGLISH SPOKEN** Yes   **FEATURES** Garden terrace in summer
RESERVATIONS Necessary on weekends   **PRICE** $$$
DIRECTIONS On the main street in the lower part of the town

Under a pink neon sign and down a narrow twisting staircase is this charming
little restaurant. (Even farther down, under a trap door, is the wine cellar, with a
ladder as steep as a submarine's; the wines are brought up with a basket pulley.) In

summer, tables are set out in a shady courtyard; in winter, the vaulted rooms are cozy and inviting without being claustrophobic.

Spinella Galeazzi is a natural cook, with a flair some women seem to have for turning simple ingredients into the most satisfying dishes. After working in a few local restaurants, she and her companion, Alberto Pescatori, decided to open their own.

"The menu follows the seasons, with an emphasis on seafood," she explained. "There is no frying, no frozen fish. I make all my own pasta. I make the most of what sparks my interest at the market." The wines are Tuscan and feature local producers, big and small. There are also estate-bottled olive oils.

On the chilly October evening when I arrived, her thick soup of mixed pulses was welcome. Chickpeas, lentils, beans, black-eyed peas, and *farro* (spelt wheat) were left whole in a puréed bean base and served with croutons, fruity olive oil, and pepper. *Pappardelle,* wide handmade noodles, came with a rich, meaty sauce with only a hint of tomato.

Main courses feature fish, though there are some meat dishes, with a number of vegetarian choices and local game in autumn. Wild boar was well stewed with black olives in a fine rendering of this oft-prepared dish. The meat was flavorful, neither tough nor dry. Roast loin of pork (*arista*) was served with sweet-and-sour onions and grapes. Fish included stockfish, grilled cuttlefish, and whole *rombo* (turbot), baked with wild mushrooms. A selection of Italian and French cheeses was a nice way to finish a bottle of wine, but there were home-baked tarts and a couple of airy creams (lemon or *zabaglione*) for those who felt the need for something sweet.

Also

APICOLTURA DR. PESCIA   SERRAGRANDE. 0586 793368

Paolo Pescia is a "nomadic" beekeeper—he takes his hives to wherever the flowers are. He has access to unspoiled, untreated areas like the Parco dell'Uccellina, and his honeys are exceptional: bitter *corbezzolo* (the "strawberry" tree); deeply aromatic *castagna* (chestnut)—even a honey called "Macchia Mediterranea" for the spontaneous plants that flower only along its coast.

He also makes an unusual drink: Idromele is fermented honey diluted with water—one of the world's earliest alcoholic beverages, made by the Mayans, Egyptians, Greeks, Vikings, and Britons, who called it mead. This version is aged in *barriques:* it's like a *passito* but has no acidity and is both sweet and dry. "It goes very well with chocolate," says master chocolate-maker Paul de Bondt (see p 135), who turned me on to it.

San Vincenzo

GAMBERO ROSSO
RESTAURANT

PIAZZA DELLA VITTORIA, 13 57027 SAN VINCENZO
TELEPHONE 0565 701021   FAX 0565 704542

OPEN Lunch and dinner   **CLOSED** Monday, Tuesday; November   **CREDIT CARDS** Visa, MC, Amex   **ENGLISH SPOKEN** Yes   **RESERVATIONS** Necessary   **PRICE** $$$$$–$$$$$$
OTHER Five guest rooms available   **DIRECTIONS** The restaurant overlooks the town's small port

One of the pleasures of eating in the restaurant of a really great chef is to see how his or her cusine evolves over time and how it improves. A recent lunch at Fulvio Pierangelini's was the confirmation of both. His almost obsessive commitment to fine-flavored, perfect ingredients has long been the foundation on which he has constructed his considerable reputation; his talent is indisputable, and now he seems to have relaxed into it—with exceptional results.

The restaurant is perfectly situated, overlooking the charming little port of San Vincenzo. The well-appointed dining room is luminous and quite romantic, with its quintessentially Mediterranean view of nothing but sea. The interior is tasteful and elegant, a tone set by Emanuela Pierangelini, who also takes the orders. There is an extensive, hand-picked, reasonably priced wine list with many older vintages. In addition to the regular *carte*, a *degustazione* (tasting) menu features the "classics of the Gambero Rosso."

In June, lunch began with a roselike swirl of pale yellow creamed *stoccafisso* (stockfish) topped with thin shavings of mild but fragrant truffle and delicate but fragrant olive oil. A cloud of loose whipped potato was paired with a plump sautéed scallop. Like Pierangelini's often-copied but never equalled *passata di ceci*—chickpea soup served with red shrimp (*gamberi rossi*)—the idea is not complicated, but the refined results seem hard to duplicate. Round ravioli were stuffed with onions sweet from their slow cooking, enhanced by Modena's barrel-aged *aceto balsamico tradizionale*—which has nothing in common with its industrial namesakes—and Parmesan cheese.

"Everyone who comes here wants to eat fish," admitted Fulvio Pierangelini, a mountain of a man, shy but with an uncompromising directness. "But in fact, the most interesting dishes to come out of my kitchen are the meats—like the pigeon." His *piccione in casseruola* is, indeed, legendary.

I was intrigued by the idea of lamb baked *in crosta di argilla*. It was just that: a gray clay parcel was cracked open to reveal the paper-wrapped meat inside, which had retained all its juices in the cooking. It was sliced and served with fried grated potatoes, fresh peas and fava beans scented with rosemary, and the chef's intense *jus*. A sampling of the remarkable local and French cheeses from the restaurant's selection followed.

I repeat an earlier assertion that Pierangelini's *biscotto soffice* is one of the best chocolate desserts I have ever eaten. A cross between a soufflé and a mousse, it is served right from the oven, scalding hot, sumptuously rich, near black from the concentration of its chocolateness. The intensity of the cocoa extract and depth of flavor are unforgettable.

"To create a great restaurant," said Pierangelini, "you must do everything yourself. You need culture to get beyond a certain level in cooking. I was lucky, I had no bad habits: I had never been a waiter or a cook. I have combined classical rigor with free choice and construction—consequently, only my emotions go into my recipes."

Suvereto

AZIENDA AGRICOLA ORLANDO PAZZAGLI
OLIVE OIL

VIA S. LEONARDO, 29 57028 SUVERETO
TELEPHONE 0565 829333   FAX 0565 828196
WEB SITE www.piastraia.it

OPEN By appointment only   **CREDIT CARDS** None   **DIRECT SALE** Yes, by appointment
ENGLISH SPOKEN No   **DIRECTIONS** In the town center

Orlando Pazzagli has a beautiful private *orciaia*, the room traditionally used for storing olive oil in terra-cotta urns (*coppi*), which have now all but disappeared. Some of these vast handmade pots from Impruneta have survived for more than a hundred years. "Every year they are cleaned out using vinegar and sawdust," explained Pazzagli, who has his own mill nearby for grinding olives, which is open to visitors during November, when the oil is made. In addition to his fine olive oil, he sells vegetables preserved in oil—*sott'olii*.

OMBRONE
RESTAURANT

PIAZZA DEI GIUDICI, 1 57028 SUVERETO
TELEPHONE 0565 829336   FAX 0565 828297
E-MAIL gian.bini@tiscalinet.it

OPEN Lunch and dinner   **CLOSED** Monday and Tuesday for lunch in summer; Monday in winter; February   **CREDIT CARDS** Visa, MC, Amex   **ENGLISH SPOKEN** A little   **FEATURES** Outdoor terrace in summer   **RESERVATIONS** Recommended in summer   **PRICE** $$$–$$$$
OTHER The couple runs a cooking school   **DIRECTIONS** In the town center, near the Comune

Giancarlo Bini has long been a key figure in Maremman gastronomy. An expert wine and oil taster, his Ombrone restaurants (first in Grosseto, now here) attract food and wine lovers. His wife, Lella, the restaurant's cook, runs the Caterina de' Medici cooking school.

Some years ago Bini created his Salotto—a collection of thirty-eight Italian artisan producers. "The Salotto is my personal choice of the foods and wines I like best," he explained. "It's not about business, but about the culture of food-making." It holds one or two meetings per year; foods and wines are tasted and a feeling of solidarity enforced.

This restaurant is set in a thousand-year-old former olive mill. A summer terrace overlooks the arched façade of Suvereto's medieval *comune*. The food is unpretentious and wholesome; Lella is a natural cook and seems at her best when working with the primary ingredients of the Maremma: wild herbs, tangy sheep's cheeses, pulses, and grains.

My early spring dinner began with piping hot *scamorza* cheese melted over spinach and salted anchovies. Some excellent *crostini* followed—a selection of savory toppings on crusty country bread—then a soup, described by Lella as a *cacciucco* of mixed pulses and grains; it was delicious, thick, earthy, and satisfying. "*Gnuddi*" of spinach and ricotta looked like green speckled bird's eggs. In fact, they are like pasta stuffing without the pasta—cloud light, with the perfumed accent of fresh sage. They were exceptional.

Second courses followed in the country mode: a well-done duck breast was cooked with Vin Santo; *faraona* (guinea fowl) was stewed simply with mushrooms, carrots, and wine. Desserts are homemade.

The Binis are unique in offering their guests separate menus for oils, vinegars, sugars, and coffees. They have an interesting wine cellar and an informal room downstairs for young diners. As we concluded our visit, Giancarlo turned to me and smiled. "There you have it," he said. "This is our little kingdom."

GUALDO DEL RE   NOTRI, 77 57028 SUVERETO
WINE   TELEPHONE 0565 829888, 829361   FAX 0565 829888
                                              WEB SITE www.gualdodelre.it

---

OPEN 9:00–12:00, 14:00–18:00; tastings and *cantina* visits by appointment   **CLOSED** Sunday
CREDIT CARDS Visa, MC   **DIRECT SALE** Yes   **ENGLISH SPOKEN** A little
DIRECTIONS Follow signs from Suvereto

The wine-producing area near Suvereto is unlike any other Tuscan wine zone. For one thing, the land is only a few kilometers from the sea and is practically flat; fields of artichokes and vegetables give way to a few acres of vineyards at the foot of big electrical pylons. The story of how a handful of local producers turned Suvereto's winemaking around and became rising wine stars is an interesting one. Gualdo del Re's young owner, Maria Teresa Cabella, explained, "At the end of the 1970s the steel factories at Piombino were feeling the effect of Italy's industrial crisis. Twenty years earlier the countryside had been abandoned in favor of the factories. But people began to have second thoughts."

Two forward-thinking men, Suvereto's mayor, Walter Gasperini, and a wine-maker, Marco Stefanini, were convinced that the area could make good wines if the farmers would concentrate on quality rather than quantity. They held meetings, and Maria Teresa, her husband, Nico Rossi, and his parents were among the first to become interested in the idea.

"It meant changing everything," she said. "Planting new vineyards, building serious cellars—a huge investment of time and money. And we were both still working at the factory." In 1983 Gualdo del Re (the name means the "king's hunting woods") bottled its first wines; they now come under the Val di Cornia DOC. By 1990 the couple had left their other jobs to run the winery.

"For us the biggest satisfaction is that our wines are liked," Maria Teresa asserted enthusiastically. "Wine is one of the few products that you can follow from birth to sales—we oversee the vines, follow the wine into the cellar, through its aging, and into the bottle. We even do our own sales trips." Over time the winery has increased to its current 20 hectares (48 acres) of vineyards.

"Initially, we didn't want to overthrow tradition, so we planted better clones of the existing Sangiovese as the mainstay of our big red Gualdo del Re, and concentrated on Vermentino, which was once a traditional grape used along the coast, for our white Valentina," Maria Teresa said. Recently they have been drawn more to making single-varietal wines: Re Nero is pure Merlot, while Federico Primo is pure Cabernet Sauvignon, made in collaboration with Barbara Tamburini, one of Italy's rare female enologists.

TUA RITA
WINE

NOTRI, 81 57028 SUVERETO
TELEPHONE 0565 829237   FAX 0565 827891

OPEN Visits and tastings by appointment only   CREDIT CARDS None
DIRECT SALE Yes, subject to availability   ENGLISH SPOKEN No
DIRECTIONS Follow signs from Suvereto

A few years have passed since Rita Tua, Tua Rita's owner, made wines from the cellar of her little house. In the meantime the success of her wines—and the incessant demand for them—has led her and her husband to build a new, more professional *cantina* and increase the extent of their vineyards to nearly 20 hectares (48 acres). The results are already extremely positive, with Redigaffi, their great Merlot, winning top marks wherever it goes.

"At the outset we didn't really plan on making wine, but nothing else would grow here," confessed the lively Rita. "I suppose you could say that our situation is the opposite of the imposing French wine chateaux: they are perfect but to me lack soul. Here it is all very personal and more homey."

She and her husband, Virgilio Bisti, began by taking winemaking courses. In 1988 they planted their first vineyards to Cabernet and Merlot and hired a professional winemaker, who has since been replaced by Stefano Chioccioli. The couple even sold their weekend house on Mount Amiata to buy *barriques*. Giusto di Notri was the result, a well-balanced, concentrated super-Tuscan that put them on the map. The arid, mineral-rich terrain and long hot summers give the wines great structure and character, yet they remain approachable. Perlato del Bosco is Sangiovese, while Lodano is a "curious" white, as Rita described it—a blend of Traminer, Riesling, and Chardonnay aged in *barriques*. "The Traminer gives this wine more perfume," she said, "but the Chardonnay makes it mellow."

"If we had realized what the investment in human and financial terms would be, we would never have gotten into it," confided Rita. "But now we are hooked, and there is so much demand for our wines, we never have enough to go around."

Vada

IL DUCALE
RESTAURANT

PIAZZA GARIBALDI, 33 57018 VADA
TELEPHONE/FAX 0586 788600

OPEN Lunch and dinner   **CLOSED** Monday; holidays in January   **CREDIT CARDS** Visa, MC, Amex
ENGLISH SPOKEN A little   **RESERVATIONS** Recommended on weekends and for dinner
PRICE $$$–$$$$ **DIRECTIONS** In Vada's main square

This restaurant has an eclectic, almost Victorian interior filled with rugs and roses, plants and antiques, lace and chintz. The rooms are lofty: they once housed the Grand Duke of Tuscany's carriages.

The kitchen features seafood only from the local Tyrrhenian Sea—no farm-raised or imported fish here. Sample the area's celebrated *cacciucco*—the Livornese counterpart to *bouillabaisse*—as only top-quality fish are used for this all-in-one dish (including lobster and shellfish). Il Ducale suggests serving it with one of Tuscany's big reds.

In *triglie con agro di limone,* red mullet fillets are cooked with garlic, parsley, and lemon. The fish is firm-fleshed under its scarlet skin. *Pesce spada con cipolle borrettane* is a delicious dish of swordfish topped with a Mediterranean stew of flat onions, potato, tomato, and rosemary. The recipe is from the sixteenth century, explained Altero Giomi, the owner. *Crostino di polpo in cacciucco* is exotic: crisp toast is topped with *piccante* but tender octopus stained a deep reddish brown.

Il Ducale offers many pasta and fish combinations. The fish are allowed to express their natural flavors without being dominated by forceful sauces. In *spaghetti con tartufi di mare,* shellfish in the clam family are simply chopped and served in a light sauce without parsley or garlic. There is a full aroma of the sea—delicate but fishy. Sea bass (*branzino*) is cooked with a little fresh tomato and tossed over *farfalle,* pasta bows. Olive oil is used judiciously; it is sensed by the palate but does not overpower. Finally, *sarago,* a local member of the bream family, is served pure—no sauce, no oil, no lemon. Its soft, creamy-white flesh is clear-tasting and delicate, offering a fine contrast to the other colorful flavors. A good-size wine list concentrates on whites from Italy and abroad.

Venturina

CALIDARIO   0565 851504; RESTAURANT 0565 851240

This is my favorite thermal bath: a sulphur-free spring of blood-temperature water feeds a dramatic pool that is open all day (8:30–midnight). The restaurant and bar make great pizzas, just what you feel like after an invigorating evening swim.

CHAPTER 7

The Island of Elba

When people think of Elba, they think of Napoleon. Although he spent only a few months there two hundred years ago, he has been credited with encouraging the island's viticulture and reforming its administration. He might also, it would appear, be thanked for putting it on the map.

Elba is an arid mountainous island, but it is not barren. Its lower ranges are covered by dense *macchia Mediterranea,* the bushy scrub that flowers so magically in spring and lends the summer air its aromatic *profumi.* Fennel and rosemary, prickly pear and fig grow wild. Up higher are woods of chestnut, acacia, and umbrella pines. Remarkably pure honeys of thistle-flower, herbs, or *corbezzolo* (the "strawberry tree") ensue—there are no pesticides or pollutants in the wilderness. Read labels carefully. Unless a honey jar specifies it was produced on Elba, it almost certainly was not.

There are fewer fishermen on Elba now than there once were. And, sadly, vendors no longer hawk spicy boiled *polpo* (octopus) along the beaches. But there is good fish to be found in some restaurants and fish stores. Among the species that are caught locally are the blunt-headed *gallinella* (a type of gurnard), purplish octopus the size of one's hand, slim anchovies, and striped, oval-bodied *sarago* (a kind of bream). In the hills, wild boar and other game forage for food. On summer nights the boar come down to feed on ripe grapes and figs and may occasionally be seen.

A recent renewal of winemaking traditions on the island has led to some good wines: Elba Bianco and Rosso, Ansonica—all DOC—and the rare and highly aromatic Aleatico *passito,* an intense cherry-red dessert wine. The real thing is fairly costly, but don't be tempted by the cheap imitation, labeled Aleatico *vino liquoroso;* it is produced elsewhere and is thick with additives and sugars.

The best time to visit Elba is in early summer or autumn; in August the island is overwhelmed with campers, beachgoers, and tourists. Elba, which is part of the

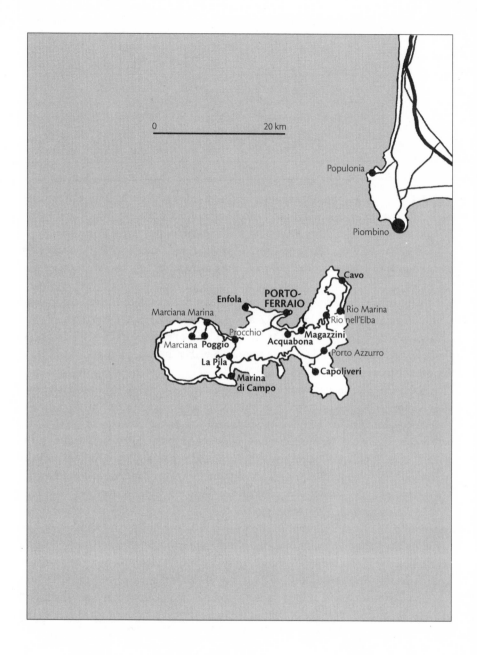

Boldface type indicates towns that are included in this chapter.

province of Livorno, is reached by ferry from Piombino (about one hour away) or by small plane.

AZIENDA PROMOZIONE TURISTICA
CALATA ITALIA, 26
57037 PORTOFERRAIO
0565 914671, FAX 0565 916350
E-MAIL info@mail.arcipelago.turismo.toscana.it
SUMMER 8:00–20:00; WINTER 8:00–14:00, 15:00–18:00

Acquabona

ACQUABONA
WINE

ACQUABONA 57037 PORTOFERRAIO LIVORNO
TELEPHONE/FAX 0565 933013
E-MAIL acquabona.elba@tiscali.it

OPEN June–September 10:00–13:00, 15:30–19:30; by appointment only during rest of year. Tastings are possible; *cantina* visits and groups by appointment   **CREDIT CARDS** None
DIRECT SALE Yes, minimum of six bottles per sale   **ENGLISH SPOKEN** Yes
DIRECTIONS Acquabona is on the main road from Portoferraio to Porto Azzurro, about halfway between them; it is signposted

Acquabona is run by three friends from Milan and Florence who, in the 1980s, accepted an invitation from the estate's owners to relaunch the disused winery. Now the results are showing: Acquabona's wines are among Elba's best. It is a pretty estate, a little inland: 13 hectares (32 acres) of vineyards alongside high avenues of eucalyptus trees near the island's golf greens. The *cantina* is tiny, crammed full of vats and equipment. Capitani, Fioretti, and Lucchini intend to extend it.

Acquabona makes ten wines, including two grappas. Acquabona di Acquabona is an aromatic yet fresh-tasting white made from the Vermentino grape that has long been known on the Livornese coast. The affordable Elba Bianco DOC is a drinkable white of primarily Procanico (Trebbiano Toscano) grapes. Elba Rosso DOC is of Sangioveto; in good years the best grapes are kept for the Riserva Camillo Bianchi, which is aged in *barriques*—small French oak casks.

The sought-after Aleatico dell'Elba DOC is a rich sweet *passito* wine particular to Elba and the Maremman coast. Acquabona's is a heady wine of an intense berry red, with aromas of violets and roses. The grapes for this wine are sun-dried on racks in ventilated greenhouses before being pressed. Aleatico is best savored on its own.

Wonderful honey is also made on the estate by beekeeper Luciano Pasolini from Officinalia at San Gimignano (see p 287).

Capoliveri

IL CHIASSO
RESTAURANT

VIA N. SAURO 57031 CAPOLIVERI LIVORNO
TELEPHONE/FAX 0565 968709

OPEN Dinner only from Easter to mid-September   **CLOSED** Tuesday in spring and autumn
CREDIT CARDS Visa, MC, Amex   **ENGLISH SPOKEN** Yes   **RESERVATIONS** Always recommended
PRICE $$$$ **DIRECTIONS** In the center of the old town of Capoliveri

---

This is a restaurant for people who like eating out. The atmosphere is lively and *simpatico*. The food (mostly fish) is fresh, unfussy, and delicious. It is served by agile waiters who navigate tables grouped a bit haphazardly—indoors and out—on either side of a narrow stepped alley (*chiasso*, in the local dialect). Il Chiasso's host, Luciano Casini, is a colorful character, warm and affable in his white linen and sandals. For twenty-five years, in these well-lit humble rooms, he has fed an international clientele of summer travelers. "The Capoliverians were dominated by the Saracens, by the Turks—by everybody," he exclaimed good-naturedly. "But we have remained welcoming. I have always wanted Il Chiasso to keep its friendly trattoria feel."

As for the food, the aromas, colors, and tastes are pure Mediterranean. Fish of all sizes are married simply to fresh local ingredients. Mollusks are sautéed and brought to the table in copper pots, steaming and aromatic. Spaghettini are dressed with light flavorful sauces of fresh anchovies, lobster, sea bream, or tuna. There are linguine with pesto and rice blackened by squid ink.

Whole fish are baked to order: Casini grabs a glistening specimen under the gills and presents it to the table before cooking. Of the authentic Elban recipes, I tasted excellent *acciughe ripiene*, once a favorite dish of Casini's mother. Two fresh anchovy fillets "sandwich" a delicate ground fish stuffing; they are lightly fried, then simmered in a sauce of fresh cherry tomatoes, garlic, and herbs. Elba's *cucina povera* is also responsible for *polpo con patate*. Young octopuses are boiled before being stewed with potatoes and rosemary. The result is a spicy purple mixture of succulent octopus and flavorful potatoes. "So many of the island's traditions have been lost since tourism hit," Casini said sadly.

Meat dishes and nicely grilled vegetables are available for those not wanting fish. Desserts are homemade: in the popular *misto di frutta flambé*, fresh fruits are dipped in hot caramel sauce and served over ice-cream. Casini's handwritten wine list is eclectic.

Also

AZIENDA AGRICOLA MOLA   MOLA. CAPOLIVERI. 0565 958151

This winery produces a good verion of Elba's Aleatico DOC—the *passito* made from the red grapes of Aleatico. This and its other wines are available from the estate's shop on the SP 26 at Piano di Mola. Farm produce is also for sale in summer.

Cavo

BALLINI APICOLTURA   VIA DELLA PARATA 57030 CAVO LIVORNO
HONEY   TELEPHONE/FAX 0565 949836
                                           E-MAIL aballini@elbalink.it

OPEN 8:00–20:00   **CLOSED** Never   **MAIL ORDER** Queen bees may be ordered by mail
CREDIT CARDS None   **ENGLISH SPOKEN** A little   **DIRECTIONS** From Rio nell'Elba, take the mountain road (not the coastal road) toward Cavo. A few kilometers before Cavo there are signs for honey; the laboratory is a few meters off the road, down to the right

Roberto Ballini was a champion bicycle racer before he took to beekeeping more than twenty years ago. An attractive man, he now works with his two sons making honey and breeding queen bees. "Making honey is an erratic business," Ballini explained. "We felt it was better to branch out and to breed queens, which can only be done in areas as geographically pure and isolated as this." The queen leaves the hive to be fertilized, and she may mate with as many as eight drones: the only way to ensure purity of breed is to be certain there are no other bees around when she comes out.

The rarest Elban honeys are *rosmarino, cardo,* and *corbezzolo.* As many as thirteen species of rosemary grow wild on the island. The light amber honey is delicate and aromatic, without being overly sugary. *Cardo* is made from the nectar of the indigenous thistle, *Galactites tomentosa.* Bright amber in color, this lustrous honey is neither too sweet nor too strong, yet has a distinctive character. The *corbezzolo* plant, *Arbutus unedo,* grows wild in the *macchia Mediterranea.* This bush (known also as the "strawberry tree") has the unusual capacity to produce its flowers and fruit simultaneously, in late autumn. The honey, a deep golden amber, is the strongest of the three. Its bittersweet and exotic taste surprised me, like incense, or resin. The aftertaste clung to the tastebuds for a long time, like a drop of perfume on the tongue.

Ballini, like every other beekeeper I have met, devotes a lot of time to combating varroa, the parasite now devastating the world's bee population. "Bees have such extraordinary intelligence," he said. "Their communication system is very sophisticated—I feel sure that once they realize they are under attack they will transmit the information to each other on how to survive."

Enfola

EMANUEL
RESTAURANT

57037 ENFOLA LIVORNO
TELEPHONE/FAX 0565 939003
E-MAIL emanuelrist@elbalink.it

OPEN Lunch and dinner from Easter to late September   **CLOSED** Wednesday in spring and autumn
CREDIT CARDS Visa, MC, Amex   **ENGLISH SPOKEN** Yes   **FEATURES** Beachside dining garden
RESERVATIONS Recommended   **PRICE** $$–$$$ **DIRECTIONS** From Portoferraio, follow signs to
Enfola; go all the way down to the beach

Emanuel is situated in a romantic spot. Enfola is a cluster of houses on an unspoiled beach overlooking a bay dotted with sailboats, against a backdrop of mountains. The restaurant, with its shaded terrace, is right on the beach, with a garden for summer dining. The clean-lined dining room has picture windows framing the view. The restaurant is run by an earnest young couple, Anna Lauria and Alberto Zanoli.

At lunchtime there is a pleasant outdoor barbecue for simply grilled fish, to eat with cheeses and vegetables. A good-value *menu degustazione* also exists, with no hidden service or cover charges. This is primarily a fish restaurant, though some meats are served. The cuisine is traditional Mediterranean and Elban, with modern touches. Seafood antipasti are a specialty here and worth trying. An unusual assortment included sautéed shrimp tossed with sliced mushrooms, cherry tomatoes, arugula, and balsamic vinegar, and *totani alla diavola*—tender squid served hot with a touch of *peperoncino*. Mussels on the half shell were steeped in herbed tomato sauce and cooked on a griddle. Beaten egg was then spooned into each shell, cooked only by the heat of the mussels—a traditional Elban recipe.

I preferred the *secondi* to the *primi* in this restaurant. A delicate fillet of *rombo* (turbot) was topped by a crust of paper-thin sliced potatoes that reminded me of *pommes Anna*. *Pesce spada con capperi* was equally good. A thin slice of swordfish was dipped in egg and bread crumbs flavored with capers and sage before being sautéed. For dessert, a *mantecato* of melon was a sorbet flavored surprisingly with white port and chili. Frozen *mattonella* from Dai Dai (p 157) came with a warm *zabaglione* sauce. The wine list includes a good range of whites, a few reds, and a group of meditation wines.

La Pila

CECILIA
WINE

LA CASINA LA PILA 57034 CAMPO NELL'ELBA LIVORNO
TELEPHONE 0565 977322   FAX 0565 977964
E-MAIL gcamerini@tin.it

OPEN 9:00–12:00, 15:00–19:00; tastings are possible; *cantina* visits by appointment for a small fee
CLOSED Sunday; Saturday in winter   **CREDIT CARDS** Visa, MC, Amex
DIRECT SALE Yes, minimum of six bottles per sale   **ENGLISH SPOKEN** A little
DIRECTIONS Azienda Agricola Cecilia is on the main road between Procchio and Marina di Campo, by the airfield

Cecilia is one of Elba's most significant wine producers, along with La Chiusa and Acquabona. Housed in a large pink building, it is surrounded by flat vineyards. As the ultramodern vinification cellars reveal, the emphasis of this winery is on technology. Cecilia's owner, Giuseppe Camerini, is an engineer who has raised the standard not only of his own wines, but also of the island's: he led the campaign to get Aleatico its DOC status, succeeding in 1994.

Coming from a winemaking background in the Veneto region, Camerini decided in 1989 to modernize and expand his family's holdings on Elba. Presently he has 5 hectares (12 acres) of vineyards but buys grapes from around the island. His cellars are equipped with sophisticated temperature controls—indispensable for making white wines in a hot climate.

Cecilia produces Elban DOCs Rosso and Bianco (with their *barrique*-aged della Casina versions), the indigenous white Ansonica, and red Aleatico—from which a highly aromatic sweet *passito* wine is made. Ansonica is particularly difficult to work: the delicately flavored, thick-skinned grapes are very low in acidity and oxidize easily. Camerini described this pale but fairly rich wine poetically: "It is ephemeral . . . it may last as long as a morning."

Magazzini

LA CHIUSA
WINE, OLIVE OIL

MAGAZZINI 57037 PORTOFERRAIO LIVORNO
TELEPHONE/FAX 0565 933046
E-MAIL lachiusa@elbalink.it

OPEN 9:00–12:00, 17:00–19:00 in summer; 9:00–12:00, 16:00–17:00 in winter; tastings and *cantina* visits possible   **CLOSED** Sunday   **CREDIT CARDS** None   **DIRECT SALE** Yes
ENGLISH SPOKEN A little   **DIRECTIONS** Magazzini is on the main road between Portoferraio and Bagnaia; Tenuta La Chiusa is clearly signposted

Tenuta La Chiusa is one of Tuscany's most beautiful wine estates. From the road, an avenue of olive trees leads you gently through ordered vineyards to the historic villa, its flower-laden gardens, and the sea. The house of a noble Florentine family twice visited by Napoleon Bonaparte, La Chiusa overlooks Portoferraio across the bay.

The winery, its atmospheric cellars, and its shop are well set up for visits. Giuliana Foresi Castelli and her husband have 9 hectares (22 acres) of vineyards. They produce Elba Bianco DOC, Elba Rosso DOC, and Rosato, a rosé. Two *passito* wines are made from Elba's most characteristic vines, Aleatico and Anzonica.

The rare Anzonica (as La Chiusa spells it) is a dessert grape formerly popular for blending with other white wines to give added body and color. The varietal known as Anzolia (or Inzolia) is still present in Sicily and may have originated in the Middle East. La Chiusa's *passito* is like a delicate, lightly sweet sherry. It should be drunk before meals as an *aperitivo*, or afterward, but not with food.

La Chiusa makes an exceptional extra-virgin olive oil, gold-green and fresh scented. Unusually for Tuscany, the olive picking is machine aided, as the trees are planted on flat ground. The olives are sent by boat to a *frantoio* on the mainland, returning to the island as oil.

Marina di Campo

GARDEN BAR   VIA VENEZIA, 12. 0565 976036. OPEN 7 A.M.–1 A.M.

Right on the seafront, this large lively bar is always a crush in summertime. It makes the best *brioches*, breakfast pastries, and cappuccino in the area. Cakes and pastries may be bought to eat standing at the counter, as most Italians like to do, or arranged in a *vassoio* (tray) to take home. Garden Bar also makes good clean-tasting fruit gelati.

Poggio

PUBLIUS   57030 POGGIO LIVORNO
RESTAURANT   TELEPHONE 0565 99208   FAX 0565 904174

OPEN Lunch and dinner March 20–November 10   **CLOSED** Monday in winter
CREDIT CARDS Visa, MC, Amex   **ENGLISH SPOKEN** Yes   **FEATURES** Panoramic dining terrace
RESERVATIONS Recommended for dinner   **PRICE** $$$$ **DIRECTIONS** From Marciana or
Marciana Marina, follow signs to Poggio; the restaurant is visible as you enter the village

---

Publius is a restaurant with a view. From its perch in the unspoiled village of Poggio, it offers its guests a breathtaking panorama of Elba's mountainous seascape. An airy glassed-in dining terrace makes the most of this location, especially at lunchtime.

This restaurant's menu is now divided between meat and fish. Antipasti include homemade *funghi sott'olio* (preserved wild mushrooms), a "mousse" of local herbs, and liver-topped *crostini* flavored with rosemary, bay, and Vin Santo. Two fish-based *primi* use *tagliolini,* fine egg noodles. In one, the pasta is stained with tomato, complementing the gray-green artichoke hearts and shelled clams (laudably grit free). In the second, yellow noodles are sauced with firm-fleshed sea bream and arugula and sweetened with mint.

Spigola (bass) fillet is wonderful baked in a *cartoccio* of foil with cherry tomatoes, olives, rosemary, and olive oil—the decisive flavors of the Mediterranean. Stockfish baked with potatoes and green olives is a rustic Elban dish. Meats are roasted over a wood fire. For dessert, Publius offers cakes and homemade *semifreddi,* or iced desserts. The wine list features the best Elban and other Tuscan wines. There is a friendly sommelier on hand to help with the choice.

Portoferraio

PESCHERIA LA LAMPARA	**VIA CARDUCCI, 174 57037 PORTOFERRAIO LIVORNO**
FISH	**TELEPHONE 0565 914286**

OPEN July and August 8:00–13:00, 17:15–20:00; September to June 8:00–13:00
CLOSED Sunday afternoon in July and August; Sunday in winter   **CREDIT CARDS** None
ENGLISH SPOKEN No   **OTHER** Another fish shop, Da Cesare at Via Carducci, 14, is owned by the same proprietor.   **DIRECTIONS** Via Carducci is one of the main roads into Portoferraio, coming from the west; the shop is near the hospital

This small fish shop is one of Elba's most reliable. It sells to the public and to some of the island's best restaurants. The staff, a group of jolly women wearing white coats and rubber boots, has a fast turnover of fish and shellfish. In Italy fish is often sold ungutted, so ask for it to be *pulito.*

Mussels and clams arrive in net bags and are cleaned in a noisy machine. Long-bodied flying squid (*totani*) come in varying sizes: larger for stuffing or grilling, smaller for pan-frying. Many odd-looking creatures taste delicious: *la gallinella,* a rosy-colored, square-headed fish has good flavor, as does the beautiful speckled moray eel, *murena.*

CHAPTER 8

Chianti Classico and Its Wines

Chianti Classico contains some quintessentially Tuscan landscapes: medieval wine castles surrounded by gray-green olive groves and hillside vineyards punctuated by dark cypress trees. This chapter visits twenty-eight of Chianti Classico's finest wineries, as well as food producers, shops, and restaurants.

The area known as Chianti Classico is a hybrid of sections of the provinces of Firenze and Siena established from the point of view of its wine. This is the heart of Tuscany, with the Chianti hills acting as a natural boundary for a delineation first shaped in 1716 by the Grand Duke of Tuscany. The overall area for Chianti production is much larger, stretching farther into the provinces of Siena and Firenze, and into Pisa, Arezzo, and Pistoia.

If the word Chianti once conjured the image of straw-covered wine flasks on red-and-white-checked tablecloths in trattorias the world over, nothing could less represent modern Chianti's wines. Even as recently as 1967, when the area was first given its DOC status (*Denominazione di Origine Controllata*), up to 30 percent of the blend in this professedly red wine based on Tuscan Sangiovese grapes was still permitted to be white grapes. Since then a lot has changed.

Thanks to early dissenters with this "recipe" for Chianti—some of whom began making superior "alternative" or "super-Tuscan" wines entirely of red grapes (including the foreign Cabernet Sauvignon) and aging them in French oak *barriques* to resounding international acclaim—pressure was put on the denomination body to rethink the laws governing Chianti. In 1984 new DOCG regulations (that added stricter "guarantees" to the original laws) allowed for Chianti's wines to be made with very few white grapes (2 to 5 percent) for those who cared to reduce them. In August 1996 the decree went one step further, enabling producers to make their Chianti entirely from red grapes.

Chianti's current grape types are Sangiovese (Sangioveto), 75 to 100 percent; Canaiolo Nero, 0 to 10 percent; Trebbiano and Malvasia (white grapes), 0 to 6 percent; and other approved red grapes, including Cabernet Sauvignon, 0 to 15 percent.

A new amendment, which should be approved by 2002, will see a further change: a minimum of 80 percent Sangiovese, with up to 20 percent other red

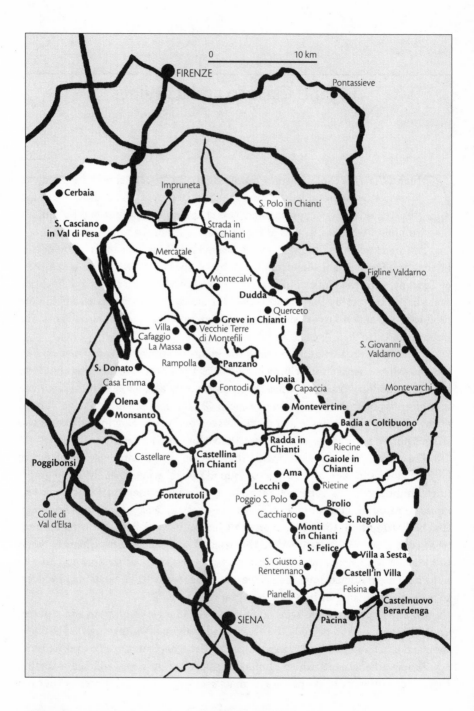

Bold typeface indicates towns that are included in this chapter.

grapes (both autochthonous and allochthonous)—and white grapes being entirely phased out within five years.

The IGT denomination (see p 24) is useful for producers whose wines do not fall within the Chianti Classico specifications—for instance, an equal blend of Sangiovese and Cabernet Sauvignon becomes an IGT, as it does not contain enough Sangiovese to be Chianti, yet it indicates that those grapes were grown in Tuscany.

Global warming has altered the climate in Chianti, and the new regulations should also soon permit irrigation of newly planted or extremely stressed vineyards in the case of prolonged drought.

The world of Chianti production is complex: many but not all of the finest producers are part of the Chianti Classico Consortium, whose symbol is the black rooster. Many also produce nondenomination *vini da tavola,* the so-called super-Tuscans, that were inspired by the great wines of Bordeaux and usually command high prices. (Some of these now come under the IGT denomination.) The winemaking philosophy of an estate cannot be understood by reading its labels. The estates included in this chapter (and in the rest of the book) have been selected based on their good reputations, but the list is by no means all-inclusive. Many other fine estates exist.

Anyone interested in visiting more than one or two estates should get a copy of the Chianti Classico Consortium's excellent map of the area, showing all the major Chianti producers, both in and out of the consortium. It is invariably best to make an appointment before visiting a winery; many are quite small and do not have staff readily available for drop-in visitors, unless arrangements have been made. I strongly recommend visiting them; it is always an enjoyable and instructive experience, as wine producers are generous with their knowledge and their passion for their wines.

CONSORZIO DEL MARCHIO STORICO CHIANTI CLASSICO
VIA SCOPETI, 155
S. ANDREA IN PERCUSSINA
50026 SAN CASCIANO VAL DI PESA
FIRENZE
055 8228501, FAX 055 8228173
WEB SITE www.chianticlassico.com

Ama

CASTELLO DI AMA
WINE

LECCHI IN CHIANTI 53010 GAIOLE IN CHIANTI SIENA
TELEPHONE 0577 746031   FAX 0577 746117
WEB SITE www.castellodiama.com

OPEN Visits and tastings by appointment only   **CLOSED** Saturday, Sunday
DIRECT SALE No, but Ama's wines are sold in Lecchi and other local *enoteche*
ENGLISH SPOKEN Yes   **DIRECTIONS** The Castello di Ama is on the road between
Lecchi and Radda

The guiding force behind the successful Castello di Ama is a young woman, Lorenza Sebasti. "The vine is a plant that needs us," she explained as we viewed the vineyards from Ama's eighteenth-century villa. "Left to its own devices, it dies. Great wines require the best situation for plants—including reducing chemical treatments. We are lucky: we have the sun, the first factor for healthy plants. So you really taste the fruit in our wines."

Lorenza's family, with three others, bought the estate in 1972. Under the initial management of Silvano Formigli, modern cellars were installed and Ama began making quality wines. Ninety hectares (222 acres) of vineyards are now in production. "Ama was among the first in Chianti to apply an entrepreneurial attitude to vine-growing, winemaking, and marketing," she said.

In 1982 they adopted the Bordeaux double-lyre system in some vineyards: each plant is allowed two principal growing stems and attached to a wooden V structure resembling the musical instrument—giving a high-density result from fewer plants. "Also, our vineyards' names appeared on the labels. We said: 'Yes, this is a Chianti Classico, but that's not all!' We were stressing our grapes' provenance when most people were still cutting their wines with grapes from other regions."

Ama's name was built on its Sangiovese wines: the Chiantis, their Riservas, and *crus,* but other varietals have been successful. Vigna l'Apparita, an award winner of pure Merlot, spends fourteen months in French *barriques* and twenty-four in the bottle. A deeply concentrated wine, it celebrates rich fruit in perfect balance with its wood. Ama impresses with its commitment to quality, its style, and its beauty. Despite its size, it produces fine wines—reds, whites, and Vin Santo—and thick green extra-virgin olive oil.

Badia a Coltibuono

BADIA A COLTIBUONO
WINE, RESTAURANT,
COOKING SCHOOL

53013 GAIOLE IN CHIANTI SIENA
TELEPHONE WINERY 0577 749498;
RESTAURANT 0577 749424; SHOP 0577 749479;
FAX WINERY 0577 749235; RESTAURANT 0577 749031
WEB SITE www.coltibuono.com

OPEN Winery visits by appointment only; restaurant lunch and dinner; shop, on entrance road to Badia, 9:30–13:00, 14:00–19:00   **CLOSED** Restaurant Monday, November–February; shop Sunday, January 15–March 1   **CREDIT CARDS** Visa, MC   **DIRECT SALE** Yes, from shop
ENGLISH SPOKEN Yes   **RESERVATIONS** Recommended   **PRICE** $$$
OTHER English-language cooking school   **DIRECTIONS** Badia a Coltibuono is off the Chiantigiana SS 408, 5 kms north of Gaiole

Badia a Coltibuono is well known to foreigners. The magnificent villa, situated in a former abbey, is the home of the successful food writer Lorenza de' Medici Stucchi. Coltibuono includes winemaking activities, a farm shop, a restaurant, and a deluxe cooking school.

The winery is very large (producing one million bottles annually from 50 hectares/123 acres of vineyards) and has recently improved its wines, thanks to Roberto and Emanuela Stucchi Prinetti, who run the winery; they recently were joined by winemaker Luca D'Attoma. Badia's ultramodern *cantina* in Chianti has been completed and is now fully operational.

Another of the Stucchi children, Paolo, runs the restaurant, which features a fresh cuisine of traditional Tuscan dishes tailored to its international clientele. Lorenza's cooking school is costly, but it offers a unique opportunity: students live in the grand villa during the week's course and dine in several stately homes—an unforgettable experience.

I was interested to learn of Lorenza's early career: "I wrote popular Italian cookbooks and articles for years," she recounted. "In the mid-eighties I met an American couple attending a cooking class in Firenze. They described learning to make pasta and preparing menus, and I thought, I could do that, too." Badia's cooking school was born; several stylish cookbooks have followed.

Brolio

CASTELLO DI BROLIO—
BARONE RICASOLI
WINE

BROLIO 53013 GAIOLE IN CHIANTI SIENA
TELEPHONE 0577 7301   FAX 0577 730225
WEB SITE www.ricasoli.it

OPEN Shop Monday–Friday 8:00–12:00, 13:00–19:00 (17:00 in winter), Saturday–Sunday 11:00–19:00.
Tastings possible; *cantina* visits and guided tastings by appointment only
CREDIT CARDS Visa, MC, Amex   **DIRECT SALE** Yes   **ENGLISH SPOKEN** Yes
DIRECTIONS The shop is inside the large cellar compound down the hill from the castle

The history of Brolio Castle is closely linked to that of Chianti wine. The Ricasolis, one of Italy's oldest winemaking families, have resided at Brolio since 1141 despite its being destroyed a few times over the centuries. In the 1840s, the "Iron Baron" Bettino Ricasoli began experimenting with imported French varietals. In 1874 he wrote a "recipe" for Chianti, an "important red wine," establishing Sangiovese as its primary ingredient, with a smaller percentage of red Canaiolo. If the wine was to be drunk young, he recommended adding white grapes to it, Malvasia or Trebbiano.

In 1963, almost a century later, this formula, white grapes and all, became law with the first Chianti DOC appellation. Filippo Mazzei of Fonterutoli (see p 196), Brolio's current director, sees it as a misunderstanding: "The white grapes were extraneous to Chianti if the intention was a wine fit for aging—they weakened Sangiovese's character." Other winemakers agreed, and recently this "new" white-less Chianti was finally ratified by the DOCG body.

Since 1960, Brolio Castle's fortunes have fluctuated. Its stories of multinational takeovers, extravagant investments, near bankruptcies, and secret coups reads like something out of the movie *Wall Street*. The fortuitous final result was that Baron Francesco Ricasoli (a former fashion photographer) and his friend Filippo Mazzei, armed with enthusiasm, quick thinking, and luck, rescued the enormous estate at the eleventh hour and now run it. "Things happened fast," explained Mazzei. "But Francesco was determined to save Brolio. We and our enologist, Carlo Ferrini, agree about making great wines here."

The huge industrial cellars remaining after the Seagrams takeover are now filled with *barriques*—a sure sign that the shift from quantity to quality has occurred. Many of the 220 hectares (540 acres) of vineyards have been replanted. Brolio now produces two lines of wines. The Castello di Brolio collection features a fine Chianti Classico, "Castello di Brolio"; Casalferro, a super-Tuscan Sangiovese *cru*; Torricella, of Chardonnay grapes fermented in *barriques;* and a mature Vin Santo. The second line, Barone Ricasoli, has a wider range of improved wines at moderate prices.

Castell'in Villa

CASTELL'IN VILLA
WINE, RESTAURANT

53019 CASTELNUOVO BERARDENGA SIENA
TELEPHONE 0577 359074; RESTAURANT 0571 359356
FAX 0577 359222
WEB SITE www.castellinvilla.com

OPEN Shop Monday–Saturday 9:00–13:00, 15:00–18:00 Easter to November; tastings and *cantina* visits by appointment only; restaurant dinner only, Sunday lunch
CLOSED Shop Sunday; restaurant Monday   **CREDIT CARDS** Visa, MC   **DIRECT SALE** Yes
ENGLISH SPOKEN Yes   **RESERVATIONS** Recommended   **PRICE** $$$–$$$$
OTHER A convent in the castle grounds has been converted into a comfortable *agriturismo*
DIRECTIONS From Castelnuovo Berardenga, go toward Gaiole; after 4.5 kms turn left. The winery is then signposted

Castell'in Villa is an austere cluster of buildings in southern Chianti with fine views of Siena. Here, Principessa Coralia Pignatelli and her husband "came thirty years ago to put our roots together," she explained.

The princess, a classically elegant Greek woman wearing a raw silk jacket, said her late husband had foretold she "would end up living in the country and producing wine. I didn't believe him then. But it turned out to be true." He was an Italian ambassador; together they lived in many countries. Since his death she has remained at Castell'in Villa, making wines and, more recently, running a restaurant and *agriturismo*.

Most of the estate's 54 hectares (133 acres) of vineyards are planted to Sangiovese, with some Cabernet Sauvignon for her "table wine," Santacroce. But her affections lie with Chianti. "I am a Sangiovese fanatic," the princess admitted. "I particularly like young old wines—old wines that are still young and lively. Like my 1971 Chianti Classico Riserva."

She now has a new wine, Poggio delle Rose Chianti Classico Riserva. "This is my baby," she said as we tasted the exceptional 1997. "It is made from a selection of Castell'in Villa's own Sangiovese clones, and like any good mother, I feel a special bond with it."

Her wines (for she is the winemaker) are the fruit of low-yield, selected grapes ripened in the hot sun of Castelnuovo Berardenga—wines that are warm, rich, and balanced.

The restaurant is beautiful, with the spare modern look that characterizes the princess' sophisticated style. Natural materials, walnut and cypress woods from the estate, are used strikingly: a long "table of life" made by the sculptor Cecco Buonanotte is the focal point. "I love the idea that people who do not know each other can sit and eat together. It creates an atmosphere of happiness. For the Greeks, hospitality is very important, complementing the activities of a farm. Here we serve simple, seasonal foods, as pure and good as the wines. That is the life-affirming message it represents."

Castellina in Chianti

L'ALBERGACCIO
RESTAURANT

VIA FIORENTINA, 35 53011 CASTELLINA IN CHIANTI SIENA
TELEPHONE 0577 741042   FAX 0577 741250
E-MAIL posta@albergacciocast.com

OPEN Dinner Monday–Saturday; lunch also Monday, Friday, and Saturday
CLOSED Sunday; November   **CREDIT CARDS** None   **ENGLISH SPOKEN** A little
FEATURES Outdoor summer terrace   **RESERVATIONS** Recommended in summer   **PRICE** $$$
DIRECTIONS Just outside the town center, going toward San Donato in Poggio

L'Albergaccio is in a restructured stone barn. In cool weather you eat under the rafters, in summer on the garden terrace. The young proprietors have been attentive to detail—not just in material things, but in researching fine ingredients. The studied wine list features the wines of Tuscany, grouping them by towns.

During my February visit, co-owner Francesco Cacciatori proposed home-cured *salumi* and *stuzzichini d'inverno*, winter taste-whetters, as antipasti (each season has its own). There were fried sage leaves, creamy-centered polenta topped with leeks, and *zolfino* beans (see p 372) with cured pork shoulder preserved in oil. The fine-skinned beans were wonderfully tender, the meat rather oily. The *salumi* included delicate-textured *finocchiona*, marbled head cheese (*soppressata*), and an ethereal slice of *lardo di Colonnata* (see p 33) served on warm bread.

The *primi*, which included ravioli stuffed with salt cod (*baccalà*) on puréed beans, confirmed the restaurant's commitment to unusual taste combinations. Light *gnocchetti* of ricotta came with shaved winter truffle and thyme. *Pici con digiune d'agnello* were homemade pasta with a robust sauce of lamb's intestines topped with pungent pecorino cheese. A *fagottino* (little crèpe bundle) contained diced pigeon and was sprinkled with crunchy fried leek rings. Flavorful wood pigeon (*colombaccio*) was simmered in wine, water, and vinegar, spiced with cloves, and sweetened with onion. The restaurant's desserts are a triumph of technique and taste—the pistachio tart, caramel-scented *bavarese*, and air-light ricotta mousse with orange sauce were all excellent.

ANTICA TRATTORIA "LA TORRE"
RESTAURANT

PIAZZA DEL COMUNE
53011 CASTELLINA IN CHIANTI SIENA
TELEPHONE 0577 740236   FAX 0577 740228

OPEN Lunch and dinner   **CLOSED** Friday; early September   **CREDIT CARDS** Visa, MC, Amex
ENGLISH SPOKEN Yes   **RESERVATIONS** Recommended for dinner   **PRICE** $$
DIRECTIONS In the town center, under the *Comune*

This popular trattoria has been in the Stiaccini family since 1895. They are generous and unpretentious, as is the food, with the simplest things being the best.

The busy dining room hosts a nice mix of locals and foreigners, young and old. The menu offers standard choices with some exceptions: in winter, hot antipasti included fried polenta topped with meat sauce, spinach frittata, chicken *vol-au-vent*, and *crostini*. Assorted *salumi* are another option. *Primi* include pastas (cannelloni, *pappardelle* with wild boar or mushroom sauce, *penne piccanti*) and thick Tuscan bread soups. In summer there are more vegetable-based dishes. Roasted meats are a specialty: veal, pork, chicken, guinea fowl, and pigeon. I tried an interesting local dish, *lesso rifatto con cipolle*. This is a *cucina povera* recipe using leftovers from *lesso*, boiled beef. Traditionally, the cooked meat is stewed with inexpensive ingredients: onions, tomatoes, and herbs. It was good: the slightly stringy meat was well-flavored and nicely spiced. Homemade desserts include *pinolata*—a pie filled with custard, plumped raisins, a layer of cake, and toasted pine nuts. The wine list contains some good Chiantis.

CASTELLARE	**PODERI DI CASTELLARE 53011 CASTELLINA IN CHIANTI SIENA**
WINE	**TELEPHONE/FAX 0577 740490**
	E-MAIL isodi@tin.it

OPEN Shop 8:00–18:00; visits and tastings by appointment only   **CLOSED** Never
CREDIT CARDS Visa, MC   **DIRECT SALE** Yes   **ENGLISH SPOKEN** Yes
DIRECTIONS From Castellina go toward Poggibonsi; after 800 meters follow signs to the left

Castellare is a 20-hectare (49-acre) winery owned since 1979 by Milanese journalist Paolo Panerai. Working with Tuscan winemaker Maurizio Castelli, he produces concentrated, new-style wines that are popular in the United States.

Castellare is a pretty place, with spectacular views of the valley above Poggibonsi. Panerai lives and works in Milan, but he has invested heavily in the estate; modern cellars were nearing completion when I visited. Castellare's shop sells his attractively presented wines (each year a different wild bird is featured on the labels), plus oil and vinegar produced for him at Volpaia (p 220).

Of the wines, I Sodi di San Niccolò is the best known. A super-Tuscan of 85 percent Sangioveto with 15 percent Malvasia Nera, it is made from grapes of mature vines and produced only in good years. The wine's lengthy aging is in *barriques*, with a year in the bottle. This well-structured, complex wine commands high prices.

Castellare's commitment to Sangiovese is also apparent in its Chianti Classico. White grapes have been eliminated, resulting in a rich, fruity red wine of intensity with good aging potential. For the whites, French grape varieties have been substituted for the Italian: Canonico is made of pure Chardonnay, Spartito of pure Sauvignon, and Le Ginestre is a blend of the two.

Also

On Saturday mornings at Castellina's weekly market, look out for Duccio Fontani's unusual stall. Duccio cultivates more than thirty types of aromatic herbs on his small organic farm outside Castellina (tel: 0577 740662), and he dries and combines them in wonderful ways.

ENOTECA LE VOLTE   VIA FERRUCCIO, 12. 0577 741314 FAX 0577 742891

In Castellina's main pedestrian street, this well-stocked wine store sells all the local stars, as well as oils, books, and wine paraphernalia, including a neat two-bottle canvas bag.

Castelnuovo Berardenga

DA ANTONIO   VIA FIORITA, 38 53019 CASTELNUOVO BERARDENGA SIENA
RESTAURANT   TELEPHONE 0577 355321

OPEN Lunch and dinner   **CLOSED** Monday; Tuesday for lunch; when the sea is too rough to fish
CREDIT CARDS Visa, MC   **ENGLISH SPOKEN** Yes   **RESERVATIONS** Recommended
PRICE $$$$ **DIRECTIONS** In Piazza Matteotti, in the town center

Antonio Farina is a curious character. "I'm a man of the sea," he said, but he nonetheless opened a fish restaurant as far from the sea as Tuscany gets: in the heart of Chianti. Still, he cooks and sells only the day's catch, which arrives from the coast's best markets. "In high seas [when no fishing is possible] my restaurant closes," he exclaimed.

Antonio's way is to prepare different fish dishes each day. Customers sit down, he cooks, and the food is brought out to them. If there is a menu, I never saw it. Anyone who is not open to this formula will probably be happier somewhere else. Antonio is a natural chef, and his food is often wonderful—though in the busy season the standard can be a bit uneven.

On a quiet evening in February, my dinner began with a quick succession of seafood antipasti. Thin slices of raw *fragolino* (a sea bream) scented with winter truffle arrived on a searing-hot plate, cooking as it came. Minuscule *rossetti* (transparent gobies) were fried in a quick *frittellina*—like a small pancake; it tasted richly of the sea. Blanched *calamaretti* (young squid) were slit and opened; they looked like white rose petals and came, warm, on a green bed of peeled baby fava beans. They were tender and silky—an early celebration of spring. A fried fillet of *nasello* (hake) was coupled with the decisive flavors of the south—cherry-tomato *concassé*, earthy, sharp capers—that made the fish seem sweet. Fragile wild asparagus spears were chopped and tossed with chunks of *pescatrice* (monkfish), olive oil, and lemon. Spaghetti had a light sauce of fresh tomato and flaked *triglie* (red mullet). The *fragolino* reappeared, poached and filleted without being topped and tailed, served with bitter baked radicchio. *Scampi e gamberi rossi* (pink and red shrimp) were charbroiled.

There is a detailed list of wines, its emphasis on whites from Tuscany and beyond. Indeed, the room is lined with bottles—not surprising for a seaside restaurant firmly anchored in Chianti's vineyards.

FATTORIA DI FÈLSINA
WINE

STRADA CHIANTIGIANA SS 484
53019 CASTELNUOVO BERARDENGA SIENA
TELEPHONE 0577 355117   FAX 0577 355651
E-MAIL felsina@dada.it

OPEN Shop Easter to October 10:00–19:00; winter: 8:00–12:30, 13:30–17:00; tastings usually possible; cellar visits by appointment only   **CLOSED** Sunday   **CREDIT CARDS** Visa, MC   **DIRECT SALE** Yes   **ENGLISH SPOKEN** Yes   **DIRECTIONS** Fèlsina is just outside Castelnuovo Berardenga, on the road toward Gaiole

---

"To understand Fèlsina's wines is to understand its lands, its *terroir*," affirmed Giuseppe Mazzocolin, the estate's director. Fèlsina is in a border zone at the southern edge of the Classico denomination that marks the changeover from vineyards to wheat fields. It was bought in 1966 by the late Domenico Poggiali, who first understood its potential. The large estate of 342 hectares (845 acres), of which 52 (128) are planted to vineyards, comprises eleven farms surrounded by woods and vineyards. At its heart is the winery, striking for the austere grandeur of its buildings: aligned on three sides of a square courtyard, they suggest a setting for outdoor theater. "Each *podere*, or farm, within the estate has an identity that remains in the wines that are made there, like Rancia or Fontalloro," explained Mazzocolin as we visited them.

Fèlsina's wines are the fruit of a winemaking "marriage of true minds" between Mazzocolin and enologist Franco Bernabei. They have planted most of the estate's vineyards to Sangiovese, Tuscany's native grape variety and the basis of Chianti Classico. Both of Fèlsina's great *crus*, Vigneto Rancia (a Chianti Classico Riserva) and Fontalloro (a modern table wine), are of Sangiovese. They are rich, powerful wines with an elegance that transcends their earthy tones.

Mazzocolin resists the idea that great modern wines must be made from "international" (that is, French) grape varietals. "There has to be room for every type of wine," he asserted with the conviction of a modern-day humanist. "You could think of it as a giant *cru* of a thousand faces! Cabernet Sauvignon is not the only answer. We in Tuscany have Sangiovese—and we're proud of it!"

However, Sangiovese is not all that Fèlsina produces under its Berardenga label. Maestro Raro is deemed by some critics to be the best Cabernet Sauvignon in Tuscany. I Sistri is a *barrique*-aged Chardonnay, while the winery's sister estate, Castello di Farnetella, produces a delicately fruity Sauvignon Blanc.

"After all these years of working with it, wine remains a mystery to me," concluded Mazzocolin with the softness of inflection that reveals his Venetian origins. "I may understand it from a scientific point of view, but nonetheless each year I am amazed by the near-magical transformation of fruit juice into wine."

BENGODI	**VIA DELLA SOCIETÀ OPERAIA, 11**
WINE BAR, RESTAURANT	**53019 CASTELNUOVO BERARDENGA SIENA**
	TELEPHONE 0577 355116

OPEN Wine bar 11:00–midnight; kitchen open for lunch and dinner   **CLOSED** Monday; January
CREDIT CARDS Visa, MC, Amex   **DIRECT SALE** Yes, of wine and oil   **ENGLISH SPOKEN** Yes
RESERVATIONS Recommended   **PRICE** $$–$$$ **DIRECTIONS** In the main square

This relaxed wine bar occupies three little rooms on the ground floor of a house in the square. It offers a flexible formula: come in for a glass of wine and *bruschetta* any time of day, or have a snack or full meal for lunch or dinner. The kitchen is open till 10:30 P.M. The menu offers an à la carte selection and two well-priced four- or two-course menus that include a different glass of wine with each course. The food is uncomplicated but fresh, with soups and pastas, main courses, and a nice selection of local artisan cheeses.

The wine list is long and unusual, as it is grouped both by vintages and by winery. Most of the 650 wines are Tuscan, with several vintages available from many estates. My waiter was very knowledgeable about wine and enthusiastic about small, up-and-coming wineries.

Cerbaia

LA TENDA ROSSA	**PIAZZA DEL MONUMENTO, 9/14**
RESTAURANT	**50020 CERBAIA VAL DI PESA FIRENZE**
	TELEPHONE 055 826132 FAX 055 825210
	E-MAIL tendaros@tin.it

OPEN Lunch and dinner   **CLOSED** Sunday; Monday for lunch; August   **CREDIT CARDS** Visa, MC,
Amex   **ENGLISH SPOKEN** Yes   **RESERVATIONS** Recommended   **PRICE** $$$$$$
DIRECTIONS In Cerbaia's main square

La Tenda Rossa was a film, but here the movie's "red tent" has given way to a luxurious restaurant with a shiny red door. Inside is a modern environment of muted colors, soft lighting, curtain dividers, expensive objets, and comfort reminiscent of the romanticism of the 1970s in Italy.

The restaurant is run by three couples and their three daughters. The young women, who dress alike, are beautiful, efficient (they are all qualified sommeliers and serve the tables), and rather formal. Of the six parents, two host the restaurant, the others cook.

La Tenda Rossa is noted for its food and wine. The wine lists are bound volumes filled with rare and remarkable Italian and French vintages. As for the food, it is ambitious and adventurous: first-rate ingredients (many homegrown) are combined in complex ways. This taste layering is reflected in the menu descriptions: "black ravioli of pork with flowers of green cabbage lightly scented with garlic and foie gras of goose," runs one *primo*. As a daughter lifts the silver cloche from your dish, she repeats its title entirely.

The food is elaborately presented. Breaded fillets of red mullet are fanned below a "flower" of black olives, asparagus, onion strips, and candied tomatoes. Four saffron-crusted shrimp decorate a puréed soup of domestic mushrooms, swirled with fragrant olive oil. Heart-shaped ravioli of a translucent milk pasta are stuffed with pounded crustaceans and sauced with a delicate "mousse" of haricot beans. Thin rolls of pasta perfumed with wild fennel come with a "white" sauce of ground guinea fowl and rosemary, the well-flavored sauce successfully complementing the herbed pasta. Two jumbo red shrimp are neatly wrapped with pancetta and tied with pineapple-sage on a bed of black-edged eggplant "ribbons." A perfectly cooked lamb chop is crusted with toasted slivered almonds, its sweetness cut by sharp fresh goat's cheese and beet greens.

"*La Tenda Rossa* was an adventure film," explained the restaurant's genial host, Silvano Santandrea. "We embarked on a gastronomic adventure—and we are still on it!"

Dudda

CASTELLO DI QUERCETO
WINE

DUDDA LUCOLENA 50020 GREVE IN CHIANTI FIRENZE
TELEPHONE 055 85921   FAX 055 8592200
WEB SITE www.castellodiquerceto.it

OPEN 8:00–12:00, 13:00–17:00; visits and tastings by appointment only   **CLOSED** Saturday and Sunday, except by appointment   **CREDIT CARDS** Visa, MC, Amex   **DIRECT SALE** Yes   **ENGLISH SPOKEN** Yes   **DIRECTIONS** The Castello is signposted off the Figline-Greve road, near Sùgame. Follow the unpaved road through the oak wood to the end

The Castello di Querceto is a fairly large winery in a stately villa dating to 1200, set in well-kept grounds with peacocks. The estate is owned by the François family, who for years have produced a range of high-quality wines. Having most of its 45 hectares (111 acres) of vineyards high up in the Chianti hills gives Querceto's wines full bouquets and elegance. "They may have less structure than wines from lower ground, and be less masculine," Alessandro François's nephew Paolo Zucconi told me, "but they are not lacking in *profumi*."

In addition to its Chiantis and their reserves, the estate makes La Corte, a single-vineyard wine of pure Sangiovese aged in *barriques*. Il Querciolaia blends 65 percent Sangiovese with 35 percent Cabernet. Il Cignale is another high-profile *vino da tavola*, of Cabernet with a touch of Merlot. The Castello is also known for its *acquavite*, distilled from fresh *vinacce* (wine-soaked grape residues) by Nannoni (see p 229–230).

Fonterutoli

CASTELLO DI FONTERUTOLI
WINE

53010 FONTERUTOLI SIENA
TELEPHONE 0577 73571   FAX 0577 735757
WEB SITE www.fonterutoli.com

OPEN Shop 10:00–21:00; tastings are possible; cellar visits by appointment only   **CLOSED** Tuesday
CREDIT CARDS Visa, MC, Amex   **DIRECT SALE** Yes   **ENGLISH SPOKEN** Yes
FEATURES The estate runs an Osteria in the village   **OTHER** Six apartments available for holiday
rentals   **DIRECTIONS** Fonterutoli and its shop are on the main road from Castellina to Siena

---

Filippo Mazzei tells good stories about his ancestors. Ser Lapo, a fourteenth-century gentleman, was a writer and notary and an ambassador in Florence for Francesco Datini, a key financier of his day. "Ser Lapo was passionate about wines," recounted Filippo Mazzei enthusiastically, "if Datini was not. One of my favorite letters of his from 1394 reads: 'Don't worry about the price of that wine; it may be expensive, but its goodness will restore us.'" He was also the author of the first document citing Chianti as a wine type (see p 85 for his connection to Carmignano). Several centuries later, Filippo Mazzei (1730–1816) took Tuscan vines and olive trees to Monticello, met George Washington, and was present at the signing of the Declaration of Independence.

The present Filippo Mazzei's grandfather relaunched the historic *borgo* of Fonterutoli and its wines. In 1924 he was among the Chianti consortium's founding members. "I got involved when I was still at university," explained Filippo Mazzei, who is also director of Brolio (p 188). "My father, like Sergio Manetti and the Antinoris, became interested in making new-style wines. Very early, he planted foreign vines here."

Fonterutoli is a self-contained village. A modern *cantina* is in the works, but for now, each cottage houses a barrel or two of its award-winning wines.

The Mazzei brothers have been instrumental in changing the attitudes of premium producers within Chianti: if, several years ago, these wineries were abandoning the Chianti denomination in favor of the more flexible super-Tuscan "table wines," now there is a swing in the other direction, and much of the best Sangiovese goes into special Chianti Classico *crus* and Riservas.

Fonterutoli's wines are now among Chianti's finest, thanks to the endeavors of the three Mazzei brothers and enologist Carlo Ferrini. Their great wines include Siepi, a super-Tuscan *cru* of Sangiovese and Merlot aged in *barriques*, which continues to win top accolades in Italy and beyond. No less powerful is the Chianti Classico Castello di Fonterutoli Riserva, of primarily Sangiovese grapes. It is a concentrated, modern wine that is, however, clearly bound to its birthplace. The normal Chianti Classico and Poggio alla Badiola are fine Sangiovese-based wines; both are affordable and a pleasure to drink.

Gaiole in Chianti

RIECINE
WINE

RIECINE 53013 GAIOLE IN CHIANTI SIENA
TELEPHONE 0577 749098   FAX 0577 744935
E-MAIL riecine@chiantinet.it

OPEN 10:00–12:30, 14:30–17:30; visits, tastings, and sales by appointment only
CREDIT CARDS None   **DIRECT SALE** Yes   **ENGLISH SPOKEN** Yes
DIRECTIONS From Gaiole, go north toward Montevarchi. Before reaching Badia a Coltibuono, there is a small turn to the right; follow the unpaved road to Riecine

When talking to the late John Dunkley, the Englishman who created Riecine, you were always aware of his passion for making wine. "The glory of a simple wine is like a peach still warm from the tree: it is a celebration of simplicity and purity. The further you get away from your pure, simple wine, from your 'grape juice fermented,' the more you lose. One of the exciting things about winemaking is that you don't need volume to make your mark."

Make his mark he did. With their small estate of 4 hectares (10 acres), Dunkley and his late wife, Palmina Abbagnano, were among the first foreigners (though she was Italian) to bring new blood into Chianti's winemaking. "At first, it was fun. We did it to please ourselves," he recalled. "Our first harvest, in 1972, was awful. To make good wine you need perfect grapes—but we didn't have them. They were mildewed from the rain. By the following year we had learned our lesson—we even won a prize."

Things became more serious: better equipment was brought in, the cellar improved. So did the wines. By the mid-seventies they had stopped adding white grapes to Chianti—way ahead of the *disciplinare* and of almost everyone else. They did all the work themselves, "me in the cellar, Palmina driving the tractor," and began making a name with their concentrated, perfumed, elegant wines. In 1982 La Gioia di Riecine was born, their *vino da tavola* of pure Sangiovese. "La Gioia and our Chianti come from practically the same grapes," Dunkley explained. "The Chianti is aged in big wooden barrels whose wood does not really affect it, but

Gioia is put into *barriques*. This smaller wood changes the nature of the wine: it acts like putting a skeleton into the wine onto which the other things are hung. It also makes it capable of long aging." La Gioia is a rich, mellow wine with "that recognizable dryness in the nose, that wonderful dustiness."

Before he died in 1998, Dunkley set the stage for Riecine's future by pairing his young partner and winemaker, Sean O'Callaghan, with a new American partner, Gary Baumann. Dunkley, whose intelligence and wit are much missed, made no bones about enjoying the fruit of his labors. "The joy of being small is that you can have a quality-control session twice a day—at lunch and dinner."

RIETINE   **53013 GAIOLE IN CHIANTI SIENA**
WINE   TELEPHONE 0577 731110   FAX 0577 738482

OPEN Tastings, sales, and visits by appointment only   **CREDIT CARDS** None   **DIRECT SALE** Yes
ENGLISH SPOKEN Yes   **DIRECTIONS** From Gaiole, go south on the Chiantigiana for 2 kms. Go left over the small bridge and up past *Cantina Geografica* to Rietine; the winery is just beyond the central square of the village

---

Galina and Mario Gaffuri-Lazarides are a Swiss couple who in 1988 bought a 13-hectare (32-acre) vineyard just south of Gaiole. "We were lucky," explained Galina, who is of Greek origin. "We found this south-facing vineyard all in one piece." They produce an unusual "table" wine: Tiziano contains equal parts of Merlot and Lambrusco and is matured in *barriques*. The couple also produces an all-red Chianti Classico and its reserve. Galina was justly proud of the 1999 Chianti Classico, as it reflected the improved quality of the grapes from newly replanted vineyards. "I like to think of it like this," the engaging Galina admitted. "Chianti Classico is an eating wine, to enjoy every day with dinner. On Saturday you drink the Riserva. On Sunday, or your birthday, you want a special wine, like the powerful, rich super-Tuscans."

Also

BIANCHI SELF-SERVICE   VIA RICASOLI, 48. 0577 749501

Bianchi's is a wonderful grocery store in Gaiole that sells everything, from great home-baked bread (including one Etruscan) to ingredients for a picnic or feast. There are now also tables out in the piazza for light meals and snacks. The Bianchi family would win my prize, if I had one, for being the most patient and friendly shopkeepers with non-Italians.

Studio Fernandez (tel: 0577 749363) is on the road between Gaiole and Radda at Le Conce. This small pottery is run by Olivier Fernandez and his lovely wife, Margherita. At their farmhouse they make and sell their modern ceramics and sculptures.

Greve in Chianti

ANTICA MACELLERIA   **PIAZZA G. MATTEOTTI, 69/71 50022 GREVE FIRENZE**
FALORNI   **TELEPHONE 055 853029   FAX 055 8544521**
MEAT: SALUMI   **WEB SITE www.falorni.it**

OPEN 8:00–13:00, 15:30–19:30   **CLOSED** Never   **CREDIT CARDS** Visa, MC
DIRECT SALE Yes   **ENGLISH SPOKEN** Yes   **DIRECTIONS** In Greve's main square

It's not hard to spot Falorni's butcher shop in Greve's market square: a stuffed wild boar stands guard outside. Inside there are baskets of *salumi*, meat counters, and pre-1914 photographs of the shop, which was *antica* even then. The current generation are active campaigners for "real" food—artisan butchers who use only quality meats from animals raised in the surrounding and central Italian countryside. The interior is divided between fresh meats and the brothers' range of homemade *salumi* (vacuum packed for easy transportation). On weekends, tourists flock to it in droves (or buses), stocking up on the packages. (U.S. laws forbid the importing of meats, so Americans will have to do their tasting while in Europe.)

Wild boar culled from the local woods (there is an overpopulation now) are turned into tasty little salamis joined with strings. Pork products include fennel-scented *finocchiona* (one of the fattiest of the *salumi*), and classic *salame Toscano*. "My father taught me that to make this kind of *salame* well," stated Lorenzo Bencistà, one of the Falorni descendants, "you have to spend twenty years working with someone who knows how. Everything is important: selecting the cuts of meat, dosing it with salt, garlic, and spices, and kneading the mixture."

Fresh meats include fine local Chianina beef—for the best *Fiorentina* T-bones—as well as pork, duck, rabbit, and guinea fowl. I asked whether the chickens were free-range (tough to find in Italy). "We used to keep them," admitted Lorenzo, "but we gave up—it was too costly. Now we buy battery chickens like everybody else. My advice to anyone who wants a 'real' chicken is to raise it themselves!"

The enterprising brothers have now opened a large underground wine bar with food in historic 1890 wine cellars in central Greve. You prepay for a magnetic card that allows you to help yourself to wines and foods set out in the refurbished cellars. A novel idea! Le Cantine di Greve in Chianti, Piazza delle Cantine, 2. 055 8546404. Open 10:00–19:30.

MONTECALVI
WINE

VIA CITTILE, 85 50022 GREVE IN CHIANTI FIRENZE
TELEPHONE/FAX 055 8544665

OPEN By appointment only   **CREDIT CARDS** None   **DIRECT SALE** Yes
ENGLISH SPOKEN Yes   **DIRECTIONS** From Greve, go toward Firenze; after 1 km, Montecalvi is on the right, before the gas station

---

I am grateful to Bernadette and the late Renzo Bolli for giving me my first official *vendemmia*—grape harvest. I volunteered, and they accepted. So for one hot October's day I joined forces with them and a group of locals and picked grapes. It was an instructive experience. I learned how to select good bunches from bad ones (rejecting the powdery blue mold that can make the wine bitter), how the grapes are destalked and crushed. It is back-breaking work, but also great fun. And not for nothing do we have the expression "I heard it through the grapevine": in Tuscany they call it *radio vigna*—radio grapevine—because by being there you find out the latest gossip about everyone in the area!

When the Bollis bought their house in 1988, it was completely abandoned. The vineyards had been planted in 1932 and were overrun and diseased. The position was excellent, though, right in the heart of Chianti Classico. They decided to replant local Sangiovese using the high-density system for their delicious, drinkable wine, Montecalvi. It is matured for one year in wooden barrels and one in the bottle.

"When we started," explained Renzo Bolli, "the *disciplinare* for Chianti Classico still obliged the blending of white grapes into the Sangiovese. I had never liked those wines—they seemed astringent to me—so we decided to opt out of the DOCG and to make a 'table wine' of pure Sangiovese. The good thing about being small is being flexible." Montecalvi is a wonderful wine, potent, elegant, and decidedly Tuscan.

VECCHIE TERRE DI MONTEFILI
WINE

VIA SAN CRESCI, 45 50022 GREVE IN CHIANTI FIRENZE
TELEPHONE 055 853739   FAX 055 8544684
E-MAIL ten.vecchie-terre-montefili@inwind.it

OPEN Visits and tastings by appointment only, by phone or fax one week ahead
DIRECT SALE No, but you can buy the wines at Gallo Nero *enoteca* at Panzano or Greve
ENGLISH SPOKEN Yes   **DIRECTIONS** From Panzano go toward Mercatale; the winery is on the right after about 5 kms

---

Vecchie Terre di Montefili is one of Chianti's rising stars. The story of its ascent is a familiar one: Roccaldo Acuti, a successful textile industrialist from Prato with a penchant for wine, bought the run-down farm in 1979. Its vineyards were semi-abandoned. He hired a winemaker, Vittorio Fiore, and invested heavily in plants and cellar equipment. Then, in an unusual twist, his young daughter, Maria, decided to run the winemaking business, which she does with her companion, Thomas Paglione, who oversees the *cantina*. The estate is still growing: it currently has 12 hectares (30 acres) of vineyards in a lovely setting, high in the Chianti hills, with house and farm buildings flanked by vineyards. Maria Acuti is a well-traveled, friendly young woman. Her house is tasteful and welcoming.

Vecchie Terre's big wines are its Chianti Classico (of pure Sangiovese; it is well structured, fruity, and drinkable), Anfiteatro IGT (a single-vineyard wine of pure Sangiovese), the white Vigna Regis (of Chardonnay, Gewürtztraminer, and Sauvignon), and Bruno di Rocca IGT (a blend of 60 percent Cabernet Sauvignon and 40 percent Sangiovese; it is also a super-Tuscan). Bruno di Rocca is a powerful wine that has been put up at tastings with Sassicaia and Solaia and come away on top. I asked Maria about its name: "My father, Roccaldo, wanted to buy an estate in Montalcino. When we chose Chianti instead, he dedicated this wine to that dream: Bruno (for Brunello) di Rocca (for Roccaldo)."

ENOTECA DEL CHIANTI	PIAZZETTA SANTA CROCE, 8
CLASSICO "GALLO NERO"	50022 GREVE IN CHIANTI FIRENZE
WINE STORE	TELEPHONE/FAX 055 853297

OPEN 9:30–12:30, 15:30–19:30 (till 20:00 in summer)   **CLOSED** Wednesday
CREDIT CARDS Visa, MC, Amex   **DIRECT SALE** Yes   **ENGLISH SPOKEN** A little
DIRECTIONS At the narrow end of the town's central square

This useful shop stocks wines from the Chianti Classico consortium's members and a good selection of nonmembers. Some space is dedicated to other Tuscan denominations: Vernaccia di San Gimignano, Brunello di Montalcino, and so on. Super-Tuscans from the best estates are available. The list is large, so have an idea of what you want before going in. The staff will provide information, but few tastings are allowed. Prices should be the same as at the nearby wineries. The *enoteca* also stocks extra-virgin olive oils from many Chianti estates, Vin Santo, grappa, and vinegar.

Also

Nerbone. 055 853308. This popular market stall from Firenze (see p 92) recently opened a branch in Greve's central piazza. It's a great place for sandwiches and snacks.

Lecchi

IL POGGIO
RESTAURANT

POGGIO SAN POLO LECCHI 53010 GAIOLE SIENA
TELEPHONE 0577 746135   FAX 0577 746120

OPEN Lunch and dinner   **CLOSED** Monday; January   **CREDIT CARDS** Visa, MC, Amex
ENGLISH SPOKEN Yes   **FEATURES** Outdoor summer terrace
RESERVATIONS Recommended in summer   **PRICE** $$
DIRECTIONS From Lecchi, go toward Poggio San Polo; the restaurant is signposted

Il Poggio is an airy restaurant on top of a hill (*poggio* means "hill" in Tuscany). In nice weather, a large shaded terrace with climbing roses provides views of vineyards. This busy restaurant offers many Tuscan favorites, cooked simply but well, and made to go with Chianti.

The mixed *antipasto Toscano* includes *finocchiona* and prosciutto and assorted *crostini*—whose chicken-liver topping comes with a candle-warmer, a nice touch. *Bruschetta di pomodoro* uses flavorful tomatoes, crunchy bread, and just enough rubbed garlic. The *primi* are very good. Il Poggio's kitchens are staffed by local women who handmake the pasta. *Tortelli* filled with spinach and ricotta are a fresh summer choice, but there is also a stiff *ribollita*, the peasant soup of vegetables and bread. I found a good range of vegetable dishes at Il Poggio, enough to satisfy my vegetarian friends. These selections change seasonally. The best meats are the simplest: steaks or chicken grilled over an open fire. They are, however, highly salted—so be sure to ask for them *senza sale* if salt is a problem. Of the desserts, some are homemade. Of these, tiramisù is light, cool, and satisfying, and the *panna cotta* (baked cream pudding) comes nicely balanced by a sweet strawberry sauce.

Monsanto

CASTELLO DI MONSANTO
WINE

CASTELLO DI MONSANTO
50021 BARBERINO VAL D'ELSA FIRENZE
TELEPHONE 055 8059000   FAX 055 8059049
WEB SITE www.castellodimonsanto.it

OPEN 8:00–12:30, 14:00–18:00; visits and guided tastings by appointment only
CLOSED Saturday, Sunday; three weeks in August   **CREDIT CARDS** Visa, MC, Amex
DIRECT SALE Yes   **ENGLISH SPOKEN** Yes   **DIRECTIONS** From Poggibonsi, go toward Barberino; after the roundabout, turn right toward Monsanto and Olena

Monsanto is a stately eighteenth-century villa set in a beautiful English-style garden. The estate, with more than 50 hectares (123 acres) of vineyards, has long been in the Bianchi family, and Fabrizio Bianchi has long been a key character in Chianti. He was among the first to eliminate white grapes from the Chianti blend and to explore the use of *barriques*. His single-vineyard Chianti Classico Riserva, Il

Poggio, was an early Chianti *cru*. Bianchi is a jolly, energetic man with a wry sense of humor. He is a great expert about wine and a tireless innovator. "He is the one who makes all the experiments here," laughed his charming daughter, Laura, "and I am the one who has to sell them!"

The Bianchis have created a spectacular *cantina*, with a long wide descending tunnel lined with stones retrieved from the vineyards. "The *barricaia* took three men six years to make," Laura explained.

Monsanto's wines are concentrated and pure. The 1993 Chianti Classico Riserva is smooth and fruity but lacks the intensity of color Chianti sometimes has. "In bad years Sangiovese has no depth of color," explained Bianchi, "which is why deeply pigmented grapes such as Colorino are often added to it." Monsanto produces no "normal" Chianti, but only the Riserva and the *cru*, Il Poggio. This comes from 5 hectares (12 acres) of vineyard positioned up at 310 meters. "This wine should stay in wood for three years," Bianchi continued. "Putting it in *barriques* for a period has the same effect but shortens the time." It spends a further year in the bottle. The estate has, in recent years, introduced some new-style *vini da tavola*. "Fabrizio Bianchi" is a wine of pure Sangiovese, mellow, structured, and rich. Tinscvil, an Etruscan word meaning "votive offering to the daughter of Jupiter," is a blend of 75 percent Sangiovese with 25 percent Cabernet Sauvignon; Nemo is pure Cabernet Sauvignon. In great years there is also a fine sweet Vin Santo.

Monti in Chianti

CASTELLO DI CACCHIANO
WINE, OLIVE OIL

CACCHIANO 53010 MONTI IN CHIANTI SIENA
TELEPHONE 0577 747018   FAX 0577 747157
WEB SITE www.chianticlassico.com/cacchiano

OPEN 8:00–12:00, 13:00–17:00; *cantina* visits and tastings by appointment only
CLOSED Sunday   **CREDIT CARDS** Visa, MC   **DIRECT SALE** Yes, Monday–Saturday
ENGLISH SPOKEN Yes   **OTHER** Guest apartment available for weekly rentals
DIRECTIONS From Gaiole, take SS 408 south toward Siena for 5.5 kms. Turn left onto SS 484 toward Brolio. After 5 kms, turn right toward Cacchiano

---

Cacchiano is an imposing, austere medieval castle commanding extraordinary views of its surrounding countryside. It was constructed by the Ricasoli-Firidolfis in the tenth century as part of Brolio Castle's fortifications against the Sienese Republic, and it has been in the same family ever since.

The castle's winemaking activities are now run directly by Giovanni Ricasoli, with the help of the enologist Federico Staderini. Cacchiano is known for its "traditional style" Chianti Classico DOCG, with, in good years, the acclaimed Millennio Riserva. In what is a sign of the growing prestige attached to the great Chianti

Classicos, RF, Cacchiano's big super-Tuscan wine of Sangiovese, will now be abandoned; its grapes will be used to enrich Millennio.

Cacchiano's delicious Vin Santo is also of the traditional type, made from 100 percent Malvasia grapes that are partially dried on racks for four to five months before being pressed and sealed in casks of 30 to 200 liters. "Every five years or so" they take it out and bottle it. The estate sells a fine extra-virgin olive oil, pressed from hand-picked olives. "We use primarily the Corregiolo olives with a little bit of Moraiolo and Leccino added, because the best pollination is possible when there are several types," explained Baroness Elisabetta Ricasoli-Firidolfi, Giovanni's mother.

SAN GIUSTO
A RENTENNANO
WINE

MONTI IN CHIANTI 53010 GAIOLE IN CHIANTI SIENA
TELEPHONE 0577 747121   FAX 0577 747109
E-MAIL sangiustorentennano@chiantinet.it

OPEN 8:00–12:00, 14:00–18:00; visits and tastings by appointment   **CLOSED** Sunday
CREDIT CARDS None   **DIRECT SALE** Yes   **ENGLISH SPOKEN** Yes   **OTHER** Several farmhouses available for holiday rentals   **DIRECTIONS** The winery is signposted from SS 408, the Chiantigiana, about 12 kms south of Gaiole

---

They have been called "vikings" and *capitani di ventura*—indeed, the brothers Francesco and Luca Martini di Cigala do seem like two young men with a mission. Self-taught winemakers and hands-on farmers, they took the wine world by storm in 1991 when their super-Tuscan of pure Sangiovese, Percarlo 1985, went up against some of France's greatest wines in a blind tasting—and won. But these are no Johnny-come-latelies.

For centuries, Fattoria San Giusto a Rentennano belonged to the Barons Ricasoli at Brolio Castle, acting as a fortified stronghold until it was destroyed at the end of the fourteenth century. One hundred years later, a country villa was built above its remaining buttressed walls. Since the early 1900s, the Martini di Cigala family has been related to the Ricasolis by marriage. Enrico Martini di Cigala inherited the property in 1957 and began improvements. After his death in 1992, his sons took over. Francesco bottled San Giusto's first Chianti in 1981; Percarlo was born in 1983. Some vineyards are on tufa, which lends the wines their structure and aging power. The reds are robust and full, becoming increasingly elegant over time.

I know I am not alone in being mad for San Giusto a Rentennano's Vin Santo, but tasting it came as a revelation. Totally unlike the lean, "dry sherry" Vin Santi, Martini di Cigala's aromatic, amber wine is sweet, rich, and seductive. "Most Tuscan Vin Santo is made from primarily Trebbiano grapes," explained Francesco, "but Trebbiano is less able to mature fully and leads to those thin, dry wines. Ours uses mainly Malvasia grapes with a higher sugar content." The harvested grapes are dried for four months on cane racks to further concentrate their sugars. The wine is sealed into small chestnut-wood *caratelli* along with the "mother" yeasts that feed the wine throughout its long fermentation. They are placed in the *vinsantaia*, usually a space under the roof where the wine can experience seasonal temperature changes. The aging lasts four to six years. Seven to eight kilos (sixteen lbs) of grapes are required to make each liter of Vin Santo.

Olena

ISOLE E OLENA VIA OLENA, 15 OLENA 50021 BARBERINO VAL D'ELSA FIRENZE
WINE TELEPHONE 055 8072763 FAX 055 8072236
E-MAIL isolena@tin.it

OPEN Sales, visits, and tastings by appointment only CREDIT CARDS None DIRECT SALE Yes
ENGLISH SPOKEN Yes DIRECTIONS From Poggibonsi, go toward Barberino; after the roundabout, turn to the right toward Monsanto and Olena

Paolo De Marchi's father bought Isole e Olena in the 1950s, and since Paolo took it over in 1976, he has become one of the most respected winemakers in Chianti, if not in Italy. The estate, with 42 hectares (104 acres) of vineyards, is at the western edge of central Chianti Classico.

De Marchi is a young, energetic man with a refreshingly open mind. He told me that he loves having foreign students working for him, because they bring "a little of the outside world" to him. This contact with other cultures has certainly pushed him to be more adventurous with his own: De Marchi was one of Tuscany's first serious experimenters with the "foreign" grape varieties Syrah, Cabernet Sauvignon, and Chardonnay, making the decision to vinify and bottle them each separately. If the Cabernet has achieved great results, De Marchi now seems less convinced about the Syrah. "I now believe that Cabernet will become part of Tuscany's tradition, because it is showing excellent results here," he said.

Sangiovese is more traditionally Tuscan. From it De Marchi makes his excellent Cepparello, maturing the wine for fourteen months in French *barriques,* and the Chianti Classico DOCG—another great wine of primarily Sangiovese grapes. De Marchi also makes an opulent Vin Santo of 75 percent Malvasia and 25 percent Trebbiano grapes.

Paolo De Marchi is a keen researcher into the best clones and growing conditions for his vines, as the perennial earthworks around the estate can testify. His passion for his work is apparent. I interviewed him in autumn as the *vendemmia* (harvest) was due to start, with thunder and lightning crashing down around us. Each time the rain fell harder or seemed to be hail, I could feel his disappointment at the prospect of the grapes being ruined. "It only takes a few hours like this to undo a year's work," he admitted.

Pàcina

PÀCINA
WINE

53019 CASTELNUOVO BERARDENGA SIENA
TELEPHONE/FAX 0577 355044
WEB SITE www.pacina.it

OPEN Sales, visits, and tastings by appointment only   **CREDIT CARDS** None   **DIRECT SALE** Yes
ENGLISH SPOKEN Yes   **OTHER** Three apartments available for holiday rental
DIRECTIONS From Castelnuovo Berardenga, go toward Pianella, then follow signs for Villa Pàcina

Located just outside the Chianti Classico border, the stately ex-convent at Pàcina has produced wines for centuries. Since 1987, however, the winemaking has taken a more professional turn. Giovanna Tiezzi, her husband, Stefano Borsa, and their young winemaker, Giovanna Morganti, have helped Pàcina be "reborn" as an organic farm. No sulphur dioxide is used in the vinification, and only copper and sulphur are used to treat the vines.

Pàcina's red Chianti Colli Senesi is *profumato* and well structured—it needs time to evolve. It is aged in double *barriques*, twice the volume of the more commonly found small oak casks. I asked Giovanna Morganti, who is the daughter of the late Enzo Morganti (see p 216), about wines made by women. "It is lovely working with other women," she said. "I don't know if this can be felt in the wine, but there has been a change in our way of working: there is a greater sensibility in relation to the earth, and we hope this will be reflected in the wines."

Panzano

ANTICA MACELLERIA
CECCHINI
MEAT, SPECIALTY FOODS

VIA XX LUGLIO, 11 50020 PANZANO IN CHIANTI FIRENZE
TELEPHONE 055 852020   FAX 055 852700
E-MAIL macelleriacecchini@tin.it

OPEN 9:00–19:00   **CLOSED** Wednesday, Sunday afternoon   **CREDIT CARDS** None
ENGLISH SPOKEN A little   **DIRECTIONS** In the town center, off Piazza Bucciarelli

The first thing that strikes you in this tiny butcher's shop is the beauty of everything in it: a deep basket of rosemary, an arrangement of homegrown vegetables, the pâtés with their jewel-like aspics, hanging garlands of peppers, hanging peppered hams—all have been put together with the eyes and the hands of an artist. There is wonderful music, a wicker sofa under a shelf of cookbooks, and the *profumi* of herbs, spices, and the salt-cured pork that is so particularly Italian. Even the meat here is wholesomely displayed.

"What interests me," explained Dario Cecchini as he added spices to a batch of hand-kneaded *salsicce*, "is the authentic *cucina Toscana*. I have spent years compiling a menu of these specialties. When you come to my shop you can taste them."

The counter is full of appetizing foods: herb-scented *lardo* for spreading on hot bread, goose spiced with coriander, galantine of duck with Marsala, pigeons stuffed with juniper, a Renaissance pâté with prunes. There also are excellent Chianina steaks and other meats.

Dario, a large, vital young man with a ready smile and large, nimble hands, is as decisive in his ideas as he is in his work. "There are two types of people," he asserted as he guided the sausage meat into its casings. "Those who look for memories of their childhood in their food, and those who look for power—eating oysters and foie gras. The only thing that upsets me," he admitted, tying off the plump sausages neatly, "are the people who come in and take pictures here without even saying hello or tasting anything." By the time you visit, Dario may have completed his extension: the little shop will be enlarged to add a tasting room "for friends."

IL VESCOVINO
RESTAURANT

VIA CIAMPOLO DA PANZANO, 9 50020 PANZANO FIRENZE
TELEPHONE/FAX 055 852464

OPEN Lunch and dinner; in February lunch is by appointment only   **CLOSED** Tuesday; January
CREDIT CARDS Visa, MC, Amex   **ENGLISH SPOKEN** Yes   **FEATURES** Summer terrace
RESERVATIONS Recommended in summer   **PRICE** $$$ **OTHER** Mimmo Baldi also runs a
cooking school   **DIRECTIONS** From Panzano's center, go toward Panzano Alto; the restaurant
is at the edge of town, signposted

Il Vescovino's summer terrace overlooks Chianti's beautiful winemaking valley, the Conca d'Oro. "When we opened in 1987 we felt like pioneers," recounted Mimmo Baldi, the owner and chef. "The area was still depressed, and the mayor encouraged us to open a restaurant, not a trattoria." Fresh ingredients were hard to get: Panzano is a drive from everywhere. Baldi comes from the Amalfi coast and wanted to cook fish, not just Tuscan "land" dishes. "We kept to simple but good food," he explained. "Homemade pastas, fresh breads, and terrines—a novelty here then." The menu changes with the seasons. There is usually a choice of *primi*, and fish and meat courses, both Tuscan and original in style. Baldi cooks with spontaneity and flair.

In early February the restaurant was not fully open, but I tasted *tagliolini* noodles with porcini mushrooms in a shallow short-crust "basket." The pasta was very fine, and the earthy mushrooms were matched with sharp, aromatic *nepitella*—a wild herb. Pancetta bacon chunks were roasted until crisp and served with chard stalks (*coste*), stewed with onions and spicy tomatoes. Dessert was a deep chocolate soufflé with chocolate sauce. Not surprisingly, Baldi's wine list features many local stars—wines are also available by the bottle from his wine bar, Enoteca Baldi (see p 211).

TENUTA FONTODI
WINE

VIA SAN LEOLINO, 87 50020 PANZANO IN CHIANTI FIRENZE
TELEPHONE 055 852005   FAX 055 852537
WEB SITE www.fontodi.com

OPEN 9:00–12:00, 14:00–18:00; tastings are possible; group tastings and *cantina* visits by appointment only   CLOSED Saturday, Sunday   CREDIT CARDS Visa, MC   DIRECT SALE Yes
ENGLISH SPOKEN Yes   OTHER Four apartments available for holiday rental
DIRECTIONS From Panzano, go toward Radda; Fontodi is on the left after 2 kms

The natural amphitheater surrounding Panzano is the Conca d'Oro—the golden bowl. On its slope is Tenuta Fontodi, the vineyards and olive groves of Domiziano and Dino Manetti. Since 1968, the Manettis have gained recognition for their fine wines and progressive management, and the estate has kept growing: it now has 67 hectares (165 acres) of vineyards. Fontodi is a winery worth visiting. The wines are great, the handsome buildings and *cantine* well appointed, and the staff welcoming. A room is set apart for tasting.

The winemaking is done by the young Giovanni Manetti and enologist Franco Bernabei. Two wines have elicited international accolades. Flaccianello della Pieve was one of the leaders of the super-Tuscan "table wines"; of pure Sangiovese, this well-structured, concentrated wine is matured in small French casks. Vigna del Sorbo is an elegant Chianti Classico *cru* of Sangiovese and Cabernet Sauvignon grown in the homonymous vineyard; it, too, is matured in *barriques*. Case Via is the estate's big Syrah, a powerful wine with elegant tannins. In good years these wines rank among Tuscany's very best.

Fontodi produces a smooth Chianti Classico and a fine Riserva, as well as an interesting white wine, Meriggio, a blend of Pinot Bianco and Sauvignon grapes matured in oak casks. The Tenuta bottles its own extra-virgin olive oil.

LA MASSA
WINE

VIA CASE SPARSE, 9 50020 PANZANO IN CHIANTI FIRENZE
TELEPHONE/FAX 055 852722
E-MAIL fattoria.lamassa@tin.it

OPEN Visits and tastings by appointment only   DIRECT SALE No   ENGLISH SPOKEN A little
DIRECTIONS From Panzano go toward Mercatale; after 500 meters, turn left, then take the right fork in the road. La Massa is on the right down the unpaved road

Giampaolo Motta is young, smart, funny, Neapolitan, and irrepressibly enthusiastic. He makes some of Chianti's best wine. The madcap story of how his dream to own a winery became a reality would fill a book, but here it is in a nutshell:

While working in his family's leather factory in Naples, Motta had a crisis of confidence, came to Tuscany, and encountered John Dunkley, "who was inspirational." Then came a spell at a giant Chianti winery, "where I learned almost nothing," paired with an old *contadino* who ate bread and onions for lunch and spoke in monosyllables. The apprenticeship continued at Rampolla: "Luca has a fine palate and passion for wine, but after four years in Tuscany I still had not risked my capital."

A vast holding in the Conca d'Oro went on sale following a bankruptcy, with 40 hectares of vineyards, "and I was looking for 4 or 5!" After much ado, half was sold off, leaving Giampaolo Motta with 27 hectares (67 acres) of some of the finest vineyards in Chianti. Now he is planning a new *cantina*.

"Our first *vendemmia* was in 1992—the worst harvest for fifty years." With winemaker Carlo Ferrini, he decided to salvage only the best grapes from the sodden vineyards. "We made a tiny amount of very good wine." Motta called it Giorgio, for his grandfather, who had secretly helped him; Primo, for his first wine. It is a Chianti Classico, as is his other wine, La Massa. Giorgio Primo contains only first-choice Sangiovese grapes. "We wait till very late to harvest, when the fruit is ripe, sweet, and concentrated, so the wines are really *morbido*, mellow. The French believe you should bottle a mellow wine, not an undrinkably tannic one; the bottle is only a glass container—it can't completely alter a wine's characteristics."

Motta's wines are particularly mellow, with concentrated fruit and balanced, but present, wood. "*Barriques* are fine, but often overused. The wood should be like a crutch under the coat—there, but out of sight." Giorgio Primo spends eighteen months in *barriques*, old and new. La Massa, of second-choice Sangiovese grapes, spends one year in wood and is also fruity and rich. Both have taken the wine world by storm. "To make wine has always been my dream. Now that I'm doing it, I'm very happy—*felicissimo!*"

CASTELLO DEI RAMPOLLA
WINE

SANTA LUCIA IN FAULLE 50020 PANZANO IN CHIANTI FIRENZE
TELEPHONE 055 852001   FAX 055 852533
E-MAIL castellodeirampolla.cast@tin.it

OPEN 8:00–12:00, 13:00–17:00; visits, sales, and tastings by appointment only
CLOSED Saturday, Sunday   **CREDIT CARDS** None   **DIRECT SALE** Yes   **ENGLISH SPOKEN** Yes
DIRECTIONS From Panzano, go toward Mercatale; after 500 meters, turn left before the white church and follow the yellow signs to Rampolla, which is at the end of the dirt road

---

The Rampolla estate, with its lovely grounds and views of the Conca d'Oro valley, is one of Chianti's most striking. The castle has belonged to the Rampolla family since 1739. Until recently it was run by Matteo di Napoli Rampolla, who had taken over after his father, Alceo's, death, but another brother, Luca, has now taken charge. If all this change initially led to speculation about the future of Rampolla's wines, recent vintages have confirmed that the estate is definitely on an upward turn again. In part, that is thanks to the renowned enologist Giacomo Tachis.

When I talked with Luca, who is a serious, gentle young man, he explained that he hoped to move the farm toward a more *biodinamico* (biodynamic) approach by using organic manures and as little chemical treatment of the vines as possible.

In addition to their Chianti Classico in both the "normal" and Riserva versions, the Rampollas produce two of the greatest super-Tuscans: Sammarco, of Cabernet Sauvignon grapes with a small percentage of Sangiovese added, a full-bodied "table" wine matured in *barriques;* and La Vigna di Alceo, of Cabernet Sauvignon with 15 percent Petit Verdot, which has been called one of Italy's greatest reds. It is the fruit of vineyards Alceo planted a few years before his death.

VILLA CAFAGGIO
WINE

VIA SAN MARTINO, 5 50020 PANZANO IN CHIANTI FIRENZE
TELEPHONE 055 8549094   FAX 055 8549096
E-MAIL basilica.cafaggio@tiscalinet.it

OPEN Visits and tastings by appointment only   **DIRECT SALE** No, but wines are available from the *enoteche* at Panzano   **ENGLISH SPOKEN** Yes   **DIRECTIONS** From Panzano, go toward Mercatale; after 3 kms, turn left and follow signs to the winery

---

Stefano Farkas was behind the wheel of a tractor, ploughing a soon-to-be-planted vineyard. Thousands of *barbatelle*, young grape vines, had arrived from France (where they had been grafted) and were waiting under a tarpaulin in the barn. "In, the next ten years there will be a giant improvement in Chianti's wines," declared Farkas, Villa Cafaggio's dynamic director and the moving force behind its award-winning wines. "Twenty years ago, when many of Chianti's vineyards were planted, no one understood about clones or American rootstocks. Everything was very haphazard. Now those who are keeping up with the times—and the research—will be in a postion to make truly great wines here."

In 1967 Farkas's father bought the estate at the western end of the Conca d'Oro valley, one of Chianti's most perfect natural sites for vine growing. Today Farkas and Girelli, a wine producer from Trento, are partners. Big investments have been made, both in the planting of Sangiovese, Merlot, and Cabernet and in the modern cellar, with its temperature-controlled presses and neat rows of *barriques*. A room used to store the bottled wines was cool. "The *invecchiamento,* or aging, in bottles is just as important as that in wood," he explained. "Too high a temperature in here and the wines would age too quickly."

The estate is known for its great reds: Chianti Classico and its Riserva; Cortaccio, of 90 percent Cabernet with 10 percent Sangiovese; and San Martino, of pure Sangiovese. They are noted for their concentration of flavor, balance, and ability to age. "In making red wines," Farkas concluded, "the most important thing is to start with perfect, ripe, and healthy grapes. If you don't, there's nothing you can do."

ENOTECA BALDI
WINE BAR, SPECIALTY FOODS

PIAZZA BUCCIARELLI, 25 50020 PANZANO FIRENZE
TELEPHONE 055 852843
E-MAIL enotecabaldi@tin.it

OPEN 10:00–22:00   **CLOSED** Holidays in winter   **CREDIT CARDS** Visa, MC   **DIRECT SALE** Yes
ENGLISH SPOKEN Yes   **DIRECTIONS** In Panzano's central *piazza*

Mimmo Baldi's latest venture (see Il Vescovino restaurant, p 207) is this wine bar. Tuscan wines are available to drink at the *enoteca* or to take out. Homemade snacks (prepared at the restaurant) are served at all hours. Specialty foods include artisan pastas, biscuits, jams, preserved vegetables, and olive oils.

Poggibonsi

LA GALLERIA
RESTAURANT

GALLERIA CAVALIERI VITTORIO VENETO, 20
53036 POGGIBONSI SIENA
TELEPHONE 0577 982356

OPEN Lunch and dinner   **CLOSED** Sunday; August   **CREDIT CARDS** Visa, MC, Amex
ENGLISH SPOKEN Yes   **RESERVATIONS** Recommended   **PRICE** $$$
DIRECTIONS The restaurant is in an arcade between Via del Commercio and Piazza Indipendenza, in the modern area of the town to the north of the historic center

---

This restaurant occupies the base of Poggibonsi's only "skyscraper," a rather unprepossessing fourteen-story 1970s construction. But don't be put off by the bland exterior. Owner-chef Michele Targi and his wife, Letizia Cappelli, opened La Galleria in 1991, and Targi, a friendly, soft-spoken man, trained in some of Firenze's best-known restaurants. He inherited his passion for wine from his father, a wine and oil salesman. The interesting wine list features Tuscany, but it includes other regions as well. Prices are fair.

The food is refined and creative, yet recognizably Tuscan, with a very good selection of fresh fish. A choice of tasting menus—including one of goat's cheeses from Ville di Corsano (p 301) served with sweet *vino muffato*—complements the seasonal à la carte selection. In early summer, antipasti included brine-cured pork loin; imported smoked goose breast; fresh-tasting tomato *bruschetta;* and a cold salad of tripe, raw onion, potatoes, string beans, and basil that afforded a stimulating mixture of tastes and textures.

Of the *primi, taglierini alla Galleria* was fine noodles tossed with a crunchy pesto of walnuts, pine nuts, basil, and tomatoes. Pennette had a tangy sauce of goat's cheese and shredded arugula. *Fusilli con pomodori acerbi* was equally good, with a tart yellow-green sauce of unripe tomatoes and herbs. Desserts are homemade and beautifully presented. The tiramisù is deliciously light; the unusual Medici pudding, a chilled baked custard, is studded with rice and raisins.

Also

GELATERIA IL VENTAGLIO   PIAZZA FRATELLI ROSSELLI, 11/12. 0577 981033

This is one of my favorite *gelaterie*, with a friendly family making a large assortment of the freshest fruit and *crema* ice creams. It's worth a detour if you're in the area on a hot day.

Radda in Chianti

RISTORANTE LE VIGNE   PODERE LE VIGNE 53017 RADDA IN CHIANTI SIENA
RESTAURANT   TELEPHONE 0577 738640   FAX 0577 738809

OPEN Lunch and dinner   **CLOSED** Tuesday in winter; some winter holidays
CREDIT CARDS Visa, MC, Amex   **ENGLISH SPOKEN** A little   **FEATURES** Summer garden dining
RESERVATIONS Recommended in summer   **PRICE** $$ **DIRECTIONS** From Radda's center, go
toward Gaiole. Le Vigne is signposted on the right just beyond Radda

---

This restaurant is surrounded by vineyards. Its summer terrace is tree-shaded and breezy. For cooler weather there is a large indoor dining room. Le Vigne is a good place for families: in summer children are free to play in the garden. The restaurant caters to foreign tourists, and the menu is multilingual, but the young staff is spread a bit thin at peak hours.

The menu is not large, but it offers Tuscan favorites. *Crostini* are topped with creamed field mushrooms; mixed *salumi* is the popular trio: *salame, finocchiona,* and prosciutto. *Primi* include *pici all'aglione,* local thick spaghetti with a garlicky tomato and leek sauce, and decent pasta *al pesto. Secondi* are typically Tuscan: rabbit with olives, duck with rosemary, lemon-roasted chicken, and stewed wild boar, plus imaginative vegetable sides. Desserts are fairly good. The wine list features Chianti-produced wines.

CERAMICHE RAMPINI   CASA BERETONE DI VISTARENNI
TABLE CRAFTS: POTTERY   53017 RADDA IN CHIANTI SIENA
TELEPHONE 0577 738043   FAX 0577 738776
WEB SITE www.rampiniceramics.com

OPEN 9:00–18:00   **CLOSED** Sunday   **CREDIT CARDS** Visa, MC, Amex   **MAIL ORDER** Ceramics
can be shipped overseas   **ENGLISH SPOKEN** Yes   **DIRECTIONS** From Radda, go toward Gaiole.
After 2 kms take the right-hand fork, toward Gaiole. Rampini's studio is signposted on the left as you
go down the hill, after 1 km

Giuseppe Rampini is a craftsman continuing a Renaissance ceramic tradition. The powerful Medici families commissioned dinner services for ceremonial events destined to be used only once, and they had different plates designed for each season. "The Medicea plates often had simple decorations in blue on a white ground," explained Rampini. "This blue glaze [*blé*] was derived from cobalt. It came from the Far East and was as costly as gold."

Working with his grown-up children, Rampini offers some of these designs in simplified form, plus a range of colorfully decorated platters, bowls, and pitchers, some of which recall Arcimboldi's sixteenth-century fruit and flower compositions. All use lead-free glazes. The clay stock is found along the Arno River.

Rampini's showroom is reached by going up the external staircase of the studio; it is filled with multicolored ceramics. Pieces can be bought directly or custom ordered. There are usually some seconds for sale at reduced prices.

PODERE CAPACCIA　　　　　　　　　　　　CAPACCIA 53017 RADDA IN CHIANTI SIENA
WINE, OLIVE OIL　　　　　TELEPHONE WINERY 0577 738385 OFFICE 0574 582426
　　　　　　　　　　FAX 0574 582428　　WEB SITE www.poderecapaccia.com

OPEN Monday–Saturday 9:00–12:00, 14:00–17:00; Sunday 9:00–13:00, 14:00–19:00; visits and tastings by appointment only　　CREDIT CARDS Visa, MC　　DIRECT SALE Yes　　ENGLISH SPOKEN Yes
DIRECTIONS From Radda, go northeast toward Castello d'Albola; turn left toward Capaccia 1 km after the turning for Montevertine

When I first met him, Giampaolo Pacini was the Tuscan president of the Movimento del Turismo del Vino, an association that organizes winery open days and promotes wine tourism. His small estate is perched on a steep little hill near Radda. The road up to the cluster of medieval buildings is not the greatest, but once there, it feels like stepping back centuries in time. "When we bought Capaccia there was not a roof left on," explained the hospitable Pacini. "The village was abandoned for at least seventy years. Bit by bit we are reconstructing it. As for the vines, they had grown wild and climbed up over the olive trees!"

Working with the experienced winemaker Vittorio Fiore, Pacini has planted mainly Sangiovese in his 3 hectares (8 acres) of vineyards. The *cantina* is squeezed into several little workers' cottages, but it includes ultramodern equipment. A soft press for white grapes is used for Pacini's reds. Another building serves as a tasting and sales room. Wines, fine olive oil, and homemade products are on sale. Pacini is a food historian and enthusiastic cook; he and his wife run Tuscan food seminars.

Capaccia concentrates on two red wines: a classic Chianti Classico, of Sangiovese with a little red Canaiolo (with its Riserva in great years), and Querciagrande IGT, a wonderfully rich, warm, fruity super-Tuscan of pure Sangiovese matured in small French casks for about fifteen months. An interesting newer wine is Spera di Sole, a late-harvest wine of Trebbiano and Malvasia picked in December and matured in tiny Slavonian oak barrels for one year (as for Vin Santo), after which the wine in the barrels is topped up for two years so less oxidation occurs. A final year is spent in *barriques*. The result is a wine whose *profumi*—of honey, almonds, and vanilla—are intact.

I asked Giampaolo Pacini how he had become interested in winemaking. "My father was a wine merchant," he recalled, "and one of my earliest memories is of the earthy, grapey wine smell in my father's car—in those days a lot of wine was sold *sfuso*, unbottled, so it must have spilled out. As a child I loved that smell, and I guess I still do."

FATTORIA DI MONTEVERTINE
WINE

MONTEVERTINE 53017 RADDA IN CHIANTI SIENA
TELEPHONE 0577 738009   FAX 0577 738265

OPEN Visits by appointment only   **CLOSED** Saturday, Sunday   **CREDIT CARDS** None
DIRECT SALE Yes, subject to availability   **ENGLISH SPOKEN** Yes   **FEATURES** Museum of
Rural Chianti   **DIRECTIONS** From Radda, go northeast toward Albola. Montevertine is signposted
from that road, on the left

The wine world suffered a great loss in 2000 with the death of Sergio Manetti. A man of many qualities, he had a larger vision for Chianti than did most of his contemporaries—who have now caught up with his avant-garde ideas. He will be much missed.

In his amusing book *Vino e Cucina,* a collection of "erogastronomic digressions," Manetti regretted the passing of the wine-drinking era of his youth. He recalled the sign posted by a bartender in Poggibonsi: If I can't sell it, I drink it. "He was right," commented Manetti. "I have admired him ever since, and I have made it my motto."

Coming from anyone else, that might have seemed like a surprising philosophy. But Sergio Manetti was not just anyone, especially not in Chianti. For it was he, back in 1971, who thought to age his wine of pure Sangioveto (the indigenous Chianti grape) in *barriques*. He called it Le Pergole Torte ("the crooked posts" in Tuscan dialect), gave it a bold, painterly label, and launched a new era in Chianti. Le Pergole Torte revealed the potential of Tuscany's native grape, putting it alongside the so-called international varietals, Cabernet and Merlot. It is an elegant wine of concentrated fruit and flavor made to age gracefully.

Working with his trusted friend, the winemaker Giulio Gambelli, his son Martino, and son-in-law Klaus Reimitz, Manetti also produced the single-vineyard wine Il Sodaccio (Sangioveto), Montevertine (Sangioveto and Canaiolo), and its Riserva. "M" is a white wine aged for four years in small oak casks; Bianco di Montevertine is a more traditional white of Trebbiano and Malvasia; and Il Maggio is the estate's recent dessert wine, of Trebbiano and Malvasia grapes dried on the vine before being aged in small oak casks. The estate has 7 hectares (18 acres) of vineyards. Its costly wines are always in high demand, but they are not made in enormous quantities.

Montevertine is a place of culture: you see it in the house and sculpture garden, in the sea of vines supported by crooked wooden posts, and in the little museum of objects of everyday country life.

Also

Podere Terreno (tel: 0577 738312), on the road that leads to Volpaia, is a winery with an unusual *agriturismo*—a country house that accepts paying guests. Each night the guests dine at a long communal table presided over by the farm's owners, Roberto Melosi and Sylvie Haniez, who are among Chianti's most hospitable hosts. The food is abundant and good, the wine flows freely (and is improving all the time), and the conversation is always multicultural.

San Casciano in Val di Pesa

EMILIO   VIA DEI FOSSI, 3. 055 820691

In his small artisan's shop, Emilio Nesi restores furniture, recanes chairs, and makes and sells lovely baskets. Look for wine flasks covered with olive and willow, as well as the teardrop-shaped, flat fig-drying baskets that make attractive fruit holders.

San Donato in Poggio

CASA EMMA   CORTINE SAN DONATO IN POGGIO
WINE   50021 BARBERINO VAL D'ELSA FIRENZE
                          TELEPHONE 055 8072859, 8072239   FAX 0571 667707
                                             WEB SITE www.casaemma.com

---

OPEN Monday–Saturday 9:00–19:00; Sunday 9:00–12:00; tastings from April to October
CREDIT CARDS Visa, MC   **DIRECT SALE** Yes   **ENGLISH SPOKEN** Yes
DIRECTIONS From San Donato, go toward Castellina; Casa Emma is on the left after about 1 km

---

Casa Emma shows what can happen when an ambitious young winery is paired with the experience of a good winemaker. In the space of a few years, Nicolò D'Afflitto, the winemaker, has transformed Casa Emma from a hardworking estate selling most of its wine unbottled to a winery that in 1997 won its first coveted *"tre bicchieri"* award—the top rating given by the Gambero Rosso-Arcigola Italian wine guide. Fiorella Lepri and family have made considerable investments in the winery, whose neat, well-exposed vineyards surround the house. "When we came in 1973 there was nothing up here but rocks and grass," Fiorella recalled. "Now we have 18 hectares [44 acres] of specialized vineyards and an efficient modern *cantina.*" In addition to two types of Sangiovese, the winery now produces some Merlot. The winery's position is high, at more than 400 meters (1,300 feet), and well ventilated—which makes for concentrated wines rich in perfumes. Casa Emma makes Chianti Classico, its Riserva (the 1993 and 1995 were award winners), and Soloìo, of pure Merlot matured in *barriques,* which has also won Italy's highest accolades.

How does it feel to gain such recognition? "We knew we had a great product," Fiorella admitted. "But we never expected to win—the little guy rarely does. Now we will try to maintain our high standards and, who knows, we might win it again someday."

Also

Marco Felluga, the great white wine producer from Friuli, is venturing into the red: his first wine from the new estate in Chianti, at San Nicolò a Pisignano, is out: Sorripa is Sangiovese with a little Cabernet Sauvignon and Merlot. 055 828834. Web Site www.marcofelluga.it.

San Felice

SAN FELICE
WINE, RESTAURANT

SAN GUSMÈ 53010 CASTELNUOVO BERARDENGA SIENA
TELEPHONE WINERY 0577 359087/8
RESTAURANT 359260   FAX 0577 359223
E-MAIL borgosfelice@flashnet.it

OPEN Sales 9:00–12:00, 14:00–18:00; April to October; wine sales from *borgo* shop 8:30–20:00; *cantina* visits and tastings by appointment only   **CLOSED** Saturday, Sunday   **CREDIT CARDS** Visa, MC   **DIRECT SALE** Yes   **ENGLISH SPOKEN** Yes   **FEATURES** San Felice has a *relais* hotel and a restaurant   **RESERVATIONS** Necessary for restaurant   **PRICE** $$$$$ restaurant   **DIRECTIONS** San Felice can be reached from SS 484 (Gaiole–Castelnuovo Berardenga) or from the south; follow signs

San Felice is a complex of 750 hectares (1,800 acres) surrounding a lovely medieval *borgo* now owned by an insurance company. It includes one of Chianti's most important wineries, with 220 hectares (543 acres) of vineyards. Of these, 18 (45) are dedicated to viticultural research. "San Felice has this research facility thanks to Enzo Morganti, who came here in 1968," explained Leonardo Bellaccini, the estate's young winemaker. "He was general manager until his death in 1994. He was a keen scientist and forward thinker when it came to vineyards and their problems."

Early on, Morganti created Vigorello, his first "alternative" red of 70 percent Sangiovese and 30 percent Cabernet Sauvignon and a precursor to today's super-Tuscans. (Today this award winner also contains a little Merlot.) He began selecting clones of Sangiovese and other varietals that are now planted on the estate.

Morganti's fascinating experimental vineyards are called Vitiarium. He collected hundreds of Tuscany's "minor" varietals, with wonderful names like Colorino, Lacrima, Volpola, and Pugnitello. "The original notion was just to conserve these plants for historical reasons," continued Bellaccini, "but we realized that some had very personal qualities when made into wine." Indeed, Pugnitello has given such good results that it is being planted in several of the estate's vineyards, and its first wine promises great things.

San Felice makes three important Chianti Classicos, all Sangiovese based: the "normal," a popular wine to drink young (within two to three years); Il Grigio, a Riserva that Bellaccini called a "strategic" wine, offering good value for money; and Poggio Rosso, a Riserva *cru* from vineyards that were once Morganti's, of 90 percent Sangiovese with 10 percent Colorino. It is an elegant, perfumed wine of balance and structure. The estate's list includes Ancherona (a *barrique*-fermented Chardonnay), and Belcaro, an interesting blend of 70 percent Vermentino grown in the Maremma with Sauvignon Blanc from Chianti. There is also an extra-virgin olive oil milled in the winery's own *frantoio*. San Felice also has important holdings at Montalcino, Campogiovanni, where it produces a fine Brunello.

A word about the restaurant: the *borgo* has a fine restaurant that serves clients from the hotel as well as from outside; they recommend booking well in advance in high season. The setting is lovely, with a pretty, peaceful outdoor terrace for an *aperitivo* or dining in warm weather. The menu offers two *degustazione* multicourse choices in addition to the main menu. The chef seeks out quality local and seasonal ingredients and combines them in interesting—and sometimes ambitious—ways to complement the more traditionally Tuscan repertoire. Pastries and breads are all baked on the premises. The service is professional and friendly. The wine list, as one would expect, has a good range—including San Felice's!

Also

PODERE LE BONCE   SAN FELICE. 0577 359383. gmorganti@nettuno.it

Giovanna Morganti is an enologist, daughter of the late Enzo Morganti, who helped create San Felice (see last entry). She now has a small estate of her own, where she produces a fine Chianti Classico, Le Trame, using an organic cultivation system. She also has an apartment for summer rentals on her property.

San Regolo

TRATTORIA SAN REGOLO   SAN REGOLO, 33 53013 GAIOLE IN CHIANTI SIENA
RESTAURANT   TELEPHONE/FAX 0577 747136

OPEN Lunch; dinner Saturday, Sunday, and holidays   **CLOSED** Monday   **CREDIT CARDS** None
ENGLISH SPOKEN A little   **RESERVATIONS** Recommended   **PRICE** $$$
DIRECTIONS In the village center

San Regolo is a tiny village near Brolio Castle. The trattoria, run by the Fabbri family, has a luminous dining room overlooking the imposing castle and its vineyards. The cuisine is strictly Tuscan, beginning with a selection of assorted *crostini* or *salumi*. The seasonal homemade vegetable soups are thick and satisfying. Hand-made egg noodles, tagliatelle, are served with a choice of hearty sauces: the mushroom has a deep woodsy flavor from locally found porcini. Ravioli filled with ricotta and spinach and sauced with sage and butter are delicate despite the fairly thick pasta. At San Regolo, the best main courses are the simplest: steaks and chops grilled over aromatic wood embers, *alla brace*. Roasted meats are sliced thin and served with savory gravy. A warning to the salt conscious: the Tuscans like their food highly salted, but the kitchen will reduce it if asked when ordering.

Desserts are homemade. The wine list reads like a local road map—Cacchiano, Brolio, Ama, San Felice, Fèlsina. The Fabbri women do the cooking, leaving the serving to Carlino and his nice son, Fabrizio. This is the kind of relaxed, friendly restaurant that it is always a pleasure to go back to.

Villa a Sesta

LA BOTTEGA DEL TRENTA
RESTAURANT

VIA SANTA CATERINA, 2 VILLA A SESTA 53019
CASTELNUOVO BERARDENGA SIENA
TELEPHONE 0577 359226

OPEN Lunch and dinner Saturday, Sunday; dinner only Thursday, Friday, Monday
CLOSED Tuesday, Wednesday; holidays in January and November   **CREDIT CARDS** Visa, MC, Amex
ENGLISH SPOKEN Yes   **FEATURES** Outdoor dining courtyard   **RESERVATIONS** Necessary
PRICE $$$$–$$$$$ **DIRECTIONS** The restaurant is in the village of Villa a Sesta

This restaurant is situated in a flowery courtyard. There is no sign, and the only menu, or indication of pricing, is outside the front door. Diners are expected to eat a complete four-course meal; those not in the mood for so much food will be better received elsewhere. The long and complicated menu is recited aloud. The restaurant's chef, Madame Stoquelet, is French, though she has lived in Italy for years. Her cooking reflects this binationalism.

This restaurant's fusion cuisine can be very good: antipasti feature the locally appreciated stuffed goose neck. *Primi* include celery-filled ravioli with piquant Gorgonzola sauce and subtle spinach and ricotta *malfatti*, which are like the filling from ravioli without the pasta casing, set off here by shavings of pungent truffle. In the main courses, the French influence is particularly apparent. Succulent duck baked slowly with wild fennel has the uncomplicated refinement of French country cooking. The boned saddle of lamb is wrapped in a crust with spinach and is of the cut and type of lamb that is rarely seen in Italy. Our "vegetarian" plate was a disappointment, as the smoky-flavored eggplant rolls contained ham.

Desserts are expertly handled with the sophistication of French *patisserie*. A delicate almond *cialde* is accompanied by a velvety white chocolate mousse, and the lemon mousse tart is cool and frothy, served with a sharp fresh strawberry sauce. Wines are well chosen, but the service left much to be desired.

Volpaia

CASTELLO   **PIAZZA CISTERNA, 1 VOLPAIA 53017 RADDA IN CHIANTI SIENA**
DI VOLPAIA   **TELEPHONE 0577 738066   FAX 0577 738619**
WINE, OLIVE OIL, VINEGAR   **WEB SITE www.volpaia.com**

OPEN Shop 9:00–20:00; cellar visits and tastings by prior written request only   **CLOSED** February
CREDIT CARDS Visa, MC, Amex   **DIRECT SALE** Yes   **ENGLISH SPOKEN** Yes
OTHER Two villas, five apartments for holiday rental; English-language cooking school
DIRECTIONS From Radda, go toward Greve; Volpaia is signposted to the right after about 4 kms

---

"Wine is a food," asserted Giovannella Stianti Mascheroni. "In Tuscany it was a food you lived on, a pleasurable but vital part of daily life. What seems to be missing now is the story behind it. My wine reflects my tastes, my philosophy—that is why it takes a lifetime to make."

Everything at Volpaia—wine, oil, vinegar, even label design—was conceived with the same spirit by Giovannella and her husband. The extra-virgin olive oil, for example, is made of hand-picked, homegrown olives milled in their own *frantoio*. It uses modern Sinolea machinery that draws the oil free from the mass, ensuring that only the *"fior, fiore,"* or choicest part, is extracted. And it really is excellent.

"We have researched everything," continued the tall, elegant Giovannella, "and selected the best, then we have brought it to Volpaia." That has been no mean feat. For in the medieval village that is Volpaia, some rather "out-of-the-way things" have happened. Not that you would notice from the outside, for the buildings' original exteriors have been rigorously maintained. The change is inside: open any of the small wooden doors into the village's houses and you will be confronted with an image that reminded me of the very large Alice crammed into the very small White Rabbit's house. Behind one, a stone cottage has been gutted and filled with a giant stainless steel fermentation tank, complete with overhead walkways. Behind another, a tiny church is stuffed with vast wooden barrels; another hides stacks of new French *barriques*. So it goes on, each door revealing a part of the complex whole. "We had to lower the big tanks in through the roofs with a crane," laughed Giovannella as she saw my amazement. "And there are miles of underground tubing, so the wines are never transported outside."

For the winemaking, the couple is assisted by the experienced enologist Maurizio Castelli. Their fine range includes Chianti Classico; its Riserva; Coltassala, of Sangioveto and Mammolo grapes, which has now become a Chianti Classico Riserva *cru*, and Balifico, of Sangioveto and Cabernet, both of which are aged in *barriques;* the white Bianco DOC Val d'Arbia, a blend of Trebbiano, Malvasia, and Chardonnay; and a wonderful rich Vin Santo.

VOLPAIA'S ARTISAN VINEGARS

Volpaia is the only winery in Tuscany presently licensed to make vinegar. By law, winemaking facilities must be situated some distance from those making vinegar. At Volpaia the traditional system is used.

"To make good vinegar, you must start with good wine," explained Carlo Mascheroni, the estate's owner, "and transform it slowly. That way its components, its perfumes, will remain in the vinegar."

Wine turns to vinegar with the help of oxygen—the vinegar-making bacteria need air to live. This good wine is impregnated with specially grown cultures and then aerated by being pumped slowly and repeatedly through a tank containing *trucioli*—wood shavings, of oak and chestnut, and grapevine trimmings. This motion breaks up the wine and feeds the bacteria that thrive on enzymes in the wood. The pumped wine is kept at a steady temperature of 35°C/95°F. After about twenty days it will have become vinegar. A secondary fermentation may then be initiated, using a "mother" culture, to enhance the vinegar's secondary bouquet.

Volpaia's red and white wine vinegars are aged in *barriques* previously used for winemaking. The vinegar absorbs noble tannins from these oak barrels, which "infuse the bouquet with extraordinary elegance," Mascheroni said. They are then given a final treatment. Five groups of *aromi*, natural flavors, are used to perfume the vinegars: groups of herbs, flowers, and spices are placed in muslin bags and left to macerate in the vinegars for about two months. The final vinegars are numbered from one to five: 1 Herbs; 2 Spices; 3 Kitchen Garden; 4 Flowers; 5 Fresh. These subtle yet characterful vinegars are available at Volpaia and make wonderful additions to any creative cook's palette.

CHAPTER 9

Grosseto and the Maremma

*G*rosseto is the capital of a large province divided between coastal plains and the Metalliferous Mountains. Much of what is now the Maremma, a fertile terrain favored by agriculture, was once swampland infested with malarial mosquitoes. Projects to drain and reclaim (*bonificare*) this land were carried out by the Etruscans and the Romans, but not until the twentieth century was the mission successfully completed.

The coast and hills held Etruscan cities: Vetulonia, Roselle, and Saturnia (still a renowned spa), with Tarquinia, Vulci, and Tuscania just over Tuscany's southern border in Lazio. The tufa hills are rich in iron ore and other metals, which the Etruscans extracted and worked. Many tomb sites still exist in this beautiful countryside rich in ancient culture; the towns of Pitigliano, Sorano, and Sovana are fascinating to visit.

If the Maremma was once an untamed land of cowboys (*butteri*), game, and natural hazards, today it offers some of the region's most glorious countryside. In spring the gently rolling hills are full of wildflowers: small pink gladioli, blue clouds of borage, scented wood cyclamen, rock roses and alium, thyme and fennel. Sheep graze on aromatic grasses in hill pastures; their pecorino cheeses are sweet and fresh. Wild boar, roebuck, and smaller game live in the woods and in the natural reserve, Parco dell'Uccellina. The local cooking is rustic but flavorful, with peasant soups such as *l'acquacotta* and stews of game and wild mushrooms in the hills, and spicy octopus and other appetizing seafood on the coast. Massa Marittima, the jewel of the Maremma, is a medieval town with a splendid Duomo; it makes the best *panforte*, Tuscany's classic honey and spice confection.

In recent years there has been an explosion of new viticulture in the Maremma: the successes of Morellino and the wines of Bolgheri have encouraged many important wineries from northern Italy and Tuscany to invest in vineyards here.

AZIENDA PROMOZIONE TURISTICA
VIA FUCINI, 43 C
58100 GROSSETO
0564 414303, FAX 0564 454606
www.grosseto.turismo.toscana.it
aptgrosseto@grosseto.turismo.toscana.it

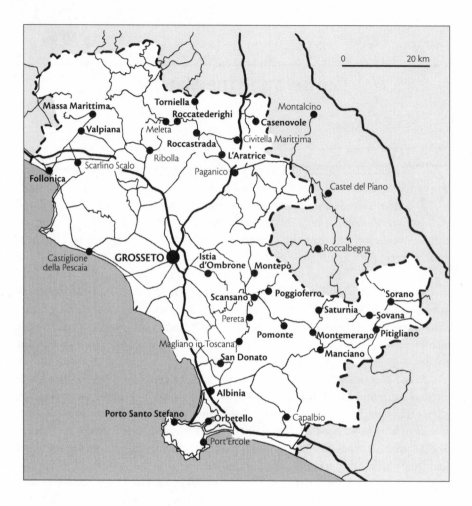

Boldface type indicates towns that are included in this chapter.

Albinia di Orbetello

LA PARRINA
CHEESE, WINE

KM 146 SS 1 AURELIA LA PARRINA 58010 ALBINIA
TELEPHONE 0564 862636   FAX 0564 862626
WEB SITE www.parrina.it

OPEN Shop 8:00–13:00, 15:00–18:00 (till 20:00 in summer); farm and *cantina* visits by appointment only   **CLOSED** National holiday afternoons   **CREDIT CARDS** Visa, MC, Amex
MAIL ORDER Yes   **ENGLISH SPOKEN** Yes   **OTHER** La Parrina has three shops in Rome
DIRECTIONS From Orbetello, turn right off SS 1 Aurelia at km 146 beside Cacciatore restaurant. After about 2 kms, turn right onto the eucalyptus-lined dirt road leading to the farm

---

La Parrina is a lovely estate. Set in the low hills north of Orbetello, the picturesque farm buildings are framed by orchards and rose-covered walls. A well-run farm shop sells its cheeses, wine, produce, extra-virgin olive oil, and honey. La Parrina specializes in dairy products; its cheeses are made in a converted schoolhouse. Every day, the small dairy transforms the milk obtained from sixty goats and six hundred sheep.

Tuscan goat's cheeses, *caprini*, are subtle in flavor; they are salted less than their French counterparts. The *caprino nella cenere* is rolled in vegetable ash; it is very creamy—almost like fresh ricotta in its delicate sweetness. The small round *caprino stagionato* is matured; it has a flakier consistency with the same creaminess but no sharpness of flavor. Small *caprini*, flavored with truffles, peppercorns, or ash, also come preserved in olive oil in attractive glass jars. They keep well and make great presents. La Parrina's range of sheep's cheeses include the soft white spreadable *stracchinato;* the pliable, slightly sweet *cacciotte;* and the piquant, molded and matured *guttus*, their homage to French Roquefort. There also are thick tangy yogurts sold plain or flavored with fresh fruit. Shoppers are welcome to sample the cheeses.

The farm is run as ecologically as possible without conforming to the strictest organic standards; whenever possible, environmentally friendly practices are followed.

La Parrina started making wine in 1950 and in 1971 obtained Parrina DOC status for its red and white wines. The Riserva is a robust wine of 70 percent Sangiovese and 15 percent each of Cabernet Sauvignon and Pinot Nero; it is aged for three years, with eight months in *barriques*. The white is produced from Trebbiano Toscano, Malvasia, and Ansonica, a varietal that originated in Sicily as Inzolia. This interesting grape also stars in one of two new DOCs that recently were formed here: Ansonica Costa dell'Argentario DOC was created in 2000; Vialetto is a white Capalbio DOC (established in 1999) of pure Trebbiano. These drinkable wines are a good value in their category. La Parrina is even making a type of balsamic vinegar using must from its grapes aged for six months in small wooden casks at Modena—it does contain some wine vinegar (the strictly "traditional" *balsamico* does not), but it is still a nice vinegar.

Casenovole

NUOVA CASENOVOLE
BIODYNAMIC FARM,
OLIVE OIL, BEEF

CASENOVOLE 58030 CIVITELLA PAGANICO
TELEPHONE 0564 908951   FAX 0564 908912

OPEN Shop 9:00–13:00, 14:00–18:00; farm visits by appointment   **CLOSED** Sunday
CREDIT CARDS None   **DIRECT SALE** Yes, of dried goods (no meat)   **MAIL ORDER** Yes
ENGLISH SPOKEN Yes   **DIRECTIONS** From the Siena-Grosseto road (SS 223), exit at Casale di Pari;
follow signs to the farm

Nuova Casenovole is a large biodynamic farm producing organic grains, olive oil, and, unusually for Italy, raising organic beef. It is set in some of Tuscany's most beautiful countryside. I say "unusually" because organic meat hardly exists in Italy, despite the work of some of its European partners, and despite the health threats that have blighted meat recently. Indeed, the concept of what constitutes a dignified life for an animal generally leaves a lot to be desired in Italy. So Nuova Casenovole is a welcome, and important, exception.

Ironically, the farm began with purely commercial objectives. "We didn't make a committed, philosophical choice for this type of system," explained the farm's director, Riccardo Micheli. "We researched possibilities to make this vast tract of land profitable, and this solution worked best." Over time, however, the positive results are converting the unbelievers.

Nuova Casenovole is run using Rudolf Steiner's biodynamic model. The farm operates as a "closed cycle": crops are grown using only farm-produced natural fertilizers (manure); in turn, the animals eat only these cereals as supplements to their grazing pastures. As a biodynamic enterprise, the farm is under the strict auspices of Demeter, the German organization that controls all procedures, from planting to sales.

The most striking validation of this system is to be found with the animals themselves. A walk through their barns at feeding time (I visited in early spring, when the cows were calving) shows how completely different their lives are from their contemporaries'.

The cattle are grouped in "families": each bull living amid a herd of twenty-five cows. Calves also stay within the group for as long as they feed from their mothers. Each herd, with its bull, spends most of the year out at pasture. So there is no stress. You sense this peacefulness immediately. The animals rarely get sick, as they are contented and have no space restrictions. This is a boon for both animals and breeders.

"Conventional breeders spend an average of 1.100 lire per day per animal on veterinary expenses," Micheli said. "Whereas our cost is ridiculously low, at 23 lire per day, including the four dogs that guard the herds. The paradoxical thing is that veterinary rules for Italian animals are much stricter than other European countries'. Hormones are forbidden here [unlike in other countries]. Yet when it comes to the animals' living conditions, things are still primitive."

The cattle, of mainly the Limousin breed, are butchered at fourteen to sixteen months. The meat is not sold on the farm, so I couldn't taste any, but I was assured that the difference between it and conventional beef was "night and day"—and it's not hard to believe.

The farm also produces extra-virgin olive oil from its own olives and mill, as well as five types of hard wheat for the making of pasta. These goods are sold on the farm.

Follonica

PODERE SAN LUIGI
OLIVE OIL

I POGGETTI 58022 FOLLONICA
TELEPHONE 0566 51350   FAX 035 798283

OPEN Sales by appointment only   **CREDIT CARDS** None   **DIRECT SALE** Yes
ENGLISH SPOKEN No   **DIRECTIONS** From Follonica, go toward Massa Marittima. After about 1 km, pass the Metanauto station; at the next curve, follow the dirt road between two white arrows in the road to the farm

When it is well made, Maremman extra-virgin olive oil is sweet and full, qualities conferred to the olives by the mild climate and sea breezes. It is less bitter and less aggressive than the oils made on higher ground, but it still has a satisfying freshness. Antonio Perico's oil is some of the best I have found of this type. His 30 hectares (74 acres) of olive groves are situated just inland from Follonica, off the country road that leads to Massa Marittima. His olives are hand-picked and pressed in a modern *frantoio* nearby.

Perico's oil is available only privately: such is the demand that he has no trouble selling it. The family villa is just a few minutes' drive from Follonica, and the charming farm manager will meet clients there by appointment. The oil is available in bottles and 5 kilo (8.8 lb) cans.

DA SANTARINO
RESTAURANT

PIAZZA 24 MAGGIO, 21 58022 FOLLONICA
TELEPHONE 0566 41665

OPEN Lunch and dinner   **CLOSED** Tuesday in winter; October   **CREDIT CARDS** Visa, MC
ENGLISH SPOKEN A little   **RESERVATIONS** Recommended   **PRICE** $$–$$$
DIRECTIONS By the covered market in the town center

Santarino's fish trattoria is a local tradition at Follonica. Family run for more than thirty years, it is an unpretentious, informal place. The dining rooms, with their wooden booths and hunting-lodge decor, are always bustling.

A prime attraction is the *polpo lesso* (boiled octopus). It comes one to a plate (hand size), as tender as chicken, drizzled with olive oil and a hint of hot *peperoncino*. Pasta specials depend on fish availability, but there is always *spaghetti con scampi* (Mediterranean shrimp from Sardinia) or *vongole* (clams), tossed simply with garlic, parsley, and olive oil. Main courses are uncomplicated: the day's catch is broiled, baked in *cartoccio*, or poached. *Orata* (gilt-head bream), *dentice* (sea bream), and *spigola* (sea bass) are popular, as are *astice* (lobster) and *aragosta* (clawless spiny lobster). The house wines are local.

PIZZICHERIA MARRINI   VIA BICOCCHI, 85 58022 FOLLONICA
SPECIALTY FOODS: PASTA   TELEPHONE 0566 40093

OPEN 7:00–13:30, 16:00–20:30   CLOSED Wednesday afternoon; Sunday in winter; November
CREDIT CARDS Amex   ENGLISH SPOKEN No   OTHER Catering available for parties
and weddings   DIRECTIONS Via Bicocchi runs parallel to the sea, a few blocks inland

---

Renzo Marrini's family started producing fresh egg pasta in 1937. Stuffed pasta is made daily, with seasonal fillings of artichokes, asparagus, and pumpkin, with fish in summer. The business has expanded into a complete *gastronomia*, offering both ready-cooked dishes and local specialty foods. A large counter features home-cooked dishes: pastas and regional soups like *acquacotta* and *cacciucco*, pasta sauces, main courses, and desserts. Tuscan *salumi* and cheeses are also available. Packages of dried mushrooms and herbs make attractive gifts to take home. The Marrinis also stock Italian wines from many regions.

Also

Follonica has a lively covered market that is open Monday to Saturday (summer 9:30–13:30, 17:00–20:00; winter 9:30–13:30). It sells everything from bread and cheese to fruit and meat. Many stalls carry local produce: tender salad greens, fava beans (*baccelli*) to eat raw with pecorino, and wild herbs brought from the country. The area is also famous for its spring *carciofini* (tiny artichokes) for preserving in olive oil. Look for Pescheria Pallino, the market's best fish stall.

GELATERIA CARIBIA   VIALE ITALIA, 212. 0566 60059

Follonica's most popular *gelateria* is not its most central, but it's a nice walk along the beach road. The family-run *gelateria's* specialty is *gelato al forno*, a variation on baked Alaska. They also make refreshing *granite* of fresh fruit, ice-cream cakes, and a range of unusual gelato flavors.

Grosseto

HERBONATURA
HONEY

VIA TRIPOLI, 41 58100 GROSSETO
TELEPHONE 0564 417677

OPEN 9:00–13:00, 16:00–20:00   **CLOSED** Saturday afternoon in summer, Monday morning in winter   **CREDIT CARDS** Visa, MC   **ENGLISH SPOKEN** A little   **OTHER** Rossi's workshop is at Viale Caravaggio, 62 (tel: 20459). Honey is also available from there
DIRECTIONS The shop is just east of the walls of the old town, by the Teatro Moderno

This shop belongs to one of the Maremma's best beekeepers and sells honeys and other natural and herbal products. Novaro Rossi and his family travel around Tuscany with their hives practicing "nomadic" beekeeping.

In Italy, single-flower honeys must contain at least 50 percent of nectar from the named species. When the chestnut tree flowers in June, any hives located in a chestnut wood will then produce "chestnut" honey. After the flowers fade, the hives are emptied and relocated. Maremman species include *erica* (broom), rosemary, and *sulla*, a wildflower in the clover family. An unusual honey from higher ground is *melata di abete:* In hot humid weather, pine trees "sweat," exuding a sticky resin that attracts the bees. They transform it into an intense amber honey with a decisive resinous flavor. Add it to plain yogurt.

Rossi started working with bees as a hobby more than twenty-five years ago. It soon became a way of life. "Working with bees is a labor of love," his wife admitted. "But once you get to know them you realize they are better than most normal families!"

IL CANTO DEL GALLO
RESTAURANT

VIA MAZZINI, 29 58100 GROSSETO
TELEPHONE 0564 414589

OPEN Dinner only   **CLOSED** Sunday   **CREDIT CARDS** None   **ENGLISH SPOKEN** A little
RESERVATIONS Necessary   **PRICE** $$ **DIRECTIONS** In the old town

Nadia Svetoni, an ex-ceramicist, opened her personal little restaurant within the town's sixteenth-century Medicean walls in 1992. She may have banished tablecloths (she says they intimidate some local young diners), but the mood is feminine in this unusual vaulted space.

A self-taught cook with a penchant for vegetarian food, Nadia bases her menu on local specialties. Standard *crostini* of wild boar or chicken livers complement her selection of vegetable tarts. In winter she favors hearty soups of *farro* (spelt wheat) or chickpeas. Her pasta is handmade nearby and is very good. A brown rice risotto with grilled vegetables and wild mint sounded better than it was. Main courses vary but include chicken, stewed rabbit, wild boar, and at least one vegetable dish. A fresh ricotta mousse with wild berries makes a light, fragrant dessert.

Nadia works from a tiny kitchen, prepreparing as many dishes as possible, with slightly uneven results. But her price-to-quality ratio is good, and the service is friendly and attentive. She is also planning to open a shop for organic products.

MAREMMA MARKET   VIA TEANO, 3 58100 GROSSETO
SPECIALTY FOODS: SUPERMARKET   TELEPHONE 0564 23424   FAX 0564 23492

OPEN 8:00–13:00, 16:00–20:00   CLOSED Sunday   CREDIT CARDS Visa, MC
MAIL ORDER Yes   ENGLISH SPOKEN A little   DIRECTIONS From Grosseto's center go toward Scansano on Via Scansanese. Turn left onto Via Teano at the outskirts of Grosseto

---

This is an enterprising modern supermarket selling primarily Maremman products. Formerly a fruit warehouse, the building was modernized in 1993 when a cooperative of about a hundred local food producers launched this new venture. The result is a well-organized store with displays of locally grown fruits and vegetables, cheeses, *salumi*, fresh Maremman meat, wine, olive oil, and dried goods. Many fine producers and cooperatives are represented, including some organic ones. The service is friendly and helpful, the prices are competitive. All in all, a great store.

Also

BAR OLIMPICO   VIA BRIGATE PARTIGIANE, 32. 0564 415325

A short walk south of the old town, this unassuming bar is known for its homemade gelati. The *creme* assortment is particularly good: creamy and not too sweet. There is a deep, rich chocolate, *panna cotta, cremino,* chocolate mint, and one amusingly called *il dolce della suocera* (the mother-in-law's dessert), with a crumbly-crunchy topping.

Istia d'Ombrone

FATTORIA LE PUPILLE   PIAGGIE DEL MAIANO 58040 ISTIA D'OMBRONE
WINE   TELEPHONE 0564 409517   FAX 0564 409519
WEB SITE www.elisabettageppetti.com

OPEN Monday–Friday 8:00–17:00; Saturday by appointment; visits and tastings by appointment only
CLOSED Sunday   CREDIT CARDS Visa, MC, Amex   DIRECT SALE Yes, subject to availability
ENGLISH SPOKEN Yes   DIRECTIONS The winery is on the main road between Istia and Veselle, 1 km south of the bridge at Istia, on the right

---

Fattoria Le Pupille is perched up on top of a dome-round hill, one of two that are known locally as "the pupils"—*le pupille* seem like eyes staring up at the sky. The estate has been in the same family since the nineteenth century, but its role as trendsetter in the up-and-coming Maremman wine area of Scansano began in 1978, when Alfredo Gentile began aging the local Sangiovese and Alicante in

French *barriques* for the Morellino di Scansano and engaged the interest and services of Tuscany's most celebrated winemaker, Giacomo Tachis (he advised there until 1995). They experimented with the Bordeaux varietals, Cabernet Sauvignon and Merlot, and conceived southern Tuscany's finest super-Tuscan, Saffredi. It has become an award winner: an intense, concentrated wine of structure and elegance that set a standard for Maremman wines that is still being held.

Elisabetta Geppetti has run the estate since Alfredo's death. In 1997 she was joined by her husband, Stefano Rizzi, and recently they moved their headquarters to an attractive seventeenth-century house and built a big new *cantina* near Istria d'Ombrone. New vineyards have been planted in addition to those at Scansano, for a total of 60 hectares (148 acres). Their first wine has already proved its worth: Poggio Valente, a *cru* of Morellino from a single vineyard, has won Italy's coveted *"tre bicchieri"* (three glasses) award. The couple has had several consultants, but now they work with Christian Le Sommer, an experienced French enologist.

"Our wines already had their own character that is linked to this terrain, but we wanted fresh imput on them, to make them more elegant," Elisabetta explained as we walked through the large new *barricaia*. "We also have adopted a new work policy in the vineyards," she continued. "Each member of our team is responsible for one vineyard and makes many of the primary decisions for it—and this too has led to better results."

Geppetti is a believer in Sangiovese and other authocthonous grapes, such as Alicante and Malvasia Nera—indeed, a new wine is being made of these two. The winery is known for its great red wines, but it also makes a desert wine. Le Sommer has worked at Chateau d'Yquem, and Le Pupille's new version of Solalto, its late-harvest wine, should give delicious results.

L'Aratrice

DISTILLERIA ARTIGIANA DI NANNONI
GRAPPA, VINEGAR

FATTORIA DI LITIANO L'ARATRICE 58048 PAGANICO
TELEPHONE 0564 905204   FAX 0564 905580

OPEN 8:00–12:00, 14:00–18:00   **CLOSED** Saturday, Sunday; August   **CREDIT CARDS** Visa, MC
DIRECT SALE Yes   **ENGLISH SPOKEN** No   **DIRECTIONS** The dark red distillery is on the road that runs north-south between the Paganico-Roccastrada and the Civitella-Roccastrada roads, north of L'Aratrice

---

Gioacchino Nannoni could be called the father of Tuscany's "designer" grappa. Nannoni, a spirited man with twinkling eyes, learned his craft in northern Italy, where the concept of single-grape-variety grappa was not unknown. "Twenty-five years ago," he explained, "nothing of quality was being done in Tuscany. I believed a great grappa could be made from Brunello, as was being produced in Piedmont from Barolo."

The first experiments were made in 1972 in collaboration with Montalcino's Altesino. Fresh *vinacce,* the wine-soaked grape residues left over from the wine-making process, were distilled; the resulting grappa retained the perfumes specific to Brunello. Other fine Tuscan estates followed suit.

"Great grappa depends on having high-quality, fresh *vinacce,*" Nannoni continued. "The rest hinges on the type of still and the distiller's experience."

The *vinacce* are first distilled directly by steam—in this "tumultuous" process, everything is extracted from the grape residues. A second, indirect, distillation is more delicate, allowing the grape's perfumes to remain in the grappa. The third and final distillation takes place in a copper column 3 meters (about 3 yards) high. The distiller then separates the "heart" of the grappa from its "head" and "tail" (both the first and last parts of the distillate are full of impurities and must be discarded). Nannoni revealed his trick for doing this: "Mother Nature comes to the rescue of distracted distillers," he chuckled. "At the top of the distilling column is an outlet called the 'mushroom,' covered over with fine netting, where the vapors escape. When the grappa passes the 'head' and enters the 'heart,' or middle section, a cloud of minuscule flies is attracted to its sweet, aromatic fumes. When he sees those flies the distiller knows the good part of the grappa has been reached. He can open a valve and siphon it into a vat. Once the flies disperse he shuts it off, excluding the impure 'tail.'"

Grappa, like wine, improves with age. Colorless grappa matures in the bottle and is sold after seven to eight months. Golden *riserva* grappa is aged in small wood *barriques* for three to five years and acquires a more complex aroma. Nannoni recommends that grappa be drunk within four to five months once the bottle has been opened.

From his distillery, Nannoni sells named Tuscan estate *grappe* as well as his unusual and delicious *aspretti,* under the Rossana Rosini label. These are fruit vinegars with a difference. The *aspretto di mora,* for example, is made from 90 percent blackberry juice with 10 percent distilled blackberry spirit added; the mixture is fermented as vinegar, filtering through beech-wood shavings to acquire enzymes. The *aspretti* are matured in small wooden kegs for one to two years before being bottled. The blackberry *aspretto,* reddish-brown in color, has a full bouquet of mellow fruit balanced with a hint of acidity.

The vinegars come in several flavors. With their distinctive fruit accents, *aspretti* are great in cooking: try sprinkling a few drops on meat, poultry, or game before serving. They may even be added to cocktails for a note of fruity sharpness.

Manciano

CASEIFICIO SOCIALE MANCIANO
CHEESE

PIANO DI CIRIGNANO 58014 MANCIANO
TELEPHONE 0564 609137, 609193   FAX 0564 609043
WEB SITE www.caseificio-manciano.com

OPEN Shop 7:30–13:00; tours by appointment only   CLOSED Sunday   CREDIT CARDS Visa
ENGLISH SPOKEN A little   DIRECTIONS From Albinia, take SS 74 toward Manciano. Do not take
the first right turn for the Caseificio, which appears after 18 kms. Continue for 5 kms, turning right
toward Vallerana (across the road from a trattoria). After 4 kms you will pass a sign saying "Chiarone
Scalo 4." Take the second left turn after it. The Caseificio is 100 meters down this road on the right

This cooperative was formed in 1961 and now has five hundred members; it pools
the resources of local sheep and cow farmers. The factory combines artisan techniques with modern technology to produce its large quota of cheeses, which are
exported to Europe and the United States.

Fresh milk is computer tested and pasteurized before being "transformed"
into cheese. The Pecorino Toscano DO (*Denominazione di Origine*) is considered an
"eating" cheese when it has matured for 30 to 60 days. The consistency is smooth
and compact, with an aromatic sweetness characteristic of sheep's milk. Left to
mature for more than 120 days, it becomes *stagionato;* still a cheese to eat rather
than grate, it remains tender while acquiring a saltier, decisive sharpness. The
Maremma's pastures give sheep's milk a distinctive flavor, more refined and less
forceful than its Sardinian counterparts.

Other cheeses include Saturnella, a delicate *caciotta* of mixed sheep's and cow's
milk, aged for only two weeks, and a fresh-tasting creamy ricotta of mixed milks.

MANLIO & CLARA VITICOLTORI: LA STELLATA
WINE

VIA FORNACINA, 18 58014 MANCIANO
TELEPHONE 0564 620190   FAX 0564 620190
WEB SITE www.web.tiscalinet.it/lastellata

OPEN Visits, sales, and tastings by appointment only   CREDIT CARDS None   DIRECT SALE Yes
ENGLISH SPOKEN A little   OTHER Three apartments for holiday rentals
DIRECTIONS La Stellata is on SS 74, about 3 kms from Manciano toward Pitigliano

Abbiamo fato una scelta di vita e di vite: "We chose our life and our vines." In 1983
Clara Divizia and Manlio Giorni left Rome, moved to the Maremma, and started a
vineyard. "We were not wine experts then, just looking for a different way of life.
The passion for winemaking has grown on us," admitted Clara.

And they are good at it. Under their label, La Stellata, they produce a Bianco di
Pitigliano DOC called Lunaia that was one of the first interesting white wines from
the Maremma. Relatively *profumato*, it has the slightly bitter aftertaste characteristic of grapes grown on tufa.

"A lot of our decisions are made while the grapes are still on the vine," explained Clara. The *potatura verde,* or green pruning, reduces the quantity of grapes to favor the quality of those that remain. Working with winemaker Massimo Albanese, they have replanted some vineyards to red grape varieties, from which they produce two Lunaia reds: one is sold young and sees no wood; the other is aged in large barrels. Half of their 5 hectares (12 acres) of vineyards are planted to Trebbiano Toscano, the mainstay of Lunaia, with some Malvasia, Grechetto, and Verdello. Clara and Manlio also make grappa. They live in a colorful house full of cats and dogs, and they welcome visitors.

Massa Marittima

LE LOGGE
PASTRY

PIAZZA GARIBALDI, 11/13 58024 MASSA MARITTIMA
TELEPHONE 0566 901827; BAKERY 0566 919923
FAX 0566 905849   E-MAIL pasticcerialelogge@libero.it

OPEN Winter 6:00–20:00; summer 6:00–midnight   **CLOSED** Tuesday except in July and August
CREDIT CARDS Visa, MC   **MAIL ORDER** Yes   **ENGLISH SPOKEN** Yes
DIRECTIONS The *pasticceria* and bar are under the arched portico up the hill from the Duomo

Panpepatus was a medieval delicacy savored by ecclesiastics with Vin Santo at Christmas. They valued the dense confection for the rarity of its ingredients: nuts and candied fruits, pepper and Oriental spices. Dominated by Siena for three hundred years, Massa Marittima justly makes claims on this Sienese specialty. The late Giuseppe Schillaci was an experienced *pasticciere* when he began making it. He perfected an original recipe from 1300.

Legend dictated that the confection be as hard as glass, softened at a fire before eating. The modern *panforte,* literally "strong bread," is made just soft enough to chew. In their small bakery, the Schillacis handmake it in dark (*nero*) and light (*bianco*) versions, using the finest ingredients. The results are excellent: their *panforti* are exquisitely refined—a cut above their Sienese counterparts.

"The recipe for the light *panforte* called for 15 percent almonds," explained Giuseppe's son Paolo. "We increased it to 28 percent of top-quality Pugliese almonds." *Panforte* comes in flat cakes, cut into thin wedges before eating. It is a complex taste experience: the *bianco* features aromatic almonds in a warmly spiced golden paste with highlights of candied citrus; the deeply spiced dark *panforte* includes toasted hazelnuts, cocoa, pepper, cinnamon, and candied melon. Both are delicious. The bakery also makes great *cantucci* and *cavallucci* biscuits. Next door, in Via Goldoni, 5A, the Schillacis also run a specialty foods shop.

Le Logge's *panforti* are named for *Il Balestro,* a traditional crossbow contest between Massa Marittima's neighborhoods that is held in Piazza del Duomo, where the *pasticceria* is situated. Paolo Schillaci won it in 1995. The *balestra* is held on the first Sunday after May 20, and on the second Sunday of August.

TAVERNA DEL	VIA NORMA PARENTI, 12 58024 MASSA MARITTIMA
VECCHIO BORGO	TELEPHONE/FAX 0566 903950
RESTAURANT	

OPEN Dinner only   **CLOSED** Sunday evening in winter; Monday   **CREDIT CARDS** Visa, MC, Amex   **ENGLISH SPOKEN** A little   **RESERVATIONS** Recommended   **PRICE** $$$
DIRECTIONS From the Duomo, go down the small street to the left; the Taverna is on the left

Claudio Bindi is a devotee of all things Maremman. A fine selection of *salumi* from Monte Amiata, rustic soups of grains and pulses, succulent grilled mountain lamb, stewed boar and rabbit—the classics of this hearty country cuisine—are served with style, accompanied by a fine selection of local vintages. Claudio's wife, Grazia Innocenti, is an *appassionata* of the kitchen, a natural cook with a flair for vegetables and desserts. The combination works.

MORIS FARMS	FATTORIA POGGETTI CURA NUOVA 58024 MASSA MARITTIMA
WINE	TELEPHONE 0566 919135 FAX 0566 919380
	WEB SITE www.morisfarms.it

OPEN Winery sales 8:00–17:00; tastings and visits by appointment   **CLOSED** Saturday, Sunday
CREDIT CARDS Visa, MC   **ENGLISH SPOKEN** Yes   **DIRECTIONS** From Scarlino, go toward Massa Marittima; the winery is on the right: follow the avenue of cypresses

Moris Farms was one of the first wineries to understand the potential of the Maremma for quality winemaking. The Moris family had long had large holdings in the Maremma, but until the 1980s their wines were produced for quantity. "We took over my wife's father's farm in 1978," explained Adolfo Parentini. "In 1988 we brought wines to Vinitaly—Italy's prestigious wine fair—and realized we were way behind. We had to greatly improve or close."

They improved: new vineyards were planted, grape yields dramatically reduced, winemaker Attilio Pagli consulted, and modern cellaring methods applied. Beautiful buildings were restored for wine tasting and hospitality. Two *enoteche* selling their wines, bottled and not, were opened in Massa Marittima, Via Butigni, 1 (tel: 0566 901599) and Follonica, Via Lamarmora, 30 (tel: 0566 40617).

Moris Farms produces a fine Morellino di Scansano DOC and its Riserva. Avvoltore, a forceful Sangiovese-Cabernet super-Tuscan, set a standard for other modern-style wines in the area. Recently the list has been extended to include Moris Moteregio di Massa Marittima: of pure Sangiovese, it is positioned between the Morellino and its Riserva, spending some time in wood.

A curiosity: At the Cura Nuova farm, wild boar are raised. Being bred in captivity seems to have tamed the piglike animal's wildness: I found them snoozing lazily in the sun.

Montemerano

DA CAINO
RESTAURANT

VIA CANONICA, 3 58050 MONTEMERANO
TELEPHONE 0564 602817 FAX 0564 602807
WEB SITE www.dacaino.it

OPEN Lunch and dinner **CLOSED** Wednesday; Thursday lunch; holidays in January and July
CREDIT CARDS Visa, MC, Amex **ENGLISH SPOKEN** Yes **RESERVATIONS** Necessary
PRICE $$$$$ **DIRECTIONS** In the village center

Caino is one of the Maremma's, if not Tuscany's, most refined and admired restaurants, and the cooking there seems to improve with each year. Two rooms without views are subtly lit and decorated in discreet, traditional style, with exposed rafters, terra-cotta floors, clean-lined chairs, and fine china. Maurizio Menichetti is a skilled sommelier, his wife, Valeria, a self-taught chef. A warmly attractive, modest woman who brings to mind a Maillol sculpture, Valeria cooks everything in her tiny kitchen, aided by two women.

The large menu includes two *degustazione,* or tasting, menus—of "creative" recipes or of classic Maremman dishes. Everything is prepared with care and attention to detail. Many vegetables are homegrown, breads are homemade, and Valeria's *sott'olii* are exceptional—these and her other preserves are on sale in the restaurant shop.

Valeria's spring sampler began with a hot Mediterranean "pudding" of eggplant, red peppers, and zucchini, accompanied by cold fresh tomato sauce and peppery olive oil. Pigeon terrine looked like a jewel on the plate: rosy pâté was studded with black truffles and pale pigeon breast on a bed of wild leaves. The flavor was refined—gamy, but subtly so.

Pasta dishes were wonderful. Thin handmade egg pasta was formed into *tortelli*—like round ravioli—and stuffed with a delicate filling of fresh sheep's cheese and pear. They were sprinkled with poppy seeds and accompanied by a fine beet sauce. *Pappardelle* noodles scented with fresh herbs were sauced with guinea fowl *in bianco* (without a tomato base) with a bit of Parmesan to bind it. The meat course was memorable. A soft greenish "crust" of finely ground artichokes encased a brilliantly tender loin of lamb, pink-centered with seared edges. The almost caramel-sweet meat went perfectly with its savory coating.

Valeria's golden-topped *crème brûlée di ricotta* was fragrant from local ricotta and vanilla; a hot little chocolate pastry "drum" opened to release its own sauce. It was served with pineapple sorbet. Well-executed *piccola pasticceria,* intricate small cookies and candies, ended this interesting meal of complex flavors. The exceptional wine list includes Tuscany's and the Maremma's best—ask to visit Maurizio's new aging cellars around the corner from the restaurant; they are spectacular.

TRATTORIA DA VERDIANA
RESTAURANT

STRADA SCANSANESE 58050 MONTEMERANO
TELEPHONE 0564 602576

OPEN Lunch and dinner   **CLOSED** Wednesday; vacations variable   **CREDIT CARDS** Visa, MC
ENGLISH SPOKEN A little   **FEATURES** Summer dining terrace   **RESERVATIONS** Recommended
for dinner and on weekends   **PRICE** $$$ **DIRECTIONS** From Montemerano, go toward Scansano
on the SS 322; the restaurant is on the right after the turnoff toward Saturnia

---

This reasonably priced country trattoria is run by a mother and her son and daughter-in-law. Sergio Ciampani hosts, and his wife, Anna Rita, cooks—very well. The menu is unusually imaginative, and not just for rural Tuscany. The Ciampanis have sought out high-quality ingredients and put them to good use.

In the spring, *antipasti* included nice salad combinations: goat's cheese with roebuck prosciutto and bitter green radicchio; arugula with fresh porcini mushrooms; and smoked prosciutto of goat with pear, pecorino, and arugula; plus, there was a tempting wild-mint frittata. An airy *gnocco* of ricotta and semolina was delicately fragrant and granular; its vivid green sauce was of field borage and nettle. Chestnut-flour tortelli were speckled like bird's eggs. Their sweetness complemented the stuffing of fennel-scented wild boar. Vegetable-based soups included artichoke.

Some rustic game recipes followed: mountain lamb flavored with marjoram; hare with onions; local venison marinated in apple vinegar and herbs; and wood pigeon baked with green olives. Vegetarian dishes included eggplant cooked with thyme, *porcini* with mint and baked tomatoes, stewed zucchini, and wild salad leaves. Fresh goat's cheese came with aromatic chestnut honey. And to finish, a palate-clearing sorbet of pink grapefruit.

The good wine list contains some big reds to match the robust meat cookery. The restaurant is attractive, airy, and colorful, with a few tables outside in summer.

Montepò

CASTELL DI MONTEPÒ
WINE

PANCOLE 58054 SCANSANO
TELEPHONE 0577 847121, 0564 580231   FAX 0577 847131
E-MAIL bsanti@sienanet.it

OPEN All week; visits by previous appointment   **CREDIT CARDS** No   **DIRECT SALE** Yes
ENGLISH SPOKEN Yes   **DIRECTIONS** Montepò is signposted from the SS 322 between Scansano
and Grosseto, near the village of Pancole

Jacopo Biondi Santi has launched into an ambitious new venture. In 1998 he bought the imposing eleventh-century castle at Montepò and its surrounding property from the nephew of the writer Graham Greene. The monolithic castle's position is unique: it sits on a naturally impregnable pinnacle within a 360-degree amphitheater of woods, vineyards, and fields.

"In the Middle Ages, this was one of the biggest farms in Tuscany, with 400,000 hectares [988,000 acres]," Biondi Santi explained as we toured the new vineyards in a Jeep. "But now the farm totals a more modest 360 hectares [889 acres]. As soon as we came here, I had a complete set of analyses done—of soil, sun exposure, drainage, et cetera. I discovered it has its own microclimate, protected from the sea by the hills that surround it."

Working with the senior enologist Vittorio Fiore, Biondi Santi started planting 30 hectares (74 acres) of vineyards, to Sangiovese, Merlot, and Cabernet Sauvignon. Within five years he hopes to increase that to 80 (197). "For now, I am planting varieties that will go into my existing wine list, but I also want to experiment with local grape types such as Ciliegiolo," he said.

The estate produces a Morellino di Scansano DOC, and the elegant Montepaone IGT of Cabernet Sauvignon vines that were planted by the Greenes. These wines complement the others in Jacopo Biondi Santi's stable: Sassoalloro IGT of pure Sangiovese; and super-Tuscan Schidione IGT, of Sangiovese, Cabernet, and Merlot. "I hope that something of my family's 200 years of experience making elegant wines from Sangiovese at Montalcino (see p 311) will have passed into my DNA," he laughed, as we drove back up the steep road to the castle.

Orbetello

ORBETELLO PESCA LAGUNARE
LAGOON FISH, RESTAURANT

VIA LEOPARDI, 9 58015 ORBETELLO
TELEPHONE 0564 860288

OPEN Shop Monday–Saturday morning. Restaurant dinner only every evening mid-June–September 10 (outdoors); winter Friday–Sunday   **CLOSED** Lunch; weeknights in winter
CREDIT CARDS None   **DIRECT SALE** Yes   **ENGLISH SPOKEN** A little
RESERVATIONS Appreciated   **PRICE** $$–$$$ **DIRECTIONS** In the town center, on the laguna shore

If you are in search of the real flavors of the sea and the authentic cuisine of the Maremman coast, don't miss this place. Local fishermen of the lagoon have formed a cooperative and set up shop to sell their fish, with a restaurant operating in the evenings. "Our lagoon's fish have a clean, protected environment and feed from the plankton and small fish that are particular to these waters," explained one of the fishermen, Rodolfo.

The shop sells both the fresh catch of the day and the "transformed" products the cooperative specializes in: *bottarga di cefalo,* dried gray mullet roe; *cefalo affumicato,* smoked gray mullet; and *anguilla sfumata,* eel that is pickled, dried, and dressed with a very *piccante* tomato sauce.

As for the restaurant, it started casually. "We began with a *sagra,* or weeklong festival, dedicated to our fish and their recipes," Rodolfo said. "It was such a success that it was prolonged—and now we do it all summer long."

The waterfront by the little port is used for fishing in the morning. Then it is "cleaned up a bit" and set with as many tables as will fit. "The kitchen is small, but we're well organized," he laughed. In cooler weather the restaurant moves indoors to the town's handsomely restructured ex-abbatoir. The recipes are the real thing—those the fishermen's wives have cooked in this area for generations.

Pitigliano

IL LABORATORIO DELL'ERBORISTA
HERBAL PRODUCTS

VIA ZUCCARELLI, 31 58017 PITIGLIANO
TELEPHONE 0564 615450, 619417

OPEN 9:00–12:30, 16:30–19:00   **CLOSED** Monday, some Sunday mornings   **CREDIT CARDS** None
MAIL ORDER Yes   **ENGLISH SPOKEN** No   **DIRECTIONS** In the town center

This small herbalist's shop is on the narrow street that leads down through the town's old Jewish ghetto to the newly refurbished synagogue. The enterprising women who run it, Costanza Giunti and Fiorella Campana, complemented their university degrees with long apprenticeships and studies of the local flora. Using pesticide-free plants they have grown or picked themselves, they distill extracts and tinctures in their laboratory. Their beauty products include carrot cream (for dry skin), sage and thyme skin tonics, and nettle shampoo.

Edible products include local honeys, tomato-based vegetarian pasta sauces, and homemade jams that seemed to me oversweet and overcooked, as is so often the case in Italy.

MACELLERIA GIOVANNINO
MEAT: SALUMI

VIA ROMA, 76 58017 PITIGLIANO
TELEPHONE 0564 616108

OPEN 7:00–13:00, 16:30–19:30   **CLOSED** Sunday; Monday and Wednesday afternoon
CREDIT CARDS None   **ENGLISH SPOKEN** No   **DIRECTIONS** In the town center

Enrico Polidori was hand-twisting a string of little pork sausages as we talked: "My grandmother was famous for these. In those days the shop was run by women; the men did the heavy butchering. Now it's different: I serve in the shop and prepare the meat. I think women like to have a man to talk to when they do their shopping."

His grandmother also made the rare *culatello di cinghiale,* prepared from the top round of wild boar's leg. Polidori gets the boar from local hunters, or when some are culled to keep the numbers down. A most unusual *salume* is *prosciutto di tacchino,* a scaled-down version of the familiar salt-cured ham made not from pork but from a turkey's leg.

OSTERIA IL TUFO ALLEGRO
RESTAURANT

VICOLO DELLA COSTITUZIONE, 2 58017 PITIGLIANO

TELEPHONE 0564 616192

OPEN Lunch and dinner   **CLOSED** Tuesday; Wednesday lunch   **CREDIT CARDS** Visa, MC, Amex
ENGLISH SPOKEN Yes   **RESERVATIONS** Necessary on weekends   **PRICE** $$$
DIRECTIONS In the town center

Domenico Pechini's *osteria* is well named: it's an informal, cheerful place to enjoy sensitively cooked Maremman dishes, and its lower cellars have been carved out of the tufa cliff. Indeed, you can descend five levels below the street if you visit Pechini's ambitious wine collection, which offers the best wines from the area, central Tuscany, and beyond. Drink the wines with your meal or buy bottles to take home.

I found the food delicious: this is country fare at its best, neither too rustic nor too refined. A smooth rabbit terrine is wrapped in eggplant slices, flavored subtly with black olives, and baked. Warm chicken liver mousse is served with Vin Santo jelly and set off by thin slices of *capocollo*, a salt-cured pork shoulder *salume*. Pechini works well with native herbs: a broth of fresh white beans is delicately perfumed with marjoram, while *tagliolini* are dressed with soft chunks of sheep's ricotta, tomato, and wild fennel. His saddle of rabbit is moist and flavorful, stuffed with garden greens and served with *fagioli del Purgatorio*, a variety of delicately skinned beans that grow only nearby, at the lake of Bolsena. Finish your meal—and your wine—with a selection of great local cheeses, including the *caprini* from La Parrina (see p 223).

CANTINA COOPERATIVA
DI PITIGLIANO
WINE

VIGNAGRANDE 58017 PITIGLIANO

TELEPHONE 0564 616133   FAX 0564 616142

WEB SITE www.cantinadipitigliano.it

OPEN Shop 8:00–13:00, 15:00–18:00; *cantina* visits and tastings by appointment only
CLOSED Sunday   **CREDIT CARDS** None   **DIRECT SALE** Yes   **ENGLISH SPOKEN** Yes
FEATURES Kosher wine is produced here   **OTHER** Winery shop is in Via Santachiara (di Sorano),
Pitigliano, open Monday to Saturday and Sunday afternoon   **DIRECTIONS** From Pitigliano, take the
SS 74 toward Orvietto; the Cantina is on the right after about 1 km

---

Pitigliano was once known as the "Little Jerusalem." An imposing medieval town carved directly from the tufa cliff it sits on, its origins go back beyond the Etruscans to the Bronze Age. Pitigliano's Jewish community, which first settled there around 1500, swelled over the next few centuries to more than five thousand before meeting a violent end at the hands of the Fascists in World War II, despite the resistance of the local people. The town is proud of its Jewish heritage, and in recent years it has refurbished the synagogue and renovated the former "ghetto." That explains why Pitigliano's large Cantina Cooperativa lists two kosher wines among its products, a Bianco di Pitigliano DOC, and a red table wine, *della Piccola Gerusalemme*. The entire winemaking process for these wines is carried out by a Jewish team overseen by a rabbi from Livorno.

The large cooperative was founded in 1954 with eleven members; it now comprises six hundred local wine growers and 1,250 hectares (3,087 acres) of vineyards. Its annual output is around 12 million liters. It recently hired the talented enologist Attilio Pagli as its consultant. The Cantina's signature wine, Bianco di Pitigliano DOC, is a dry white with the *amarognolo*, or slightly bitter, aftertaste characteristic of grapes grown on volcanic tufa. By definition it consists of primarily Tuscan Trebbiano grapes, but now up to 20 percent Chardonnay, Sauvignon, Grechetto, Greco di Tufo, and Malvasia grapes is also allowed. Ildebrando Bianco di Pitigliano Superiore DOC is the cooperative's best white, of 70 percent Trebbiano with Malvasia and Chardonnay; it sees no wood. Duro Persico is an unusual white of the Verdello grape. There are also a few good new reds, including Sovana Superiore DOC, of pure Merlot, that has just been launched.

Also

GHIOTTORNIA   VIA ROMA, 41 AND 58. 0564 616907

Lida Manetti's delicatessen features Maremman specialties from local producers: sheep's yogurts from La Parrina (p 223); fresh ricotta and pecorino from Sorano (p 246); *salumi* made by Manetti's husband, Enrico Polidori (p 237); *salse* and bottled organic vegetables from La Selva (p 242); coffee from Le Piantagioni del Caffè (p 119); and local wines.

Poggioferro

FRANTOIO ANDREINI   VIA AMIATINA, 25 58050 POGGIOFERRO
OLIVE OIL   TELEPHONE 0564 511002   FAX 0564 511075

OPEN Always: the family lives upstairs; sales are year round, no set hours; *frantoio* open November to December   **CREDIT CARDS** None   **ENGLISH SPOKEN** No   **DIRECTIONS** The *frantoio* is on the main road through the village; ring the bell in the courtyard behind the row houses

Andreini produces excellent Maremman olive oil. Situated in a rural village above Scansano, the family-run *frantoio* extracts oil using superior modern Foligno and Sinolea machinery. Andreini cultivates some olives and buys others from trusted growers. He mills for third parties and bottles two extra-virgin oils under his own label: top-of-the-line Mignola, from Scansano olives, and Maremma Toscana, from olives grown throughout the Maremma.

Olives are hand-picked and brought to the mill as quickly as possible. Leaves are removed by aspiration, and the olives washed in cold water. In a room that is kept warm at 20°C (68°F), they are slowly crushed to a pulp by stainless-steel hammers. "This may take up to thirty minutes," explained Stefano Andreini. "Olives are a fruit—they must not be handled too aggressively."

His best Mignola oil, from olives in his Fontelinda grove, then drips out of the mass of pulp by gravity; it is neither pressed nor spun free. This liquid is given a final centrifugal spin to remove the water content. "This is the 'flower' of the oil—the best part," he asserted. Indeed, the green-gold oil's bouquet is as sweet and fresh as newly cut grass. The flavor is full and balanced, with a pleasing taste of olives and a faint peppery aftertaste. Andreini said, "It is fruity but not too arrogant."

Olive oil must be handled carefully. "It is alive. Left in a hot place, it ferments." Keep it cool (but not refrigerated) and stored in the dark. Andreini's oils may be tasted and bought directly, with a range of sizes and prices available.

Pomonte

FIORENZO CARLUCCI
CHEESE

ON SS 322 AT JUNCTION FOR POMONTE 58050 POMONTE
TELEPHONE 0564 599000

OPEN 7:00–21:00 Tuesday to Sunday, from the van   CLOSED Monday   CREDIT CARDS Visa, MC
ENGLISH SPOKEN No   DIRECTIONS The turnoff to Pomonte is on the main road from Scansano to Manciano. The bar and cheese van are at that junction

---

Fiorenzo Carlucci formerly sold his cheeses by driving from town to town. He still makes cheese, selling it from his van, but he no longer travels. The old van now sits beside his daughter Alessandra's bar, and customers drive to him. If there is no one in the van when you arrive, ask in the bar.

Carlucci's cheeses are made of 100 percent sheep's milk from his own herd. *Pecorino fresco,* a young cheese with an aromatic fresh taste, is delicate and creamy. The *semi-stagionato* (half-matured) pecorino is delicious, with a soft, slightly crumbly texture, light salt content, and faintly nutty taste. In the mature *stagionato,* the salt is more emphatic and the texture denser without becoming rubbery— unlike the "Pienza-style" industrial pecorini. Other cheeses include a meltingly fresh ricotta, and walnut- or *peperoncino*-flavored pecorini. They are sold by weight, whole or by the piece.

Porto Santo Stefano

IL FORO
RESTAURANT

BANCHINA TOSCANA (GALLERIA VALLE)
PORTO SANTO STEFANO 58019 MONTE ARGENTARIO
TELEPHONE 0564 814138

OPEN Dinner only   CLOSED Monday; January   CREDIT CARDS Visa, MC, Amex
ENGLISH SPOKEN Yes   PRICE $$$ DIRECTIONS From the seafront at Porto Santo Stefano, take the small slip road along the shore to the left (with your back to the sea). The restaurant is along that road a little ways, by the Giannutri ferry ticket office

---

This pleasant family restaurant and pizzeria is situated near the water's edge. From the long windowed room you can watch the port as you eat. The food is just right for the seaside: wholesome platters of pasta tossed with chunky fish sauces followed by simply cooked local fish.

Spaghetti with mixed seafood—small calamari, clams, mussels, and other shellfish—in a light tomato sauce sprinkled with parsley is good. So is the *fritto misto mare:* shrimp, calamari, and little fish deep-fried in a light batter. *Triglie* (red mullet), *San Pietro* (John Dory), and *gallinella* (gurnard) are nicely cooked over a wood grill and served with big wedges of lemon. The owner is not keen on the farm-raised fish the markets are full of, like the *spigola* (sea bass). "They are bland and too expensive," he said. He prefers the less fancy but more flavorful (and certainly more colorful) "secondary" fish of the Tyrrhenian Sea.

Also

To see some of these weird and wonderful Mediterranean fish, walk along the seafront to the cluster of fishmongers whose large storefronts extend into the street. "Da Roberto" is one (open 8:00–20:00, closed Monday, tel: 0564 812693).

TRATTORIA DA ORLANDO   VIA BRESCHI, 8. 0564 812788. CLOSED WEDNESDAY

Walk to the western end of the port and up a short rise (you'll see the signs there) to this family-run trattoria that specializes in cooking the day's catch with care and serving it on a breezy, vine-covered terrace overlooking the sea. The short wine list has some interesting offerings.

Roccastrada

AZIENDA AGRICOLA   VENTURI, 36 58036 ROCCASTRADA
POGGIO OLIVETO   TELEPHONE 0564 577257   FAX 0564 577394
OLIVE OIL, FRUIT

OPEN 9:00–12:30, 14:30–19:00   CREDIT CARDS Visa, MC   DIRECT SALE Yes, of fruit in season and oil   ENGLISH SPOKEN Yes   OTHER Rooms available for holiday rental
DIRECTIONS The farm is halfway between Roccastrada and Ribolla; there is a yellow sign and a short avenue of pine trees to the farmhouse

---

This farm is positioned above the Grosseto plains and the sea. It has pretty buildings, an old well, a tiny chapel, and friendly white Maremman sheepdogs.

The Curatolo family uses the *lotta guidata* system of pest control to monitor the olive fly on its 40 hectares (98 acres) of olive groves; they also use predators, keeping chemical spraying to a minimum.

The Curatolos have their own *frantoio*. From late October they make and sell fine unfiltered extra-virgin oils. The *frantoio* may be visited during the late autumn. This farm also specializes in unsprayed strawberries from greenhouse and field, cantaloupes, and watermelons.

Roccatederighi

MELETA
WINE

MELETA 58028 ROCCATEDERIGHI
TELEPHONE 0564 567155   FAX 0564 567146
E-MAIL meleta@tin.it

OPEN Shop 9:00–12:00, 15:00–19:00; *cantina* visits by appointment   **CLOSED** Saturday afternoon;
Sunday   **CREDIT CARDS** None   **DIRECT SALE** Yes   **ENGLISH SPOKEN** Yes
DIRECTIONS Meleta is on the road between Roccatederighi and Tatti

---

The Meleta estate is now entirely dedicated to the production of fine wines, as it no longer breeds gourmet eating pigeons. The company was started by a Swiss couple, Peter Max Suter and his wife, Erica. Until his untimely death in 1994, Suter had ambitions to produce world-class wines from this largely undervalued part of the country. The estate is perched high above the reclaimed swamps of the Maremma. The vineyards were planted with no expenses spared: Suter set his sights high. "He wanted to create wines that could compete on an international level," Roberto Tonini, the farm's director, told me. Suter's wife now runs the estate.

The emphasis at Meleta is on efficiency and modernity: the colorful wine labels have abstract paintings on them. Suter was advised by Franco Bernabei, one of Tuscany's best winemakers. Rosso della Rocca is a super-Tuscan-style blend of Cabernet, Sangiovese, and Merlot. Bernabei vinified and matured each variety separately for up to two years before assembling the wine. Other wines include the new Massaio, of pure Merlot, and Bianco della Rocca, of pure Chardonnay matured in French *barriques* of differing ages. In the summer of 2001, Luca D'Attoma, a talented winemaker of the younger generation, replaced Bernabei at Meleta; time will tell how the wines will differ.

San Donato

AZIENDA BIO-AGRICOLA LA SELVA
FARM PRODUCE: ORGANIC

STRADA PROVINCIALE 81, SAN DONATO
ALBINIA 58010 ORBETELLO
TELEPHONE 0564 885799, 885669
FAX 0564 885722

OPEN Shop 8:00–12:00, 15:00–20:00; daily in summer; Monday, Wednesday, Saturday in winter
CLOSED Sunday; Tuesday, Thursday, Friday in winter   **CREDIT CARDS** Visa, MC
DIRECT SALE Yes   **ENGLISH SPOKEN** Yes   **OTHER** Six rooms on the farm available for
holiday rentals   **DIRECTIONS** From SS 1 Aurelia turn inland (east) at the Corte dei Butteri bar; the
farm is on the left, after 3 kms

If it is true that we are what we eat, then Karl Egger is the best example anyone could find for converting to organic foods. A large, friendly man with an almost volcanic amount of energy, Egger has for many years been an active, though often isolated, champion of organic fruits and vegetables. A native of Germany, he was among the first to settle in the Maremma and to start (in 1980) cultivating and selling this kind of produce.

His beautiful farm of 345 hectares (850 acres) is positioned between the sea and the foothills below Scansano. A seven-year crop-rotation system is used on the farm, with no chemical fertilizers or pesticides. In addition to a full range of vegetables and fruits, cattle and sheep are raised; most of this meat is sold by private order. Grapes are grown for making into robust organic wines.

An attractive farm shop is filled with baskets of freshly picked produce. The walls are lined with jars of Egger's preserves and pulses. There is no delay between the picking of the ripe vegetables and their cooking. For the "Tuscan antipasto" line, sliced zucchini, eggplant, and peppers are grilled in a machine that removes up to 75 percent of their water content, then stored in olive oil, ready for eating. La Selva's tomato sauces, some made by the Ciarlo family (p 158), are wonderful, with all the sweetness of the ripe fruit. There are savory eggplant spreads for vegetarian *crostini*, red pepper purées to use on pasta, and cooked chickpeas and *farro*—the spelt wheat Egger said the Romans used to conquer the world.

Saturnia

GROSSETO'S THERMAL WATERS

The Metalliferous Mountains are famous for their sulfur springs, whose waters have healing powers. The natural warm springs in this area were frequented by the Etruscans and Romans, and today they offer full spa facilities. Terme di Saturnia is a modern hotel-spa with a large natural waterfall nearby (tel: 0564 601061; fax: 601266). Farther north is the hotel-spa Terme di Petriolo, Civitella Paganico, Pari (tel: 0564 908871/2; fax: 908712).

BACCO E CERERE
SPECIALTY FOODS, RESTAURANT

VIA MAZZINI, 4 58050 SATURNIA
TELEPHONE/FAX 0564 601235

OPEN Shop 9:00–13:00, 16:00–19:30; restaurant lunch and dinner Saturday and Sunday, dinner only Monday and Wednesday to Friday in summer; lunch and dinner Thursday to Monday in winter
CLOSED Shop Tuesday; restaurant Tuesday in summer; Tuesday and Wednesday in winter
CREDIT CARDS Visa, MC, Amex   ENGLISH SPOKEN A little   FEATURES Garden wine bar
RESERVATIONS Recommended on weekends   PRICE Restaurant $$–$$$
DIRECTIONS In the center of Saturnia

Bacco and Cerere (the god of wine and the goddess of grain) are the symbolic figureheads of this gastronomic center. On the ground floor, Eugenio Piccini has a small wine bar and shop selling selected artisan foods, cookbooks, and handmade kitchen objects. Upstairs, his son Federico runs a restaurant. The shop has been in business for more than fifteen years.

"Each product tells a story," Eugenio Piccini told me. "I have spent years helping people who still make foods as our grandfathers did." Under his creamy yellow Saturnia label, Piccini sells preserved vegetables, dried mushrooms, jam, honey, cheese, pasta, olive oil (his own), and more. There is a good range of wines, particularly Maremman and Tuscan, and the wine bar offers a chance to taste them. Customers can select from the assortment of cheeses (including Fiorini's pecorini, see p 263) and *salumi* to eat inside or out with local bread and wine.

Upstairs, the small, airy restaurant has nice wooden chairs and embroidered curtains. After an antipasto of mixed *salumi* or *crostini*, the menu offers seasonal *primi* of a Maremman character. *Zuppa di ricotta* is a thick spinach soup enriched with sheep's ricotta. Other wholesome starters include soups of fava bean or spelt wheat and handmade pastas.

Meats come from small local suppliers—a *contadino* who might have a few extra chickens or ducks, or a hunter selling native game. They are grilled, roasted, or stewed with wild herbs from the surrounding hills. Wild boar comes well cooked in a spicy sauce. *Agnello in buglione* is a rustic dish of assorted cuts of lamb with rosemary, garlic, hot pepper, tomatoes, and wine. (*Buglia* is a local term for "mixture" or "tangle.") Desserts are handmade by Signora Piccini. There are no great local desserts, so her repertoire comes from farther afield.

Scansano

CANTINA COOPERATIVA DEL MORELLINO DI SCANSANO
WINE

SS 322 SARAGIOLO 58054 SCANSANO
TELEPHONE 0564 507288   FAX 0564 507785
WEB SITE www.cantinadelmorellino.it

OPEN Shop 8:30–12:30, 14:00–18:00   **CLOSED** Saturday and Sunday   **CREDIT CARDS** Visa, MC
DIRECT SALE Yes   **ENGLISH SPOKEN** A little   **DIRECTIONS** On the SS 322, 1 km from Scansano going toward Grosseto; the building is set back from the road on the right

---

In recent years the area around Scansano has seen an explosion of new viticulture, with many important wineries from the north of Italy and Tuscany buying land here. This cooperative began in 1973 when a renewed interest in Maremman wines brought 40 small producers together. They decided to pool grapes and production costs and to organize distribution for the wines. The enrollment fee was 10.000 lire (about $6). Today the members number 151, with more than 340 hectares (840 acres) of vineyards. The *cantina* produces 40 percent of all Morellino made. In 1977 the first wines appeared; in 1978 Morellino was granted DOC status.

"A noted red wine was produced here by the Etruscans," explained Benedetto Grechi, the *cantina*'s president. "We believe it was named Morellino much later—noblemen coming to Scansano to buy wine had horses of the Morello breed." Morellino di Scansano is a red wine of 85 to 100 percent Sangiovese grapes, with the remaining percentage of other black varieties. A deep ruby red, it has a full bouquet, moderate tannins, and austere warmth to its flavor. It is best served at 18°C (65°F), and goes well with red meats. Its Riserva spends at least one year in Slavonian oak barrels. A more modern-style version, of pure Sangiovese, is fermented in steel vats and matured for one year in *barriques*. A young version, Vin del Fattore, is designed to be drunk within one year of production. The *cantina*, whose enologist is currently Attilio Pagli, has two distinct lines: one for the mass market at economical prices; the other, of higher-quality wines, at competitive prices.

ERIK BANTI
AZIENDA AGRICOLA VINOSO
WINE

FOSSO DEI MOLINI 58054 SCANSANO
TELEPHONE 0564 508006   FAX 0564 508019
WEB SITE www.erikbanti.com

OPEN 8:30–12:30, 14:00–17:00   **CLOSED** Saturday and Sunday   **DIRECT SALE** Yes
ENGLISH SPOKEN Yes   **DIRECTIONS** The *cantina* is 400 meters outside Scansano, going toward Manciano

---

Erik Banti is considered responsible for having launched Morellino di Scansano as one of Tuscany's key wines. An articulate, extroverted wisp of a man, he was a photographer, racing driver, and travel agent before becoming a winemaker. "I came here from Rome," he recounted in perfect English, "wanting to make a great wine. I took it to the country's top restaurants—including Gualtiero Marchesi and Pinchiorri—and they went for it." He had transformed a *contadino* wine, robust and drinkable but with little finesse, into one fit for an international audience.

Banti has gradually been buying land, and currently he owns 35 hectares (86 acres), with 15 (37) more rented. He also buys selected grapes from around Scansano. His best wines are *crus*, single-vineyard Morellinos named Ciabatta IGT and Aquilaia IGT, which are made only in great years. Ciabatta, of pure Sangiovese, is matured for thirteen to eighteen months in Slavonian oak barrels and sold three years after harvesting. Aquilaia, of Sangiovese with 20 percent Grenache added, is sold after two years; it spends twelve to fifteen months in French oak *barriques*. A recent series is called Annoprimo, Annosecondo, Annoterzo . . . one for each year, of Sangiovese with a little Merlot. The "normal" Morellino is a wine to drink young—though all of Banti's wines may be cellared successfully for at least five years. At their best, his wines have great concentration and body while remaining deliciously drinkable. The enterprising Banti also plans to open a fancy food and wine store.

Also

PANIFICIO PASTICCERIA GUALTIERO BERNARDINI   VIA XX SETTEMBRE, 40.

I found several unusual breads in this bakery, including a crusty small *schiacciata*, oval and flat, with a central slash to keep it crunchy. *Schiacciata con ricotta* has soft cheese blended into the dough. *Pane fritto con zucchero* was just that: deep-fried crusty bread sprinkled with sugar—simple but delicious. It is special to Scansano.

Sorano

CASEIFICIO SOCIALE	VIA LA FRATTA, 54 58010 SORANO
COOPERATIVO SORANO	TELEPHONE 0564 633002, *CASEIFICIO;*
CHEESE	0564 633748 SHOP
	FAX 0564 633093 *CASEIFICIO*

OPEN Shop summer 8:30–13:00, 17:00–19:30; winter 8:30–13:00, 16:00–19:00   **CLOSED** Shop Sunday   **CREDIT CARDS** Visa, MC   **DIRECT SALE** See below. The cheeses are also sold in grocery stores throughout the Maremma   **ENGLISH SPOKEN** A little   **DIRECTIONS** The Caseificio's cheeses are sold from its shop in Via Pitiglianese, on the road from Sorano to Pitigliano, on the right after less than 1 km

This dairy cooperative was formed in 1963 and now numbers 125 members, producing sheep's and cow's milk from local pastures. The wild herbs and grasses the animals eat give the milk an aromatic quality that is maintained in the cheeses.

This *caseificio* makes very fine eating (as opposed to grating) pecorino: perfectly smooth, it has a slight sweetness to complement the distinctive sheep's milk flavor. It is sold *da taglio* (matured for thirty to ninety days before eating), and *da serbo* (for eating or grating, a semihard version that may be matured for four to twelve months). The large, modern dairy makes excellent, delicate ricotta of pure sheep's milk or mixed cow's and sheep's milk. *Stracchino* is a fresh, slightly acid spreadable cheese of cow's milk.

BANDARIN	VIA ROMA, 7 58010 SORANO
TABLE CRAFTS: POTTERY	TELEPHONE/FAX 0564 633143

OPEN 9:00–13:00, 14:30–18:30 or later   **CLOSED** Almost never   **CREDIT CARDS** Visa, MC   **ENGLISH SPOKEN** No   **DIRECTIONS** Via Roma is the main street in the old part of Sorano

In 1980 Beatrice Bandarin, a ceramicist and art school teacher, opened this potter's studio. In 1984 her students Moreno Migliorelli and Laura Corsini took the business over. They sell a range of colorful hand-painted plates, bowls, and mugs decorated with delicate flowers and leaves. Half-glazed terra-cotta pitchers spattered with green are remakes of the rustic peasant ware once used in the local kitchens, now, sadly, so hard to find.

Also

SALUMIFICIO SA.SO.   VIA LA FRATTA, 57. 0564 633185

Giuliano Fratini salt cures pork products. His fine *capocollo* (boned shoulder) is aged for forty days; many of his *prosciutti* are sent to be aged near Parma; *salame Toscanello* is made of ground lean shoulder of pork, with 30 percent belly fat added.

Sovana

SASSOTONDO   PIANI DI CONATI, 52 58010 SOVANA
WINE: ORGANIC   TELEPHONE 0564 614218   FAX 0564 617714
E-MAIL sassotondo@ftbcc.it

CREDIT CARDS No   **DIRECT SALE** Yes   **ENGLISH SPOKEN** Yes   **OTHER** Four rooms available for holiday rentals from April to October   **DIRECTIONS** Take the road to Sovana from Pitigliano; after 3 kms (at km 2), Agriturismo Sassotondo is signposted to the left; follow the dirt road for 2.5 kms to the farm

---

I first tasted Carla Benini and Edoardo Ventimiglia's unusual wine of exclusively Ciliegiolo grapes at Pane e Vino in Firenze (see p 102), and I was so intrigued that I drove down to the Maremma to meet them. "Ciliegiolo is a red grape varietal that was traditionally used in a blend with Sangiovese," said Carla, "but we bought a 4.5-hectare [11-acre] vineyard already planted with it and decided to make it into a wine of its own. The locals all thought we were crazy!" This single-vineyard wine, San Lorenzo IGT, is matured in new French oak *barriques* for one year, then spends a year in the bottle. It is aged in the couple's spectacular cellar, which was carved out of the tufa hillside in the 1930s. "This area was used by the Etruscans for their cellars and burial sites because the stone is so soft to cut into," Edoardo explained. The well-structured wine has a light but distinctive peppery note, to complement the red fruit tones and cherry flavor to which the grape owes its name.

Carla and Edoardo bought the 72-hectare (178-acre) farm in unspoiled country-side "by accident" and moved there from Rome in 1990. "We started off thinking this would be a summer home, but the passion for making wine made us abandon the city altogether," said Carla. The couple now grows some crops as well as grapes and olives, all of which are cultivated organically. "People used to think that organic wines couldn't be good, but now they see it as a plus," explained Edoardo.

In an area known, if anything, for its white wine, Bianco di Pitigliano, Carla and Edoardo are producing more reds than whites—helped by the talented enologist

Attilio Pagli. Sovana DOC Franze is 70 percent Sangiovese, with 25 percent Ciliegiolo and 5 percent Merlot. "It's made to drink young, and is very territorial," Carla explained. It spends one year in second-passage *barriques*. Sassotondo Rosso is a blend of Ciliegiolo and Alicante, while Sassotondo Bianco is a Bianco di Pitigliano of primarily Trebbiano, with 20 percent each of Sauvignon and Greco di Tufo grapes added.

Torniella

SALUMIFICIO SILVANO MORI
MEAT: SALUMI

VIA S. GIROLAMO, 1 58030 TORNIELLA
TELEPHONE 0564 575436   FAX 0564 575100
WEB SITE www.salumificiomori.com

OPEN 8:00–13:00, 16:00–19:00   **CLOSED** July   **CREDIT CARDS** Visa, MC   **MAIL ORDER** Yes
DIRECT SALE Yes   **ENGLISH SPOKEN** Yes   **DIRECTIONS** The shop is in Torniella's main square

---

"Wild boar, *cinghiale*, is a difficult meat to work," Silvano Mori explained. "It is very lean. Without enough fat, *salumi* tend to toughen. But it is a traditional Maremman specialty." Mori's *salumi* are some of the best I tasted in Tuscany. His small boar sausages, *salsicce di cinghiale*, are excellent: tight-grained and peppery, with a good meaty flavor that is strong without being gamy. They require no cooking and are best sliced finely with unsalted Tuscan bread. They are sold loose or preserved in jars of sunflower oil—to stop them from drying out. I also liked Mori's *salamella*. This narrow pork *salame* is evenly spiced and made without an excess of fat. His *finocchiona* is large, unusually compact, and peppery; it is matured for two months or more. Mori also makes a fine *prosciutto Toscano*—tender and not overly salty.

Silvano Mori, a friendly, spirited artisan, keeps scrupulously clean workshops that conform to E.U. requirements; his products may be exported. He uses no additives or preservatives.

Valpiana

LA NOVELLA
SPECIALTY FOODS

VIA MASSETANA VALPIANA 58020 MASSA MARITTIMA
TELEPHONE 0566 919005   FAX 0566 919194
WEB SITE www.lanovella.it

OPEN 8:30–12:30, 16:00–19:30   **CLOSED** Sunday; Wednesday afternoon in winter
CREDIT CARDS Visa, MC, Amex   **MAIL ORDER** Yes   **ENGLISH SPOKEN** A little
DIRECTIONS The shop is in the former Cantina Sociale on SS 439, the main road between Follonica and Massa Marittima

---

When Valpiana's Cantina Sociale, or cooperative winery, closed down in 1985, four of its young employees decided to save the building. They took it over and sought out the area's best food products: olive oils, *salumi*, and wines. Starting as a distribution network, they supplied restaurants and food shops.

Their shop offers a fine selection of specialty foods: pecorini and *salumi* from the hills around Massa, preserved vegetables and fruits, sauces, and vinegars. La Novella's own label, La Ceppaia, appears on many items made for the shop by local food artisans. Local olive oil is well represented; buyers can choose between La Ceppaia's modern extraction system oil and the more traditional stone-ground types. La Novella has not forgotten its enological roots: it sells inexpensive but drinkable local wine *sfuso* (unbottled) for those who bring their own containers, as well as a selection of reasonably priced Maremman labels.

CHAPTER 10

Mount Amiata

ount Amiata is southern Tuscany's highest mountain. On a clear day it can be seen from points north of Arezzo—a distinctive group of four soft peaks more than a thousand meters above sea level. The highest of these, Monte Labbro, reaches 1,193 meters (3,914 feet). Of volcanic rock and clay, the wide-based mountains straddle two provinces: Grosseto and Siena. Once famous for its mercury mines, Amiata experienced an economic slump when, in the 1960s, the mines' closing coincided with the disbanding of the *mezzadria* share-cropping system. Thousands of hectares of cultivated holdings were abandoned as the *contadini,* or peasants, left the hillsides to seek work in the industrial cities.

Now, many years later, Mount Amiata's economy is being revived. An area of great natural beauty and resources, the mountain's unspoiled countryside and picturesque towns are attracting tourism throughout the year. In summer the statuesque beech and chestnut forests offer a cool respite; the autumn woods abound with wild mushrooms, chestnuts, and game; winter snow brings skiing; in spring the hedgerows are thick with wildflowers, and there are wonderful paths for hiking or biking.

Sheep graze in herds in the sloping pastures; Amiata is famous for its herb-sweet sheep's cheeses. Mushrooms, from the celebrated *fungo porcino* to the rarer *ovolo,* are prepared in myriad ways. Rustic mountain *salumi* of wild boar are made here, as are bitter herb liqueurs from medieval recipes. The unusual local olive oil is used in many hearty dishes of the mountain's *cucina povera*—a cuisine of seasonal ingredients cooked simply to enhance their decisive natural flavors.

AZIENDA DI PROMOZIONE TURISTICA DELL'AMIATA
VIA ADUA, 25
53021 ABBADIA SAN SALVATORE
SIENA
0577 775811, FAX 0577 775877
info@amiata.turismo.toscana.it

Boldface type indicates towns that are included in this chapter.

Abbadia San Salvatore

**FORNO BAFFETTI
& CONTORNI**
BREAD

VIALE ROMA, 32 53021 ABBADIA SAN SALVATORE SIENA
TELEPHONE 0577 778298

OPEN 7:00–12:30, 16:00–19:30   **CLOSED** Wednesday afternoon, Sunday
CREDIT CARDS None   **ENGLISH SPOKEN** No   **DIRECTIONS** In the town's central square

This busy bakery offers an assortment of baked goods. *Biscotti all'anice* are a surprisingly tasty salty-sweet combination. Anise seeds are added to a salted bread dough that is shaped like a pretzel and boiled like a bagel before being baked. "They are good for the digestion," explained baker Luigina Baffetti. "Anise helps settle the stomach. We eat them as snacks—plain or dunked in wine."

Schiacciata, or *ciaccia*, as it is called here, is flat crusty bread sprinkled with coarse salt and oil before baking. Here it is topped with *i friccioli*, little pieces of pork fat that become brown and crunchy in the oven. I also liked the rosemary version.

Abbadia's special cake, *la ricciolina*, is an elaborate affair of meringue, chocolate, almonds, and pastry. It is gooey, terribly sweet, and madly popular with the locals.

**LOMBARDI
& VISCONTI**
HERBAL PRODUCTS: LIQUEURS

ZONA ARTIGIANALE "LA MINIERA" VIA AMMAN, 51
53021 ABBADIA SAN SALVATORE SIENA
TELEPHONE 0577 777092

OPEN 10:00–12:00, 17:00–19:00, mid-June to September   **CLOSED** October to May
CREDIT CARDS None   **DIRECT SALE** Yes; liqueurs also sold at Bar dei Tigli, Piazza 20
Settembre, 37, in Abbadia   **MAIL ORDER** Yes   **ENGLISH SPOKEN** No
DIRECTIONS From Abbadia, go toward Monte Amiata; after 1 km turn left into La Miniera

The tradition of transforming aromatic herbs into liqueurs to stimulate the digestion dates at least to the Middle Ages. The Italians are fond of these often very bitter alcoholic drinks (called *amari*) and like to collect them. They come in decorative bottles and make an interesting addition to the liquor cabinet, primarily for use as after-dinner "digestives."

This small artisan company makes liqueurs from dried herbs without artificial colors or extracts. Each liqueur contains different herbs, which are grown on an herb farm in northern Italy. Stilla, made from a recipe first used by Abbadia's monks, comprises five types: Asiatic karkadé (a kind of hibiscus), *Mentha piperita*, *melissa* (balm), *Artemisia absinthium* (Roman absinthe), and rhubarb. The resulting liqueur is bright yellow-gold, fairly sweet in its fiery herbal impact, and has a pleasantly bitter aftertaste. Elisir Lucrezia is altogether a lighter affair: made from just basil and sage, it is a refreshing, perfumed *digestivo* for a summer's lunch. Sage, or *salvia*, is known for its healing properties; its bitterness is tempered by the basil's peppery sweetness.

To make the liqueurs, dried herbs are macerated in a mixture of alcohol and water for five to fifteen days. The herbs are filtered out and the liquid is blended with distilled water and sugar. The resulting mixture is fairly cloudy. It is clarified through *farina fossile*, a ground-stone powder, and then through the same type of carbon filters as those used in winemaking. The liqueurs, with an average alcohol content of 30 percent, are then aged for several months.

Dried mushrooms, herbal mixes, and honey are also on sale from the shop in the Miniera complex, which is in what was once the town's famous mercury mine.

As this book went to press, the company was unsure if it would be moving soon, so phone before going there.

IL CANTINONE
RESTAURANT

VIA ASMARA, 14/16 53021 ABBADIA SAN SALVATORE SIENA
TELEPHONE 0577 776552

OPEN Lunch and dinner   **CLOSED** Wednesday in winter   **CREDIT CARDS** Visa, MC
ENGLISH SPOKEN No   **RESERVATIONS** Recommended in summer and on weekends
PRICE $$ **DIRECTIONS** Near Piazza della Repubblica

Il Cantinone was once an inn. It is a large space with the dark wooden beams characteristic of mountain architecture. The kitchen, run by Maurizio Bisconti, serves uncomplicated country fare with some refinements. Spring *primi* were wholesome and satisfying. *Zuppa di verdura* was a thick mix of seasonal vegetables with beans and rice. Homemade *tortelli* were stuffed with fragrant sheep's ricotta and spinach and topped with Parmesan and torn arugula. Wide *pappardelle* noodles came with a sauce of tender artichokes. The best season for wild mushrooms is autumn, particularly for the prized porcini, though some do grow in spring and summer.

Meats such as *coniglio* (rabbit) or *agnello* (lamb chops) were grilled or deep fried. Others were stewed simply with wine. Everything was well salted, as is the custom in rural Tuscany. For dessert there was thick homemade *panna cotta* (baked cream pudding) and a bowl of fresh fruit. The house wine is an uncomplicated red from Montalcino, served in pitchers. The service is relaxed but attentive.

PINZI PINZUTI
SPECIALTY FOODS,
WINE, OLIVE OIL

VIA CAVOUR, 30 53021 ABBADIA SAN SALVATORE SIENA
TELEPHONE 0577 778040
E-MAIL pinzi.pinzuti@iol.it

OPEN Shop 8:30–13:00, 16:00–20:00; wine bar 9:00–13:00, 16:00–20:00, 21:00–23:00 in summer
CLOSED Wednesday afternoon; Sunday in autumn and winter   **CREDIT CARDS** Visa, MC
ENGLISH SPOKEN A little   **DIRECTIONS** Near the abbey

Take one step into Marcella Pinzuti's treasure trove of a store and you will be overwhelmed by the quantity of bottles, jars, and assorted curiosities cohabiting in such a tiny space. There are hundreds of wines, *grappe,* olive oils, and liqueurs, as well as unfilled decorative bottles. There are vegetables in oil and nuts in honey; jams made from quince, figs, or chestnuts; and packages of pasta, cookies, dried herbs, and spices.

This is more than a provision store: it is a personal, hand-picked accumulation, and a very feminine one. Marcella Pinzuti is a soft-spoken woman of great delicacy, and this is her domain. Among the bottles are traditional baskets and rare woven flasks, made especially for her by a few elderly *contadini.* There are dried flower arrangements, carefully assembled gift boxes, and much more.

Marcella's father, Lido, makes wine and olive oil and runs his own *frantoio.* I was very impressed by him. A courteous white-haired man, he seemed much younger than his years, thanks to his passionate commitment to his land.

"In my childhood it was still the Middle Ages," he recounted. "The men worked in the mine all day and then came home to work the land. Each family had a little strip planted with a few vegetables, vines, and olives. If you were lucky, you had a donkey to help with the loads. It was backbreaking. But most of the land here was cultivated then. It looked very different, with all those well-tended terraces. I have never forgotten it."

In the 1960s everything changed. People left the countryside to seek employment in the cities. The *mezzadria,* or sharecropper, system collapsed. Nobody wanted to work the land anymore.

For years Lido Pinzuti nurtured a dream to recultivate a large piece of a devilishly steep hillside whose nickname in Italian means "hell." "It took me ten years to coax all the families who owned the strips into selling them to me," he asserted. "Some of the old-timers only agreed because they too wanted to see the land come alive again." Walking around Pinzuti's steeply terraced vineyards and thriving olive groves, you would never guess what went into taming the wildness of the terrain. Some of the biggest boulders had to be blasted with dynamite.

Pinzuti's vines and olives are grown organically. He has built a *frantoio* with traditional stone wheels for grinding the olives. It's an amazing achievement, of interest to anyone who cares about the land, its present, and its past. Appointments to visit the *frantoio* and farm may be made through the shop.

Also

FATTORIA CORTEVECCHIA   VIA CASE NUOVE, 16. 0577 779358

This butcher shop sells meat from animals raised on its large farm nearby. Pork, chicken, beef, and eggs are also available, as is game, which must be ordered.

Arcidosso

RISTORANTE AIUOLE
RESTAURANT

AIOLE VIA PROVINCIALE
58031 ARCIDOSSO GROSSETO
TELEPHONE 0564 967300   FAX 0564 966747

OPEN Lunch and dinner   **CLOSED** Monday   **CREDIT CARDS** Visa, MC, Amex
ENGLISH SPOKEN A little   **RESERVATIONS** Recommended   **PRICE** $$–$$$
DIRECTIONS The restaurant and hotel are on the main road between Arcidosso and Santa Fiora,
3.2 kms from Arcidosso

I had a really enjoyable meal at this restaurant because of its convivial atmosphere and the excellent home cooking of Signora Rossana Bargagli Quattrini. The restaurant, on the ground floor of the Quattrinis' thirty-room hotel, is run by Rossana with her family and son, Ugo. Rossana's cooking celebrates the bounty of the woods and fields, against the backdrop of Monte Amiata's verdant landscape.

"I love to go searching for wild mushrooms or herbs," explained the vivacious Rossana. "Even after working in the kitchen it relaxes me." Whatever she comes back with—be it spring *prugnoli,* the first mushrooms of the year, earthy porcini, young nettle shoots, or wild aparagus tips—she transforms in simple but delicious ways.

In spring an antipasto "salad" of creamy beige *prugnoli,* with their delicate, cucumber-like flavor, is served with shavings of Parmesan, lemon juice, and fragrant olive oil. There are *crostini* toasts topped with frail asparagus or mushrooms, and a bowl of the little black *olivastra Seggianese* olives. Used primarily to produce oil in the nearby town of Seggiano, some of the olives are dried near the fireplace in wicker baskets and then soaked in garlic- and orange-flavored water before eating. They are unlike any other olive, an intense mixture of sweet and bitter.

The restaurant is hosted by Ugo, whose nickname is "Pampini." He is tall and distinguished, with his bushy mustache, and an expert on Tuscany's *cucina povera* and on local artisan foods. Let him advise you about the day's *primi*—such as Rossana's fine *fiocchi di neve,* or snowflakes. These exquisite little balls are made of potato, local sheep's ricotta, and eggs. They are floured and poached but remain incredibly light, served simply with grated cheese and butter. Her pasta is hand rolled and as fine as any I've had: *tortelli* are stuffed with ricotta and nettle and served with a little meat sauce; noodles are married to woodsy mushrooms.

Main courses feature meat and game, including some classics of Tuscan country cooking: *capriolo in salmì,* stewed roebuck, tender but still moist in a rich reddish sauce; delicately seasoned roast suckling pig; wild boar; local sausages; chestnut polenta; and meats grilled simply, *alla brace.*

Save room for cheese. Orange-crusted, delicately salted local pecorino is perfectly married to lemon-infused honey, while creamy sheep's ricotta is coupled with a purée of sweet chestnuts. "We call these dishes *companatico*—literally, 'to go with bread'—because in the old days that was all you had," explained Ugo. "If you were lucky there was cheese or honey to accompany it, which acted as main course and dessert."

Desserts are homemade. The wine list is extensive. Ugo bottles their Montalcino house red. The extended Quattrini family eats at a big table in the dining room, and, in the off-season at least, it is lovely to see Rossana sit down afterward to play cards with her friends.

Bagnolo

MULINO IMPERO BELLINI
FLOUR MILL

VIA FRATELLI ROSSELLI, 43
58037 BAGNOLO GROSSETO
TELEPHONE 0564 953003

OPEN 8:00–12:30, 15:00–19:00 **CLOSED** Wednesday afternoon, Sunday; June
CREDIT CARDS None **DIRECT SALE** Yes **ENGLISH SPOKEN** No
DIRECTIONS In the village of Bagnolo, on the main road from Santa Fiora to Piancastagnaio

For anyone interested in the past, this old-fashioned, fully operational flour mill is worth visiting. Opened in 1928 by the present millers' grandfather, it still uses postwar machinery and some original stone grinding wheels. The Bellini brothers, Luciano and Lorenzo, mill flour for local bakeries using an ingenious machine that reminded me of *Charlie and the Chocolate Factory*.

The Maremman grain undergoes eight procedures while being sped along pneumatic tubes and hoisted on pulleys. After cleaning it is wetted to raise the moisture content before grinding, or the delicate inner kernel, *il fiore*, would be scorched. The grain is cracked, separated from the bran, and ground to "0" or "00" grade flours for use in baking or pasta making. Coarser grinds are used for animal feed.

The two original stone mills are now used only for grinding corn, chestnuts, and organic grain. The chestnuts, once a staple food of the mountain population, are smoke-dried until hard enough to be ground. The large French stone wheels each have a different configuration of grooves hand-chiseled on their flat sides that determine the thickness of the grind once the grain is crushed between the top and bottom stones. These "canals" are hammered by hand once a year to remove any impacted grain.

The miller, an open-faced, patient man who looks the part, will sell small amounts of the flours directly. He is justly proud of his machinery and happy to show it when he is not too busy.

Castel del Piano

CASEIFICIO CIOLO
CHEESE

VIA CELLANE ZONA ARTIGIANALE 58033
CASTEL DEL PIANO GROSSETO
TELEPHONE 0564 956225   FAX 0564 955108

OPEN 8:00–13:00   CLOSED Sunday   CREDIT CARDS None   DIRECT SALE Yes
ENGLISH SPOKEN A little   DIRECTIONS The Zona Artigianale is south of the town, on the road to
Arcidosso; the Caseificio is signposted

This privately owned *caseificio,* or cheesemaker, "transforms" sheep's milk from the surrounding provinces into pecorini and ricotta. About 350 quintals (34 tons) of sheep's and cow's milk is pasteurized before being made into cheese each day. Interestingly, sheep's milk is twice as fat as cow's and produces double the amount of cheese per quintal of milk.

"We make two types of pecorino here: the *Pienza* and the *pecorino tipico,*" Ciolo's manager, Claudio, explained. *Pienza* is a nearby town in the province of Siena famous for its sheep's cheese." Each is worked differently. The *Pienza* is eaten within twenty days of being made. It is whiter and a bit saltier when young. If you come up here to buy it, it also costs half the price! "The *pecorini tipici* are sold either fresh or matured. The milk is given more rennet for a longer fermentation, and the cheese loses some of the acidity it has when fresh."

The formed cheeses are brined before being laid on angled wooden boards to mature. Cedar is used, as it imparts a slightly resinous flavor to the cheeses. Maturation lasts from one to several months. The cheeses' crusts are hand-colored using natural substances. The orange color is tomato-based, and the brownish black comes from *morchia,* the dark fatty sediment from olive oil. Some cheeses are given a black plastic covering. The *caseificio*'s pecorini are available in 1 kg, 2 kg, and 2.5 kg sizes.

CORSINI BISCOTTI
PASTRY

VIA MARCONI, 2 58033 CASTEL DEL PIANO GROSSETO
TELEPHONE 0564 955250 STORE, 0564 956787 OFFICE
FAX 0564 956615
WEB SITE www.corsinibiscotti.com

OPEN 7:30–13:00, 17:00–19:30   CLOSED Tuesday; Sunday afternoon   CREDIT CARDS None
MAIL ORDER Yes   ENGLISH SPOKEN A little   OTHER Corsini has a store in Grosseto, Via
Matteotti, 12/14   DIRECTIONS In Piazza Garibaldi, the town's central square

Corsini's bakery has been a fixture in Castel del Piano since 1921. "My mother and father started making and selling bread," explained Ubaldo Corsini. "I took over when I was seventeen, and although I liked bread making, I preferred baking cookies and cakes."

Corsini, with his sons, now runs a profitable cookie business as well as the bakery. From their two factories, built in the 1960s and 1980s, the Corsinis successfully blend traditional and modern techniques.

I visited one of the factories and saw croissants being hand-rolled and bread being kneaded by old machines that are as slow as manual motion. Their yeast "mother" (which one of Corsini's four sons described as the "fifth brother") is over thirty years old. Every four hours, 365 days a year, it is "freshened" with water and flour, allowed to rise, and then divided. It even has its own special room.

I sampled several of the fifty or more products Corsini makes. The cookies are substantial, short, and not too dry, with good biting texture. Whole-wheat flour *biscotti integrali con yogurt,* shaped like an oval O, are flecked with bran, with a moist firmness in the crumb. Ridged *torciglioni* are the closest thing to shortbread: buttery in taste and crumbly in texture. *Biscottoni al latte* are thin finger cookies with a fine crumb and buttery sweetness. There is also an exciting new line of organic baked goods, such as the *farro*-flour cookies.

Corsini manages a lot better with their *crostata,* a flat jam tart, than most Italian housewives do. Italian women invariably bake these tarts for parties and fairs, and just as invariably they turn out leaden, dry, and indigestible.

I found myself eating a whole package of *pizza croccante.* About the size of an Italian railway ticket, these crisp flat breads are salted and flavored with olive oil— a cross between a cracker and focaccia. They are great alone or with cheese or olives. Some of Corsini's products are available in the United States.

FUNGOAMIATA
SPECIALTY FOODS:
PRESERVED VEGETABLES

PIAN DI BALLO 58033 CASTEL DEL PIANO GROSSETO
TELEPHONE/FAX 0564 956214
WEB SITE www.fungo-amiata.it

OPEN 8:00–12:00, 14:00–18:30   **CLOSED** Sunday   **CREDIT CARDS** None   **DIRECT SALE** Yes
ENGLISH SPOKEN A little   **DIRECTIONS** On the main road between Seggiano and Castel del Piano

---

"Come in!" cried Gastone Angeli merrily. "You have caught us at a good moment. We are waging war on the baby artichokes!"

The scene did resemble a battle: young workers were surrounded by mountains of small purple artichokes in various phases of "transformation." The factory floor was deep in discarded outer leaves. Much of this work is done by hand. "Just think," the simpatico Angeli continued, "in thirty days in late spring we trim and cook over one million artichokes. Then the season ends."

In fact, that was why I was there. I tracked Fungoamiata down after tasting their *carciofini sott'olio*—baby artichokes in olive oil. Unlike many vegetables preserved in oil—which often taste more of sharp vinegar than vegetables— Fungoamiata's let the artichoke's natural flavors dominate. There is a light tang of lemon to complement the fruity olive oil, a hint of herbs and peppers, but the star is the vegetable.

"Our artichokes are grown nearby, at Venturina by the coast," Angeli said. "We use the dark *morello Toscano* variety. They are smaller and more flavorful." The tiny artichokes are simmered for a few minutes with water, fresh herbs, lemon juice, and vinegar. Batches are tasted and seasoned individually. They are pulled off the heat when just tender and still almost crunchy in the center. "Only someone who isn't normal would do this," joked Angeli.

The Angeli family uses no chemical fertilizers when growing vegetables, and no preservatives, citric acid, ascorbic acid, colorings, or antioxidants when preserving them.

As the company's name indicates, mushrooms are featured. "Many types grow wild in the Amiata woods," Angeli explained. "The volcanic terrain naturally gives a better flavor." *Funghi* of all shapes and sizes are preserved under oil, pickled, sauced, or dried. I liked the soft gray *Pleurotos ostreatus*. They are meaty without being slimy, their delicate flavor enhanced by the fragrant preserving oil.

Fungoamiata sells many products under its own label. It also produces them anonymously for many Tuscan shops. If you see a small white rectangular sticker on the back of the jar saying "prodotto e confezionato da Az.Agr PI 0094 . . . C. Piano (GR)," you'll know it's Fungoamiata's.

Also

Cerboni's *salumificio* is one of the best on the Amiata. They do not sell directly to the public, but their products are easily found at COOP supermarkets in the Amiata section and in other local specialty shops. Vittorio and Augusto Cerboni specialize in boned *prosciutto Toscano,* three types of pork *salame* (lean, "sweet," and hot), and other salt-preserved pork products. "Our *salumi* contain less garlic than the Sienese," explained Signor Cerboni, "so they don't leave a strong aftertaste." The Cerbonis also work wild boar, making small, deeply flavored *salsiccie* (sausages).

Castiglione d'Orcia

OLEIFICIO SOCIALE COOPERATIVA
DI CASTIGLIONE D'ORCIA
OLIVE OIL

LA FONTE 53023
CASTIGLIONE D'ORCIA SIENA
TELEPHONE/FAX 0577 887184
IN WINTER: 0577 887535

OPEN November to early January　**CLOSED** Mid-January to October　**CREDIT CARDS** None
DIRECT SALE Yes, during milling season; the cooperative's oil is also available from Pane e Companatico, under the tower in the village center　**ENGLISH SPOKEN** No
DIRECTIONS Coming from Siena on the SS 2, go toward Castiglione d'Orcia, turning right at the fork before Castiglione d'Orcia. After about 4 kms, the *frantoio* is on the left

---

This 1960s cooperative olive mill has two hundred private members from the Orcia Valley. In 1993 they installed a modern extraction system and began selling their oil under the cooperative's label. During the winter olive season the *frantoio* may be visited and the new oil bought.

The *ciclo continuo* double-centrifuge system may be less picturesque than the old stone mill, but it provides a more hygienic, versatile way of producing oil. Temperatures at different stages of the process can be controlled, and the stainless-steel containers are easily cleaned and guarantee less contamination between batches of members' olives.

The cooperative's oil is very low in acidity; it is made from hand-picked Leccino, Frantoiano, and Moraiolo olives. In a blind taste test I carried out with some friends, this fruity green-gold oil, with its artichoke-like bitterness, was a favorite.

Contignano

CASEIFICIO COOPERATIVA VAL D'ORCIA
CHEESE

STRADA DELL'ORCIA CONTIGNANO 53040 RADICOFANI SIENA
TELEPHONE 0578 52012   FAX 0578 52085

OPEN 7:30–13:00, 15:00–17:00   **CLOSED** Wednesday and Saturday afternoons, Sunday
CREDIT CARDS None   **DIRECT SALE** Yes   **ENGLISH SPOKEN** No
DIRECTIONS The *caseificio* is on the outskirts of Contignano, on the road that skirts the village going north toward Chianciano and Montepulciano

This cheese cooperative has an interesting history. In the 1950s, Tuscany's feudal estates were broken up and many farmworkers moved to the cities. The *contadini* left the land they had worked for generations, including much of the Val d'Orcia and Crete Senesi hills. Meanwhile, a number of Sardinian shepherds, struggling to make a living at home, came across to the mainland. Some brought their herds. They began to reclaim the abandoned land, which was well suited for grazing, and they made sheep's cheeses, as they had in Sardinia.

In the early 1960s these independent cheese producers had difficulty competing with large private corporations. In 1964 a priest from Contignano, Don Oscar Guasconi, helped the shepherds form a cooperative. It began with ten members and today has more than ninety, though fewer are now Sardinian.

In 1995 the factory was remodeled to European Community standards. The modern cooperative now works 320 quintals (about 31 tons) of milk daily. The product line includes eleven types of cheese, from fresh ricotta to matured grating *pecorini*. Some are made from mixed sheep's and cow's milk.

This *caseificio* specializes in Pienza-style *pecorini*. Its youngest (matured one month) has a creamy white interior. The flavor is delicate, with a light sweetness. Barely salted, it has only a faint taste of sheep's milk. The mottled orange-skinned pecorino is colored with tomato paste. Matured for longer, its flavors and salt are more emphatic; smooth-textured, it is less moist than the younger cheese. The black-skinned pecorino, matured for more than two months, is yet drier and saltier. There is a real sheep's milk character to its crumbly interior, but some sweetness remains. There is a place to buy the cheeses behind the dairy.

Pescina

SILENE
RESTAURANT

LA PESCINA 58038 SEGGIANO GROSSETO
TELEPHONE 0564 950805　FAX 0564 950553

OPEN Lunch and dinner　**CLOSED** Monday; November.　**CREDIT CARDS** Visa, MC, Amex
ENGLISH SPOKEN Yes　**RESERVATIONS** Recommended　**PRICE** $$$
DIRECTIONS The restaurant is signposted from Pescina

Situated a short drive from Amiata's peak, amid monumental forests, this restaurant specializes in wild mushrooms. The family-run hotel, formerly an inn, was founded in 1830. The walls of the large, semimodernized restaurant are hung with botanical mushroom prints. Dried flowers and floating candles adorn each table.

Pasta is homemade, served with toppings that include porcini mushrooms, truffles, meat sauce, and in spring, wild asparagus. I sampled several dishes. Very thin noodles, *taglierini*, were sauced with asparagus, onion, ham, cream, and Parmesan and enclosed in a slice of Parma ham. There was even black truffle in this highly seasoned, complicated dish. Tagliatelle noodles were tender and well made, though in summer their peppered mushroom sauce lacked the intensity of autumnal porcini. *Tortellini,* tiny pasta squares stuffed with pigeon, were well flavored.

A nice salad of sliced *prugnoli* mushrooms with shavings of Parmesan cheese was dressed with the unusual olive oil from Seggiano. These delicate spring mushrooms tasted of woods, peat, and cucumber.

Main courses are mountain fare. They include roebuck and wild boar, deep-fried lamb chops, grilled porcini caps, local snails, and beef *tagliata*—always popular with Italians. Thin slices of raw beef are flash-cooked on a hot griddle. Here they were topped with arugula and balsamic vinegar or porcini and truffles.

The *semifreddo* of lemon mousse and strawberry jelly was elaborate; fresh strawberries served with balsamic vinegar was a lighter option. The wine list features Tuscany, with a limited but well-selected group from Montalcino, Montepulciano, and Chianti.

Piancastagnaio

BOTTEGA DEL BUONGUSTAIO　　　VIALE GRAMSCI, 79. 0577 786052

This specialty food shop carries a good selection of wines, spirits, and artisan foods. Local selections include *salumi* from Cerboni (p 260) and vegetable preserves from Fungoamiata (p 259).

Rocca d'Orcia

CANTINA IL BORGO
RESTAURANT

53023 ROCCA D'ORCIA SIENA
TELEPHONE/FAX 0577 887280

OPEN Lunch and dinner   **CLOSED** Monday; January and February
CREDIT CARDS Visa, MC, Amex   **ENGLISH SPOKEN** Yes   **FEATURES** Three rooms and an apartment available for holiday rental   **RESERVATIONS** Recommended on weekends
PRICE $$ **DIRECTIONS** The restaurant is in the village center

Cantina Il Borgo is situated in a picturesque medieval village, commanding great views of the wide Orcia Valley. The *borgo* is tiny, with just forty-seven residents. The restaurant faces inward: its outdoor terrace overlooks the *borgo*'s intimate piazza and restored antique well. The vaulted dining room is in an eighteenth-century carriage house. The furnishings are stark but tasteful: a terra-cotta floor has been uncovered; walls are refreshingly bare; a massive wood counter recalls the medieval style.

The menu, too, is pared down but interesting. Laura Mori, a local woman, does the cooking. The owners have sought out fine pecorini and produce wonderful olive oil. This stars in a plate of *pici con le briciole*—hand-rolled ropes of pasta tossed with sautéed bread crumbs, garlic, *peperoncino,* and oil. Ricotta and spinach *tortelli* are tossed with butter and sage; fresh sheep's ricotta always imparts a fragrance of summer fields. *Ribollita,* the twice-cooked Tuscan vegetable soup, is also available.

Main courses are meat-based and uncomplicated. *Scottiglia* is three meats stewed together: rabbit, chicken, and pork. There are steaks, roasts, and a mixed grill. I was offered crisply fried sage leaves and a delicious *sformato di carcioffi*—a kind of artichoke pudding. Here *pecorini* are served alone or with honey and walnuts. Desserts are homemade: I liked a dense apple and nut cake. There is a decisively Tuscan wine list: Montalcino, Montepulciano, Chianti, San Gimignano.

Roccalbegna

CASEIFICIO IL FIORINO
CHEESE

ZONA ARTIGIANALE PAIOLAIO 58053
ROCCALBEGNA GROSSETO
TELEPHONE 0564 989059   FAX 0564 989067
E-MAIL caseificioilfiorinosrl@tin.it

OPEN 8:00–12:30, 14:30–18:00   **CLOSED** Sunday   **CREDIT CARDS** None   **DIRECT SALE** Yes, for whole cheeses   **ENGLISH SPOKEN** No   **DIRECTIONS** From Roccalbegna, go toward Triana. After 500 meters, turn right onto a dirt road across from a group of cypress trees; the *caseificio* is pinky beige

Il Fiorino is a private, family-run *caseificio*. Working with all local sheep's milk, Duilio Fiorini makes some of the area's best *pecorini*. The dairy transforms about ten tons of milk per day. Some of this is cow's milk used in Il Fiorino's ricotta and *marzolino,* both of which are mixed-milk cheeses. Fiorini described his *pecorini* as "old-fashioned, traditional style." He explained that the difference between cheeses has less to do with the milk than with the fermentation process. "Starting with the same milk, there are over twenty ways to work it," he said.

I tried the *stagionato,* matured for a minimum of six to seven months. It has a pronounced but fine sheep's milk flavor, good texture, and a well-balanced salt content—one of the best I've tasted. The cheeses are available in the traditional round forms, usually weighing between 800 grams to 1.5 kg.

Santa Fiora

PANIFICIO MANNI
BREAD

VIA DELLA RIPA, 24 (PIAZZA 12 GIUGNO)
58037 SANTA FIORA GROSSETO
TELEPHONE 0564 977141

OPEN 8:00–13:00, 17:00–19:30   **CLOSED** Wednesday afternoon, Sunday; June, November
CREDIT CARDS None   **DIRECT SALE** Yes   **ENGLISH SPOKEN** A little
DIRECTIONS Off Piazza 12 Giugno

Hidden in the heart of the old town, this family-run bakery produces sweet and savory breads and cookies unique to Monte Amiata, if not to Santa Fiora. Much of their flour is ground by the mill at Bagnolo (p 257).

Biscotti dell'ascensione were originally made to celebrate the Ascension but are now a year-round staple. Looking like a double-tiered bracelet, these delicious crisp biscuits are made of bread dough with added egg, sugar, olive oil, lemon, and aniseed. They make good snacks because they are not too sweet, but have a refreshing taste of anise. Other sweet items include the *stinchi di morto,* crisp meringue-based biscuits with ground hazelnuts; yellow butter cookies made with granular corn flour; and *schiaccia di Pasqua,* an Easter ring cake of yeast dough flavored with aniseed.

Some savory breads are unusual: *biscotto salato lessato* is a salted bread dough seasoned with olive oil and aniseed, boiled and then baked in a pretzel shape. The *schiacce salate* are flat yeast breads mixed with fresh ricotta and olive oil or finely chopped pork rind, *friccioli.* They are baked in individual-size oval loaves with a couple of central slashes to keep their edges crisp. The most unlikely combination is the *schiaccia con friccioli e zucchero*—a salty dough blended with pork rind and sprinkled with sugar before baking.

Also

SCALA D'ORO

PIAZZA GARIBALDI. 0564 977021

This lively bar, know locally as "da Beppe," is open till late. It makes its own gelati using fresh dairy products, and they are some of the Amiata's best.

CHAPTER 11

Siena and the Crete Senesi

S iena is a territory rich with history, culture, and gastronomy. A medieval Ghibelline rival to Guelf Florence, Siena spent centuries battling to retain its independence from Tuscan and foreign domination, with limited results. It is visited today for its fine examples of Gothic art and architecture and for the Palio. This barebacked-horse race is run twice per year, on July 2 and August 16. The evening before the race each *contrada,* or town ward, holds an elaborate banquet in its streets. Places at these tables may sometimes be obtained by visitors. The beautiful town is known for its sweet baked goods, especially *panforte*—a medieval spiced confection of honeyed paste studded with nuts and candied fruits. At its best, this is a rich, perfumed sweetmeat for eating after dinner; more popular versions are oversweet and cloying.

Few areas of Tuscany are as suggestive as the Crete Senesi, the rounded limestone hills to the south of Siena likened to moonscapes. These barren hills are fit for little cultivation but offer fine grazing pastures to the flocks of sheep whose milk is made into pecorino.

Siena is also the territory of some of Tuscany's greatest wines. Half of Chianti Classico (p 183) lies within the province of Siena, as do Montepulciano, San Gimignano, and Montalcino (see chapter 12).

AZIENDA PROMOZIONE TURISTICA
PIAZZA DEL CAMPO, 56
53100 SIENA
0577 280551, FAX 0577 270676
WEB SITE www.siena.turismo.toscana.it

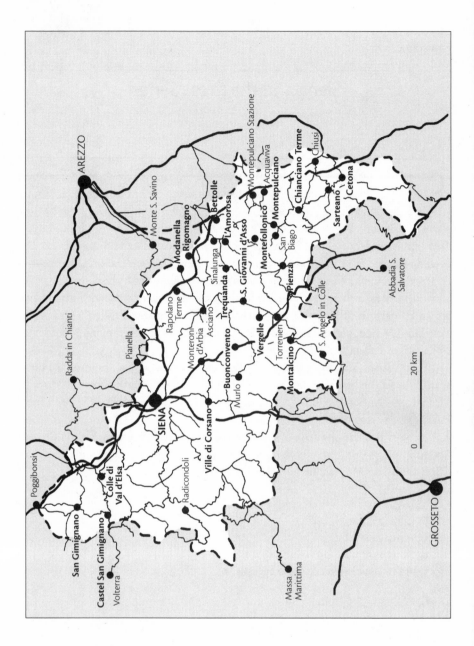

Boldface type indicates towns that are included in this chapter.

Bettolle

RISTORANTE LA BANDITA   **VIA BANDITA, 72. 0577 623447**
WEB SITE www.locandalabandita.it

Walter Redaelli was the acclaimed chef at Locanda dell'Amorosa (see p 273) for many years, until he moved to this simple country inn to start a restaurant of his own. The food is less formal here, and delicious, for great attention is paid to finding excellent ingredients to work with. The menu is strictly seasonal, the prices very good. The restaurant is signposted from the SS 326 between Sinalunga and the Val di Chiana *autostrada* exit.

Buonconvento

OSTERIA DA DUCCIO   **VIA SOCCINI, 76. 0577 807042**

This is a traditional Tuscan *osteria*, offering home-cooked, local dishes in a friendly, casual environment. Pastas are rustic and satisfying; main courses include game in season; there are fine local cheeses and an enterprising wine list.

Castel San Gimignano

CASEIFICIO   **FATTORIA BRENTINE 53034 CASTEL SAN GIMIGNANO SIENA**
EMILIO PINZANI   TELEPHONE 0577 953005 FAX 0577 953163
CHEESE: UNPASTEURIZED   E-MAIL caseificiopinzani@virgilio.it

OPEN 15:00–17:00 or by appointment   **CLOSED** Saturday and Sunday   **CREDIT CARDS** None
DIRECT SALE Yes   **ENGLISH SPOKEN** Yes   **DIRECTIONS** From Castel San Gimignano, go west toward Volterra 2 kms, past tower Monte Miccioli, then turn left for Casole d'Elsa. After 3 kms, take dirt road on left, to the *caseificio* at Fattoria Brentine

Guido Pinzani makes some of the most delicious *pecorini* in Tuscany. For more than twenty years, his has been the only sizable dairy to have committed itself to making cheese from unpasteurized sheep's milk—*pecorino di latte crudo*—because the hygiene standards for such cheeses are much higher and more difficult to maintain than those for pasteurized cheese.

"We have to be very rigorous at every stage of the production of our cheeses," Pinzani told me as we toured the dairy's spotless cooling cells. "But I have always felt it was worth doing, because the flavors of the cheeses are so much better when the milk has not been heated to very high temperatures." Take one bite of these delicate *pecorini* and you will taste the wild grasses and aromatic herbs the sheep graze on in the beautiful hills of central Tuscany.

"Two of our cheeses are made of milk from specific parts of the countryside," he continued. "Pecorino Nero, with the black covering, uses the milk of sheep that have grazed in the Balze Volterrane—the jagged hill formations near Volterra— whereas the Marzolino delle Crete comes from the softly curved Crete Senesi hills south of Siena. Each expresses the character of its terrain and its pastures."

The milk, from farms whose sheep are all carefully tested, is heated to only 38° to 40°C (100.4° to 104°F) whereas pasteurizing would take the milk to 100°C (212°F) or higher.

European Community health laws now oblige certain cheesemaking opera- tions that were once done manually to be done mechanically. "Since the move- ments in cheesemaking must be gentle, we have designed machines that imitate the rhythm of a dairyworker's hands," Pinzani said, "so the cheeses will be as close to handmade as possible." The fresh cheeses are turned and salted by hand and aged on pine boards—again, to maintain the traditional flavors.

All raw milk cheeses undergo a natural sterilization process after forty-five days—any bacteria that might have been in the cheese would automatically be killed in this time. Indeed it is illegal to sell them any younger. Pinzani sells his cheeses when they are at least sixty days old, and several are matured for longer.

In addition to his range of "normal" *pecorini*, Pinzani makes a great pecorino covered with cracked pepper, as well as a truffle-scented pecorino to which a blend of the finest black and white truffles has been added.

Cetona

LA FRATERIA DI
PADRE ELIGIO—MONDO X
RESTAURANT

CONVENTO DI S. FRANCESCO 53040 CETONA
TELEPHONE 0578 238261   FAX 0578 239220
E-MAIL frateria@ftbcc.it

OPEN Lunch and dinner   **CLOSED** Tuesday; January 12 through February   **CREDIT CARDS** Visa, MC, Amex   **ENGLISH SPOKEN** Yes   **FEATURES** Special diets accommodated with advance notice
RESERVATIONS Necessary   **PRICE** $$$$$ **OTHER** Five rooms available for guests
DIRECTIONS From Cetona, go uphill toward Sarteano. After less than 1 km, turn left to Mondo X. The Frateria is up on the right; park up beyond it

---

In 1975 a beautiful but derelict eleventh-century Franciscan convent was given to Father Eligio, a Franciscan monk, to house one of his Mondo X communities of young people with histories of drug abuse and abandonment. "Even then its exceptional qualities of peace and spiritual well-being were apparent," asserted its chef, Walter Tripoli.

Painstakingly, over many years, the buildings and grounds were restored. Today not a stone, not a flower is out of place. The convent, with exquisite clois- ters and chapels in the Gothic and Romanesque styles, has been brought back to life with a rare sense of beauty and culture. Perfectly tended grounds contain scented herb terraces, orchards, vegetable patches, and rose gardens. Mondo X, with communities throughout Italy, is almost self-sufficient, producing cheeses, organic vegetables and fruits, meats, and fish.

The remarkable setting is now matched by wonderful food, thanks to Tripoli. "I learned to cook here, after joining the community," he said. "Padre Eligio organized high-level cooking classes, bringing in master chefs in all categories. Since then I have developed my own style." The restaurant was started to raise money for the communities; it has since built a reputation on its merits. The hand-illustrated tasting menu changes daily, offering a long and interesting succession of courses using Tuscan ingredients with refinement but simplicity. The spare, elegant dining room overlooks the formal gardens.

After an artistically presented *aperitivo*, my September meal began. Perfect shrimp on a soft bed of stewed onions came with a mustard-yellow *timballino* of puréed onion. Tender rabbit fillet was topped with pine nuts, rosemary, and golden raisins plumped in Vin Santo; it went well with an earthy medley of potato, porcini mushrooms, and onion. Spinach leaves enclosed a creamy filling of barley, yellow peppers, and sweet walnuts.

Primi were vegetable-based: soft noodles with a broccoli sauce, and a painterly risotto of zucchini flowers, zucchini, and tomato. Partridge braised in red wine was served with rosemary-scented sauce and garden vegetables. Desserts, too, were delicious. A lacy butter biscuit cup, crisp with hazelnuts, contained an iced chestnut cream. For anyone who still had room, there were petits fours small enough for a doll's house served on an alabaster plate. The restaurant offers fine wines and impeccable service. The set-price menu (exclusive of wines) may not be cheap, but it provides a unique dining experience.

Chianciano Terme

IL TELAIO   PIAZZA ITALIA, 70. 0578 60593. semannu@tin.it

This linen shop has striking window displays featuring pretty tablecloths, hand towels, sheets, and more, in jacquards, linens, and cottons. Inside are tea towels with Renaissance designs, napkins, and place mats in myriad colors, as well as a good range of bolt fabrics for making tablecloths or curtains, which the shop will sew to order.

Also

Chianciano Terme has been built around its thermal baths and water, and is one of Italy's most important spas. For information contact Azienda Promozione Turistica, Piazza Italia, 67, 53042 Chianciano Terme, Siena. 0578 63648, fax 0578 63277.

Colle di Val d'Elsa

ARNOLFO DI CAMBIO
TABLE CRAFTS: CRYSTAL

PIAN DELL'OLMINO 53034
COLLE DI VAL D'ELSA SIENA
TELEPHONE 0577 928279   FAX 0577 929647
WEB SITE www.arnolfodicambio.com

OPEN 9:00–12:30, 15:30–19:00   **CLOSED** Sunday   **CREDIT CARDS** Visa, MC
DIRECT SALE Yes   **ENGLISH SPOKEN** Yes   **OTHER** Factory visits by appointment
DIRECTIONS The factory and shop are on the SS 541 8 kms south of Colle di Val d'Elsa

Colle di Val d'Elsa is renowned throughout Italy for its crystal. If the upper part of the town, Colle Alta, is a perfectly preserved medieval *borgo*, the lower area is home to some of the world's most important crystal manufacturers. Here you can buy fine lead crystal for the table in every conceivable shape and style. Most of these companies still follow traditional methods, employing master craftsmen to blow, carve, and engrave the crystal.

One of the most interesting of these laboratories is Arnolfo di Cambio, named after the prodigious Renaissance artist who was born in the town.

"In his day, Arnolfo di Cambio was a great innovator," says Gabriele Bagnasacco, whose grandfather founded the company in 1963. "Inspired by him, we have always tried to push the boundaries of crystal design." They have succeeded: "Smoke," modernist Joe Colombo's wine glass with an off-center stem, became one of the icons of Italian design in the sixties.

Under Gabriele's management, Arnolfo is once again at design's cutting edge. With art director François Burkhardt, the creative director of the Centre Pompidou in Paris for many years, he has produced a new collection of provocative crystal, like the square charger plates by Spanish designer Oscar Tusquets, and the volumetric glasses of Milanese Ettore Sottsass Jr.

"These ultramodern glasses are made by traditional methods," Gabriele said. "They really show off our 24 percent lead crystal's clarity and luminosity—as do our more classical lines."

In collaboration with the Italian Association of Sommeliers (AIS), Arnolfo has designed a new line of wine glasses called Bacco, with shapes appropriate for specific wine types. There is even a glass designed specifically to bring out the flavors of Brunello.

The company also produces some exciting china, such as fashion designer Roberto Cavalli's graphic rose plates. The factory shop features almost-perfect and end-of-line crystal at reduced prices; the perfect range is available at fine crystal shops in Colle di Val d'Elsa.

ARNOLFO
RESTAURANT

VIA XX SETTEMBRE, 52 53034 COLLE DI VAL D'ELSA
TELEPHONE/FAX 0577 920549
WEB SITE www.arnolfo.com

OPEN Lunch and dinner   **CLOSED** Tuesday; Wednesday lunch; August 1–10
CREDIT CARDS Visa, MC, Amex   **ENGLISH SPOKEN** Yes   **RESERVATIONS** Necessary
PRICE $$$$$–$$$$$$ **OTHER** Several rooms available   **DIRECTIONS** In Colle Alta

I have admired the cuisine of Gaetano Trovato for some years, and like that of many talented chefs, it seems to be improving all the time. The Trovato brothers' small, elegant restaurant is in the historic upper part of Colle di Val d'Elsa, a non-touristy, prosperous hill town famous for its crystal works.

Gaetano Trovato, one of the Jeunes Restaurateurs d'Europe, is originally from the south of Italy; his cooking combines classical technique with a personal palette of Mediterranean tastes and colors.

A recent meal there was memorable. I was struck by the beauty of a yellow stuffed zucchini flower in its green sea of courgette purée, accented by bright basil leaves and cherry tomatoes. "The eye is the first to feel the impact of a dish," says Gaetano Trovato, "so I like to make my food visually chromatic to enhance its fresh flavors. My work is an assemblage of modern cuisine and dishes from our Tuscan *territorio*."

Trovato's painterly aesthetic matches his ability to combine pure-tasting ingredients. Large *tortelli* of smooth egg pasta are stuffed with a cloud of sheep's ricotta, served in light tarragon broth, and topped with matured pecorino and fine strands of crisped carrot. Tiny mountain lamb chops are presented with "variations" of cauliflower—puréed, fried, and pastry-wrapped—and a sweet and tart compote of shallots. Frozen *zucotto* is accompanied by an exotic fruit salad and Vin Santo *zabaione*. This food is refined but real. Great wines and service complement the seasonal menus. In good weather you eat on the terrace, overlooking a field of sunflowers.

L'ANTICA TRATTORIA
RESTAURANT

PIAZZA ARNOLFO, 23 53034 COLLE DI VAL D'ELSA
TELEPHONE/FAX 0577 923747

OPEN Lunch and dinner   **CLOSED** Tuesday; end of December   **CREDIT CARDS** Visa, MC, Amex
ENGLISH SPOKEN Yes   **FEATURES** Outdoor tables in summer   **RESERVATIONS** Necessary
PRICE $$$$$ **DIRECTIONS** In the main square of Colle Bassa

This restaurant occupies a central position in the lively market square of the lower town of Colle; the weekly market takes place on Friday morning. If it was once a popular trattoria, the Paradisi family has upgraded it now to restaurant status, with carefully prepared, authentic Tuscan cuisine. Inside, the mirrored wood panelling and soft lights give the dining rooms a warm atmosphere, as do the friendly family and waiters. Enrico Paradisi is a wine enthusiast and has a model cellar below the restaurant to house his vast collection.

The food is satisfyingly genuine, using quality ingredients that are local whenever possible. The ample menu offers choices from both land and sea. In spring, I tasted steamed shrimp on chickpea purée to start, and a terrine of porcini mushrooms and truffles. *La Ribollita* was a fine version of the classic vegetable soup enriched with beans and bread, and *maccheroncetti* were large, irregular-shaped noodles in a deeply flavored pigeon sauce. Other pastas included *pappardelle* sauced with hare, and jumbo ravioli dressed with seafood. Under the heading of "Innovative Tuscan Cuisine" I chose rabbit cooked *all'Artusi*, a recipe adapted from that nineteenth-century cookery writer's classic *Science in the Kitchen and the Art of Eating Well.* The roasted rabbit loin was rolled around a filling of carrot, zucchini, and aromatic wild fennel. Coffee mousse was garnished with black and white chocolate, and with blackberries. Book ahead, and specify if you would like to eat outside in the square.

L'Amorosa

LOCANDA DELL'AMOROSA   53048 SINALUNGA
RESTAURANT   TELEPHONE 0577 679497   FAX 0577 632001
WEB SITE www.amorosa.it

OPEN Lunch and dinner   CLOSED Monday, Tuesday lunch; January 10 through February
CREDIT CARDS Visa, MC, Amex   ENGLISH SPOKEN Yes   FEATURES Outdoor tables in summer
RESERVATIONS Necessary for dinner   PRICE $$$$$ DIRECTIONS From Sinalunga, go toward
Torrita; after 2 kms follow signs to L'Amorosa

Locanda dell'Amorosa is one of the loveliest restaurants in Tuscany. It occupies the vaulted stables of a fortified medieval *borgo* of the same name, which is also a fine hotel. These quintessentially Tuscan buildings are reached along an avenue of cypress trees. The dining rooms are comfortable without being stuffy, the food is delicious, the service formal; in summer you eat in a picturesque courtyard. The restaurant's chef is committed to using Tuscany's specialties as a springboard for lighter dishes with a modern feel (and less salt than usual). His menu includes versions of rustic bread soups and *frittate* or, in late autumn, dishes devoted to the new season's olive oil.

I arrived in early summer when vegetables were plentiful: a fresh-tasting *bavarese* of tomato with tarragon was a set *coulis*, beautifully red, served with herbed vegetable strips. A zucchini flower stuffed with a cloud-light ricotta mousse was balanced with a hot compote of cherry tomatoes, olives, and basil. *Ceci e farro* was a refined chickpea and spelt wheat soup, drizzled with fragrant olive oil. *Stracci alle mille erbe*, irregular "rags" of handmade pasta, were tossed with aromatic garden herbs. Speckled gnocchi made with porcini mushrooms and black truffles were excellent, lighter and more woodsy than their potato namesakes.

Main courses were divided between fish and meats (the restaurant serves only Chianina beef). Fillet of turbot (*rombo*) was spiced with fresh ginger and served with grilled vegetables. A fanned duck breast was accompanied by caramelized onions and a sauce of balsamic vinegar and acacia honey.

A soufflé tart of L'Amorosa's lemons was nicely sharp, with its decorative salad of berries topped with caramel brûlée; it was well matched with Malvasia delle Lipari, the Sicilian dessert wine. The restaurant's wine list contains more than 130 wines, with emphasis on fine Tuscans. L'Amorosa even makes a few wines of its own.

Modanella

CASTELLO DI MODANELLA
WINE

MODANELLA 53040 SERRE DI RAPOLANO
TELEPHONE 0577 704604, 704553   FAX 0577 704740
WEB SITE www.modanella.com

OPEN 8:30–13:00, 14:30–19:00; group visits and tastings by appointment only
CLOSED Saturday and Sunday in winter, Sunday in summer   **CREDIT CARDS** Visa, MC
DIRECT SALE Yes   **ENGLISH SPOKEN** Yes   **OTHER** Houses and apartments available for holiday rentals   **DIRECTIONS** Modanella is signposted from the SS 326; look for the northeast turnoff to Modanella near Serre di Rapolano

---

Modanella is a handsome twelfth-century castle with Gothic arched vaults, a dramatic inner courtyard, and a cluster of secondary buildings and church. It once belonged to the powerful Piccolomini family of Pope Pius II.

The estate, with 25 hectares (62 acres) of vineyards, has adopted an interesting policy of winemaking. "When my company took over in 1987," explained Gabriella Cerretti, its director, "we decided to abandon Chianti and concentrate on single-variety wines." Modanella now boasts a group of four red grape varieties: Sangiovese, Cabernet Sauvignon, Merlot, and Canaiolo. They no longer produce any white wines. Each varietal is vinified and bottled separately. Most are modern style, aged in small French oak casks, and are made in conjunction with the enologist Fabrizio Ciufoli. There is a very low grape yield per plant, and that increases the concentration of flavors in the wine.

The farm is becoming increasingly organic. "With the Wine Institute of Arezzo," Gabriella continued, "we experimented by reducing chemical treatments." Modanella also sells Vin Santo, olive oil, and organic produce.

Montalcino

See chapter 12, page 303.

Montefollonico

LA CHIUSA   VIA DELLA MADONNINA, 88 53040 MONTEFOLLONICO
RESTAURANT   TELEPHONE 0577 669668   FAX 0577 669593

OPEN Lunch and dinner   **CLOSED** Tuesday; mid-January to mid-March
CREDIT CARDS Visa, MC, Amex   **ENGLISH SPOKEN** Yes   **RESERVATIONS** Necessary
PRICE $$$$$ **OTHER** Fourteen rooms available   **DIRECTIONS** The restaurant is signposted
from the entrance to Montefollonico

La Chiusa is an elegant restaurant in what were once rustic farm buildings, nestled in a painterly green setting of olive groves and gardens. The kitchen, which all visitors are invited to see, is large and welcoming and full of the aromas of home cooking. The dining room is as high as a barn, with vaulted brick arches and white walls. Allow time for your meal here, as a leisurely pace is needed to appreciate the authentic country flavors of this cuisine.

Owner Dania Masotti is unique in offering her customers a pasta-making demonstration—while they eat. Indeed, charming local ladies come in wearing aprons and bearing portable tables on which they knead and roll their *sfoglia*. It helps us appreciate what real pasta is.

In spring I was treated to a tender baked artichoke, stuffed with bread crumbs, capers, and onion. A *tortino* of mashed potato was shaped like a heart, golden and crusty on top, and delicately scented with nutmeg and pepper. I loved the pea soup: it was bright green, rich, and remarkably sweet—the essence of freshly picked garden peas. Then came the pasta, in the guise of three ricotta-filled *tortelli*, soft, savory, and flavorful. This is rustic food with a knowing sophistication. Lamb shanks were deeply roasted, till both they and their onions were almost caramelized. The dessert of hot strawberry compote was topped with ice-cream and went well with a glass of opulent Vin Santo. The wines here are primarily Tuscan, with big vintages priced accordingly.

Montepulciano

FORMAGGI SILVANA CUGUSI   SS 146 PER PIENZA VIA DELLA BOCCIA, 8
CHEESE   53045 MONTEPULCIANO
                                     TELEPHONE 0578 757558

OPEN 8:00–13:00, 15:00–19:30   **CLOSED** Never   **CREDIT CARDS** None
DIRECT SALE Yes, for whole or half cheeses; Cugusi also has a shop in Via di Gracciano nel Corso, 31,
in Montepulciano   **ENGLISH SPOKEN** No   **DIRECTIONS** The *caseificio* is off the main road
between Montepulciano and Pienza, 3 kms from Montepulciano, 10 kms from Pienza

This cheesemaker is located amid the extraordinary rounded Crete Senesi hills. The Cugusis make some of the finest sheep's cheeses in Tuscany, and their story is interesting. Rafaele Cugusi was one of the first Sardinian shepherds to bring his flock (and eight children) from Sardinia in the early 1960s to land abandoned after the sharecropping system was disbanded. It was well suited for grazing sheep; its wild herbs and grasses lent the milk a distinctive fragrance. The Cugusis bought the land for little and began making pecorino as they had at home. Today the business is run by Silvana Cugusi, an attractive, energetic young woman, and her siblings.

The Cugusis still handmake their cheeses, using milk now pasteurized to conform to E.U. standards. Their exquisite ricotta is exceptionally delicate and creamy—the secret is in its whole-milk enrichment. Ricotta is made from the whey that remains after pecorino is made. It is steam heated to 75° to 80°C (167° to 176°F) in a large cauldron, while Silvana's sister Giovanna spins it constantly by hand, for "it must never stay still" she explains. The small ricotta curds are formed by heat alone; no rennet is needed to make them set. A little salt and whole milk are added, and that is all.

The Cugusis make a range of *pecorini* (the real *pecorini di Pienza*) in different stages of maturation of up to six months. All the cheeses are turned by hand as they mature; some are rubbed once a week with *la morchia*, the murky residue from a vat of olive oil. This thick oil prevents cracking and gives a brownish crust. Sometimes ash is sprinkled over the cheeses; they may be rubbed with tomato paste, or packed under walnut leaves, each element imparting a slight but particular flavor.

A rare cheese is fresh *ravaggiolo*. This is the "first curd": one solid curd, uncut, of whole milk, placed in a small mold and left to set. It is like eating soft, set milk, and it must be consumed within a few hours of being made. Sprinkle it with salt, pepper, and a little good oil and eat with fragrant fresh bread.

IL FRANTOIO
DI MONTEPULCIANO
OLIVE OIL

VIA DI MARTIENA, 2 53045 MONTEPULCIANO
TELEPHONE MILL 0578 716305; SHOP 0578 758732
FAX 0578 758732

OPEN Shop 10:00–13:00, 16:00–19:30; mill may be visited in winter during operation
CLOSED Wednesday afternoon and Sunday in summer; the shop is closed during the milling season, when oil is sold from the mill   **CREDIT CARDS** Visa, MC, Amex
DIRECT SALE Yes; there also is a shop in Piazza Pasquino, 9   **ENGLISH SPOKEN** No
DIRECTIONS The shop is within the town walls; the mill is just outside them

---

Montepulciano's *frantoio* (olive oil mill) belongs to a large cooperative of olive growers with 650 members in the *comune* of Montepulciano. The *frantoio* presses their olives and sells oil from the cooperative's shop. Many of the growers also produce wine, as the olive harvest begins in early November, after the grapes are finished.

The recently modernized mill uses stainless-steel Alfa-Laval and Rapanelli machines. They may be less picturesque than stone wheels and presses, but they offer a more hygienic and flexible system, since members can control temperatures at each stage. There is also far less danger of contamination from one batch of olives to the next.

After being washed and freed of their leaves, the olives are effectively cut up (rather than hammered) between flat discs covered with blunt *lamelle* (little blades). The *gramola* (paste) is then lightly heated in a double-boiler system to 25° to 30°C (77° to 86°F). Without some heat, the olives will not readily render their oil, but compared to industrial methods, in which the paste is worked at very high temperatures, this still constitutes "cold" extraction, the mill's director explained. The paste is then pushed against a series of blunt blades like a comb, which gently draw the oil and olive water out by drops. For every 100 kgs of olives, only 14 kgs of oil are made. The oil and water mixture is separated by centrifuge, and it may be cotton filtered.

The *frantoio* sells several grades of oil, in sizes from 250 ml to 5 liters. Its best oil has a vivid, cut-grass flavor with the decisive "peppery" finish that characterizes central Tuscany's finest oils.

EARLY SUMMER IN MONTEPULCIANO

Montepulciano in June is divine: the fields are cropped of their first hay, golden but not yet parched. The olives are just flowering, the vines freshly green with still unpruned tendrils and their first miniature *grappole*. If the surrounding countryside is sun soaked, the town, with its warm peachy stone, is the perfect respite: hot in the sun, away from the hill breezes, cool in the shade, and almost bone chilling in the dark interiors.

Midweek few people were there, mostly foreigners, and we gently wandered up and up, diverted on either side by enticing boutiques of local foods. Here wine is king but it is also culture; there need be no apologies for so many wine stores and *cantine,* one after the other, on the way up.

The main street is wide enough to be zigzagged from side to side, but its charm lies in its steady ascent, unfolding one section at a time—you never see the whole stretch at once. Nor do you more than glimpse the extraordinary sweep of countryside as you peer past arched openings or slits between palazzi, until you reach the top, when the whole magnificent panorama is revealed.

CAFFÈ POLIZIANO
RESTAURANT, CAFÉ

VIA VOLTAIA NEL CORSO, 27 53045 MONTEPULCIANO
TELEPHONE 0578 758615
WEB SITE www.ec-net.it/site/caffèpoliziano

OPEN 7:00–1:00 A.M.   **CLOSED** Never   **CREDIT CARDS** Visa, MC
DIRECT SALE Yes, of wines   **ENGLISH SPOKEN** Yes   **FEATURES** Outdoor dining in summer
DIRECTIONS On Montepulciano's main street

Caffè Poliziano is a Montepulciano landmark. The café, with its Italian art nouveau-style decor, first opened in 1868. Its celebrated clientele has included Carducci, Pirandello, and Fellini. It went through several transformations—from *café chantant* to movie house—before its refurbishment in 1992. It is a pretty place, with lofty rooms commanding an exceptional panorama of the valley below, and a flexible one—you can have coffee, lunch, snacks, afternoon tea, dinner, or a glass of wine. There are six *primi* to choose from for lunch, plus salads and sandwiches. Three set-menu dinners—including one vegetarian—along with the regular menu are available downstairs in the evenings. Prices are fair—no cover or service charges are added—and in summer there is a beautiful outdoor terrace to eat on while you admire the view.

LA GROTTA
RESTAURANT

SAN BIAGIO 53045 MONTEPULCIANO
TELEPHONE/FAX 0578 757607

OPEN Lunch and dinner   **CLOSED** Wednesday; January and February   **CREDIT CARDS** Visa, MC, Amex   **ENGLISH SPOKEN** Yes   **FEATURES** Garden terrace   **RESERVATIONS** Recommended for dinner   **PRICE** $$$ **DIRECTIONS** San Biagio is the church below Montepulciano (to the west, off the road to Pienza, 1 km from town); drive down the avenue of cypresses to the restaurant facing the church

This restaurant is beside the lovely San Biagio church, just below the main town of Montepulciano. Its spacious dining room has walls of stone and stucco and a big fireplace; in summer you eat in the shady garden. The style is sophisticated but not stuffy. The wine list features Montepulciano (with twenty-three wineries), Tuscany, and beyond.

My June lunch began with excellent *panzanella,* the quintessentially Tuscan summer salad: soaked bread combined with tomatoes, olives, arugula, capers, celery, red radicchio, and a little onion, then chilled. *Crostini* were also far from banal: a fine, warm calves' liver pâté came with a Vin Santo sauce as pure as nectar. I began to suspect an unusually creative hand was in the kitchen. Homemade *raviolini* were stuffed with fresh sheep's-ricotta mousse (you tasted its tangy sweetness), basil, and pine nuts and topped with Parmesan flakes and herbed oil. Rabbit in sweet and sour sauce, *in agrodolce,* had Indian colors: the tender rabbit was dressed in an ocher sauce of soft onions with an edge of vinegar. Beside it a dark oak lettuce leaf held spicy ratatouille of eggplant, peppers, potato, and zucchini. The food was light and fresh tasting. (Even the garnishes were intelligent!)

For dessert, a berry tart resembled a soft *clafouti,* served with a *crème anglaise*—with an unmistakably French touch. David explained that, indeed, his mother, Pierrette Matthieu, is French and ran this restaurant for more than ten years. The marriage of French technique and Tuscan inspiration works! Recently his sister, Cristina, has taken over in the kitchen.

AVIGNONESI
WINE

VIA DI GRACCIANO NEL CORSO, 91 53045 MONTEPULCIANO
TELEPHONE 0578 724304   FAX 0578 724308
WEB SITE www.avignonesi.it

OPEN Shop daily March–October: 9:30–13:30,14:30–19:30; winery or cellar visits by prior written request only   **CLOSED** December–February   **CREDIT CARDS** Visa, MC, Amex
DIRECT SALE Yes, subject to availability, from shop or winery   **ENGLISH SPOKEN** Yes
DIRECTIONS Shop is on Montepulciano's main street

Avignonesi is what you would think of if you closed your eyes and imagined a quintessential Tuscan wine estate. The country villa—with its courtyards of sweet *tiglios,* grouped buildings, cypress avenue, herb garden, *vinsantaia,* and its surrounding sea of vineyards—has a style and beauty that is perfect yet natural. The *cantina* slopes ever downward underground, with room upon room of *barriques:* it is immaculately kept and quite spectacular. In town, an elegant sixteenth-century palazzo with antique cellars houses the winery's shop.

Ever since the three Falvo brothers merged lands to create Avignonesi, they have invested the estate with passion and ambition. It boasts a list of fine wines, from Vino Nobile and its Riservas to modern wines aged in *barriques,* like Desiderio (of 85 percent Merlot and 15 percent Cabernet Sauvignon), and Il Marzocco (Chardonnay). They make lovely extra-virgin olive oil and Occhio di Pernice, Vin Santo so rare hardly anyone has tasted it. Its cellars are well worth a visit, so make an appointment to do so.

BINDELLA
WINE

VALLOCAIA VIA DELLE TRE BERTE, 10/A 53040 MONTEPULCIANO
TELEPHONE 0578 767777   FAX 0578 767255
WEB SITE www.bindella.it

OPEN 8:30–16:00; *cantina* visits by appointment only   **CLOSED** Saturday and Sunday
CREDIT CARDS Visa, MC   **DIRECT SALE** Yes; wines also available from shop in
Montepulciano: Terra Toscana, Via Ricci, 14. 0578 757708   **ENGLISH SPOKEN** A little
FEATURES Apartments available for holiday rentals   **DIRECTIONS** From Montepulciano
Stazione, go through Acquaviva toward Tre Berte, passing over the *autostrada.* After about
1 km turn right to Bindella and Fattoria del Cerro

Rudolf Bindella, a Swiss wine importer, owns Terre di Bindella, comprising this Vallocaia estate, with 30 hectares (74 acres) of vineyards, and Borgo Scopeto in

MONTEPULCIANO'S NOBLE WINES

Vino Nobile di Montepulciano is a red wine that traditionally was made from primarily Prugnolo Gentile grapes (a local clone of Sangiovese similar to that used in Chianti), with Canaiolo Nero and Mammolo added. A small percentage of white grapes was traditionally added, but progressive wineries have eased them out (up to 10 percent is still allowed). Recent modifications to the DOCG specify that the wine must be of between 80 and 100 percent Prugnolo Gentile, with flexibility about the other red grapes: Mammolo, Canaiolo, and Colorino are the traditional types, Merlot and Cabernet Sauvignon the modern.

The DOCG was granted in 1980, and its most recent regulations offer producers more flexibility in how to age the wine: Vino Nobile must still come out two years after the harvest, but it may be matured in wood for anywhere from 12 to 18 months, with the remaining time in the bottle. The Riserva comes out after three years.

As in Montalcino, a "younger brother" exists for the Vino Nobile: Rosso di Montepulciano DOC. This uses the same grapes as Vino Nobile but is aged less and sold sooner.

Prugnolo Gentile (named for its tiny, plum-shaped grapes) affords the wine good structure and concentration of flavor, while Mammolo confers the characteristic hint of violets that distinguishes Vino Nobile from Chianti. Like all big red wines, Vino Nobile will benefit from a few years of extra cellaring.

As for the name, it may have been a case more of pomp than circumstance, but in 1685 the poet Francesco Redi declared that "Montepulciano, of all wines, is king." From royal to noble, the concept stuck—with today's wines coming closer to their lofty title than ever before.

The Vino Nobile consortium's new headquarters also house a wine bar for its producers' wines, with direct sale and tastings.

Consorzio Del Vino Nobile di Montepulciano
Palazzo del Capitano
Piazza Grande
53045 Montepulciano, Siena
0578 757812, FAX 0578 758213
Web Site www.vinonobiledimontepulciano.it

Chianti. His style is modern, technologically advanced, even experimental. His large shipshape *cantina* exemplifies a progressive attitude toward winemaking.

Vineyards are planted at high density (more than eight thousand plants per hectare), with grass beneath them as a natural deterrent to the vines' natural vigor. Cellar temperatures are controlled against summer and winter extremes. The estate's best wines are its Vino Nobile di Montepulciano (reserve and normal), Rosso di Montepulciano Fosso Lupaio, and Vallocaia, an unfiltered super-Tuscan of selected Prugnolo Gentile grapes matured in *barriques*—a powerful, elegant wine set to improve with time. Bindella recently added a Vin Santo to its list, called Dolce Sinfonia.

LE CASALTE   VIA DEL TERMINE, 2 SANT'ALBINO 53045 MONTEPULCIANO
WINE   TELEPHONE 0578 798246   FAX 0578 799714
E-MAIL lecasalte@libero.it

OPEN 9:00–12:00, 14:00–18:00; visits and tastings by appointment if possible
CLOSED Saturday and Sunday except by appointment   CREDIT CARDS None
DIRECT SALE Yes   ENGLISH SPOKEN Yes   DIRECTIONS From Montepulciano, go toward Chianciano Terme; after 4 kms at Sant' Albino village turn left on Via dei Cipressi (just before Hotel Tre Stelle); go straight for 2.5 kms; at the T-junction turn left onto the dirt road and follow it to the winery at the hilltop

Le Casalte is a modest country farmhouse perched on a hillside to the south of Montepulciano. It was bought in 1975 by Guido Barioffi, a banker from Rome who had always dreamed of making wine. He found an abandoned house and its lands long before it was the trendy thing to do and set about replanting the vineyards as perfectly as he had seen them in Piemonte, where he worked. In 1979 he took the first wine he had made to Vinitaly and surprised himself by finding a German importer for it. Today his lovely daughter Chiara lives in the farmhouse and oversees the running of the now successful winery.

"We are starting to build a new cellar, because we need more space to grow," she explained as we visited the tiny but perfectly kept existing cellars under the house. They work with a mix of traditional large barrels and smaller *tonneaux* and *barriques*.

Another recent change has been the collaboration with senior winemaker, Giulio Gambelli. "Gambelli is a wonderful person to work with," she said, "because he always respects the character of both the client and their wines." They taste the wines together every week and make decisions in tandem. "After all, my family's name is on the label, and we want the wines to reflect our philosophy."

Le Casalte makes Vino Nobile di Montepulciano, with its Riserva in great years; Rosso di Montepulciano; and a white wine of primarily Chardonnay, with a little Grechetto and Sauvignon. There is also a traditional-style Vin Santo, of Malvasia and Grechetto grapes. "I like this wine because it starts sweet and ends dry," Chiara said, as we sipped it under her shady pergola.

CONTUCCI
WINE

VIA DEL TEATRO, 1 53045 MONTEPULCIANO
TELEPHONE/FAX 0578 757006
WEB SITE www.contucci.it

OPEN 9:00–12:30, 14:30–18:30 for sales and tastings; groups by appointment only
CREDIT CARDS Visa, MC   **DIRECT SALE** Yes   **ENGLISH SPOKEN** Yes
DIRECTIONS In the town center

A visit to the Contucci cellars is de rigueur for anyone interested in Montepulciano's Vino Nobile. All the atmosphere and history is there, in those almost spooky cellars in the bowels of a sixteenth-century palazzo in the heart of town. Apron-clad male attendants act as guides on the tour, friendly and full of talk of waning moons and their importance for a wine's development.

Count Alamanno Contucci's family has played a key role in the town's history for seven hundred years. He has been president of the Vino Nobile consortium for many years. A traditionalist by tradition, he seems now to be veering toward modernity: far from the tourist track of picturesque red-and-black-painted old barrels, he is experimenting with small new oak—with optimistic results. "You need common sense in these matters," he told me. "We are finding that old and new ideas work well together."

Contucci makes three types of Vino Nobile: a *cru*, from the vineyard called Pietra Rossa, a "normal," and, in good years, a reserve. The best grapes go to Vino Nobile; the rest are used for the younger Rosso di Montepulciano. Contucci also produces Vin Santo: rich and raisiny in taste, golden amber in color.

FATTORIA DEL CERRO
WINE

VIA GRAZIANELLA, 5 ACQUAVIVA DI MONTEPULCIANO
53040 MONTEPULCIANO
TELEPHONE 0578 767722, 767700   FAX 0578 768040
E-MAIL fattoriadelcerro@tin.it

OPEN Visits and tastings by appointment only   **CREDIT CARDS** Visa, MC   **DIRECT SALE** Yes; wines also available at the shop in Piazza San Francesco, 1, Montepulciano   **ENGLISH SPOKEN** Yes
RESERVATIONS Groups of fifteen or more may eat lunch or dinner in the *cantina* by previous appointment only   **DIRECTIONS** From Montepulciano, go toward Chianciano; after 5 kms turn left at the big curve; Fattoria is after 6 kms, signposted

Fattoria del Cerro is a major force in the winemaking landscape of Montepulciano. It is one of the biggest estates, with more than 140 hectares (345 acres) of vineyards belonging to Saiagricola, a giant insurance company with holdings throughout Italy. (Italian law dictates that insurance companies must invest in property assets.) Its catalog of wines includes those geared for mass distribution; the top labels, including a fine Vino Nobile and its Riservas, win awards.

The large complex is efficiently and intelligently run (the estate participates in many winemaking experiments), but, like all corporations, it remains somewhat anonymous. Those wanting to taste or buy its wines should go there: the countryside and views are exceptional.

PODERI BOSCARELLI
WINE

VIA DI MONTENERO, 24 CERVOGNANO
53045 MONTEPULCIANO
TELEPHONE 0578 767277, 767608   FAX 0578 767277

OPEN Monday–Friday 8:00–13:00, 15:00–20:00; weekends by appointment; tastings and *cantina* visits by appointment only   CREDIT CARDS None   DIRECT SALE Yes; wines also available at the shop in Montepulciano at Via Ricci, 42 (off Piazza Grande)   ENGLISH SPOKEN Yes   DIRECTIONS From the center of Acquaviva, across from the tobacconist, take the small Via delle Vecchie Mura toward Cervognano; the *cantina* is on the right after about 1.5 kms

"Our winery began in the sixties," explained Marchese Luca de Ferrari Corradi, "because my mother, Paola, remembered the taste of wines drunk at Montepulciano with her grandfather and wanted to re-create them. Much local land was abandoned then, and most wines were pretty awful."

This passionate hobby became a full-time commitment for Paola and her sons. Poderi Boscarelli is an intimate setup: a country house sheltered by an oak wood, with cellars that have now outgrown their original small room. The atmosphere is relaxed, personal. The family members live as winemakers and are proud of the recognition their wines have achieved in collaboration with Maurizio Castelli, one of Tuscany's finest enologists.

The estate's 16 hectares (40 acres) of vineyards produce a small range of wines. The award-winning Vino Nobile Riserva, in both the normal and *cru* (Vigna del Nocio) versions, is made only in great years. They are concentrated, rich ruby wines of elegance and warmth. Boscarelli is a modern-style wine of pure Prugnolo Gentile grapes aged in small French casks. Vino Nobile, Rosso di Montepulciano, Chianti Colli Senesi, and extra-virgin olive oil are also produced.

POLIZIANO
WINE

VIA FONTAGO, 11 MONTEPULCIANO STAZIONE
53040 MONTEPULCIANO
TELEPHONE 0578 738171   FAX 0578 738752
WEB SITE www.carlettipoliziano.com

OPEN 8:00–12:00, 14:30–18:00; tastings and cellar visits by appointment only   CLOSED Saturday and Sunday; August   CREDIT CARDS Visa, MC   DIRECT SALE Yes; wines also available at Enoteca Poliziano in Piazza Grande, Montepulciano, open April–October   ENGLISH SPOKEN Yes   DIRECTIONS Reached from the Montepulciano Stazione-Nottola road, or the Gracciano-Montepulciano Stazione road, along symmetrical cypress avenues

Federico Carletti is Poliziano, and vice versa. Described affectionately as "the volcano," Carletti is passionate about his wine, and that passion is contagious. The estate is big, with more than 120 hectares (296 acres) registered to DOC and DOCG wines, but Carletti's personal involvement renders it intimate.

When he took over from his father in the early 1980s, Carletti selected the best clones of the local Prugnolo Gentile grape and replanted or grafted any weak plants. His best wines, made in collaboration with the talented winemaker Carlo

Ferrini, now consistently win top accolades. His star is a *cru*, produced only in exceptional years: Asinone is made from the estate's best Sangiovese grapes, with a little Merlot or Canaiolo added. The wine matures for eigthteen months in small *barriques*, followed by eight months in the bottle. It is a great wine: rich, complex, and compelling. Le Stanze IGT is a flexible blend of Cabernet Sauvignon, Merlot, and Sangiovese that also sees eighteen months in new *barriques*.

Carletti has changed his philosophy regarding the planting of the vines: "I am now planting at even higher density," he said as we inspected a new vineyard with grass growing between alternate rows. "The clonal selection of Sangiovese is a key factor too—great wines must be created in the vineyard."

I visited his huge new modern *cantina*, with its neat rows of small oak casks. "You have to move with the times," he exclaimed enthusiastically. "*Barriques* are the future, and it is as well to understand them. For me, the sweeter taste conferred by the French oak is better suited to Vino Nobile; the Slavonian seems more bitter."

Twenty hectares of vineyards in the Maremma, near Magliano in Toscana, are the latest addition to this exciting winery.

TENUTA TREROSE　　　　　　　　　　　　VILLA BELVEDERE VIA DELLA STELLA, 3
WINE　　　　　　　　　　　　　　　　　　　VALIANO 53040 MONTEPULCIANO
　　　　　　　　　　　　TELEPHONE 0578 724018, 724103　　FAX 0577 849316

OPEN 8:00–12:00, 14:00–18:00; tastings possible for retail buyers; cellar visits and groups by appointment only　　**CLOSED** Saturday and Sunday　　**CREDIT CARDS** None
DIRECT SALE Yes; wines also on sale at the *borgo*　　**ENGLISH SPOKEN** Yes　　**OTHER** The medieval *borgo* has holiday accommodations　　**DIRECTIONS** From the Val di Chiana exit on *autostrada* A1, go toward Perugia. Take the second exit, for Cortona, then go toward Montepulciano. After 6 kms go toward Pozzuolo; the winery is after 1 km

---

Tenuta Trerose is now owned by the Angelini family, who own a pharmaceutical corporation and whose exceptional holdings in Tuscany include the prestigious Val di Suga winery at Montalcino and San Leonino in Chianti. The family is investing heavily in them, refurbishing the buildings and maintaining a high standard of winemaking. The estate's former owner, Lionello Marchesi, modernized the winery by planting at high density in 11 hectares (27 acres) of the 55 hectares (135 acres) of vineyards. (Lasers were used to keep the rows straight.) A spacious *cantina* was built adjacent to the attractive sixteenth-century villa.

The estate, managed by Mario Calzolani, makes Vino Nobile and its two *crus*, Simposio, of selected Prugnolo Gentile grapes, and La Villa, which contains 10 percent Cabernet Sauvignon—both award winners in their best years. There is also now a modern-style Rosso di Montepulciano that includes a little Syrah and Gamay. The Tenuta has also planted non-Tuscan vines. Three interesting white wines, Busillis (Viognier), Flauto (Sauvignon), and Salterio (Chardonnay) are the fruit of this policy. Each wine is made of single-variety grapes and aged in *barriques*. Renaio is a fresh-tasting Chardonnay that sees no wood.

VALDIPIATTA
WINE

VIA DELLA CIARLIANA, 25/A 53040 MONTEPULCIANO
TELEPHONE 0578 757930   FAX 0578 717037
WEB SITE www.valdipiatta.it

OPEN 9:00–18:00; guided tastings and cellar visits by appointment   **CLOSED** Saturday and Sunday   **CREDIT CARDS** Visa, MC   **DIRECT SALE** Yes; wines also on sale at Valdipiatta's shop: Via del Poliziano, 14 and at Caffè Poliziano, both in Montepulciano   **ENGLISH SPOKEN** Yes   **OTHER** Two apartments for holiday rental available   **DIRECTIONS** From Montepulciano, follow green *autostrada* signs; after 3.7 kms, take the unpaved road to the right, signposted to the winery, following it down for 1 km

---

Tenuta Valdipiatta was taken over in 1990, and the new owners have already made a name for themselves. The setting is rural, in a valley surrounded by vineyards. The offices and vinification areas are plain, but the aging *cantina* is spectacular. It has been hewed horizontally from the hillside, like an outdoor stage setting. Inside, an avenue of large casks leads to an inner *degustazione*, or tasting, room sitting right under the mountain. This *cantina* is modern but not characterless, reflecting the forward-thinking philosophy of the estate's three young partners.

"We determined to make fine wines as ecologically as possible," explained Lauretta Bernini, the serious young agronomist. "We use no chemical herbicides and fight pests with the *lotta guidata*, or 'guided struggle,' system of natural predators and minimal spraying."

Working with Bernini and winemaker Paolo Vagaggini, Valdipiatta's owner, Giulio Caporali, has replanted select clones of Prugnolo Gentile and restored existing vineyards. The emphasis is on quality: even the Rosso di Montepulciano, often considered Vino Nobile's poor cousin, is made of select grapes and matured partly in French *barriques*. The result is a more concentrated wine than usual.

A recent collaboration with Bordeaux University's enology professor, Yves Glories, has led to marked changes in the wines. "Since 1997 our wines have become more rounded, as we are learning to temper Sangiovese's tannins with a better use of wood and more stringent pruning in the vineyard," Bernini explained. "It's an exciting project [see also Pacenti, p 325]: Professeur Glories' palate is exceptional, and he has helped us improve many aspects of our winemaking—one of which is the use now of *barriques* from Sylvain."

The company's wines are Vino Nobile, its Riserva, and Rosso; I Trefonti IGT (of 40 percent each Cabernet and Sangiovese and 20 percent Canaiolo, aged for eighteen months in *barriques*); Trincerone IGT (60 percent Canaiolo and 40 percent Merlot, aged in *barriques* for twelve months); and the white Il Nibbiano (of red Canaiolo vinified *in bianco*, Trebbiano, Grechetto, and Malvasia; it sees no wood).

ENOTECA OINOCHÓE
WINE STORE

VIA DI VOLTAIA NEL CORSO, 82
53045 MONTEPULCIANO
TELEPHONE 0578 757524

OPEN 9:00–19:00   **CLOSED** Sunday; January and February   **CREDIT CARDS** Visa, MC, Amex
DIRECT SALE Yes   **MAIL ORDER** Within Europe   **ENGLISH SPOKEN** No
DIRECTIONS In the town center

"The ancient Etruscans poured their wine into a clay *oinochóe* [vessel]," explained Chiara Bellacci, the shop's owner, "and the word inspired us when we decided to sell wines." The shop stocks all of Montepulciano's Nobile wines and a good selection of Brunello di Montalcino, Chianti, and super-Tuscans. The owners of the shop are knowledgeable and friendly. A good place to stock up on your favorite noble wines.

Pienza

TRATTORIA LATTE DI LUNA
RESTAURANT

VIA SAN CARLO, 2/4 53026 PIENZA
TELEPHONE 0578 748606

OPEN Lunch and dinner (last orders at 21:30)   **CLOSED** Tuesday; February and July
CREDIT CARDS Visa, MC   **ENGLISH SPOKEN** No   **RESERVATIONS** Always recommended
PRICE $$ **DIRECTIONS** In the town center, near the Porta al Ciglio gate

This small, family-run *trattoria*, with summer tables out in the piazza, is always packed. The menu is uncomplicated but appetizing: rustic soups, pastas with a choice of sauces (meat, tomato, truffle), including local *pici all'aglione*—thick spaghetti in a garlicky tomato sauce. Meats are roasted or grilled: steaks, suckling pig, country sausages, duck with olives. Daily specials (ask for these) include unusual vegetable dishes such as *sformato di zucchine*—a soufflé-like pudding of zucchini. Frozen *semifreddi* are a specialty. I sampled a great orange-flavored one shaped like a roulade. The portions are generous, prices fair, wines local, and the service is friendly. Sounds good, doesn't it?

LA CORNUCOPIA—
CLUB DELLE FATTORIE
SPECIALTY FOODS

PIAZZA MARTIRI DELLA LIBERTÀ, 2 53026 PIENZA
TELEPHONE/FAX 0578 748150, 748491
WEB SITE www.emporiodellefattorie.com

OPEN 9:30–13:00, 14:30–19:30   **CLOSED** Tuesday, Wednesday morning in November, January, and February   **CREDIT CARDS** Visa, MC, Amex   **MAIL ORDER** Yes   **ENGLISH SPOKEN** Yes
DIRECTIONS In the town center, on Pienza's main street

Alberto and Mara del Buono were among the earliest champions of Italy's artisan foods. Their Club delle Fattorie, literally, "farm club," is a mail-order business, which is a rarity, as Italian mail is notoriously undependable. The club offers selected gourmet foods at good prices to subscribers. "You could call us the soul and palate of the business," exclaimed the genial Alberto del Buono. "We personally travel and taste each product—and never sell anything we don't eat or drink ourselves."

Their lively shop is filled with rare honeys and pâtés, sauces and pastas, biscuits and cheeses, grappas and vinegars, oils and wines . . . a cornucopia of gourmet treats. Definitely worth a food lover's detour!

PIENZA'S CHEESES

In Italy the name Pienza is synonymous with pecorino, sheep's cheese. It is considered among the country's finest, owing to the fragrant pastures the local sheep graze on. The pretty village is stuffed with food boutiques professedly selling local artisan cheeses, often displayed maturing in ash or walnut leaves. But be warned: many are Sardinian or industrial southern Italian cheeses masquerading as local *pecorini* (they may be good cheeses, but they are rarely worth such high prices). Read the small print on the labels for production information, and be wary of any products without labels—the really small peasant producers do not sell their cheeses through these shops.

Several of the good local sheep's cheese producers (*caseificio*), who are nearby and sell to the public, are Belsedere (p 299), Crete Senesi (p 301), Cugusi (p 274), Putzulu (tel: 0577 669744), SOLP (tel: 0578 748695), and Val d'Orcia (p 261).

Also

CERAMICHE DELLA MEZZALUNA   VIA GOZZANTE, 67. 0578 748561

Dino and Fabrizio are friendly potters with a workshop under Pienza's fifteenth-century hanging gardens (ask to see these gardens' brick supports). They specialize in ceramic tiles and objects with clean geometric lines and modern colors. The short walk down to their shop from the Duomo offers breathtaking views of the Val d'Orcia.

Rigomagno

BOSSI & TURCHI
MEAT: SALUMI

RIGOMAGNO SCALO 53040 SINALUNGA
TELEPHONE 0577 663550   FAX 0577 663592

DIRECT SALE Should begin soon—phone to check; meats also available from Antonio Miccoli, Via di Città, 93. Siena; Bazar dei Sapori, Via S. Giovanni, 8. San Gimignano   **ENGLISH SPOKEN** A little
DIRECTIONS The company is by the train track at Rigomagno Scalo

Bossi & Turchi produce game *salumi,* bottled game sauces for pasta and *crostini,* and other gourmet foods. They specialize in salt-cured hams, air-dried meats (*bresaola*), sausages, salami, and more. Most game comes from former Eastern bloc countries, with some from Tuscany. Many meats are sold presliced in "modified atmosphere" packages—in which inert gasses replace the oxygen—with prolonged shelf lives, and with maroon-and-white striped labels. When I visited, the factory direct-sales point was not yet open.

I sampled a selection of game products: The small roebuck (*capriolo*) sausages have a smoky, peppery taste and a close-grained texture; they are better than the venison (*cervo*) which, though highly seasoned, has less flavor. Presliced wild boar (*cinghiale*) prosciutto has a strong pepper aftertaste and is decisively flavored and smoky. The venison is less successful, tasting bitter and of blood. The turkey (*tacchino*) *bresaola* is a pleasant surprise, as is the horse (*cavallo*) *bresaola,* which is tender and less spiced than the rest. In a private taste test, it was voted the best of this group.

San Gimignano

OFFICINALIA
HONEY, ORGANIC FRUIT

CORTENNANO, 46 53037 SAN GIMIGNANO
TELEPHONE/FAX 0577 941867
E-MAIL officinalia@hotmail.com

OPEN Always, but best to phone ahead   **CREDIT CARDS** None   **DIRECT SALE** Yes
ENGLISH SPOKEN A little   **DIRECTIONS** From San Gimignano, go toward Poggibonsi. After about 5 kms, take the left fork toward Poggibonsi; after 150 meters turn left toward Villa di Pietrafitta, up the dirt road. Officinalia is the first house uphill on the right

Luciano Pasolini and Olga Balducchi produce wonderful organic honey and grow stone fruit: apricots, plums, cherries, nectarines. They also make exceptional biodynamic fruit juices and jams, as well as a new line of vegetables preserved *sott'olio*—under oil.

I discovered their honey on Elba (p 176), where Pasolini had taken his hives for the eucalyptus flowers. Moving the bees to follow the flowering cycles of different plants is called "nomadic" beekeeping.

In May, Volterra's hills are crimson with wild *sulla* (*Hedysarum coronarium*) flowers; the resulting delicate, sweet honey has a faint lemony aftertaste. The deeply flavored, dark amber chestnut honey (*castagne*) is from higher ground. *Mille fiori* (a thousand flowers) is made in spring and summer, when many flower species bloom simultaneously. The spring version is clearer and more delicate than the aromatic summer honey.

Pasolini and Balducchi belong to the biodynamic movement. Luciano Pasolini explained: "Like organic farmers, we are committed to not using chemical fertilizers or pesticides, but the Steinerian biodynamic model is unique in its use of *preparati*, or natural preparations, sprayed onto crops to boost growth."

In the case of beekeeping, *preparati* are being used against varroa, the parasite that is attacking the world's bee population, diminishing honey yields without affecting the honey. "We are having quite a lot of success against varroa with essential oils and lactic acid," Pasolini admitted. "But the solution may come from the bees, once they learn to defend themselves."

LA BUCA DI MONTAUTO
MEAT: SALUMI

VIA SAN GIOVANNI, 16 53037 SAN GIMIGNANO
TELEPHONE/FAX 0577 940407
WEB SITE www.labucadimontauto.com

OPEN 8:30–21:00 in summer; 10:00–19:00 in winter   **CLOSED** Tuesday in winter
CREDIT CARDS Visa, MC   **ENGLISH SPOKEN** Yes   **OTHER** Six apartments for holiday rentals
DIRECTIONS In the town center

As you might guess by the wild boar "guarding" the door, this shop specializes in *salumi di cinghiale*. The farm-reared boar are transformed into sausages, hams, and salami. The meat has a more pronounced taste than pork and always seems more peppery, owing to the spices used in the curing. A close-textured *salame* is delicately scented with truffle (*al tartufo*); the deep-colored, lean cured fillet is tender and not too salty; and the little sausages in strings make ideal antipasti—just slice them into rounds and serve with a glass of Chianti. Also for sale are saffron-flavored boar *salumi* and locally produced saffron (see next entry).

The attractive shop is run by the lively Signora Capezzuoli. The shop will vacuum-pack its meats for easy conservation during inter-European travel.

L'ASSOCIAZIONE "IL CROCO"
SAFFRON

CASELLA POSTALE, 17 (FOR MAIL)
53037 SAN GIMIGNANO
TELEPHONE 0577 940986

OPEN Not open to the public   **DIRECT SALE** No; but various food shops in San Gimignano sell the saffron   **ENGLISH SPOKEN** A little

"It began lightheartedly," recounted Brunello Bertelli, president of L'Associazione "Il Croco," the "crocus" association. "In 1990 a group of us decided to try growing saffron, as centuries ago San Gimignano had been famous for it. It was even used as currency here until its cultivation was lost as an art." They got advice from the University of Firenze about how to grow the bulbs. But what exactly is saffron?

"Saffron is the red-colored stigma from the purple autumn-flowering crocus, *Crocus sativus*," explained Bertelli. "Each flower has just three of these filaments, plus three yellow ones without flavor. A productive bulb may produce up to seven flowers, so at best it will yield twenty-one saffron strands. The flowers are picked in October, just before they would have opened. They are unwrapped by hand, and the three precious stigmas are removed and dried over a wood fire."

Saffron's current market value is 25,000 euros per kilo, about $25,000 per pound; 125 flowers yield just 1 gram of saffron. Still, a little goes a long way, and it is a delicious spice. "Yes," Bertelli agreed, "it can transform many dishes and goes well with our famous wine, Vernaccia."

CESANI	PANCOLE 82/D 53037 SAN GIMIGNANO
WINE	TELEPHONE/FAX 0577 955084
	E-MAIL cesanivini@novamedia.it

OPEN Visits and tastings by appointment only   **CREDIT CARDS** None
DIRECT SALE Yes, but best to phone first   **ENGLISH SPOKEN** Yes   **OTHER** Eight rooms available for holiday rentals   **DIRECTIONS** From San Gimignano go northwest toward Certaldo. Go to Pancole, under its church, and straight on the unpaved road; the house is on the right 500 meters after the church

Vincenzo Cesani began working his small farm in the 1950s and planted his first half-hectare vineyard in 1964. A warm, friendly man more at home driving a tractor than sitting behind a desk, he explained that sharecropping families were able to buy their own land after the *mezzadria* system was disbanded. "My family had always worked the land," he explained simply. "We moved from Le Marche when I was a child, settling in these beautiful hills. At that time there was no demand for Vernaccia—local wines were sold unbottled."

The vineyards have since increased to 9 hectares (22 acres): the once-humble farm now boasts a sophisticated *cantina* and the assistance of winemaker Paolo Caciorgna, who has taken over from Luca D'Attoma. Cesani makes two Vernaccias: a selection called Sanice that includes some Chardonnay, aged partly in *barriques,* and the affordable "normal," which is very pleasant to drink. It has a flowery bouquet and is fresh-tasting and less bitter in the finish than some Vernaccias. Other wines include a red Chianti Colli Senesi. I asked Cesani how he became so interested in wine. He answered, "When we were children, after the war, there were no snacks—we dunked our bread into wine. I suppose that was how it started."

GUICCIARDINI STROZZI
WINE, APPLES

FATTORIA CUSONA 53036 POGGIBONSI
TELEPHONE 0577 950028   FAX 0577 950260
WEB SITE www.guicciardinistrozzi.it

OPEN 9:00–12:00, 15:00–18:00; cellar visits and tastings by appointment only
CLOSED Winery Saturday and Sunday; shop Tuesday   CREDIT CARDS Visa, MC
DIRECT SALE Yes; you also can buy wines at the shop in Piazza Sant'Agostino, 3/A, San Gimignano
ENGLISH SPOKEN Yes   DIRECTIONS From San Gimignano, go toward Poggibonsi. After about
10 kms, but before Poggibonsi, turn left toward Ulignano and Cusano; the winery is on the left
after 4 kms

Vernaccia di San Gimignano is one of Italy's oldest white wines, and it has been loved by popes, poets, and pilgrims. Dante mentioned it in *The Divine Comedy*: Pope Martin IV was infamous for having avidly eaten eels drowned in Vernaccia. Prince Girolamo Strozzi's Fattoria di Cusona is Vernaccia's historic home. In 1994 it celebrated its thousandth year. In 1966 Vernaccia was the first Italian wine to gain DOC status, followed in 1993 by DOCG: all wines bearing this name must be made of Vernaccia grapes grown and vinified within San Gimignano.

The wine sung by the poets was different from today's Vernaccia, a dry white wine with a nuttiness to its fruit and a signature light bitterness to its aftertaste. Modern wines are made using soft presses and sophisticated cooling systems.

Prince Girolamo Strozzi, a professor of international law, produces five types of Vernaccia on his large estate, including San Biagio—a single-vineyard wine given some contact with the skins and consequently better structured, more elegant, and fuller in flavor than the "normal"—and the Riserva, made from selected ripe grapes aged partly in *barriques*. Reds include a young, drinkable Chianti and Sòdole, a well-structured super-Tuscan of pure Sangiovese.

Vineyards and orchards surround the stately villa with its *parterre* gardens. The cellars are suitably atmospheric, with long underground tunnels now lined with *barriques*. In autumn, the estate also produces wonderful apples, sold directly from the farm. They are sweet and perfumed—I happily ate mine on the long drive home.

MONTENIDOLI
WINE

53037 SAN GIMIGNANO
TELEPHONE 0577 941565   FAX 0577 942037
WEB SITE www.montenidoli.com

OPEN Tastings, visits, sales by appointment only   CREDIT CARDS None   DIRECT SALE Yes
ENGLISH SPOKEN Yes   OTHER Eight rooms available for holiday rentals   DIRECTIONS Take the
road beside San Gimignano's Carabinieri station over 2 kms to the farm (it becomes unpaved)

"A wine cellar is a place of culture," affirmed Elisabetta Fagiuoli, the driving force behind Montenidoli, one of San Gimignano's most interesting and beautiful wineries. Indeed, you see it in the marble sculptures that people Montenidoli's cellars; you enjoy it in the art of Fagiuoli's conversation; you taste it in the wines. Elisabetta Fagiuoli is a warm, creative woman who has given San Gimignano's native wines a very personal stamp.

"When I arrived in 1965, there was nothing on top of this hill—no road, no electricity, no water. Just an old farm with overgrown vineyards and a stunning view of San Gimignano." She dug a well, struck water, and began to fashion her winery—"Sono Montenidoli" (I am Montenidoli) proclaims one of her wines. "Vernaccia is a white wine from a land of red wines, unlike the white wines from Friuli or Germany," she said. "A great white wine, even a dry one, should become *meloso*—honeylike." Her 1990 Vernaccia Fiore, tasted in 1996, did have a wonderful, honeyed richness, with full and complex *profumi*. Fagiuoli specified that her Vernaccias are wines that can age well and may be drunk over time; three of her wines are Vernaccias.

"I believe that each patch of vineyard, each vine, has a distinct character. Grapes are like flour to a baker, they give us something to work with, but it is up to us to learn how to interpret them. In my mind I have an ideal wine—and I will undoubtedly keep working toward it until I attain it."

TERUZZI & PUTHOD
WINE

FATTORIA PONTE A RONDOLINO CASALE, 19
53037 SAN GIMIGNANO
TELEPHONE 0577 940143   FAX 0577 942016
WEB SITE www.teruzzieputhod.com

OPEN 8:00–12:00, 14:00–18:00; visits by appointment only; no tastings   **CLOSED** Saturday and Sunday   **CREDIT CARDS** Visa, MC   **DIRECT SALE** Yes; twelve-bottle minimum, subject to availability; new shop located near the winery   **ENGLISH SPOKEN** Yes   **DIRECTIONS** From San Gimignano, go toward Certaldo; turn right almost immediately beyond San Gimignano. Ponte a Rondolino is signposted from there

If Guicciardini Strozzi represents Vernaccia's historical past, Teruzzi & Puthod has revealed its future potential: in twenty years Enrico Teruzzi, the company's dynamic founder, has put Vernaccia squarely on the international wine-market map. An ex-jockey whose father made his fortune patenting light switches, Teruzzi, with his French ballerina wife, Carmen Puthod, has created a wine empire from the simple farm they bought in 1974.

Grapes are grown on the estate's 96 hectares (237 acres) of vineyards, or bought locally. "The methodology required for white wines is very different from that needed for reds," explained the charismatic Teruzzi. "The French have a saying: red wine is made in the vineyard; white wine is made in the cellar. I believe it's true." The Vernaccia grape is difficult to work, tending to oxidize easily. "It is not enough to do an honest job with it," he said. "You need to stabilize and control it." To do this, Teruzzi built one of Italy's most avant-garde *cantine*. Looking rather like a moon base, this impressive "cellar" is a network of outdoor "islands" of stainless-steel tanks fed by miles of underground tubing and commanded by the latest microtechnology and computers.

"I spend 70 percent of my time planning for the future," he admitted. "Most of the day-to-day decisions I leave to my staff." Indeed, the company is run along American lines, with a young workforce given plenty of responsibility.

Teruzzi & Puthod's best-known wines are its Vernaccia di San Gimignano, in the "normal" and *barrique*-aged Terre di Tufi versions; Carmen Puthod, a modern-style white wine made from red Sangiovese grapes; and Peperino, a very drinkable red wine of pure Sangiovese. These last two also spend time maturing in small French oak *barriques*. All have achieved a loyal international following.

Enrico Teruzzi is an indefatigable adventurer. Recently he even bought 20 hectares (49 acres) of land near the coast at Suvereto. "I really want to make a great red wine, after all these whites," he said. "And down there it seems it's hard to go wrong!"

Also

BOTTEGA D'ARTE POVERA   VIA SAN MATTEO, 83. 0577 941951

The Calonaci's tourist shop sells *arte povera*, or poor art—handmade baskets, olive wood bowls and boards, terra-cotta cooking pots, recycled glass from Empoli. Look for local chestnut baskets with a wide ribbon weave, *cesti da olive* (semicircular waist baskets for olive gathering), and flat teardrop baskets for drying figs.

RISTORANTE DORANDÒ.   VICOLO DELL'ORO, 2. 0577 941862
CLOSED MONDAY EXCEPT IN SUMMER. $$$$

This is one of the better restaurants in the touristic town of San Gimignano, in a narrow street off Piazza Cisterna. It specializes in creative modern dishes as well as Tuscan recipes from past centuries—some of which are surprisingly modern themselves.

San Giovanni d'Asso

San Giovanni d'Asso hosts an annual truffle fair each November (usually the third Sunday of the month). The Fiera del Tartufo is organized by the Associazione Tartufai Senesi, whose members hunt for the truffles in the surrounding hills with the help of specially trained dogs. *Tuber magnatum pico*, the white truffle, is the most sought-after variety; it can be bought directly from its finders at the fair. For more information, call Associazione Tartufai Senesi, 0577 823213.

Sarteano

FRANTOIO TISTARELLI
OLIVE MILL, OIL AND WINE STORE

VIALE EUROPA, 106 53047 SARTEANO
TELEPHONE 0578 265425   FAX 0578 268721
WEB SITE www.tistarelli.it

OPEN 8:00–13:00, 16:00–20:00; Sunday by appointment only   **CREDIT CARDS** Visa, MC
MAIL ORDER Yes   **ENGLISH SPOKEN** Yes   **DIRECTIONS** On the main road from Sarteano
to Chianciano Terme

I was saddened to hear of the death of Mario Tistarelli, a great character and a great olive oil expert. An experienced connoisseur with a fine palate, he was an outspoken advocate for "real" extra-virgin oil. His family now runs the *frantoio* and shop that sells his company's oils, selected wines, and specialty foods.

"All this hype today about cold-pressed means nothing," he asserted when I interviewed him in 1997. "Olive oil freezes at 8°C [46°F], and for the stone-ground system of extraction to work the temperature in the *frantoio* must be at least 15°C [59°F]. Without some heat the olives will not even release their oil."

Tistarelli believed that the best oil is made using this stone-ground, mechanical press system, but only under certain conditions. "This system is more vulnerable than the modern," he explained, "and requires more attention to avoid the oil being tainted." For example, to avoid contamination, *fiscoli*, the round woven mats used in the press, must be changed frequently, and absolutely no defective olives must be accepted into the machinery. Tistarelli explained why this system is best. "The slow crushing movement and soft rhythm of the stone wheels is less stressful on the olives than high-powered modern machinery, so the oil remains sweeter."

Of Tistarelli's three types of oil, the finest, Cinque Monti, is made from local olives picked as they change color from green to black (*invaiatura*). The result is a clear green oil with a fragrant olive perfume and a well-balanced taste of artichoke. Reticchio is a blend of Tuscan olives grown at fairly high altitudes. Decisive in taste, it has the elegant bitterness that characterizes many Tuscan oils. Tistarelli's most economical line is named for his grandfather: "Signor Olio," or Mister Oil, as he was known. It is a blend of olives bought from central Italy.

Also

TENUTA DI TRINORO   0578 267110

In the unspoiled, expansive Val d'Orcia, Andrea Franchetti has established a little Bordeaux: French vines planted in French-style vineyards. His two wines, Palazzi (of Merlot and Cabernet Franc) and Tenuta di Trinoro (of Cabernet Franc with some Merlot, Cabernet Sauvignon, and Petit Verdot) are sold *en primeur* in France—but can occasionally be found in Tuscany too!

Siena

FORNO DEI GALLI—SCLAVI
BREAD

VIA DEI TERMINI, 45 53100 SIENA
TELEPHONE 0577 289073

OPEN 7:30–13:15, 17:00–19:30   **CLOSED** Saturday afternoon in summer; Sunday
CREDIT CARDS In some of the shops   **DIRECT SALE** Yes   **ENGLISH SPOKEN** A little
OTHER Sclavi's other bakeries include: Panificio Moderno, Via Montanini, 84; Forno Indipendenza,
Piazza Indipendenza, 27; Forno Antiporto, Via Vittorio Emanuele, 85; Forno Da Penny, Via Massetana
Romana, 41   **DIRECTIONS** Via dei Termini is north of the Campo

"Our *pane basso* is so good," the elderly lady at the cash desk announced proudly,
"that I eat it in the street on my way home!" It *is* very good. The "low bread" is
given two risings; it remains deliciously crisp outside and soft inside. Other specialties from this historic Sienese bakery are the *schiacciate*, (flat yeast breads) dotted
with raisins or olives or, in autumn, baked with grapes in them. A crunchy,
crumbly version, *ciaccina friabile*, is baked in large flat sheets—a great snack for
touring the city. There are breads of all types, including some using organic flours.
Sclavi produces pastries, cakes, and cookies, including the Sienese classics *panforte*
and *ricciarelli*.

ANTICA TRATTORIA
BOTTEGANOVA
RESTAURANT

STRADA CHIANTIGIANA, 29 (SS 408) 53100 SIENA
TELEPHONE 0577 284230   FAX 0577 271519
E-MAIL stocco.carmela@libero.it

OPEN Lunch and dinner   **CLOSED** Monday   **CREDIT CARDS** Visa, MC, Amex
ENGLISH SPOKEN Yes   **RESERVATIONS** Recommended for dinner   **PRICE** $$$$–$$$$$
DIRECTIONS The restaurant is between Siena and Pianella on SS 408, the main road into Chianti

This restaurant is located a few hundred yards from Siena's gates. It is run by two
young men attentive to detail in both the kitchen and the dining room. The
atmosphere is fairly formal, with careful service. Guido Bellotti and Michele
Sorrentino propose two tasting menus in addition to the main list; the shorter one
offers four full courses, includes wines, and is a good value.

During my February visit, the seasonal menu featured winter vegetables and
game—though fine T-bone steaks (*la Fiorentina*) are always available. My lunch
began with a tartare of ground sea bass with blood orange, lemon, and fennel,
though I preferred the *cappelletti* stuffed with Tuscan winter cabbage (*cavolo nero*),
and sautéed with oil, garlic, and chili pepper. The pasta was tender, the filling
unusual and good, and it went well with a sauce of puréed beans. A second pasta
was successful, though rich: *tortelli di pecorino*, pasta stuffed with sheep's cheese,
was served on a searingly hot plate, topped with truffle-scented melted Parmesan
just browned at the edges.

The young chef likes layering unusual flavors, as in the breaded *mazzancolle*
(large shrimp), served on a bed of onions braised in red wine. Quail breast *alla*

grappa might have been named *au poivre,* for its demiglace was thick with aromatic crushed pepper. It was, however, carefully cooked and tender. Fruity olive oil was liberally drizzled over it. The fine dessert was beautifully presented: *semifreddo* (frozen cream) of nougat and rum was served with a decorative caramel sauce. The wines, from various Tuscan zones, were well matched to the foods. The list read very much like the selection in this book.

IL GHIBELLINO
RESTAURANT

VIA DEI PELLEGRINI, 26 53100 SIENA
TELEPHONE 0577 288079   FAX 0577 40775

OPEN Lunch and dinner   **CLOSED** Monday   **CREDIT CARDS** Visa, MC, Amex
ENGLISH SPOKEN Yes   **FEATURES** Additional fish menu Thursday and Friday
RESERVATIONS Recommended on weekend evenings   **PRICE** $$–$$$
DIRECTIONS Via dei Pellegrini runs from the Campo to the Duomo

Il Ghibellino is perfect for a plate of pasta and a glass of wine after a morning's sightseeing. A cross between an *osteria* and a *trattoria,* Il Ghibellino offers a relaxed mood, reasonable prices, and uncomplicated local dishes. The *osteria* influence is apparent in the attention to detail and the slightly more creative cooking. The interior is spare but quite stylish: marble-topped tables are set with butcher-paper mats, the napkins are linen, the floors are traditional terra-cotta tile, and the white are walls framed by original wood beams.

The food is best when it stays within the range of *cucina povera,* the simple, hearty foods of Tuscany's countryside. *Zuppa di farro* is a well-seasoned soup of spelt wheat, and *rustici con melanzane* a satisfying bowl of handmade curlicued pasta in a tomato and eggplant sauce. I was less convinced by some of the antipasti: the fresh vegetable tart and the cheese and tomato strudel are nice ideas, but both suffered from having undercooked pastry; the red-pepper mousse seemed a bit flat.

The various meat *secondi* include local favorites rabbit and tripe; on Thursday and Friday Il Ghibellino also features a fish menu. The desserts are homemade, ambitious, and quite successful. The wine list features Tuscany and is well priced. The amiable young owners take turns on the floor, so the service is intelligent and attentive.

OSTERIA LE LOGGE
RESTAURANT

VIA DEL PORRIONE, 33 53100 SIENA
TELEPHONE 0577 48013   FAX 0577 224797

OPEN Lunch and dinner   **CLOSED** Sunday; mid-November–early December
CREDIT CARDS Visa, MC, Amex   **ENGLISH SPOKEN** Yes   **RESERVATIONS** Necessary
PRICE $$$–$$$$ **OTHER** Outdoor tables in summer   **DIRECTIONS** The street runs off
Piazza del Campo

Le Logge is Siena's most *simpatica osteria,* a favorite with locals and visitors. The dining room is high ceilinged and luminous, and in summer its tables spill out into the street. The décor is done in classic style—old-fashioned wood panelling, white tablecloths, lace curtains—but the mood is not overly formal. This is the place to have a plate of local artisan-made *salumi*, followed by a satisfying dish of pasta or risotto. Vegetables always feature well on the seasonal menu: in spring I had deep-fried artichokes and asparagus with garlicky aioli sauce, and "crunchy" baked pecorino with honey and pine nuts. There are assorted meat and fish dishes, as well as homemade desserts.

The wine list specializes in Tuscany's best. Try owner Gianni Brunelli's Rosso or Brunello di Montalcino, made by him at his winery at Montalcino (see p 320). These are fruity, drinkable wines and not overly expensive. Brunelli has also opened a fun new wine bar in Piazza del Campo (see p 297).

ANTICA DROGHERIA MANGANELLI 1879
SPECIALTY FOODS, PASTRY

VIA DI CITTÀ, 71/73 53100 SIENA
TELEPHONE 0577 280002   FAX 0577 205000
E-MAIL admanganelli@tin.it

OPEN Summer: 9:00–20:00; winter: 9:00–13:00, 15:30–19:30   **CLOSED** Wednesday afternoon in winter   **CREDIT CARDS** Visa, MC, Amex   **DIRECT SALE** Yes   **ENGLISH SPOKEN** Yes   **DIRECTIONS** Via di Città runs beside the Campo

---

This shop is a gourmet treasure trove. Its antique wood cabinets are stacked to the ceiling with edible (and drinkable) goodies of all description. Here, in the rarified spice-perfumed interior, you find everything from "designer" olive oils to truffle-scented polenta. There are herbed vinegars from Volpaia (p 220), Martelli's pasta (p 129), Falorni's *salumi* (p 199), jams and honeys, sauces and *sott'olii*—vegetables preserved in oil that make great antipasti. One room is devoted to wines, liqueurs, and grappas. A perfect place for presents and personal indulgences.

Manganelli bakes its own traditional Sienese pastries from "very old" recipes—the store has been in operation since 1879. It makes two types of *panforte*: Margherita is the paler; its thick paste has a strong presence of cinnamon and is studded with toasted almonds and green melon *canditi*. The darker version, also full of nuts, tastes of mixed Tuscan spices and is slightly more bitter. The *ricciarelli*, made of ground almond dough, are wonderful: moist and sticky, with real almond flavor.

CONSORZIO AGRARIO SIENA
SPECIALTY FOODS

VIA PIANIGIANI, 9 53100 SIENA
TELEPHONE 0577 2301   FAX 0577 280378

OPEN Winter: 7:45–13:00, 16:30–19:30; summer: 7:45–13:00, 17:00–20:00   **CLOSED** Sunday; Wednesday afternoon in winter, Saturday afternoon in summer   **CREDIT CARDS** Visa, MC   **DIRECT SALE** Yes   **ENGLISH SPOKEN** A little   **DIRECTIONS** Near Piazza Matteotti

---

This supermarket features foods from the province of Siena. It is run by the Consorzio Agrario (farmer's consortium), an organization under the auspices of the Ministry for Agriculture. It was founded in 1901 and now has four thousand members. The consortium helps producers promote their goods and sells them seeds, fertilizers, and equipment.

The supermarket stocks a range of *pecorini*, the area's famous sheep's cheeses, *salumi*, grain and honey, olive oil and wine. Many of its producers are mentioned in this book. Under the brand name Granducato, it sells members' oil and wine at reasonable prices. The consortium has a modern-system oil mill at Pianella, which is open to visitors during November and December. This consortium has several shops in the province, at Montalcino, Pienza, Buonconvento, and Chianciano Terme.

GASTRONOMIA MORBIDI 1925
SPECIALTY FOODS: DELICATESSEN

VIA BANCHI DI SOPRA, 73/75 53100 SIENA
TELEPHONE 0577 280268, 282257
FAX 0577 285077

OPEN 8:00–13:15, 17:00–20:00   **CLOSED** Saturday afternoon and Sunday
CREDIT CARDS Visa, MC   **DIRECT SALE** Yes   **ENGLISH SPOKEN** A little
OTHER A second shop is in Via Banchi di Sotto, 27; catering facilities available
DIRECTIONS On the main street leading into the north side of the Campo

Gastronomia Morbidi has offered quality foods in Siena since 1925. Armando Morbidi began as a cheese resaler. His granddaughter Patrizia said he was the first to introduce certain cheeses to Siena. The family now runs the Salcis *caseificio* near Pienza, selling its excellent pecorini in the shops.

The present shop, with its clean white vaulting, is modern and attractive. A long counter holds dairy foods, *salumi*, and a fabulous array of home-cooked foods to take out—the *gastronomia*. Recipes change daily, but there are always ready-to-eat antipasti (including seasoned olives, vegetables preserved in oil, sweet and sour onions), *primi* (pastas and thick soups), and *secondi* (roast meats, aspics, herbed fish dishes). They are sold in containers, by weight or by the piece, and make great picnic foods. There is even a wine cellar downstairs.

LIBERAMENTE OSTERIA
WINE BAR

PIAZZA DEL CAMPO, 26 53100 SIENA
TELEPHONE 0577 274733   FAX 0577 224797

OPEN 10:00–23:30   **CLOSED** Sunday   **CREDIT CARDS** Visa, MC, Amex
ENGLISH SPOKEN Yes   **RESERVATIONS** Possible   **PRICE** $–$$$

Gianni and Laura Brunelli, who run Osteria Le Logge (see p 295), have come up with a wonderful new place, and one that was missing in Siena: a stylish wine bar right in the heart of Piazza del Campo. So now you can drink a great glass of wine or cocktail and eat simple yet sophisiticated snacks as you sit out in the square and watch the world go by. Culture lovers should not miss the interior: painter Sandro Chia (who has now branched out into winemaking from his Castello Romitorio at Montalcino) has designed colorful, painterly mosaics for the floor and walls, made by the mosaic *maestri* of Ravenna. Stand at the post-modern steel bar or sit inside, and sample soups, salads, or sandwiches in a work of art.

ENOTECA ITALIANA
WINE STORE, WINE BAR

FORTEZZA MEDICEA, 1 53100 SIENA
TELEPHONE 0577 288497   FAX 0577 270717
WEB SITE www.enoteca-italiana.it

OPEN Monday 12:00–20:00, Tuesday–Saturday 12:00–1:00 A.M.   **CLOSED** Sunday
CREDIT CARDS Visa, Amex   **DIRECT SALE** Yes   **ENGLISH SPOKEN** Yes
FEATURES Summer terrace in fortress walls   **DIRECTIONS** The fortress is at the top of Siena; the *enoteca* is on the left as you enter it

The underground cellars of a Medicean fortress are the dramatic setting for one of Italy's most important wine stores. Enoteca Italiana is state run; its mandate is to promote wines from all of Italy's regions. Its vaulted brick cellars house permanent displays of more than 750 types of quality wines. A team of professional wine tasters constantly tastes and grades Italian wines to maintain the *enoteca*'s high standards. Only those attaining a score of over seventy-five points are chosen.

At the upstairs wine bar, more than eight hundred selected wines may be tasted by the glass, at modest prices. This exceptional opportunity invites comparisons between regions, grape varieties, or neighboring producers. (You can just as happily sit with a glass or bottle of wine and have lunch or a snack.) Wine may also be bought to take away.

Enoteca Italiana organizes many events and activities: guided wine tastings at all levels of expertise, concerts, exhibitions of wine-related art, a Wine Week in June, and buffets and banquets. Groups can be accommodated by prearrangement. A must for wine lovers.

Also

LORENZA DE' MEDICI SHOP   VIA DI CITTÀ, 47. TELEPHONE/FAX 0577 47755

Walking down toward the Campo recently, I noticed an attractive window display of stylish and unusual tabletop objects. I went in to see more, and found Lorenza de'Medici inside. "This is my new store," she said. "That explains it!" I said, for only someone with a very good eye would have gathered such tasteful objects together. I particularly like the earthy glazed terra-cotta plates from Puglia with their scratched-on designs, and the Palio cups—elegant coffee cups decorated with the colors and patterns of Siena's seventeen *contrade*, or districts.

GELATERIA BRIVIDO   VIA DEI PELLEGRINI, 1. 0577 280058. OPEN MARCH–OCTOBER

Stop in here for Siena's best ice creams: thirty-five flavors include some very fresh-tasting fruits, as well as creamy *mousse alla gianduja*—a chocolate-hazelnut confection.

Trequanda

MACELLERIA RICCI
(FONDO PENSIONE CARIPLO)
MEAT

AZIENDA AGRICOLA TREQUANDA
VIA TRAVERSA DEI MONTI, 4 53020 TREQUANDA
TELEPHONE 0577 662252   FAX 0577 662001

OPEN Tuesday–Wednesday 9:00–13:00; Thursday–Saturday 9:00–13:00, 17:00–20:00
CLOSED Monday, Sunday; variable winter holidays   **CREDIT CARDS** Visa, MC, Amex
ENGLISH SPOKEN A little   **OTHER** The farm may be visited by appointment
DIRECTIONS On the main Sinalunga-Montisi road at Trequanda

This butcher's shop belongs to the pension fund of one of Italy's biggest banks. Ricci specializes in pure Chianina beef, one of the world's finest breeds, raised nearby in Trequanda. The Chianina have been known since Etruscan times. They are the pale cattle with dark eyes seen pulling the plough in old Tuscan photographs. A consortium called 5R controls this and four other pure cattle breeds.

"Our beef comes from our own farm," explained Enrico Ricci, the butcher. "So there is an absolute consistency of quality. We know what the animals have been eating, so there is no danger of disease." Chianina make the best steaks for the *Fiorentina*, the Tuscan T-bone traditionally grilled over a wood fire. The ultraclean shop also sells fresh and salt-cured pork from the same farm, and wine and other products from Fondo Cariplo producers.

AZIENDA AGRICOLA BELSEDERE
DE GORI AVANZATI
SALUMI, MEAT, CHEESE

53020 TREQUANDA
TELEPHONE/FAX 0577 662307
WEB SITE www.belsedere.com

OPEN 9:00–13:00, 15:00–19:00   **CLOSED** Never   **CREDIT CARDS** None   **DIRECT SALE** Yes; the farm's products also are on sale in their shop in Siena at Via Camollia, 29.   **MAIL ORDER** By courier within Europe   **ENGLISH SPOKEN** A little   **OTHER** Several villa apartments for holiday rentals
DIRECTIONS From Trequanda, go toward Belsedere and Asciano. The farm is signposted along that road. Ask for sales assistance at the villa

This farm is nestled in the beautiful rolling hills to the west of Trequanda. It has long been noted for its fine handmade *salumi*, farm-reared meats, and *pecorini*. "This land has been in our family since 1200," explained Silvia De Gori. "My father-in-law decided to raise sheep and pigs thirty years ago, when most people were leaving the land to work in industry. It was a way of saving his patrimony—the buildings and the land."

She and her husband have built their reputation on their genuine artisan foods. "We could never have stayed in business if our products had not been of very high quality," she continued. "The competition from industrial food companies is fierce."

The farm, which also produces grain, is certified to organic standards. Fresh pork and lamb are sold. Most lamb sold in Italy is very small and scrawny, with a different flavor than American or British lamb. Signora De Gori explained that Sardinian lambs, bred throughout Italy for milk, are small by nature, and their young are butchered before they have time to develop. Sheep bred for meat, such as Belsedere's, are larger; their lambs remain with the mothers until they are eating grass.

Belsedere makes a full range of excellent pork *salumi*, from hand-salted prosciutto to lean sausages, *pancetta*, *salame*, and *finocchiona*, the fennel-scented sausage. Some are made from the rare Cinta Senese breed. Because of the small percentage of preservatives these cured meats contain, they cannot be considered organic, even if the original animals are; the excellent raw-milk *pecorini* made on the farm, however, are certified organic.

FATTORIA DEL COLLE	IL COLLE 53020 TREQUANDA
WINE, OLIVE OIL	TELEPHONE 0577 662108; 0577 849421 MONTALCINO
	FAX 0577 662202
	WEB SITE www.donatellacinellicolombini.it

OPEN 9:00–13:00, 15:00–18:00 daily   **CLOSED** Never   **CREDIT CARDS** Visa, MC, Amex
DIRECT SALE Yes   **ENGLISH SPOKEN** Yes   **OTHER** Nineteen apartments available for holiday
rentals; restaurant   **DIRECTIONS** From Trequanda go toward Asciano and Belsedere; the estate is
signposted along that road

Donatella Colombini comes from one of Montalcino's historic winemaking families (see p 317). The family possesses several farms in southern Tuscany, and recently Donatella has moved her family and some of her enological activities to this lovely property near Trequanda.

Donatella is a well-known figure in the Italian wine world: she has long been a keen promoter of Italy's wines, their culture, and the special tourism that is linked to them. "I think it is important to bring people into our wineries, to appreciate and learn about what making wine is," she said as we walked around the handsome new aging cellars being built at Colle. "That is why I have campaigned for both the Cantine Aperte, or open cellars day [the last Sunday in May], and the Wine Roads, which happily are now firmly on the map throughout Italy."

She also has been active in opening the door to women in what has traditionally been a male-dominated world. Le Donne del Vino is a now a large organization that comprises women producers, enologists, and critics, and women who play other key roles in winemaking. Her Brunello di Montalcino, Prime Donne, which is made at her Montalcino estate Casato, attests to this. "This is a wine made by women—four international women wine tasters together make the decisions about the wine's aging and vinification," she explained. "I am also setting up a vinification cellar that will be entirely run by women—the first of its kind—to prove that you don't need brawn to make wine, you need intelligence."

Her farm is fun to visit, with a lovely tasting room for receiving visitors, an *osteria* serving traditional local cuisine, and many workshops, cooking classes, and other activities. The estate produces great olive oils, grows white truffles, and makes a selection of wines.

Vergelle

CRETE SENESI
CHEESE

VERGELLE 53020 SAN GIOVANNI D'ASSO
TELEPHONE 0577 834046, 834431   FAX 0577 834046
E-MAIL info@vergelle.com

OPEN 8:00–20:00   **CLOSED** Never   **CREDIT CARDS** None   **DIRECT SALE** Yes, for whole cheeses   **ENGLISH SPOKEN** A little   **DIRECTIONS** From the Torrenieri–San Giovanni d'Asso road, follow yellow signs up the cypress avenues to Vergelle; the road is unpaved but good. The *caseificio* is in the village

This *caseificio* makes pasteurized sheep's cheeses. The beautiful area around Pienza is famous for pecorino cheeses, and this family-run business is one of several owned by Sardinian shepherds who came to Tuscany in the early 1960s.

The Cosseddu family makes unusual *pecorini* weighing about 500 grams (1 lb) flavored with herbs—mixed dried tarragon, rosemary, sage, and juniper, blended into the milky mass before the cheeses set. Other varieties include arugula (made with fresh leaves), hot pepper, dried porcini mushrooms, saffron, and olive. *Pecorini* are also preserved in jars of oil: sunflower for the herbed and olive oil for the truffle-scented cheeses. They keep for several months and make attractive presents.

Ville di Corsano

AZIENDA AGRICOLA S. MARGHERITA
GOAT'S CHEESE

50010 VILLE DI CORSANO
TELEPHONE/FAX 0577 377101
E-MAIL santamargherita@tin.it

OPEN 14:00–19:00   **CLOSED** Never   **CREDIT CARDS** None   **DIRECT SALE** Yes
ENGLISH SPOKEN Yes   **DIRECTIONS** Coming from Siena or Monteroni D'Arbia, go to Ville di Corsano, through the village to the cemetery (look for the group of cypresses). The main road curves to the right, but go straight ahead. Follow it until the road turns right, but go straight ahead again. There is a signpost from there. Follow to the end of this road, going left at the fork

Maria De Dominicis is an active defender of Italy's artisan food makers, struggling to survive in an ever more industrialized society. She herself makes some of Tuscany's finest goat's cheeses, from milk produced by her organically certified herd.

"The most important thing is to enable your animals to lead dignified lives," she asserted. "If you allow them freedom, light, and sunshine, they almost never get sick and, by extension, neither do we."

I visited her farm (situated in exquisite countryside) in late February, when many of her 130 goats were about to give birth. Maria keeps them in the barn at this time because of wolves and other predators who would attack the pregnant females and newborn kids. As we talked in the sweet-smelling barn (she described it as her *salotto*, or living room), she moved knowingly among the animals. "This one is about to give birth," she said. And, sure enough, she did—with help from Maria. "Goats are funny," she observed. "They willingly rely on humans to help them." Within minutes the baby kid was awake and mewling.

Maria started making cheese because no one wanted the goats' milk. She makes French-style cheeses, which she learned to do by reading books. These fresh, white, smooth-textured *caprini* are then flavored with herbs or toasted sesame seeds and matured in wood ash or walnut leaves. She sells them directly from the farm—there is a small organic shop on the premises—and to some of the area's best restaurants and food shops (including La Galleria, p 211).

CHAPTER 12

Montalcino and Its Wines

*T*he medieval hill town of Montalcino merits a chapter of its own: this one *comune* has 199 registered producers of Brunello di Montalcino, one of the world's greatest wines. It also has some of the most unspoiled countryside in Italy—and it will remain that way, for Montalcino was recently certified with environmental protection status by the European Community.

Montalcino is a wine lover's mecca. Many wineries welcome visitors; the town has wine shops and wine bars. There are restaurants, but fewer hotels. The steep town, with its fourteenth-century fortress, commands spectacular views.

Although each winery has its own distinct character, the producers are bonded by a commitment to do justice to their famous wine. These estates are wonderful to visit. Usually a phone call in advance is all that is needed. Many offer informal tours of the cellars or vineyards. In most, wines may be tasted and bought. Many also produce fine extra-virgin olive oil.

A selective list of Montalcino's restaurants, wine stores, and specialty food shops is included at the end of this chapter.

The Brunello Consortium, housed in the ground floor of Montalcino's *comune* building, in the town center, is friendly and helpful. They have excellent maps of the region, with the producers marked.

CONSORZIO DEL VINO BRUNELLO DI MONTALCINO
COSTA DEL MUNICIPIO, 1
53024 MONTALCINO SIENA
0577 848246
FAX 0577 849425
WEB SITE www.consorziobrunellodimontalcino.it
OPEN MONDAY–FRIDAY 8:30–13:00, 15:00–18:00

AZIENDA PROMOZIONE TURISTICA
COSTA DEL MUNICIPIO, 1
53024 MONTALCINO SIENA
TEL/FAX 0577 849331
WEB SITE www.prolocomontalcino.it
OPEN DAILY 10:00–13:00, 14:00–17:40 APRIL–OCTOBER;
CLOSED MONDAY IN WINTER

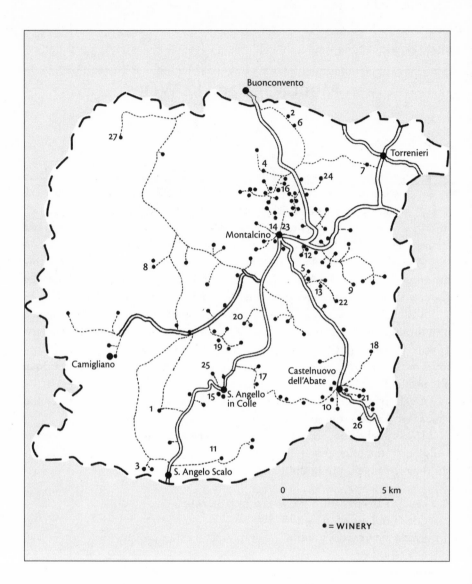

SELECTED WINE PRODUCERS KEYED TO THE MONTALCINO MAP

1   ARGIANO
2   AZIENDA AGRICOLA ALTESINO
3   BANFI
4   BARICCI—COLOMBAIA DI MONTOSOLI
5   BIONDI-SANTI
6   CAPARZO
7   CASANOVA DI NERI
8   CASTELGIOCONDO
9   CERBAIONA
10 CIACCI PICCOLOMINI D'ARAGONA
11 COL D'ORCIA
12 CONTI COSTANTI
13 FATTORIA DEI BARBI
14 FULIGNI
15 IL POGGIONE
16 LE CHIUSE DI SOTTO—GIANNI BRUNELLI
17 LISINI
18 MASTROJANNI
19 PIEVE DI SANTA RESTITUTA
20 POGGIO ANTICO
21 POGGIO DI SOTTO
22 SALICUTTI
23 SALVIONI—LA CERBAIOLA
24 SIRO PACENTI
25 TALENTI—PODERE PIAN DI CONTE
26 TENUTA OLIVETO
27 TENUTE SILVIO NARDI

Brunello di Montalcino DOCG

Brunello was Italy's first wine to be granted DOCG status (*Denominazione di Origine Controllata e Garantita*) in 1980, but its story began long before. According to historical documents, during the town's siege of 1555, Montalcino's commander, Marshal Montluc, "reddened his face with a robust vermilion wine" in order to appear less pale and food-deprived. Brunello's birth came in the 1880s when Ferruccio Biondi Santi first made a wine from just one local grape type, known then as Sangiovese Grosso, but identified genetically today as being Sangiovese. This fruit turns dark violet, earning it the local name *brunello*. Biondi Santi was ahead of his time:

nineteenth-century Tuscan wines were blends of red and white grapes, made to drink young. Biondi Santi wanted to produce a wine to age. He succeeded: in 1988 Brunello celebrated its hundredth birthday. It was toasted with a rare, still drinkable, Biondi-Santi Brunello from the vintage of 1888. Brunello is one of Italy's most prestigious wines, whose fame is linked to its longevity; it is a concentrated, complex, and elegant red wine with powerful structure. At its best, it is packed with fruit and has smoky or spicy flavors and balanced acidity and tannins.

What Makes Brunello So Special?

In part, the terrain: Montalcino's hills are situated in a zone with several distinct microclimates and soil compositions. Vines are planted at 300 to 500 meters on soils ranging from limestone to clay. Wines produced in the southeast are rich and robust, whereas vineyards in the northeast make more elegant wines.

Brunello's regulations allow a maximum yield per hectare of 80 quintals (8.8 tons) of exclusively Sangiovese grapes—and some producers go much lower. That means better but fewer bunches per plant, at the cost of pruning away half a vine's production.

Finally, the vinification and cellaring: here again, DOCG regulations are strict. Brunello must be aged a minimum of four years, of which at least two must be in wood casks. One additional year of aging and the wine becomes a Riserva. At least four months of bottle aging is obligatory for Brunello, six months for the Riserva. Traditionalists want to maintain the status quo, with the risk that much Brunello will be drunk before it is fully mature, while reformers are pushing for an "accessible" Brunello that is drinkable sooner. Some producers would like to see other red grapes, such as Merlot or Cabernet Sauvignon, permissible in the wine in small percentages; for now, these are forbidden.

Rosso di Montalcino DOC

Montalcino's second wine is considered Brunello's "younger brother" (*vino* is masculine in Italian). Rosso di Montalcino—literally, Montalcino's Red—is made of the same grapes as Brunello: 100 percent Sangiovese aged for one year. Grapes may be designated for it while still on the vine, or the immature Brunello may be "switched" to Rosso. In poor vintages some producers make little or no Brunello, putting all their grapes into Rosso for a quick turnover of cellar space and cash; in great years there is no obligation to produce it, though some of Montalcino's vineyards have now been specially designated for growing Rosso di Montalcino. A ready-to-drink, fruity red wine, Rosso di Montalcino provides wine lovers with a chance to taste some of Brunello's flavors at a third of the price.

Moscadello di Montalcino DOC

This sweet white wine is Montalcino's oldest wine, known in a different form in the Middle Ages. It is found in lightly bubbly, still, or *passito* versions.

Sant'Antimo DOC

This recent denomination was created in 1996. It is made in a delimited area around the Romanesque church of Sant'Antimo, near Castelnuovo dell'Abate. The DOC comprises both red and white wines. There are set rules about yields per hectare, but none about aging. If a wine contains more than 85 percent of one varietal (including Cabernet Sauvignon, Merlot, and Pinot Nero for red, Chardonnay, Pinot Grigio, and Sauvignon Blanc for white) that grape's name may be included on the label. This DOC contains premium "table" wines, young *novello* wines, as well as Vin Santo.

BRUNELLO: THE CONSORTIUM'S RATINGS SINCE 1970

After each vintage, Brunello is given a rating from one to five stars.

1970 ***** 1971 *** 1972 * 1973 *** 1974 ** 1975 ***** 1976 * 1977 **** 1978 **** 1979 **** 1980 **** 1981 *** 1982 **** 1983 **** 1984 * 1985 ***** 1986 *** 1987 *** 1988 ***** 1989 ** 1990 ***** 1991 **** 1992 ** 1993 **** 1994 **** 1995 ***** 1996 *** 1997 ***** 1998 **** 1999 **** 2000 ***

Wineries

ARGIANO
WINE

S. ANGELO IN COLLE 53020 MONTALCINO SIENA
TELEPHONE 0577 844037   FAX 0577 844210
E-MAIL argiano@argiano.net

OPEN Visits by appointment only   **CLOSED** Saturday and Sunday   **DIRECT SALE** No, but wines are sold at Enoteca Franci in Montalcino   **ENGLISH SPOKEN** Yes

---

Argiano is a restrained, handsome 1482 castle built around three sides of a courtyard and set amid perfect vineyards and olive groves. The castle's recent history has been checkered. Rescued from bankruptcy in 1980 by a marriage into the Cinzano family, the property was taken over by Countess Noemi Marone Cinzano after her father's death in 1990.

Determined to improve the winery's 25 hectares (62 acres) of vineyards, the young countess appointed the equally young Sebastiano Rosa as manager, entrusting the winemaking to the veteran enologist Giacomo Tachis. "When Tachis arrived," explained Sebastiano Rosa, "we tasted everything in the cellars. He liked the wines' bouquets but found them too aggressive. Our goal was to create modern wines—a Brunello that was drinkable sooner."

Grape yields were dramatically reduced and older vineyards replanted. Small French oak *barriques* are now used judiciously in conjunction with traditional larger casks. "Brunello's regulations stipulated three years' aging in wood," Sebastiano explained as we toured the castle's underground cellars. "Tachis felt that this was too long, so we balanced the older casks' neutrality with the characterful new wood of the *barriques*."

In addition to the fine Brunello, Argiano produces Rosso di Montalcino and Solengo ("lone wild boar" in Tuscan dialect), a modern-style table wine now classified as IGT Toscana. An unusual blend of Sangiovese, Merlot, Syrah, and Cabernet, the powerful Solengo is following in the footsteps of Tachis's other sensational super-Tuscans, Sassicaia, Tignanello, and Solaia.

AZIENDA AGRICOLA ALTESINO   53028 MONTALCINO SIENA
WINE   TELEPHONE 0577 806208   FAX 0577 806131
E-MAIL altesino@iol.it

OPEN Visits and tastings Monday–Saturday, best by appointment; group tastings by appointment only and with fee   **CLOSED** Sunday   **CREDIT CARDS** Visa, MC, Amex   **DIRECT SALE** Yes   **ENGLISH SPOKEN** Yes

---

Altesino is a sizable estate exemplifying one facet of present-day Montalcino. In 1969 it was bought by Milanese entrepreneurs who invested heavily in remodeling the existing buildings, planting vineyards, and creating a modern winery. They also invested in an image they hoped would appeal to a sophisticated international audience. A restored fifteenth-century palazzo sits in perfectly manicured grounds with grazing thoroughbred horses. In 1982 Altesino officially became part of a conglomerate owning a restaurant chain with outlets throughout northern Italy.

A lengthy list of wines, both red and white, is produced from Altesino's own and subcontracted local vineyards. The best exposure and terrain are on the hillside named Montosoli, which usually confers elegance to the wines; several of the company's high-end wines originate there.

BRUNELLO'S OWN GLASS

"A few years ago Brunello di Montalcino's consortium decided to have a glass custom designed for its wine," explained Stefano Campatelli, the consortium's director. "The glass often used for mature red wines was the large spherical *ballon*, but it did not bring out Brunello's best."

Brunello is made for extended aging and is characteristically high in tannins. The *ballon* shape's low, wide aperture let too many of Brunello's *profumi* escape and accentuated the astringency of the wine's tannins and its acidity. "Each area of the mouth responds to different taste sensations," explained Campatelli. "Acidity is sensed by the sides of the tongue, as are tannins, using taste buds in the sides of the mouth. So when you drink from a glass with a very wide aperture, the wine is pushed toward the outer edges of the mouth, heightening these acid sensations."

A group from the consortium, including Piero Talenti, Andrea Costanti, Nuccio Turone, and Giulio Gambelli—reputed to have the greatest palate in Tuscany—went to Austria to the crystal firm of Riedel to develop a better form. "We brought a supply of Brunellos and tasted them in differently shaped glasses," he continued. "A wide high tulip shape worked well: its narrow top trapped the bouquet released when the wine was swirled, and focused the wine's entry toward the mouth's center, where its mellow fruit is better appreciated. Using a large glass is a valid alternative to decanting or opening wines hours ahead."

BANFI
WINE, MUSEUM,
RESTAURANT

CASTELLO DI POGGIO ALLE MURA 53024 MONTALCINO SIENA
TELEPHONE 0577 840111   FAX 0577 840205, 840444
WEB SITE www.castellobanfi.com

OPEN Visits by appointment only, made at least two days ahead; reservations made from the United States must be reconfirmed two days ahead   **CREDIT CARDS** Visa, MC, Amex   **DIRECT SALE** Yes   **ENGLISH SPOKEN** Yes   **RESERVATION** Recommended for restaurants   **OTHER** Glass Museum

---

There is nowhere quite like the Banfi winery. If you want to visit an intimate, family-run *cantina*, this is not the place for you. If instead you are attracted to the grandeur of modernity, to the marriage of industry and integrity—this is it! Banfi is a giant. Literally. Its vast steel tanks and architect-designed glass structures are on such a mighty scale that they make Montalcino and its personalized estates recede to dwarfdom. You can't help but marvel at it.

Banfi is an American creation, the brainchild of leading wine importers John and Harry Mariani. The Italian American brothers bought a feudal domain and, with the great enologist Ezio Rivella, transformed it into one of the world's most innovative wineries. If an average Montalcino winery has 2 to 12 hectares (5 to 30 acres) of vineyards growing Sangiovese, Banfi has 148 hectares (365 acres), with another 600 (1,480) producing Cabernet, Chardonnay, Moscadello, Sauvignon Blanc, and other grape varieties. Its holdings stretch for miles around the medieval Castello Banfi.

Banfi's wine list reads like a catalog. It includes the prestigious Brunello Riserva Poggio all'Oro, a single-vineyard *cru* aged in large *botti* in the estate's model cellars; Centine, a fresh, fruity Rosso di Montalcino; Summus, a modern-style award winner of Sangiovese, Cabernet, and Syrah aged wisely in *barriques*; "B," a late-harvest dessert wine of Moscadello grapes; and many more. The level is consistently high.

Worth visiting are the spectacular cellars, the shop in the twelfth-century *borgo*, the restaurants—recently expanded in a restructured building—and the Glass Museum, a fascinating collection from Roman times to the present. All in all, a multicultural experience.

BARICCI—AZIENDA AGRICOLA COLOMBAIA DI MONTOSOLI
WINE

MONTOSOLI 53028 MONTALCINO SIENA
TELEPHONE/FAX 0577 848109

OPEN Daily; appointments preferred   **CREDIT CARDS** None   **DIRECT SALE** Yes
ENGLISH SPOKEN A little

My first visit to a Montalcino wine producer was to Nello Baricci. I couldn't have found a better place to begin. Any apprehension about the possibility of a snobbish reception by some of the world's finest winemakers was dispelled by Nello's lovely wife, Ada Nannetti. She was wearing an enormous straw hat and a flowery dress and had just come in from the vineyard.

"We were checking the vines for damage," she said, a little out of breath, "after last night's hailstorm." Nello himself appeared, mopping his brow from the heat. "We have always worked the land," he explained simply, "but there's no beating the weather."

Until the mid-1950s Nello was a landless *contadino,* or peasant, working the farm of a local landowner. When the *mezzadria,* or sharecropping, system ended, he was given the opportunity to buy a plot. "It was a big change for us," said Nello. "But at that time there were sponsored mortgages for people in our situation." They bought a 15-hectare (37-acre) farm on the hillside of Montosoli, now a choice wine-growing zone. Then it comprised fields of mixed crops, a few animals, and some vines. "We went along that way until 1967, when an agrarian reformer, Dr. Ciatti, taught us how to prune the vines to make better wine." Nello smiled as he thought back. "The rest is history."

In 1967 Nello was one of eighteen founding members of the Brunello Consortium, and in 1971 he bottled his first Brunello. His Brunello and Rosso di Montalcino have gained praise from wine critics; there is never enough to go around. "We now have three hectares registered to Brunello. Even if I wanted to I couldn't increase my plantings, as the land permitted to produce Brunello is strictly limited. I could only do it by buying out someone else's rights."

BIONDI-SANTI
WINE

IL GREPPO 53024 MONTALCINO SIENA
TELEPHONE 0577 848087   FAX 0577 849396
E-MAIL biondisanti@biondisanti.it

OPEN 9:00–11:00, 15:00–17:00, appointment preferred; groups pay a limited fee for tastings **CLOSED** Saturday and Sunday   **CREDIT CARDS** Visa, Amex   **DIRECT SALE** Yes, for available vintages going back to 1891   **ENGLISH SPOKEN** Yes

The approach to Il Greppo, the Biondi Santi estate, is along an extended avenue of cathedral-high centennial cypresses. Here even the notion of time has shifted and a wine's life is conceived in decades, if not centuries. The stately vine-covered villa is a house of distinguished style, but it is welcoming and accessible, just like its owner, Franco Biondi Santi, a tall, elegant man now in his seventies.

"To make a really long-living wine you must have perfect grapes," he asserted. "You must always keep the future life of your wine in mind, and not submit the grapes to anything that could adversely affect the wine in years to come." Franco Biondi Santi represents the fifth generation of professional winemakers in a family credited with Brunello's birth. Clemente Santi won prizes with a Vino Rosso Scelto (Brunello) of the 1865 vintage. His grandson Ferruccio Biondi Santi, an enologist, identified a local clone of Sangiovese, named it Sangiovese Grosso, and by 1890 had grafted it throughout his vineyards. Its wine was called Brunello. Franco's father, Tancredi Biondi Santi, established a methodology for producing Brunello and began making the wine known in Italy and abroad. His son, Jacopo, recently started a large winery in the Maremma, at Montepò (see p 235).

By harvest time each stalk in the 20 hectares (49 acres) of vineyard is left bearing just one perfect bunch of grapes. The best of these go for Brunello, the second-best for Rosso. "Our grapes are also selected by age," Franco Biondi Santi explained. "The Brunello Riserva is produced from vines over twenty-five years old. The normal Brunello uses plants of ten to twenty-five years, while the white label Rosso is made from vines under ten years of age. The Rosso di Montalcino's red label signifies a year in which no Brunello has been produced."

Despite the modern technology in the historic cellars, each stage of the wine-making process is performed with personal attention. Bottles are corked, labeled, and numbered by hand. If over time (meaning decades) a customer finds the level in a well-cellared Brunello has dropped, Biondi Santi will recork it, topping it up with wine of the same vintage.

The Biondi-Santi Brunellos have always been expensive symbols of prestige, collector's items representing the absolute guarantees of tradition and quality. Burton Anderson, in the introduction to his 1988 book on Biondi-Santi, describes his first tasting, in 1971, of the 1964 Riserva:

"It was young and aggressive, robust in constitution and rich in color, with the extract and tannins that would maintain it proudly for decades. But already it had those niceties of bouquet, those sensations of flavor, those intricate traits revealing what the experts refer to as race or breed which even an inspired amateur might recognize though perhaps not venture to explain. After years of tasting through the region's wines . . . this was a revelation. I wrote in my notes: 'At last, a Tuscan *grand cru!*'"

CAPARZO
WINE

TORRENIERI 53028 MONTALCINO SIENA
TELEPHONE 0577 848390, 847166
FAX 0577 849377
WEB SITE www.caparzo.com

OPEN 9:00–12:00, 14:30–18:00 for visits and tastings; groups by appointment only
CLOSED Saturday and Sunday   **CREDIT CARDS** Visa, MC, Amex   **DIRECT SALE** Yes
ENGLISH SPOKEN No

Giulio Consonno was one of the businessmen who bought Altesino and, in 1970, Tenuta Caparzo, then a run-down country house with a few barns and vineyards. By 1981 the estate had grown to 65 hectares (160 acres), of which 32 (79 acres) were vineyards. The choice 7-hectare (17-acre) vineyard, La Caduta, was added in 1991. The Milanese Nuccio Turone now runs the successful business in an atmosphere of innovation and experimentation. With winemaker Vittorio Fiore as consultant, vineyards were planted, including Montalcino's first Cabernet Sauvignon, and a sophisticated cellar established.

"We were the first in Montalcino to use *barriques*," recalled Turone, "for our Sangiovese-Cabernet blend, Ca' del Pazzo, presented in 1982. And we were criticized for it." But Turone and Fiore were attuned to the demands of a changing international wine market. Their white wine, Le Grance—now Sant'Antimo DOC—is considered one of Tuscany's most convincing barrel-aged Chardonnays. Also containing small amounts of Traminer and Sauvignon grapes, Le Grance was Caparzo's answer to the need for a white wine to be aged.

Their single-vineyard Brunello *cru*, La Casa, matures in barrels of differing sizes, from small *barriques* to large Slavonian casks. Three years is too long for the wine to remain in small casks, Turone explained. The fine La Caduta, of Sangiovese grapes aged for one year, is sold as a Rosso di Montalcino.

CASANOVA DI NERI
WINE

TORRENIERI 53028 MONTALCINO SIENA
TELEPHONE/FAX 0577 834455
E-MAIL giacner@tin.it

OPEN 8:00–12:30, 14:30–19:30; cellar visits and tastings by appointment only   CLOSED Sunday
CREDIT CARDS None   DIRECT SALE Yes   ENGLISH SPOKEN Yes

Giacomo Neri belongs to the new generation of Brunello winemakers. He learned about winemaking from his father, Giovanni, who bought his first Montalcino vineyards in 1971. "My father's intention here was always to make high-quality wines," he said. Within a few years Giovanni Neri had added more vineyards in strategic positions, for a current total of 35 hectares (86 acres)—including some recent additions at Castelnuovo dell'Abate that will eventually go into a new Sant'Antimo wine. Ever-better clones of the local Sangiovese grape were developed.

"He spent years researching and experimenting with smaller, more intensely flavored fruit," continued Giacomo, a strapping young man with a relaxed, friendly manner. "The individual grapes had to be widely spaced within the bunch to avoid mildew." By the mid-1980s, this selection process and the modernized cellars were paying off.

"After tasting many great foreign wines," he said, "we were convinced that without compromising Brunello's traditional qualities, it could become more approachable: a more elegant wine with softer tannins and respect for its fruit. A wine to drink now that would last."

When Giovanni died in 1991, Giacomo—by now a winemaker in his own right—took over the estate. He has made a great name for himself with his distinctive, intense, yet well-balanced wines. In addition to the normal Brunello and Rosso di Montalcino, in great years Neri produces two *crus:* Cerretalto, a rich, concentrated single-vineyard Brunello that has won all the top awards; and Tenuta Nuova, another great Brunello from a single vineyard. He also makes a delicious, atypical olive oil from *olivastra* olives.

CASTELGIOCONDO
WINE

CASTELGIOCONDO 53024 MONTALCINO SIENA
TELEPHONE 0577 848492   FAX 0577 849138
E-MAIL tecas@galli.it

OPEN Visits and tastings (only for groups of four to six) by appointment only
CLOSED Saturday and Sunday   CREDIT CARDS None   DIRECT SALE Yes, subject to availability
ENGLISH SPOKEN Yes   OTHER For larger groups or other inquiries call Frescobaldi's head office
in Firenze: 055 2381400

Castelgiocondo is the Marchesi de' Frescobaldi's holding in Montalcino (see p 107), and one of the area's largest, with more than 200 hectares (494 acres) of vineyards, of which 140 (345) are registered to Brunello. Set in the expansive countryside south of Montalcino, the austere but impeccably run estate is deservedly gaining recognition after a period of change and renovation.

"Castelgiocondo is part of the Frescobaldi group but is run autonomously," the estate's manager, Gilberto Cosci, explained. A large modern *cantina*, highly efficient but without much character, has been built. New vineyards—including some with higher-density planting—have been created with the winemaker Nicolò D'Afflitto.

The estate's wines include a classic-style Brunello, with an excellent, concentrated Riserva in great years, which may be aged briefly in *barriques*. Unusually, the Rosso di Montalcino Campo ai Sassi is a single-vineyard wine. Newer additions to the list are Lamaione, of pure Merlot, and the white Vergena, of pure Sauvignon, which also spends some time in the small oak barrels. A recent joint venture, Luce, sees Robert Mondavi as partner.

Castelgiocondo also produces olive oil. During the season, hand-picked olives are trucked every two to three days in special aerated cages to the Frescobaldi's in-house stainless-steel mill near Firenze (see Laudemio, p 117).

CERBAIONA	53024 MONTALCINO SIENA
WINE	TELEPHONE/FAX 0577 848660

OPEN Visits by appointment preferred; tastings only when owners present   **CREDIT CARDS** None
DIRECT SALE Yes, subject to availability   **ENGLISH SPOKEN** Yes

"This has always been a place for friends," the hospitable Diego Molinari said as he showed me Cerbaiona's tiny *cantina*. "But right now I wish I had a crystal ball to see into the future. We are getting older and finding it harder to manage all the work."

Cerbaiona is in one of Montalcino's most stunning positions, with a spectacular panorama of the Crete Senesi. The beautiful villa and its striking *giardino all'Italiana* have an intimacy the larger estates lack. "When we bought the place," Molinari explained, "an old *contadino* still lived here, in the almost slavelike conditions imposed by the sharecropping system." Diego and Nora Molinari came from Rome, where he had been a senior pilot for Alitalia. They planted new vineyards and in no time were winning top marks with their great Brunellos.

"I was never that interested in the Rosso di Montalcino," Molinari confided. "So recently I decided to try an experiment." He planted what he described as "a bit of salt and pepper" to add to the Sangiovese: Cabernet, Merlot, Syrah, Aleatico. "For me Sangiovese alone is no longer mysterious. I like the idea of creating a new wine. It's fun. It will be something to talk to our friends about."

CIACCI PICCOLOMINI D'ARAGONA
WINE

VIA BORGO DI MEZZO, 62
CASTELNUOVO DELL'ABATE 53020 MONTALCINO SIENA
TELEPHONE 0577 835616   FAX 0577 835785
WEB SITE www.ciaccipiccolomini.com

OPEN 9:00–13:00, 15:00–19:00; *cantina* visits and tastings by appointment only
CLOSED Saturday and Sunday   **CREDIT CARDS** Visa, MC, Amex   **DIRECT SALE** Yes, from the
side of the palazzo, appointments preferred   **ENGLISH SPOKEN** Yes

"Come down to the *cantina* and taste the wines directly from the barrel. That's the best way. A bottle doesn't necessarily need to be opened in a room with a view," said Roberto Cipresso, who was the young winemaker of Tenuta Ciacci Piccolomini d'Aragona when I first visited it (Paolo Vagaggini has taken over since then). The aging cellars turned out to be wonderfully atmospheric, dug deep below medieval Castelnuovo. The palazzo, formerly a bishop's seat, dates back to the sixteenth century, but the cellars are older.

Once the property of the Countess Elda Ciacci Piccolomini, the palace and its holdings were bequeathed in 1985 to the estate's then-manager, Giuseppe Bianchini. Under the management of Bianchini and his son Paolo, the domain has earned a reputation as one of Montalcino's best.

Many of the estate's 32 hectares (79 acres) of vineyards are planted to Sangiovese, the grape variety of Brunello and Rosso di Montalcino. Ten more were recently planted with Sangiovese, Merlot, Cabernet Sauvignon, and Syrah. Indeed, Syrah is at the heart of the estate's new wine, Fabius, a Sant'Antimo DOC.

In addition to its Brunellos and Rosso, the farm produces a super-Tuscan table wine with the provocative name of Ateo—or "atheist"—of Sangiovese grapes, with added Merlot and Cabernet, that is aged in new *barriques*. Why this name? Roberto Cipresso smiled before answering. "Ateo came from a desire to go against the current. I don't believe in the dogma or god of Brunello—I believe in our Italian grape varieties, and the challenge to do something new with them is exciting."

COL D'ORCIA
WINE

S. ANGELO SCALO S. ANGELO IN COLLE 53020 MONTALCINO SIENA
TELEPHONE 0577 808001   FAX 0577 844018
WEB SITE www.coldorcia.com

OPEN Monday–Saturday 8:30–12:30, 14:30–19:00, Sunday 8:30–12:30; limited tastings possible in estate shop; guided tastings, cellar visits, and large groups by appointment only
CREDIT CARDS Visa, MC   **DIRECT SALE** Yes, of wines and oil   **ENGLISH SPOKEN** Yes

Count Francesco Marone Cinzano's estate, Col d'Orcia, is one of Montalcino's largest. It includes 110 hectares (272 acres) of Sangiovese grapes for Brunello and Rosso di Montalcino, and a further 21 (51.8 acres) of other varieties. Its attractive villa and shipshape modern *cantine* are set in landscaped gardens.

The estate's star wine is Poggio al Vento, a Brunello Riserva of selected grapes from a single vineyard; complex and elegantly structured, it is made only in exceptional years. Olmaia, a Cabernet Sauvignon super-Tuscan that is now an IGT, is aged for eighteen months in French *barriques*. There is also a new white wine, Pinot Grigio DOC Sant'Antimo. Lovers of meditation wines will appreciate Pascena, a late-harvest sweet Moscadello di Montalcino wine. "To make this wine the white muscat grapes are left to dry on the plant until mid-October," explained Giuliano Dragoni, the estate's agronomist. A slow fermentation in *barriques* is followed by a year in wood.

Col d'Orcia participates in viticultural experiments with the University of Firenze. "The program covers all aspects of the winemaking process," explained Dragoni. "A key factor in vine growing is the vigor of the plant." Grapevines should not be too vigorous, or the plant's energy is spent making foliage rather than in enriching the fruit. "Planting in stony, dry soil is one way of reducing its vigor; another is to grow grass between the rows, providing competition for the vines."

Some techniques being experimented with are common organic practices. "We have borrowed many of their ideas to improve production—using fewer chemical fertilizers or pesticides definitely helps," Dragoni said.

CONTI COSTANTI
WINE

COLLE AL MATRICHESE 53024 MONTALCINO SIENA
TELEPHONE 0577 848195   FAX 0577 849349
E-MAIL costanti@inwind.it

OPEN Visits and tastings by appointment only; groups charged a per-glass fee for tastings
CLOSED Saturday and Sunday   **CREDIT CARDS** None   **DIRECT SALE** Yes, subject to availability
ENGLISH SPOKEN A little

The Costantis, one of Montalcino's oldest families, are based in Colle al Matrichese, a stately villa with box-hedged gardens. "First accounts of winemaking in my family are from 1550, although no one did it professionally until this century," said Andrea Costanti, who runs the estate. "In 1870 Count Tito Costanti presented two wines named Brunello at an exhibition in Siena. One was five years old, and the other two, just like present-day Brunello and Rosso."

Andrea Costanti is an articulate member of the new generation of growers. "What I find interesting about Brunello," continued Costanti, "is that it constituted a revolution in winemaking terms. Never before in Italy had a single grape variety been used to produce a wine of prestige. Tito Costanti's generation had traveled and seen the wines of Bordeaux. They too wanted to produce a red wine that could age."

Andrea Costanti trained as a geologist but took over the estate in 1983. "I took the plunge, learning as I went along." He was advised by winemaker Vittorio Fiore, but always took an active part in the decision making: "After all, my name is on the bottles."

"All three of my wines are made from Sangiovese," he asserted. "The Brunello matures for three years in Slavonian oak. It used to be a wine for long aging, but it is becoming more immediate. The Rosso is an easier wine: with ten months in French *barriques*, it's about youth and wood and is drinkable right away." The third wine, Vermiglio—now an IGT—is between the two: made of Sangiovese, it spends two years in large oak barrels and six months in *barriques*. Two fine Brunello Grappas and a decisive, fresh-tasting extra-virgin olive oil are also made. Andrea Costanti is a generous, affable young man who believes that meeting the people "behind" the wine is important. "You get right to the person," he declared. "And they to you. After all, drinking a glass of wine together is very nice."

FATTORIA DEI BARBI
WINE, CHEESE, SALUMI

FATTORIA DEI BARBI E DEL CASATO
53024 MONTALCINO SIENA
TELEPHONE 0577 848277   FAX 0577 849356
WEB SITE www.fattoriadeibarbi.it

OPEN Monday–Friday 9:00–13:00, 15:00–18:00; Saturday–Sunday 14:30–17:30; guided tastings and groups by appointment only   **CREDIT CARDS** Visa, MC, Amex   **DIRECT SALE** Yes **ENGLISH SPOKEN** Yes   **FEATURES** Restaurant   **OTHER** Vacation apartments available, call 0577 849421

A tour of the Fattoria dei Barbi's cellars is a multimedia experience. The underground labyrinth illustrates various stages of the winemaking process, as well as the history of the Colombini Cinelli family and their wines. Amid the barrels are paintings, murals, family trees, soil samples, maps, fables, and even a few videos. It all has been done with a kind of fanciful pedagogy, like a teacher thinking up amusing ways to interest and educate a class of children. I suspect a lot of this is Donatella Colombini's idea—she has a charming air of whimsy about her. The acting secretary of the Movement for Wine Tourism, she has long been a keen promoter of Italian wines (see p 300 for her other Tuscan estate).

The Colombini family traces itself back to 1200 and further, its history punctuated by an eccentric cast of characters. Of these, the brigand Bruscone and the blessed Beato Giovanni have had wines named after them. Of the classic Montalcino wines, the Fattoria's stars are the *cru* Brunello di Montalcino Vigna del Fiore Riserva, made of selected grapes from one vineyard, and the Brunello Riserva, made only in great years. These wines have benefited from the family's recent collaboration with the enologist Luigi Casagrande. The estate has 42 hectares (103 acres) given over to Sangiovese.

Fattoria dei Barbi, headed by Donatella's mother, Francesca Colombini Cinelli, hosts a restaurant specializing in local cuisine and sponsors an annual literary prize. The estate is also noted for its pecorino cheeses and the excellent *salumi* it produces from farm-raised pigs; both products can be purchased here.

HOW TO DRINK BRUNELLO

Brunello di Montalcino is matured for four to five years before being sold, but additional aging should take place in a horizontal position in a cool dark cellar, where it may remain for years. If you intend to drink an older vintage soon after buying, it is best to let it settle for a few days, ideally in a horizontal position. The wine should be drunk at 18° to 20°C (64° to 68°F). Open the bottle at least one hour before drinking, or slowly decant the wine, thereby also eliminating any sediment deposited during its aging. Any remaining wine will keep for around twenty-four hours in a corked bottle unless rubber vacuum corks are used. Both Brunello and Rosso di Montalcino are full-flavored red wines that go best with red meats, game, and cheese. Brunello also makes a fine meditation wine for sipping slowly after dinner.

FULIGNI
WINE, OLIVE OIL

VIA S. SALONI, 33 53024 MONTALCINO SIENA
TELEPHONE 0577 848039   FAX 0577 848710

OPEN Visits and sales by appointment only   **CREDIT CARDS** None   **DIRECT SALE** Yes, by appointment sales are possible from farm or villa   **ENGLISH SPOKEN** Yes

---

"Our father came here from Verona in 1925 with the Grand Duke of Tuscany, when the *mezzadria* system was still in operation. We have stuck to the traditional pairing of grapes and olives. Since his death, all six of us brothers and sisters have run the estate," said Signorina Maria Flora Fuligni.

She and her sister Matilde, both retired teachers, were showing me their vineyards. Like colorful Frank Capra characters, the two ladies carried on a spirited discussion about old times and new, stopping here and there to point out features in their beloved landscape. "Our land is very stony. But the earth is rich," explained Maria Flora. "They say that olives born on rocky soil make the best oil," interjected Matilde. "Before 1985, before the terrible winter that killed almost all our great old olive trees," continued Maria Flora, "we picked the olives using a tall ladder with thirty-two rungs. Some of those trees were two hundred years old. It was heartbreaking when they died."

They cut their trees down to the ground and waited for them to regenerate, and they are now producing oil again. Maria Flora is justly proud. "I am not a big wine drinker, but I love our oil. I use it every day. We particularly like it for *bruschetta*, drizzled onto toasted unsalted bread." Their extra-virgin olive oil is milled locally in La Spiga *frantoio* (see p 330).

The estate's elegant wines are made by Roberto Guerrini, who represents the next generation of the Fuligni family. Their atmospheric wine cellar is under the pleasantly crumbling fifteenth-century palazzo in town. Alongside the large oval *botti* containing the estate's admired Brunello and its Riserva are some of the new *barriques* used for aging their Rosso di Montalcino, Ginestreto. "This comes from a very arid, rocky vineyard of the same name. Leopardi [a nineteenth-century Italian poet] called *ginestra* [broom] 'the flower of the desert,'" said Maria Flora. "And we liked the name."

IL POGGIONE
WINE

S. ANGELO IN COLLE 53020 MONTALCINO SIENA
TELEPHONE 0577 844029   FAX 0577 844165
WEB SITE www.tenutailpoggione.it

OPEN Cellar visits and tastings by appointment only   **CREDIT CARDS** Visa, MC
DIRECT SALE Yes, from the *cantina*   **ENGLISH SPOKEN** Yes

The story of the Franceschi family's Il Poggione is inextricably bound to that of the late Pierluigi Talenti (p 326). From its creation in 1959, Talenti managed the estate, its acclaimed wines, and their policy of reasonable pricing. For many years he worked with Fabrizio Bindocci, director of the estate's 100 hectares (247 acres) of vineyards.

"Although Il Poggione's Brunellos will age well, they are made to be drunk now, rather than to be kept as collector's items," explained Bindocci. Talenti believed that *barriques*, used for many modern wines, were not for Montalcino's classic reds. "When you drink Montalcino's wines you should taste the fruit of the Sangiovese, not the wood," he told me. "For me, too much wood is a defect. Great red wines are made on the vine." Grape yield is reduced by pruning, and clones of Sangiovese are selected in an ongoing search for better quality.

The estate was one of the first to reintroduce Moscadello di Montalcino, a slightly bubbly, sweet amber wine with origins in the medieval Moscadelletto. "I was fascinated by Montalcino's oldest wine," Talenti recalled. "I sought out old vines of Moscato di Canelli for it, which is more aromatic than the Moscato di Montalcino." It should be drunk soon after being bought.

Il Poggione makes a fine Vin Santo of combined Malvasia and Trebbiano grapes. It also has its own *frantoio*, or olive mill. The estate's olives are pounded by steel hammers before being cold-pressed in a more traditional way.

LE CHIUSE DI SOTTO— GIANNI BRUNELLI
WINE

CHIUSE DI SOTTO 53042 MONTALCINO
TELEPHONE/FAX 0577 849342

OPEN All week by appointment   **DIRECT SALE** Yes, by appointment only
ENGLISH SPOKEN A little

Gianni Brunelli is one of the area's nicest restaurateurs: he runs Osteria Le Logge in Siena and recently opened a wine bar there in Piazza del Campo (see p 297). Brunelli is a colorful, affable characer, but there's nothing easygoing about his winemaking. His *cantina* is modest in size, but it is kept as perfectly as any I've visited. The property extends around a small country farmhouse that was once his grandfather's, on the northern slopes below Montalcino. With 4 hectares (10 acres) newly planted, the estate will total 7 hectares (17 acres) of vineyards, of primarily Sangiovese, with a little Merlot. You can taste Brunelli's fruity, drinkable wines at the restaurants or buy them in Montalcino.

LISINI
WINE

FATTORIA DI S. ANGELO IN COLLE
S. ANGELO IN COLLE 53020 MONTALCINO SIENA
TELEPHONE 0577 844040   FAX 0577 844219
WEB SITE www.lisini.com

OPEN *Cantina* visits by appointment only (no tastings)   **CLOSED** Saturday and Sunday
CREDIT CARDS None   **DIRECT SALE** Yes, if available   **ENGLISH SPOKEN** Yes

Set in untamed countryside on the scenic unpaved road between S. Angelo in Colle and Castelnuovo dell'Abate, the Lisini estate is among Montalcino's oldest. Farm buildings include a tower dated to 1300 and an arched brick *loggia* in the Sienese style. The family's 13 hectares (32 acres) of vineyard include some of Montalcino's finest terrain.

"Since great wine is made with great grapes," explained Lorenzo Lisini Baldi, "we prune and select them as they grow and harvest only the finest." Each vineyard and type of grape is vinified separately. The Brunello/Rosso division is decided in the cellar, once the grapes have been made into wine. This allows for a lot of flexibility: in a lesser year the winery may make no Brunello (as in 1992) and come out with only the Rosso. All the wines are matured in different-size chestnut and oak casks, but not in the smaller French oak *barriques*.

"Our wines are very *fruttato*, so we really have had no need of *barriques*, which might overemphasize their qualities," said Lisini, who is aided in the winemaking by Franco Bernabei. Lisini's excellent Brunello Riserva, made only in exceptional years, is called Ugolaia, after its vineyard. Lisini also produces a decisively fragrant olive oil, extracted at Montalcino's Frantoio La Spiga (see p 330).

MASTROJANNI
WINE

PODERI LORETO E S. PIO CASTELNUOVO DELL'ABATE 53024
MONTALCINO SIENA
TELEPHONE 0577 835681   FAX 0577 835505
E-MAIL mastrojanni.vini@tiscalinet.it

OPEN *Cantina* visits and tastings by appointment only   **CREDIT CARDS** None
DIRECT SALE Yes, if available   **ENGLISH SPOKEN** A little

The Mastrojanni estate is situated in beautiful countryside. A dirt road climbs up from Castelnuovo to the crest of the hill, revealing sweeping views of Mount Amiata and its valleys. The farm was bought in 1974 by a Roman lawyer for his son, and for years its 18 hectares (44 acres) of vineyards produced good but not exceptional wines. In 1992 winemaker Maurizio Castelli was brought in to work with Andrea Machetti, the young expert running the estate; recent wines have been very well received.

In addition to the "regular" and reserve Brunellos, Mastrojanni produces an award-winning Brunello *cru*, Vigna Schiena d'Asino, in which only small perfect grapes from a vineyard named *schiena d'asino* (the shape of a donkey's back) are used. Rosso di Montalcino and San Pio, a super-Tuscan IGT wine of 75 percent Sangiovese and 25 percent Cabernet Sauvignon grapes, complete the estate's list of reds.

"Rather than make a Vin Santo," Machetti went on, "we liked the challenge of a *passito*." Botrys is an intense dessert wine made from sun-dried grapes that is aged in *barriques* for 15 months. Golden in color and highly perfumed, Mastrojanni's *passito* is a blend of Moscato and Malvasia di Candia grapes. The winery's aromatic Brunello grappas are made from very lightly pressed grapes, the amber grappa spending three years in wood.

PIEVE DI SANTA RESTITUTA
WINE

CHIESA DI SANTA RESTITUTA 53024
MONTALCINO SIENA
TELEPHONE 0577 848610   FAX 0577 849309

OPEN Not open to the public   **DIRECT SALE** No, but the wines are sold at *enoteche* Fortezza and Franci in Montalcino   **ENGLISH SPOKEN** Yes

Although this lovely estate is not open to visits from the public, its recent history is having a significant impact on Montalcino, and I include it for those readers interested in what lies behind its fine wines.

In 1972 Roberto Bellini bought the land from the adjacent church of Santa Restituta, transforming its 18 hectares (44 acres) from the mixed-crop system into top-quality vineyards. But Bellini did more than simply modernize: his passion for wine created a cultural environment for its making, as his poetic underground cellar-stairway will attest. Then, in 1994, he sold it.

Its current owner-partner, Angelo Gaja, is one of Italy's most brilliant wine producers, a legendary figure in Piemonte thanks to what wine critic Robert

Parker has described as his "fanatical commitment to excellence." That he should be spreading his interests to Montalcino—and, more recently, Bolgheri (see p 153–154)—has caused a stir in winemaking circles.

When I first visited there, in 1996, Fabrizio Moltard was the estate's young manager; he explained the direction the winery was taking. "Clearly, Angelo Gaja shares Bellini's ideals of quality," he affirmed. "He wants to study Tuscan methods before making any radical changes, so things are evolving naturally." There are no Brunello Riservas, but in good years two Brunellos are produced, matured partly in small oak casks: Sugarille, a single-vineyard *cru*, and Rennina, of grapes from three plots.

"We don't think of *barriques* as a means of imparting a vanilla flavor to wine," stated Moltard, "but to help it grow: increasing its range of aromas and perfumes, and stabilizing its color. There is no mystery about this: you must respect tradition, but not become its prisoner—after all, successful innovation in time becomes tradition."

And other wines? "Brunello is Sangiovese's maximum expression, so there seems no point in producing a Rosso di Montalcino," Moltard explained. "A new 'table wine,' Promis, of 90 percent Sangiovese and 10 percent Cabernet Sauvignon, gives the flexibility to absorb more Sangiovese in less-good Brunello vintages."

In 2001 I asked Angelo Gaja how things were coming along in Montalcino, where he now works with Oriano Scheggi and Ilaria Marchetti. Was he satisfied with his wines from there? "Sangiovese is a grape that is even more tricky to work with than Nebbiolo," he admitted, "and so far I have only learned a few of its secrets. I will need more time before I can feel comfortable with it technically, or produce the kind of wines I have in mind.

"However," he continued, "I consider Montalcino to be 'the' Italian wine city, and I find working here fascinating. Sangiovese is a difficult beast, but I hope eventually to make a great wine here, an important wine, but one that speaks Tuscan, not Piedmontese."

POGGIO ANTICO
WINE

POGGIO ANTICO 53024 MONTALCINO SIENA
TELEPHONE 0577 848044   FAX 0577 846563
WEB SITE www.poggioantico.com

OPEN Shop daily 8:00–20:00; *cantina* visits Monday–Friday 9:00–20:00, appointment preferred; tastings only for groups of ten or more, with nominal fees   **CLOSED** Shop never; *cantina* Saturday and Sunday   **CREDIT CARDS** Visa, MC   **DIRECT SALE** Yes   **ENGLISH SPOKEN** Yes
OTHER For Poggio Antico's restaurant, see p 333

Paola Gloder's office is right in the heart of this estate; we talked against a background of soft clinking from the bottling line. This attractive, energetic young woman is herself the heart of Fattoria Poggio Antico, one of the most dynamic of Montalcino's "younger" wineries.

When her father, a Milanese stockbroker, bought the estate in 1984, Paola was a student in her twenties. He offered her the chance to run it. She was amazed: "He said, 'You are very young. You are a woman. You know no one in Montalcino. But it would be all yours for the making.' I thought it over. It meant giving up my whole life in Milan. But I loved this place, and hoped I could turn it into something great. I accepted."

She had everything to learn, but threw herself into it, winning the respect of the locals with her determination and hard work. The *fattoria* was overhauled, new *cantine* were built, and the restaurant was refurbished (see p 333). Everything was created with style, from the handsome wine labels to the "library" of old vintages in the immaculate cellars. Today Paola is helped by winemaker Carlo Ferrini.

Poggio Antico's Brunellos are characterized by an elegance imparted by the vineyards' high position, at 450 to 520 meters (1,476 to 1,706 feet). With 20 hectares (49 acres) given over to Sangiovese, and 12 more (30) recently renewed or planted, the *fattoria* concentrates on Montalcino's traditional wines, giving them a modern character. Alongside the estate's traditional Brunello, Riserva, and Rosso di Montalcino is Altero, of pure Sangiovese. "You could call this a modern Brunello," Paola explained. "It is aged in *tonneaux* [French barrels that are larger than *barriques*] and spends two of its four years in wood."

POGGIO DI SOTTO
WINE

POGGIO DI SOPRA, 222 CASTELNUOVO DELL'ABATE 53020
MONTALCINO SIENA
TELEPHONE/FAX 0577 835502
E-MAIL palmuccipds@libero.it

OPEN Visits by appointment   CREDIT CARDS Visa, MC
DIRECT SALE Yes   ENGLISH SPOKEN Yes

"I do not make a modern wine," declared Piero Palmucci proudly. "My wines are called traditional and countercurrent—but that's because they contain nothing but Sangiovese grapes. No yeasts, no concentrates, no 'international' varietals. What's important to me is to be able to taste these wines in ten years and know that they will still be fine."

We were walking through his just-built new *cantina*, with its perfect rows of large barrels, the whole scrupulously clean. "I hate *barriques*!" he laughed. "I want to taste fruit in my wines, not wood."

And fruit you do taste in his elegant, fragrant Brunello. The vineyards face Monte Amiata and benefit from long hours of sun and a heightened daily temperature range, "which adds *profumi* to the wines." His award-winning Brunello has soft, nonaggressive tannins, fine structure, and great length.

Palmucci comes from a background in shipping and lived for many years in Scandinavia. "When I came here in 1990 I looked for the most traditional, most pure winemaker, and found him in the person of Giulio Gambelli, who learned his craft from Tancredi Biondi Santi."

At harvest time, Palmucci personally checks each bunch of grapes, rejecting any that are not perfectly mature. At first, the pickers who work with him thought he was crazy to do this, but they, too, acknowledge the results in the final wines.

Piero and his wife, Elisabeth, make two wines: Brunello and Rosso di Montalcino, with a Riserva only in great years. They also make a decisive, unfiltered olive oil. "I believe you can give people pleasure in many ways," he says, "and one of them is to offer a glass of wine to someone." A great glass of wine.

SALICUTTI	**PODERE SALICUTTI, 174 53024 MONTALCINO SIENA**
WINE: ORGANIC	TELEPHONE/FAX 0577 847003

OPEN Visits by prior appointment only   **DIRECT SALE** No, but wines are available at Enoteca Fortezza in Montalcino   **ENGLISH SPOKEN** Yes   **OTHER** Rooms available for holiday rentals

When Francesco Leanza bought a small farm in Montalcino in 1990, the chances of his being able to make Brunello there seemed practically nonexistent. All planting rights for Tuscany's most prestigious wine were taken, and there seemed little hope of new vineyards being granted them. He decided to plant Sangiovese anyway, in three steep vineyards on his beautifully situated property, which offers perfect views of Mount Amiata.

"My land forms a natural *conca*—almost an amphitheater," he explained, "so the vines are protected and very healthy here. I realized that no one in Montalcino was making organic wines, but I wanted to try. For that, you must start with great grapes, grown on land that has a natural vocation for vineyards." His is sunny, yet well-drained, so there is no risk of the mists and humidity that can cause mold to form on the fruit. By not overfeeding the vines, he keeps them producing smaller amounts of higher-quality grapes—just what is needed for great wines. His gamble has paid off: within a few years he has managed to get all three vineyards accepted for producing Brunello.

Leanza also produces an intense organic olive oil. He laughed as he told me that, early on, he made one chemical treatment in the olive grove. "It was awful! I had the sensation that I was dirtying nature by spraying this stuff on the trees, and I felt so unwell I decided that would be the last time I ever did it." In 1995 he registered the whole farm as organic. His new wines began to be tasted by local experts and to win accolades from people who had not formerly believed that organic wines could be this good.

Leanza, who is Sicilian, currently makes three wines: in addition to the Brunello and Rosso di Montalcino is the red Dopoteatro IGT, of primarily Cabernet Sauvignon grapes. For aging these wines he favors *tonneaux*, French barrels a bit bigger than the ubiquitous *barriques*.

SALVIONI—LA CERBAIOLA
WINE

PIAZZA CAVOUR, 19 53024 MONTALCINO SIENA
TELEPHONE/FAX 0577 848499

OPEN Visits by appointment only   **CLOSED** Saturday and Sunday   **CREDIT CARDS** None
DIRECT SALE Yes, subject to availability   **ENGLISH SPOKEN** A little

Giulio and Mirella Salvioni make celebrated Brunellos. Yet they started making wine as a hobby, in their spare time. The land, which they inherited, is fortunately positioned at 420 meters (1,378 feet) with southeasterly exposure, conferring perfect aromas and elegance to their Sangiovese-based wines. Luckily their small vineyard is being expanded, so their winemaking capacity will double.

"If we have obtained top results," asserted the loquacious Giulio Salvioni, "it is because we believe in a drastic selection of the grapes when they are still growing on the vine." During July the Salvionis work with their enologist, Attilio Pagli, to carry out a "green harvest," leaving only two bunches per plant, one bigger than the other. At the beginning of September the vines are cleared of lower leaves, giving the grapes maximum exposure to sun and air. Only the healthiest bunches are left, in readiness for the harvest. Two *vendemmie* (harvests), are carried out: for Brunello all the smallest bunches, plus the top *orecchiette* (literally, "ears") on the bigger bunches are picked. The remaining bigger bunches are then gathered for making Rosso di Montalcino.

"If we have done our job correctly, the smaller grapes are more mature and a better color than the larger ones," Salvioni explained. "In fact they may contain a half degree more alcohol." From then on, the vinification process is identical for the two batches.

Salvioni also makes a limited amount of extra-virgin olive oil from trees he has planted, milled in the nearby *frantoio* La Spiga (p 330).

SIRO PACENTI
WINE

PELAGRILLI 53024 MONTALCINO SIENA
TELEPHONE/FAX 0577 848662
E-MAIL pacentisiro@libero.it

OPEN *Cantina* visits and tastings by appointment only   **CREDIT CARDS** None
DIRECT SALE Yes, for small amounts   **ENGLISH SPOKEN** A little

I recently had an exhilarating conversation with Giancarlo Pacenti, the talented young man now at the helm of this winery. I have admired him and his wines for some time: he has been a committed campaigner for progressive reforms in the often traditionalist seas of Montalcino, and he has been instrumental in raising the image—by raising the quality—of Rosso di Montalcino, a wine that was so often relegated to second best.

Now Giancarlo is taking another step forward. "For some time I have believed it must be possible to create a really great Sangiovese wine here in Montalcino," he began excitedly, "a wine that could hold its own against any of the world's biggest 'international' grape varietals. Previously, it was felt that in order to do this, one would need to 'cut,' 'correct,' or 'enhance' the Sangiovese with Merlot or Cabernet—that neither its color nor its body could match up to those top international wines. But I felt we must try to get pure Sangiovese, which is what this territory is really about, to attain those heights. People always say that Sangiovese alone does not have enough color to compete with those wines, but I saw no good reason why it should lose the depth of color it has when it is first vinified. And Montalcino's Sangiovese has the unique complexity, acidity, and finesse to make it great."

Pacenti sought expert advice from outside in the person of Professor Yves Glories, head of the enology faculty at Bordeaux University, who was fascinated by the challenge of working with Sangiovese.

"This is not a question of making French-style wines here," Pacenti went on. "But of applying a different methodology to our own winemaking. It has involved radical changes in the way I work and think, both in the vineyard and in the cellar. For example, each of my vineyards has been analyzed and divided into separate sections, depending on soil structure, etc. The grapes from each of these units are picked and vinified separately. After the fermentation, they are tasted, and each one is put into the wood type that best suits it: a powerful wine with lots of structure and character goes into a wood with the same characteristics. A softer, more perfumed wine goes into wood that will not cover those *profumi*." At the end, the wines can be blended as necessary to create a balanced whole whose parts have been respected individually.

"Each aspect of the wine's development is closely controlled, using a range of often very simple techniques, in such a way that the grape's natural colors and perfumes are never lost." If the first fruits of his labors, such as the intensely colored, rich yet elegant and fine-tannined 1997 Brunello (which had only then been in the bottle for one year), and the exceptionally aromatic 2000 vintage, which I tasted from the barrel in 2001, are anything to go on, Pacenti will realize his dreams sooner than he hoped.

TALENTI—PODERE
PIAN DI CONTE
WINE

S. ANGELO IN COLLE 53020 MONTALCINO SIENA
TELEPHONE 0577 844064   FAX 0577 844043
E-MAIL az_talenti@tin.it

OPEN Visits and tastings by appointment only   **CREDIT CARDS** None
DIRECT SALE Yes   **ENGLISH SPOKEN** A little

The late Pierluigi Talenti was an exceptional man, forward thinking for his time, uncompromising in his belief in Brunello, respectful and charming in his dealings with other people. He was one of the elder statesmen of Montalcino, and his death in 1999 left an unfillable void there. His son and young grandson are now running the estate, with the help of the expert winemaker Carlo Ferrini.

For more than fifty years Talenti was Il Poggione's guiding light (p 319). In 1980 its owners gave him a farm at Pian di Conte as a present. He enlarged it to 11 hectares (27 acres) of vineyards and won high acclaim for his classic Brunellos.

Pian di Conte is a very pretty place, with its handsome round tower and cluster of cypresses. It was a fittingly dignified seat for one of modern Montalcino's founding fathers. "I began to learn about wine as a boy," explained the then elderly but sprightly Talenti. "My father ran a restaurant in Romagna and occasionally brought me to Tuscany when he chose his wines."

Blessed with a perfect palate, the lively-eyed Talenti was a charter member of the Brunello Consortium and one of its main tasters. He was critical of wineries that, in order to win top ratings from wine critics, produce "special" barrels of exceptional wine only for wine fairs or tasters' samples. "Only a very scrupulous critic who double-checks by anonymously buying a bottle and tasting it can spot the difference, if there is one," Talenti concluded, shaking his head in disapproval.

His super-Tuscan wine, Talenti, created in the last years of his life, is a blend of Sangiovese, Canaiolo, and Syrah. The estate's extra-virgin olive oil, made exclusively from Corregiolo olives, has a sweet, somewhat almondy flavor. Extracted in Il Poggione's in-house olive press, the oil drips simply through a cotton filter before being bottled.

TENUTA OLIVETO
WINE

53020 CASTELNUOVO DELL'ABATE
TELEPHONE 0577 807170, 835542   FAX 0577 809907
E-MAIL oliveto.amachetti@tin.it

OPEN Visits by appointment only   CREDIT CARDS No
DIRECT SALE Yes   ENGLISH SPOKEN A little

Aldemaro Machetti is a dynamic, enterprising Sienese banker who fell in love with a country house and an extraordinary piece of land near Castelnuovo dell'Abate. It was in the countryside where, many years before, his grandfather had come to work the land. The views from the house are breathtaking, commanding a full panorama of the extended Orcia valley, with Monte Amiata directly across from it.

"I remember my grandfather saying that the wines from this hillside were the best in the area," Machetti said, "so I began dreaming of making wine here myself." The decisive moment came when he befriended Roberto Cipresso, the talented young winemaker who revitalized the wines of the nearby estate, Ciacci Piccolomini. They tested the soil and found it to be perfect for planting Sangiovese. In 1997 the first vineyards were dug, and in 1998 the first results began to appear: Il Roccolo is a Rosso di Montalcino of richness and elegance, with exceptional fruit to its palate. It is aged in *tonneaux*—French barrels twice the size of *barriques*. "The more I learn about wine, and the more I taste," he said, "the less I want to be aware of the wood in a great wine. It may be useful for fixing the color and giving structure, but I don't want it to cover the fruit."

In addition to the Rosso, Machetti produces a Brunello whose first release was in 2002. Based on the barrel tastings, it promises to be a great wine. He also produces Il Leccio IGT, a premium Tuscan red of Sangiovese grown in three rented vineyards around the Val d'Orcia.

Machetti recently bought another estate across the valley near Sarteano, where he is planting Cabernet Franc, as in Bordeaux. There's no stopping him now!

TENUTE SILVIO NARDI   CASALE DEL BOSCO 53024 MONTALCINO SIENA
WINE   TELEPHONE/FAX 0577 808269
                                  E-MAIL tenutenardi@tin.it

OPEN Cellar and vineyard visits available by appointment   DIRECT SALE No, but wines are available from local wine shops   ENGLISH SPOKEN Yes

---

Emilia Nardi is a very attractive young woman, and she is at the helm of one of Montalcino's oldest and largest wine-producing farms. Her family is in the agricultural machinery business and bought the Montalcino farm in the 1950s.

"The Biondi Santi and Colombini families, who were of course already important producers of Brunello, urged my father to make wine too," explained Emilia as we toured some of the vineyards in a Land Rover. "Our first vintage was 1958."

Since she took over, Emilia has been giving the vast estate a more modern direction. "These days, there is much more information about how to make quality wines," she said. "You need to do a lot of research to find the solutions that suit your land best—on grape types, soil analysis, and cellaring techniques. For instance, in our tests we discovered that an old, stony, disused vineyard called Vigneto Sassi had the potential for making great wines, so we have completely replanted it with clones of our own Sangiovese grapes." The estate currently has 80 hectares (197 acres) of vineyards.

"Every farmer loves his own products and wants them to be appreciated," she continued. "But what is also important is to produce a wine that is recognizably one's own, that has an imprinting of this place, this *terroir.*" The farm has some west-facing vineyards, which will confer greater fragrance and fruitiness to the wines. "My dream is to make wines that will seem like drinking silk," she said. "I love wines that are round, smooth, and warm."

The estate's wines include a single-vineyard Brunello from Vigneto Manachiara; the normal Brunello and Rosso di Montalcino, which are reasonably priced; Chianti Colli Senesi; and Vin Santo. It also produces extra-virgin olive oil.

Restaurants, Wine Stores, and Specialty Food Shops

CAFFÈ 1888
FIASCHETTERIA ITALIANA
CAFÉ, WINE BAR

PIAZZA DEL POPOLO, 6 53024 MONTALCINO SIENA
TELEPHONE 0577 849043   FAX 0577 847137
E-MAIL fiaschetteria.italiana@tin.it

OPEN 7:30–24:00   **CLOSED** Thursday in winter; February   **CREDIT CARDS** Visa, MC, Amex
ENGLISH SPOKEN No   **DIRECTIONS** In the town center, by the *comune*

"This is one of only five *fiaschetterie* left in Italy with original nineteenth-century decor," Gianfranco Tognazzi told me proudly. It is a gem: red velvet banquettes, marble tables, Thonet chairs, and mirrored walls set the mood in Montalcino's favorite café. In warm weather, tables spill out into the piazza, in the shadow of the historic commune building. It is the place for a morning cappuccino and *brioche* (croissant), or an *aperitivo* any time of the day.

Being situated in Montalcino, the café features wines. (It was orginally opened by Tancredi Biondi Santi.) Many Brunellos are sold by the glass, and the back room is like a wine bar, with snacks to accompany a bottle of the town's historic wine.

APICOLTURA FRANCI E TASSI
HONEY

CAPANNA 53024 MONTALCINO SIENA
TELEPHONE 0577 848546, 848205

OPEN 9:00–13:00, 15:00–20:00   **CLOSED** Wednesday afternoon in winter   **CREDIT CARDS** None
DIRECT SALE Yes; also, Franci's shop faces the fortress   **ENGLISH SPOKEN** No   **DIRECTIONS**
From Montalcino, go toward Torrenieri. About 500 meters after the Siena fork, turn left at the big curve. There is a sign. Follow the central dirt track for 100 meters to the warehouse shop

"I am eighty-six-and-a-half years old," the late Guido Franci told me proudly when I interviewed him in 1997. He was an extraordinary character, a slice of a life now gone, so I am leaving this entry as a tribute to him. "I have been a beekeeper for sixty-one years." A small, wiry man with lively eyes, Franci was the "grandfather" of Tuscan apiculture. "When I started, the countryside was full of wildflowers; there were no pesticides, so the bees were never sick. But working for a *padrone*, we couldn't travel much." By the 1940s he had his own business and was practicing "nomadic" beekeeping. "You bring the hives to each type of flower as it blooms. When those flowers finish, you remove the honey and go elsewhere."

With his son-in-law Tassi, who has carried on the business, Franci sold local and non-Tuscan honeys, such as Sicilian orange blossom. *Sulla,* made from a crimson clover found in southern Tuscany, is a delicately flavored sweet honey with a whiff of wheat fields; eucalyptus has a deeper character and a lingering aftertaste. Other single-flower honeys are chestnut, acacia, clover, heather, and *marruca*.

Sadly, Franci's old age was spent battling a parasite called varroa, which kills bees but does not affect the honey. "I'm still hopeful that we will find a strain of bees strong enough to resist. Each year I carry out experiments, but it's slow work. And you need a lot of time," he said, smiling a little wistfully.

FRANTOIO LA SPIGA
OLIVE MILL, WINE STORE

VIA CIRCONVALLAZIONE, 212
53024 MONTALCINO SIENA
TELEPHONE/FAX 0577 848611

OPEN Shop 9:00–13:00, 14:30–19:30; *frantoio* November and December   **CLOSED** Thursday
CREDIT CARDS Visa, MC, Amex   **DIRECT SALE** Yes   **ENGLISH SPOKEN** No
DIRECTIONS The shop and mill are on the outer road circling Montalcino, halfway up the hill

La Spiga is a modern-style olive mill, or *frantoio*. This being Montalcino, it is also a wine shop—La Spiga's olive growers are mostly wine producers; their oil and wine are available at reasonable prices. Several grades of oil are sold with La Spiga's label. The cooperative has 117 members and was formed in 1952.

In November and December, the freshly picked olives arrive in airy plastic crates. The leaves are sucked away and the olives rinsed. In a large stainless-steel Sinolea machine they are pounded and churned at a maximum temperature of 25°C (77°F). A system of tiny metal blades enables oil to drip free of the mass. The final centrifuge separates oil from water. All parts are stainless steel, easy to clean, and hygienic. The oil may be drip-filtered before bottling. During the milling season, the *frantoio* runs twenty-four hours a day and may be visited.

FORNO LAMBARDI
PASTRY, BREAD

VIA S. SALONI, 54 53024 MONTALCINO SIENA
TELEPHONE 0577 848084

OPEN 8:00–13:00, 17:15–1:30   **CLOSED** Wednesday afternoon, Sunday   **CREDIT CARDS** None
DIRECT SALE Yes   **ENGLISH SPOKEN** No   **DIRECTIONS** In the town center

Lambardi, an old-fashioned bakery, is tucked into the narrow street leading to Montalcino's *comune*. It specializes in bread, pastries, and handmade pasta but is famous for its dried biscuits.

Montalcino's classic cookies are *ossi di morto* (dead man's bones). Bite into one, and you will see why. These brittle biscuits are light as a feather, despite being studded with chewy almonds. They are so good it's impossible to eat just one. Other Sienese favorites are honey-enriched *cantucci, ricciarelli,* and *panforte.*

Along with salted and unsalted (*sciocco*) Tuscan bread, I found unusual *schiacciatine con uvetta*. Crusty flat rounds of oiled bread with raisins, they are best eaten in the morning, because they dry out fast.

BOCCONDIVINO
RESTAURANT

**VIA TRAVERSA DEI MONTI
53024 MONTALCINO SIENA
TELEPHONE 0577 848233   FAX 0577 848340**

OPEN Lunch and dinner   **CLOSED** Tuesday; November   **CREDIT CARDS** Visa, MC, Amex
ENGLISH SPOKEN Yes   **FEATURES** Outdoor summer terrace   **RESERVATIONS** Recommended
on weekends   **PRICE** $$$ **DIRECTIONS** Coming from Siena and the north, on the left 1 km
before Montalcino

This enjoyable, family-run restaurant overlooks Montalcino's vineyard-covered slopes and, farther north, the Crete Senesi hills. It has a very nice atmosphere and is one of my favorites in the area. There is a breezy outdoor terrace in summer. The menu offers many Tuscan favorites, as well as some more ambitious fare. *Gnocchi di Mario*—Mario is the owner—are sauced interestingly with truffles and a "cream" of cheeses. *Carabaccia,* a "hymn to the onion" as Mario described it, is a thick oniony soup with a crust of cheesy bread. Eggplant-stuffed ravioli come with a tangy fresh tomato sauce, and homemade *tagliolini* noodles are dressed with butter and truffles. In the main courses, *scaloppine* are paired with balsamic vinegar, lamb with artichokes, marinated wild boar with little toasts. There is now also a good-value lunch menu that allows many tastes of different dishes.

BocconDivino means a sip of wine and a divine mouthful; its interesting international wine list encourages comparisons between Montalcino's and foreign wines.

OSTERIA DI PORTA AL CASSERO
RESTAURANT

**VIA DELLA LIBERTÀ, 9 AND VIA RICASOLI, 32
53024 MONTALCINO SIENA
TELEPHONE 0577 847196**

OPEN 9:00–24:00   **CLOSED** Wednesday; January   **CREDIT CARDS** Visa, MC, Amex
ENGLISH SPOKEN No, but an English menu is available   **FEATURES** Outdoor dining in summer
RESERVATIONS Recommended at peak times   **PRICE** $$ **DIRECTIONS** Near the fortress

This relaxed family eating house is furnished simply with attractive marble tables and wooden chairs. In summer, eat out in an awning-covered courtyard. Service can be haphazard when the restaurant is full, but food is available all day, so time your meal before or after peak times.

Homemade soups and pastas are good, including local *pinci*—thick, hand-rolled spaghetti. The menu offers assortments of cheese, *salumi,* salads, or grilled vegetables, and a few hot egg or meat dishes. Desserts are *cantucci* with Vin Santo or home-baked tarts. Pitchered wine is red or white, but there is more choice for those who want it. This is a low-pressure and friendly place—the kind welcomed by many travelers.

OSTERIA DEL VECCHIO CASTELLO
RESTAURANT

PIEVE DI SAN SIGISMONDO
POGGIO ALLE MURA 53024 MONTALCINO
TELEPHONE/FAX 0577 816026

OPEN Lunch and dinner   **CLOSED** Tuesday; mid-February to mid-March   **CREDIT CARDS** Visa,
MC, Amex   **ENGLISH SPOKEN** Yes   **RESERVATIONS** Necessary   **PRICE** $$$$–$$$$$
DIRECTIONS The restaurant is signposted from the Montalcino–S. Angelo Scalo road; it is 11 km
southwest of Montalcino

When I first ate at Osteria del Vecchio Castello, it was hidden away on the top of
Mount Amiata in a tiny rural village. That did not stop its owners—Alfredo Sibaldi
Bevilotti, connoisseur and lover of wines, and his wife, Susanna Fumi, devotee of
fine cooking, present and past—from making a big name for themselves. People
drove all the way up the mountain just to eat in their intimate dining room.

Recently, they left the mountain and moved the restaurant down to
Montalcino, where their presence has greatly enhanced the restaurant scene. Now,
finally, they have a bit of room in which to spread out. The lovely old stone buildings around the Romanesque church make a fine place for a meal, with a pretty
courtyard for summer *aperitivi*.

Inside, the rooms are furnished with antiques, and of course with wines—for
Alfredo has assembled a truly impressive list, of a caliber that was lacking in
Montalcino's other restaurants. Great attention is paid to the selection of crystal
glasses and decorated plates.

Luckily, the food has not changed substantially from the way it was at Triana.
Susanna prepares purely seasonal produce with flair, using local ingredients, cultivated or wild, and stimulated both by her collections of antique recipe books and
by her imagination. A late-spring tasting menu went like this:

A *sformato* of nettle (*ortiche*) was served with a warm pecorino sauce. The delicate green mousse, less sweet than spinach but less sour, had sharper accents of
parsley. It was meltingly soft. The airy cheese sauce confirmed the sensations of
fresh-smelling pastures.

In contrast, the next courses were earth-inspired. Fawn chestnut-flour ravioli
were stuffed with pork and aromatic rosemary; sheep's-ricotta gnocchi came with
shavings of pungent truffles and field mushrooms. The wine, a rare Morello aged
in chestnut wood from Franceschini at Scansano, complemented these deep,
woodsy flavors. The meat course, *peposo*, came from an antique cookery book: a
favorite dish of Brunelleschi's, it dates back to 1430. Made of Chianina beef, salt,
garlic, wine, and abundant pepper, it requires six hours of marination, six hours of
cooking, and a day to rest. The resulting rectangles of highly stewed beef are very
salty, very peppery. Quite interesting. After I had finished, there were fifty peppercorns left on my plate.

A remarkable cheese platter followed. It included a lighter-than-air goat's *ravaggiolo;* pecorino aged under ash for a slight smokiness; a satisfyingly salty goat's

cheese from Ville di Corsano (p 301) served here with sweet fig jam; and a very ripe cow's cheese reminiscent of Camembert. They were matched with a deliciously clear-tasting 1975 Marsala. Fragrant homemade sorbets and other desserts followed.

RISTORANTE POGGIO ANTICO	**POGGIO ANTICO 53024 MONTALCINO SIENA**
RESTAURANT	TELEPHONE/FAX 0577 849200

OPEN Lunch and dinner	**CLOSED** Monday; January	**CREDIT CARDS** None
ENGLISH SPOKEN Yes	**RESERVATIONS** Necessary	**PRICE** $$$$–$$$$$
DIRECTIONS In Poggio Antico winery (see map p 304)		

This is one of Montalcino's best restaurants, and worthy of a detour. Situated in the landscaped grounds of Poggio Antico estate, with great views of the Val d'Orcia, it is reached along a quintessentially Tuscan avenue of cypress and maritime pines. Its elegant, clean-lined interior has a terra-cotta floor and modern picture windows. The service is attentive and not too formal; the gracious Patrizia Leonardi, wife of chef Roberto Minnetti, explains the dishes and, in her role of sommelier, serves the wines.

The food is quite elaborate, with a modern feel despite traditional roots. The normal and tasting menus change seasonally; there is no obligation to have numerous courses. My June tasting-menu lunch was accompanied by a succession of lovely freshly baked rolls.

Minnetti's *panzanella* salad was bready and cool. An unexpected flavor made the taste buds sit up: Was it fish? The next dish looked like a flower on the plate: paper-thin slices of cured pork loin (*lombo*) were arranged around a kind of apple-fig chutney; the sweet-spicy fruit complemented the strong, salty meat. A very rich "parfait" of duck and goose liver was voluptuous and velvety, with a honey-sweet sauce of reduced Moscadello, Montalcino's historic sweet wine. The *gnocchetti*'s "white" wild boar sauce contained not tomato but grated zucchini and carrot. Pigeon with herbed beef stuffing and Vin Santo vinegar was succulent and successful. The desserts were refined and fresh flavored.

A more recent meal was superb: a succession of light fish dishes was infused with the flavors of the Mediterranean and was produced with the essential artistry of a talented, experienced chef. As for the wine list: I expected, in such a fine restaurant at Montalcino, to find a stimulating selection of Brunellos. Instead, the list's only Brunellos were Poggio Antico's, with a token pair of Montalcino "table" wines—a limitation imposed on the restaurant by the mother estate. That is a shame. To preclude the possibility of comparison or choice seems shortsighted, no matter how good the estate's own wines are.

ENOTECA LA FORTEZZA
WINE STORE, WINE BAR

PIAZZALE FORTEZZA 53024 MONTALCINO SIENA
TELEPHONE/FAX 0577 849211
WEB SITE www.enotecalafortezza.it

OPEN Winter: 9:00–18:00; summer: 9:00–20:00   **CLOSED** Monday in winter
CREDIT CARDS Visa, Amex   **DIRECT SALE** Yes   **ENGLISH SPOKEN** Yes
FEATURES Tickets for the fortress's ramparts are on sale from the *enoteca*
DIRECTIONS The shop is inside the fortress; enter through the large gate in the piazza

A fourteenth-century fortress is a dramatic location for a wine bar, and it is a perfect place to sample or buy Montalcino's great wines. The bar and shop are within the walls of the 1362 monument, situated at the top of the town. On nice days you can sit in the peaceful inner courtyard sipping wine and listening to medieval music. What could be nicer?

In the warm, vaulted brick interior, more than one hundred Brunello producers are represented—a breathtaking array. Wine is sold by the glass from many bottles (not Riservas or other premium wines), so you can compare producers or choose a favorite before investing in a few bottles to take home.

To accompany the wines, Mario Pianigiani and Marzio Giannelli have selected excellent local cheeses and *salumi*. They are sold whole or served in sandwiches. The *enoteca* carries locally produced olive oils, honeys, and biscuits as well. There are tables inside and out.

ENOTECA OSTERIA OSTICCIO
WINE STORE, WINE BAR

VIA MATTEOTTI, 23 53024 MONTALCINO
TELEPHONE/FAX 0577 848271
WEB SITE www.osticcio.com

OPEN 9:00–20:00   **CLOSED** Sunday   **CREDIT CARDS** Visa, MC, Amex
DIRECT SALE Yes   **ENGLISH SPOKEN** Yes   **PRICE** $$ **DIRECTIONS** In town center

Tullio and Francesca Scrivani's *enoteca* has become one of the most serious wine shops in Tuscany. The selection of fine wines is impressive, as is their policy of offering glasses of four Brunello or Rosso di Montalcino wines (you decide which you want to taste) at very reasonable prices. You can browse the stacks for bottles to take home, or sit at a travertine table overlooking the panoramic view and have a light meal with your wine. There are wonderful cheeses and *salumi* to try from Tusany's best artisan producers. The Scrivanis are active members of Slow Food.

Also

HOTEL-RISTORANTE IL GIGLIO   VIA SALONI, 5. 0577 848167. hotelgiglio@tin.it

This small, family-run hotel is one of my Tuscan favorites, and its restaurant offers fine home cooking by Signora Anna and wonderful wines chosen by her husband, Mario, who is an *appassionato di vino*. Open for dinner only; closed Tuesday.

LE ANTICHE TELE DI ALESSIA SALVIONI   VIA MAZZINI, 27. 0577 849338

Brunello-producer Giulio Salvioni's daughter has a lovely linen shop on Montalcino's main street, featuring the woven colored cloths of Busatti (see p 341, 344). A great place to find affordable, unbreakable presents.

OSTERIA BASSO MONDO at Castelnuovo dell'Abate is a fine place to get sandwiches filled with pecorino cheese or *salumi* made locally by Vasco Sassetti, which are also sold by Enoteca La Fortezza, at Montalcino. Instead of eating at the adjacent restaurant, I recommend a picnic in the vicinity of the exquisite Romanesque church of Sant'Antimo, very nearby.

CHAPTER 13

Arezzo, Its Hills and Valleys

*A*rezzo is one of Tuscany's largest provinces, dominated geographically by three wide valleys: Val di Chiana, Valdarno, and Casentino. The latter two are valleys of the river Arno, separated by the monumental Pratomagno mountain range. The landscape is varied, with the Casentino providing unspoiled mountain scenery, while the reclaimed valley of the Chiana canal is flat but punctuated by remarkable hill towns that were once strategic Etruscan holdings: Cortona, Arezzo, and Chiusi, to the south. The Casentino's rural villages offer hearty country cooking with goat's and sheep's cheeses, wild mushrooms, and herbs.

The Val di Chiana is a key industrial and agricultural plain, with fruit orchards, crops, and cattle raising—especially of the sought-after Chianina breed. I expected to see a lot of these animals in this area, but most are reared indoors, with little possibility of outdoor grazing. The lower slopes around the central valleys are planted with olive groves for making fine extra-virgin oil. There also are organic growers of vegetables and the Aretino's yellow bean, *zolfino*.

Art lovers will associate this province with Piero della Francesca. Indeed, the Piero "tour" includes Sansepolcro, his birthplace; Monterchi, site of the extraordinary *Madonna del Parto* fresco; and Arezzo, where in the 1450s Piero painted his great masterpiece, the *Legend of the True Cross* fresco cycle. This recently was completely restored, as was the Cimabue Crucifix—and both can now be seen close up by appointment (0575 900404).

AZIENDA PROMOZIONE TURISTICA
PIAZZA DELLA REPUBBLICA, 22
52100 AREZZO
0575 377678, FAX 0575 20839
E-MAIL info@arezzo.turismo.toscana.it

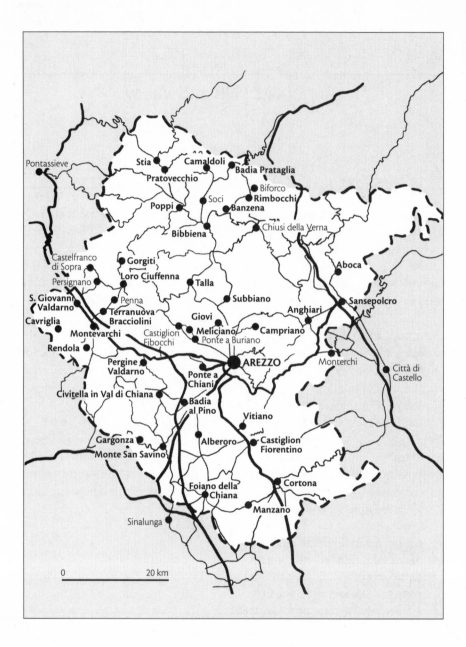

Boldface type indicates towns that are included in this chapter.

Aboca

ABOCA
HERBAL PRODUCTS

SS 258 ABOCA 52037 SANSEPOLCRO
TELEPHONE 0575 7461   FAX 0575 749130
WEB SITE www.abocausa.it

OPEN Shop 9:00–13:00, 16:00–19:00   **CLOSED** Monday morning; Sunday except before Christmas
CREDIT CARDS None   **DIRECT SALE** Yes   **MAIL ORDER** Yes   **ENGLISH SPOKEN** Yes
DIRECTIONS From Sansepolcro, take SS 258 toward Aboca. L'Erboristeria di Aboca is on the left after about 6 kms

---

Of the many places I visited for this book, Aboca is among those that most impressed me. Set in virgin countryside, Aboca is an extensive farm producing organically grown herbs for medicinal and culinary use. If the Italians are not often very informed about the organic-foods movement, they do widely believe in the curative use of herbs. One has only to look at the vast number of *erboristerie* to see that Italians are almost as likely to resort to herbal remedies as pharmaceutical ones.

Valentino Mercati's Aboca is a large farm comprising the growing fields for more than ninety varieties of herbs and flowers, the laboratories for "transforming" them, and a sophisticated center for research. The herbs are sold dried (for use in teas) or as essential oils, tinctures, or concentrates. Many are combined in "complex" capsules—such as the Energo (energy giving) formula, which includes the essential oils of sage and rosemary with cinnamon, ginseng, royal jelly, seaweed, pollen, and wheat germ. There are herbal products to aid dieting, energy, sleeping, and toning.

The company's shop sells much of the range. A resident herbalist gives advice about the products (they can provide an English-speaking expert). Aboca also produces wonderful honey—gathered by the bees that pollinate the fields of beautiful flowers. Some Aboca products are now available in the United States from selected practitioners.

Alberoro

TORREFAZIONE CAFFÈ DONATELLO
COFFEE, COFFEE SHOP

VIA LEOPOLD DI TOSCANA, 13
ALBERORO 52040 MONTE SAN SAVINO
TELEPHONE/FAX 0575 848497
E-MAIL gena@ats.it

OPEN 8:00–13:00, 15:00–19:30   **CLOSED** Saturday afternoon; Sunday
CREDIT CARDS None   **ENGLISH SPOKEN** A little   **OTHER** Home delivery
DIRECTIONS On the road between Arezzo and Foiano della Chiana

---

Maurizio Sestini is a coffee roaster. He buys green coffee beans from the equatorial countries and roasts them in a propane gas oven that leaves no residual odors. The coffee is sold in his quaint shop by the kilo, ground to order. The range goes from 100 percent Arabica (the most expensive) to 100 percent Robusta (which costs less but is closer to industrial) or any combination in between. Water-decaffeinated coffees are available. Sestini also sells his irresistibly aromatic coffee in single-portion "pods" (*cialde*), like tea bags, and the special coffee pots that go with them.

Anghiari

LOCANDA AL	**VIA SAN LORENZO, 21 SORCI 52031 ANGHIARI**
CASTELLO DI SORCI	TELEPHONE 0575 789066, 1678 67089 FAX 0575 788022
RESTAURANT	E-MAIL lsorci@ats.it

OPEN Lunch and dinner   **CLOSED** Monday evening   **CREDIT CARDS** Visa, MC, Amex
ENGLISH SPOKEN A little   **RESERVATIONS** Recommended on weekends   **PRICE** $$ adults
(including wine), $ children   **OTHER** Houses available for holiday rentals; banquets and receptions
catered   **DIRECTIONS** From Anghiari, go toward Monterchi; after 3 kms turn right to Castello

The medieval Castello di Sorci is dramatically positioned above a wide valley. Its nearby *locanda*, or inn, houses a big, lively restaurant. The style is nicely done rustic; this is a great place to come in a group or family. There is a special reduced price for children, and the adult's fixed price is both reasonable and all-inclusive, comprising a four-course menu of traditional local recipes. All the pasta is handmade. There are no freezers.

A typical dinner begins with platters of *crostini*, Tuscan canapés, spicy tomato *bruschetta* on country bread, and mixed *salumi*. *Primi* include tagliatelle noodles, potato gnocchi, *ribollita*, or risotto. Main courses feature mixed roasted meats and seasonal vegetables. For dessert a local cake, *torcolo*, is served with Vin Santo. Red and white wine and water are on the tables and included in the price.

Primetto Barelli is a lively, elderly gentleman with twinkling eyes. His father was a shoemaker, and he was a farmer before buying the *castello* more than twenty-five years ago. "It took fifteen years to fix it up," he admitted, "but I have revolutionized the restaurant trade by my all-inclusive price. It has meant that entire families can afford to eat out, and well."

The *castello* is also a cultural center, housing musical concerts and a study center for the culinary traditions of the central Apennine mountains.

BUSATTI VIA MAZZINI, 14 52031 ANGHIARI
TABLE CRAFTS: LINENS TELEPHONE 0575 788424 STORE; 788013 OFFICE
FAX 0575 789819   WEB SITE www.busattitessuti.it

OPEN Summer: 9:00–13:00, 16:00–20:00; winter: 9:00–13:00, 15:30–19:30   **CLOSED** Monday morning
CREDIT CARDS Visa, MC   **MAIL ORDER** Yes   **ENGLISH SPOKEN** Yes
DIRECTIONS Off Corso Matteotti, in the town center

Anghiari is an unspoiled medieval hill town of particular interest to linen enthusiasts. After spotting the Busattis' shop in Arezzo (p 344), I was determined to see their mill, which also sells to the public.

"Weaving natural local fibers has been a tradition in Anghiari for centuries," explained Signora Busatti Sassolini, whose family has run the business since 1842. "My family created a niche for itself producing high-quality linens for the table, bed, and bath."

The Busatti palazzo comprises an attractive shop, offices, and the looms in the basement. I was taken down to see them, crowded into a large, deafeningly noisy room worked by local women. Some of the fascinating machinery predates World War II.

Upstairs, the shop sells mainly Busatti fabrics (with others from neighboring regions), finished as hand or dish towels, tablecloths, napkins, and more. Many have elaborate woven borders in medieval designs, knotted fringes, or open-worked hems. Fabrics may also be bought by the meter (about one yard) for customers who want to make their own; the bolts are wide enough for making bedspreads, tablecloths, or curtains.

Arezzo

PANE E SALUTE CORSO ITALIA, 11 52100 AREZZO
BREAD TELEPHONE 0575 20657

OPEN 7:30–13:00, 16:30–20:00   **CLOSED** Sunday; Wednesday afternoon in winter; Saturday
afternoon in summer; August   **CREDIT CARDS** None   **ENGLISH SPOKEN** No
DIRECTIONS In the town center

This is a hundred-year-old bakery on the street leading up to Piazza Grande. You'll know it by the delicious aroma of baking bread that wafts out into the street. The *forno* used to be wood-burning, until a health regulation some years back made them convert to modern ovens. "Now they have decided that wood ovens are not dangerous after all," explained Iride Magnani, the shop's owner, "but we can't keep ripping out our ovens every time the bureaucratic wind changes."

One of her specialties is the *pan di romarino*, a bread dough studded with rosemary and raisins. The *schiacciata* also reigns here: flat, crunchy, and salt-topped, it marries perfectly with cheese and *salumi*. Eat it early in the day—by nightfall it will already have lost its sparkle. I also spotted Irish soda bread, dried rounds of bread for *bruschetta*, and loaves of soya, corn, and hard wheat flours.

The bakery was under threat of closure last time I spoke to them: the landlord would prefer to have an international clothes chain store there instead. Let's hope the bakers survive.

UN PUNTO MACROBIOTICO HEALTH FOODS, RESTAURANT	**SHOP VIA G. MONACO, 42 52100 AREZZO** **RESTAURANT PIAZZA SAN GEMIGNANO, 1** **TELEPHONE 0575 302420 SHOP; 0575 350530 RESTAURANT**

OPEN Shop 9:00–13:00, 15:30–17:30; restaurant lunch Monday–Friday 12:00–14:00, dinner Thursday–Saturday 20:00–21:30   **CLOSED** Sunday; two weeks in August   **CREDIT CARDS** None   **ENGLISH SPOKEN** A little   **PRICE** $ **DIRECTIONS** In the town center

Un Punto Macrobiotico has been a mainstay in the Italian macrobiotic movement since the 1980s. The shop in Sansepolcro opened in 1991, this one in 1994. At lunchtime there is a nice mix of people in the small restaurant: families with children, elderly people, office workers, students. Everyone is welcome, macrobiotic or otherwise.

For a modest sum you can have the set-price lunch, usually a soup and a mixed vegetable and pulses platter—Italian style, of course. There are daily pastas and a few desserts. Foods are strictly seasonal and, whenever possible, local. The shop sells a variety of macrobiotic and other health foods: unpasteurized miso, rices and grains, natural jams and juices. The center also organizes macrobiotic cooking classes.

IL GELATO ICE CREAM	**VIA DEI CENCI, 24 52100 AREZZO** **TELEPHONE 0575 300069**

OPEN 10:30–13:10, 13:45–23:30 (till 20:30 in winter)   **CLOSED** Wednesday; November or January   **CREDIT CARDS** None   **ENGLISH SPOKEN** A little   **DIRECTIONS** Off Corso Italia, in the town center

Il Gelato makes good gelati using fresh milk, eggs, sugar, and fresh or frozen fruits. Of the custard-based gelati, I liked the *crema di riso*. It is textured with grains of rice boiled in milk before being sweetened. A hint of lemon spices this grown-up child's dessert. Best summer fruits include fig and mixed berries.

ANTICA OSTERIA L'AGANÌA
RESTAURANT

VIA MASSINI, 10 52100 AREZZO
TELEPHONE 0575 295381

OPEN Lunch and dinner   **CLOSED** Monday; June   **CREDIT CARDS** Visa, MC, Amex
ENGLISH SPOKEN No   **RESERVATIONS** None accepted   **PRICE** $$
DIRECTIONS In town center, off Corso Italia

L'Aganìa is full of local color—it's the only phrase that springs to mind. Run by a group of friendly women who have worked there for years, the *osteria* serves the Italian equivalent of "down-home cooking." The dining room is just below street level. It is painted a warm reddish brown and decorated with a motley mix of old pictures, pitchers, photos, wine bottles, and strings of peppers and garlic. In autumn, each table held a vase containing rosemary, bay, sage, and one pink rose.

At lunchtime there is a lively atmosphere. No reservations are taken, so get there early for the first sitting. The food is unpretentious and appetizing: an antipasto platter of cold cuts with homemade meatballs; nourishing soups of chickpeas, *farro* wheat, or vegetables; pasta, polenta, or gnocchi with a good choice of sauces; simply roasted meats, such as rabbit scented with wild fennel and served with roast potatoes, or local favorites of tripe or sausages; and for dessert, fresh fruit, a pie, or some *cantucci* biscuits.

MORINI
TABLE CRAFTS: KITCHENWARES

PIAZZA SAN JACOPO 52100 AREZZO
TELEPHONE 0575 23277   FAX 0575 323231
WEB SITE www.acantodomu.com/morini link

OPEN Summer: 9:00–13:00, 16:00–20:00; winter: 9:00–13:00, 15:30–19:30   **CLOSED** Sunday; Monday in winter, Saturday afternoon and Monday morning in summer; August   **CREDIT CARDS** Visa, MC
MAIL ORDER Yes   **ENGLISH SPOKEN** Yes   **DIRECTIONS** At the beginning of Corso Italia

Morini is a top contender for my best kitchen and tablewares shop. It covers the whole range, from basic kitchen tools through specialist equipment, fine china, and crystal. You can tell by looking at the stylish window displays that the shop has a serious commitment to the art of the table.

Morini's has been a fixture in Arezzo since the 1930s. The basement is a cook's paradise: you'll find everything from high-tech utensils to pressure cookers, from French gratin dishes to Alessi's stainless-steel-lined copper saucepans (expensive but fabulous). There are oven thermometers and Parmesan graters, Tuscan bean pots and picnic baskets. The china and glass departments feature world leaders and fine Italian design objects, such as Alessi (including the wooden Twergi range), Aldo Rossi's lighthouse, and Fornasetti.

BUSATTI
TABLE CRAFTS: LINENS

CORSO ITALIA, 48 52100 AREZZO
TELEPHONE 0575 355295

OPEN 9:00–13:00, 15:30–19:30   **CLOSED** Sunday; Monday morning; one week in August
CREDIT CARDS Visa, MC, Amex   **ENGLISH SPOKEN** Yes   **DIRECTIONS** In the town center

Linen lovers should make a pilgrimage to this store. Renaissance griffins, floral arabesques, and simple stripes are woven from natural cotton and linen, wool, and hemp (*canapa*) in the subtlest shades. Most come from the Busatti artisan loom in Anghiari (p 341). Fabrics are also sold by length for home sewing at lower prices. Treat yourself (or a friend) to an original piece of Italian style.

DIANA DE MORI
TABLE CRAFTS: LINENS

CORSO ITALIA, 72 52100 AREZZO
TELEPHONE 0575 27505 EVENINGS

OPEN 10:00–13:00, 16:00–19:30   **CLOSED** Sunday (except the first Sunday of the month); Monday
CREDIT CARDS None   **ENGLISH SPOKEN** A little   **DIRECTIONS** in the town center

In her very personal shop, Diana De Mori has garnered linens—old and new—yarns, tablecloths, and the like. She has a great eye and has chosen beautiful, rare, and simple fabrics of natural materials. Here you can find the rust-printed kitchen linens from Emilia Romagna, with their bold stenciled designs, and other artisan weaves. Some of the rarest items are costly, but worth the money for their quality. There is no name to the shop, but if it is not raining De Mori hangs a few fabrics up outside the door. The shop is always open the first Sunday of the month, when the antiques market is in town.

ACETIFICIO ARETINO
VINEGAR

VIA ROMANA, 76 52100 AREZZO
TELEPHONE 0575 903244   FAX 0575 900925
E-MAIL aretino@etr.it

DIRECT SALE No, but the vinegar is sold in local wine stores and Esselunga supermarkets

There are few vinegar makers in Tuscany—a separate building and license are now required to produce it. This *acetificio* is a semi-industrial plant that transforms Chianti wine into wine vinegar; white wine vinegar is made from the local Bianco Vergine Valdichiana. The vinegars are good quality and less expensive than the "designer" vinegars that use the traditional system.

"We work with Chianti that has spent six months in wooden casks," explained Signor Verdi, one of the brothers who runs the *acetificio*, "which gives the vinegar a richer flavor."

Air (which naturally contains vinegar bacteria) is pumped into the wine; it is then kept in continuous motion for twenty-four hours to distribute these bacteria, at temperatures below 40°C (104°F). Since wine contains many trace elements of metals (iron, copper, zinc) that would cause the vinegar to oxidize, it is filtered. The top-of-the-line red Chianti vinegar is then aged for one year in wooden casks before being bottled. "Our system is less picturesque than the old-fashioned methods," Verdi continued. "But it is more hygienic and more stable—our vinegars do not have problems with oxidization or fermentation; they remain crystal clear for at least one year."

Acetificio Aretino doesn't sell directly to the public, but it's not difficult to find its vinegars locally. Its best "Chiantigiano" products come in tall, square bottles.

Also

PANETTERIA TAVANTI   BORGO SANTA CROCE, 15-17

This small grocery store sells wonderful bread *cotto a legna*—baked in a wood oven. It is in an unspoiled part of town that is fun to explore.

ELENA CACCIALUPI   VIA MADONNA DEL PRATO, 25

This old-fashioned shop sells seeds to eat or plant, dried beans, ground polenta, pulses, and grains.

On Saturday mornings, Arezzo's large street market includes a farmer's market. It's in a parking lot across Viale Mecenati from the Esselunga supermarket, and you'll find homegrown vegetables, fruit, eggs, and other country sundries.

Whenever wild mushrooms are to be found in the woods and fields in early summer and autumn, the mushroom collectors gather on the corner of Via Garibaldi and Corso Italia to sell them from cardboard boxes or baskets. There are many types on display; even if you can't cook them, it makes for an interesting scene.

Badia al Pino

BOSCOVIVO TARTUFI	**VIA DEI BOSCHI, 34 BADIA AL PINO 52040**
SPECIALTY FOODS:	**CIVITELLA IN VAL DI CHIANA**
TRUFFLE PRODUCTS	TELEPHONE 0575 410696, 410388 FAX 0575 410381
	WEB SITE www.boscovivo.com

OPEN 9:00–13:00, 14:30–19:00   **CLOSED** Saturday and Sunday; August   **CREDIT CARDS** Visa, MC, Amex   **DIRECT SALE** Yes   **MAIL ORDER** Yes   **ENGLISH SPOKEN** Yes
DIRECTIONS From the Arezzo exit of A1 *autostrada*, take first right toward Badia al Pino; the company is after 4 kms

---

"We started small," recounted Franca Bianchini Landucci. "I was a teacher and my husband had a full-time job, but we loved going searching for truffles. Then we began selling them: fresh, preserved, and in sauces." That was back in 1982. Signora Landucci now has a small factory employing twenty-six people who service a worldwide client list.

Boscovivo has a large catalog: truffle-scented pastes and oils, meat and game sauces for *crostini*, plus preserved vegetables and honeys bought from other suppliers. Boscovivo's Tuscan specialties use the brand name "Le Ricette di Caterina." They include rich pasta or canapé sauces of chopped liver or game. Gift packs are also available.

As for the truffles, several types are used: white, *Tuber magnatum pico;* white spring truffle, *Tuber albidum pico;* black, *Tuber melanosporum vitt.;* summer, *Tuber aestivum vitt.* They come from various parts of Italy. "The white is the most delicate—the best for *primi*," Franca explained. "Whereas the black is more pungent and better for use with meats."

Boscovivo also sells excellent Chianina beef, bred locally by registered breeders. It must be specially ordered.

Badia Prataglia

PASTICCERIA ANNA
SNACK BAR, PASTRY

VIA NAZIONALE, 35 52010 POPPI
TELEPHONE 0575 559121

OPEN Summer: 8:00–13:00, 15:00–1:00 A.M.; winter: 8:00–13:00, 15:30–20:00
CLOSED Tuesday   **CREDIT CARDS** None   **ENGLISH SPOKEN** No
DIRECTIONS On the main road through the village

After a nice hike in the pure mountain air, you'll be in the mood for a slice of pizza or a *schiacciata* with mushrooms on it. This little Swiss-style snack bar also makes some great *tortelli di patate*, the potato-stuffed pasta famous in this area. There is also a range of pastries.

Banzena

IL BIVIO
RESTAURANT

BIVIO DI BANZENA, 65 BANZENA 52010 BIBBIENA
TELEPHONE 0575 593242

OPEN Lunch and dinner   **CLOSED** Monday; holidays variable   **CREDIT CARDS** None
ENGLISH SPOKEN A little   **RESERVATIONS** Recommended for dinner and on weekends
PRICE $$–$$$ **DIRECTIONS** From Bibbiena, take SS 208 for La Verna; the restaurant is after 9.5 kms

A *bivio* is a fork in the road, and Il Bivio is situated at one on the road that winds up the hillside to the Franciscan sanctuary of La Verna. Il Bivio doubles as a simple country bar; travelers can stop in for a coffee or snack. Behind this bar is an interesting restaurant.

With his wife and her family, Lorenzo Giuliani has created a fine menu of local dishes, *cucina tipica*, with recipes that are traditional in origin yet modern in feel. It offers many reasonably priced choices. The wine list features some of the less well known wines of the area; Giuliani is a qualified sommelier and author of a book about the wines of Arezzo. "Part of the work of a sommelier," he explained, "is to *abbinare*, or match, each dish with a wine that best complements it."

The restaurant, with its light wood and exposed stone interior, is a mixture of informal and formal. The customers include serious food lovers and locals on a night out; Giuliani is a fine host to all.

In autumn, I began with a pastry tart filled with artichoke and potatoes. A *pappa* of yellow pumpkin and *farro*, spelt wheat, was a thick golden soup, both sweet and fiery, thanks to its fresh basil and *peperoncino*. Delicate ravioli contained a vivid green filling of wild herbs and ricotta and came with truffle-speckled cream. *Svaccheroni col pizzichino* used a local curate's recipe from 1637: *maccheroni* was served with a very "stinging," matured pecorino cheese sauce. This was apparently popular on fasting days, when meat was forbidden.

Main courses include roasted meats and steaks and stewed wild boar. Duck was moist and flavorful, with a good crispy skin; guinea fowl was braised with rosemary. Giuliani explained that these game birds were free range and reared locally. Pastries were fine: a golden-topped ricotta tart on biscuit crust was studded with nuts and raisins; lemon *torta* was sharp and dairy free. Homemade *semifreddi* blended fresh fruits into a frozen cream base.

Bibbiena

APICOLTURA CASENTINESE
HONEY

VIA DEL ARTIGIANO, 10/12 52012 BIBBIENA
TELEPHONE 0575 536494   FAX 0575 536029
E-MAIL apicas@elledi.it

OPEN 8:00–12:00, 14:00–18:00   **CLOSED** Sunday   **CREDIT CARDS** None   **DIRECT SALE** Yes
ENGLISH SPOKEN A little   **DIRECTIONS** From Bibbiena, go toward Soci; after 2 kms follow signs for Zona Industriale Ferrantina, where the company is situated

This company sells twelve typically Tuscan honeys. It owns two thousand hives; other honey is bought locally or from the south of Italy. Alberto Ricci, the company's young director, explained about some of the other products of beekeeping.

Flower pollen is a complete substance. "All life starts here," said Ricci. It is rich in amino acids, minerals, and vitamins. Royal jelly is the queen bee's food. Ricci described propolis as "the first miracle of beekeeping." A resinous gluelike material obtained by bees from the buds of some plants (such as poplars), propolis is used by them to seal the cracks in their hives and to disinfect them. Propolis is an anti-inflammatory agent and a natural antibiotic; the Egyptians used it for embalming mummies.

The company moves its hives around for "nomadic" collection—going to an area when a particular type of plant is in flower. Ricci explained that it was difficult to guarantee that honey was organic, "as you can never know what a peasant has sprayed his fields with." However, all the honeys are analyzed before being sold.

I was particularly struck by the *melata di abete*. This deep amber, runny honey has an intense resinous taste and great richness of flavor. It is made by the bees from the *abete*, an evergreen in the pine family. The bees are attracted to the resin released by the trees and produce this "honey" from it. Other typically Tuscan honeys are acacia, chestnut, *sulla, erica*, sunflower, and clover.

Camaldoli

ANTICA FARMACIA DEI MONACI CAMALDOLESI   52010 CAMALDOLI
HERBAL PRODUCTS   TELEPHONE 0575 556143

OPEN 9:00–12:30, 14:30–18:00   **CLOSED** Wednesday in winter   **CREDIT CARDS** None
ENGLISH SPOKEN No   **DIRECTIONS** Camaldoli is signposted from Poppi

A winding drive up into the Casentino forest leads to Camaldoli, the monastery founded in the eleventh-century by St. Romuald. Some of the monks chose to take vows of silence and live as hermits here, isolated from the rest of the world in tiny cells. Others established an important pharmacy and hospital, making herbal cures and liqueurs.

The pharmacy, with its original walnut paneling, is from 1543. The monks' alembics and other equipment are on view in the atmospheric rooms, which are still intact, serving today as the monastery's gift and souvenir shop. Here you can find a range of herbal products, honeys, and jams packaged for the monks by local producers. There are also some of the bitter herbal elixirs that the monks once made.

Campriano

LA CAPANNACCIA   ANTECCHIA, 51 52100 CAMPRIANO
RESTAURANT   TELEPHONE 0575 361759

OPEN Lunch and dinner   **CLOSED** Sunday evening; Monday; August   **CREDIT CARDS** None
ENGLISH SPOKEN A little   **FEATURES** Outdoor terrace in summer
RESERVATIONS Recommended at lunchtime and on weekends   **PRICE** $$–$$$
DIRECTIONS From Campriano, the restaurant is signposted; take the winding road to La Capannaccia, a thatched stone building set back from the road

La Capannaccia is a lively country trattoria. Its large picture windows overlook the beginning of the Casentino hills; in summer there is a vine-covered terrace. This is the only thatched restaurant I have seen in Tuscany. This rustic trattoria is popular and does a busy lunchtime trade. The atmosphere is informal, the helpings generous, the food wholesome, and the prices reasonable.

My autumn lunch began with mixed *crostini* topped with liver paste, ham, and spicy tomato sauce. *Primi* included fluffy polenta heaped with mushrooms, wide *pappardelle* noodles with a well-seasoned sauce of coarsely ground hare, penne with a piquant *arrabbiata* sauce, and a compact risotto with *funghi porcini*. Second helpings were available.

Meat lovers will appreciate the main courses. There were platters of grilled chicken, steak, sausages, rabbit, and ribs cooked in the giant open fireplace. To accompany them were *fagioli*—white Tuscan beans stewed with sage—or fried potatoes.

Desserts included satisfyingly sweet tiramisù, *affogato al caffè*—ice cream with hot espresso coffee poured over it—and *cantucci* biscuits dunked in Vin Santo. Anyone wanting help digesting all of this should have an *amaro*, the bitter herbal liqueur favored by the Italians as a *digestivo*.

Castiglion Fiorentino

COOP PRO.AGRI.A VIA COSIMO SERRISTORI, 53 52043 CASTIGLION FIORENTINO
MEAT TELEPHONE 0575 680226

OPEN 8:00–13:00, 16:30–19:30 **CLOSED** Wednesday afternoon; Sunday
CREDIT CARDS None **ENGLISH SPOKEN** A little **DIRECTIONS** From Castiglion Fiorentino,
take SS 71 toward Arezzo. After about 2 kms turn left toward Manciano, Lucignano, and the green
autostrada sign. The shop is on the right after about 300 meters, set back in its own parking lot

---

Produttori Agricoli Associati is a small cooperative run by two farming families. They raise (but do not breed) cattle, pigs, and sheep for meat they butcher and sell at this shop. On their farm, 5 kms away, they also grow the grains for the animals' feed.

"We kept hearing about the meat that was being imported from other countries," explained Tiziana Palazzoni. "It was full of hormones, and now we know that even the animals' feed may not be very trustworthy. It made us quite angry, so we decided to form this cooperative and supply fine meats to the local population whose provenance we could guarantee."

That was ten years ago, and the cooperative is now going strong. They buy young calves of the Chianina or Charollais breeds and raise them for from eight to twelve months before butchering. As members of the Carni Bovine DOC consortium, their meats are rigorously checked; no hormones are used. In the cheerful shop homemade *salumi* are sold in addition to the fresh meats. There are artisan-made cheeses and other local products—olive oil, honey, and wine.

AZIENDA AGRICOLA "IL MORO"
PRODUCE: ORGANIC

VIA MONTECCHIO, 301B
PIEVUCCIA 52043 CASTIGLION FIORENTINO
TELEPHONE 0575 651370

OPEN 8:00–19:00   **CLOSED** Saturday and Sunday   **CREDIT CARDS** None   **DIRECT SALE** Yes
ENGLISH SPOKEN A little   **OTHER** One simple apartment available for holiday rentals
DIRECTIONS From Castiglion Fiorentino, go toward Cortona. Turn left toward Pievuccia at third set
of traffic lights. Go through S. Lucia, over a humpbacked bridge, and continue about 1 km to the
church on the right. Four hundred meters after the church at Pievuccia, cross the green bridge on
the right, then take two right turns to the cream-colored house on the right

Alberto Bennati is a certified (AIAB) organic grower. On his small farm he produces broccoli, beets, celeriac, potatoes, melons, pumpkins, and strawberries. In keeping with organic regulations, he uses no chemical sprays or fertilizers. "When it comes to the bugs," he said, "either we pick them off by hand (as in the case of the cabbage caterpillars) or else we spray with the so-called Bordeaux mixture used for the vines, of copper and sulphur. The amazing thing is that within just a few years of the land being worked organically, both diseases and pests have radically diminished."

In addition to crop rotation, the earth is enriched with animal manure and with "green manure." Here plants such as annual lupins or comfrey are grown over the winter. As soon as they flower they are cut and left on the ground for two to three days before being dug under. This is one of the best fertilizers: the plants' roots fix nitrogen in the ground, and the green stems offer organic material for gradual breaking down in the soil. It is not too easy to find this rural farm, but it will be worth it to anyone who wants to taste great vegetables.

Also

Near the Il Moro farm, the Materazzi family (tel: 0575 651095) produces organic wines, olive oil, and *farro*, spelt wheat.

Cavriglia

LA LOCANDA CUCCUINI
RESTAURANT

AIA 52022 CAVRIGLIA
TELEPHONE 055 9166419
WEB SITE www.locanda-cuccuini.com

OPEN Lunch and dinner   **CLOSED** Sunday for dinner; Monday; holidays in winter
CREDIT CARDS None   **ENGLISH SPOKEN** Yes   **FEATURES** Summer terrace
RESERVATIONS Recommended   **PRICE** $$$ **OTHER** Eight rooms available for holiday rentals
DIRECTIONS From Cavriglia, follow signs for Aia; the Locanda is signposted

Stefano Cuccuini worked in Paris before coming home to open this restaurant in 1996. His country house now hosts a friendly, informal, but cultured restaurant, with an outdoor terrace for hot weather. Cuccuini is bright and refreshingly well traveled. "In Paris in the 1980s everybody was interested in Franco-Italian restaurants," he recalled. "But now I think we want a return to the kinds of foods our grandmothers prepared." Indeed, he has dedicated his restaurant to his grandmother. It was she who inspired both the *locanda*'s cooking and its spirit of hospitality.

I loved the food at this restaurant. Cuccuini's is a cuisine of clear flavors and fine ingredients; it is modern and pure, yet authentic. He proposes a very reasonably priced "combination" of three or four courses that includes the service charge, with a choice of five or six dishes for each course. The menu keeps up with the seasons.

In November, the antipasti were *bruschetta* toasts topped with eggplant and olives, Tuscan *salame* and figs, or warm fillets of herring served with cold parsleyed potatoes. "For us Italians," he exclaimed, "pasta is hot bread in search of a flavoring." His was wonderful. A *semplicissimo* plate of speckled buckwheat spaghetti (*grano saraceno*) came dressed only with freshly pressed olive oil and garlic. It was aromatic, uncluttered, and delicious. His grandmother's *tortellacci* had a delicate pale orange filling of pumpkin, buttery and sweet. Other *primi* included a risotto of radicchio and local sausage meat, and noodles cooked with hare.

Main courses went from *baccalà* (salt cod) to tripe, grilled cheese with vegetables to anchovy-scented steak. I tried a tender chicken fricassee with a yellow egg and lemon binding, and a more decisive duck (*anatra muta*) stewed in wine, served with braised *rochietti*, a kind of celery. Dessert was frothy, sharp lemon curd on a piece of very flaky pastry. The wines are local and good. I look forward to going back.

Civitella in Val di Chiana

RISTORANTE DEI LAGHI	**VIA TROVE, 27 52040 CIVITELLA IN VAL DI CHIANA**
RESTAURANT	**TELEPHONE 0575 448201, 448031**

OPEN Lunch and dinner   **CLOSED** Wednesday; August   **CREDIT CARDS** Visa, MC
ENGLISH SPOKEN Yes   **FEATURES** Trout fishing; children's playground, outdoor dining in summer
RESERVATIONS Necessary on weekends   **PRICE** $$ **DIRECTIONS** From Civitella, go toward
Badia Agnoano; the restaurant is clearly signposted after 4 kms

This hunting lodge–style restaurant and pizzeria is set in the woods and surrounded by small lakes and streams—with trout fishing available. There also is a large outdoor garden with a dining terrace and kids' playground. The rustic interior is dominated by an enormous copper-hooded open fireplace that warms the whole room in winter. Here the restaurant's owner acts as grill chef, cooking meats and local mushrooms. The Del Cucina family has run this restaurant for more than twenty-five years; I imagine the collection of stuffed game birds that decorates the dining room dates back that far.

This is a great place for mushroom lovers. In autumn there were excellen *crostini di funghi*: charcoal-scented toasts topped with fine slices of raw mushrooms. The rare *ovoli* were sprinkled with coarsely grated Parmesan cheese, fruity olive oil, and black pepper; the stronger porcini had a garlic-rubbed toast. They number among the best *crostini* I have tasted in Tuscany. In addition, there were *funghi fritti, alla brace,* or *trifolati*—fried, grilled, or stewed. Mushrooms appeared in pasta sauces too.

The restaurant's other specialty is, not surprisingly, meat cookery. A basket next to the fireplace holds logs cut to size for the imposing *camino.* Diners are provided with sharp knives. The fresh, quality meats—fillet steaks, chops, ribs, and *la Fiorentina,* the T-bone (now served from younger animals)—are brushed with herbed oil and salted before being broiled. It is a spectacular scene, with the glowing red embers and the appetizing aroma of roasting meat. Juicy porcini mushroom caps are given the same treatment and are a delicacy. Some game is also prepared, including wild boar and pheasant. There are seasonal vegetable accompaniments.

Most diners seem to drink the house red, but other wines are available. When the dinner service is finished, the friendly family leaves the kitchen and settles in the dining room to eat its meal.

Cortona

AZIENDA AGRICOLA RISTORI
OLIVE OIL

VIA SANTA MARGHERITA, 9 52044 CORTONA
TELEPHONE 0575 603571, 0584 23261, 075 5725260

OPEN Sales by appointment only   **CREDIT CARDS** None   **DIRECT SALE** Yes
ENGLISH SPOKEN A little   **OTHER** Holiday rentals available   **DIRECTIONS** In the town center

Silvio Ristori has long been an important personage in the food and wine world of Arezzo. He is a qualified sommelier and oil expert (he helps run local oil courses), and produces fine extra-virgin olive oil from his olive groves around Cortona of the classic Tuscan blend of Frantoiano, Leccino, and Moraiolo olives, processed in a *frantoio* nearby.

"The oils from these regions," he explained, "are very forceful: green, *fruttato,* and with a pleasant, characteristic bitterness. They go well with thick rustic soups like the *ribollita,* or on fresh salads—but not with fish, which they tend to overpower."

CASTEL GIRARDI
RESTAURANT

CASTEL GIRARDI, 61 52044 CORTONA
TELEPHONE 0575 691030

OPEN Lunch and dinner   **CLOSED** Tuesday   **CREDIT CARDS** Visa, MC
ENGLISH SPOKEN A little   **FEATURES** Outdoor summer terrace, children's playground
RESERVATIONS Recommended in summer   **PRICE** $$; pizza $ **DIRECTIONS** From the top of
Cortona, go toward Città di Castello; the pizzeria is on the main road after 5 kms

On a clear day you really can see for miles from this modest family-run trattoria. Perched high on a hill above Cortona, its panorama extends across the Val di

Chiana into Umbria. Children are welcome (there is a little playground) and there is no problem about having just pizzas or pasta—the menu even offers a reasonably priced *tris* of three pastas.

Some daily specials do not appear on the menu. In spring and autumn, local wild mushrooms are featured in "salads"—sliced raw and served with shavings of Parmesan, oil, and pepper. They may be porcini or the rarer *ovoli:* firm-fleshed, orange-skinned mushrooms that taste wonderfully peaty. Pizzas have paper-thin crusts in these parts and come with many toppings. Although they are in no way Tuscan specialties, they are popular with kids (and with whoever is paying the bill). The restaurant also offers mixed vegetables grilled over wood embers, the usual assortment of meat dishes, a good range of desserts, and some local wines.

IL FALCONIERE
RESTAURANT, RELAIS

SAN MARTINO, 43 52044 CORTONA
TELEPHONE 0575 612679   FAX 0575 612927
WEB SITE www.ilfalconiere.com

OPEN Lunch and dinner   **CLOSED** Wednesday in winter; November   **CREDIT CARDS** Visa, MC, Amex   **ENGLISH SPOKEN** Yes   **FEATURES** Summer outdoor terrace with view
RESERVATIONS Necessary for dinner and on weekends   **PRICE** $$$$–$$$$$
OTHER Il Falconiere, a *relais,* has nineteen rooms to rent within the villa's grounds
DIRECTIONS The restaurant is off SS 71 between Castiglion Fiorentino and Cortona, about 3 kms north of Cortona; it is clearly signposted from the main road

Il Falconiere is one of this area's most elegant restaurants: a picturesque seventeenth-century villa set in perfectly manicured grounds with cypress trees and flowers. The restaurant is in the *limonaia,* once used for wintering lemon trees. The summer dining terrace offers painterly views of Cortona and its vineyard-covered hillsides.

Il Falconiere's owners are strikingly young. Within a few years of inheriting the property, Silvia and Riccardo Baracchi have brought the complex up to *relais* (a luxurious small country hotel) standards. The well-appointed dining rooms have vaulted brick ceilings and warm terra-cotta floors and are decorated with fine murals and paintings. "We wanted to create a refined, comfortable environment," explained the attractive Silvia, "one where the food matched its setting."

Being both a sommelier and a talented cook, she is ambitious about the restaurant's scope. The cuisine is based on Tuscany's native ingredients—wild herbs, local game, seasonal produce—but they are elaborated on creatively. The autumn antipasti included a delicate *baccalà* tartlet with a purée of rosemary-scented chickpeas. A soufflélike hot *budino* of bread crumbs and cheese came with a cool sauce of sweet pears. A mold of cardoons and sun-dried tomatoes was served with a creamy onion sauce. Quite a few of the *primi* were fish-based. A slice of corn polenta was topped with mixed shellfish and wild mushrooms. I preferred the woodsy colors and aromas of pumpkin-stained pasta with a savory pheasant stuffing and sauced with red wine and juniper.

Main courses were again divided by sea and land. A fine fillet of turbot (*rombo*) was topped with crunchy deep-fried celery and porcini mushrooms. The boned rabbit, rolled around pistachios and carrots, was highly salted, but the rosemary lamb with its purée of garlic was wonderfully tender. Other *secondi* featured pheasant, pigeon, beef, and locally gathered porcini.

Desserts were elaborate and beautifully presented. A rich hot chocolate pudding came with an airy chocolate mousse. A rustic frozen *semifreddo* had crunchy bread crumbs and chocolate chips in it and it was surrounded by a voluptuous vanilla sauce. Much of the extensive wine list is Tuscan, with a complement of foreign wines. The service, as would be expected in a restaurant of this caliber, is excellent.

L'ETRURIA
PIAZZA SIGNORELLI, 21 52044 CORTONA
TABLE CRAFTS: POTTERY
TELEPHONE 0575 62360

OPEN 9:00–13:00, 15:30–20:00   **CLOSED** Monday in winter   **CREDIT CARDS** Visa, MC
ENGLISH SPOKEN A little   **DIRECTIONS** In the town center

Cortona has several little shops selling terra-cotta tableware. They all claim that the pieces are locally made, but I have my doubts (the nearby Umbrian town of Deruta supplies china shops all over the country with this kind of rustic ware). But that doesn't stop the pieces from being pretty enough to take home. This shop has some good garlic pots pierced with airholes, a range of *zabaglione*-colored dinnerware with olive-green trim, and a series of plates with indigo borders around central scenes of rabbits or birds. Years ago I bought a small, one-handled pottery colander here; it was glazed off-white and punched full of draining holes, just perfect for rinsing berries. I have it still.

ENOTECA ENOTRIA
VIA NAZIONALE, 81 52044 CORTONA
WINE BAR, SPECIALTY FOODS
TELEPHONE 0575 692007

OPEN 9:30–13:30, 16:00–20:00 (later in summer)   **CLOSED** Tuesday   **CREDIT CARDS** Visa, MC
DIRECT SALE Yes   **ENGLISH SPOKEN** No   **DIRECTIONS** In the town center

---

This *enoteca* is one of Cortona's principal meeting places for locals. Since 1985, Imola, the owner, has run this friendly, informal wine bar and shop, selling a selection of reasonably priced Tuscan wines and local artisan foods. You can sit at the little counter or at one of the tables in the back while you drink a glass of wine (interested buyers can taste the wines before purchasing a bottle) or eat a *panino* filled with one of Imola's well-selected food finds. She sells wild boar *salumi* and pecorini and ricotta from Mateassi (see next entry) to eat with *ciaccia*—local slang for *schiacciata*, a flat crusty bread—and other breads made nearby in a wood-burning oven.

Foiano della Chiana

CASEIFICIO MATEASSI
CHEESE

VIA DI CORTONA, 66A 52045 FOIANO DELLA CHIANA
TELEPHONE/FAX 0575 649101

OPEN 8:00–13:00, 15:00–19:30   **CLOSED** Sunday   **CREDIT CARDS** None   **DIRECT SALE** Yes, for whole cheeses   **ENGLISH SPOKEN** No   **DIRECTIONS** From Foiano, go toward Cortona; the *caseificio* is on the right, 500 meters after the stop junction, behind a beige private house

---

This family-run *caseificio* makes cheeses from sheep's and cow's milk. In early summer the sheep provide a lot of milk, so the company's *pecorini* are 100 percent sheep's; later in the year some cow's milk may be added into it. All the sheep's milk comes from Tuscany and nearby Umbria. Mateassi's pasteurized *pecorini* are sold fresh, semiseasoned (one month) and fully seasoned (three to six months). The dairy also produces a delicate sheep's milk ricotta that is sold on the day it is made, as well as a milder but less sweet cow's milk ricotta. Other cheeses vary with the seasons.

When I visited there was no company sign visible from the road, even though the small factory shop is well frequented; they said they are planning to put one up soon.

Gargonza

CASTELLO DI GARGONZA
RESTAURANT, WINE

GARGONZA 52048 MONTE SAN SAVINO
TELEPHONE 0575 847021;
LA TORRE RESTAURANT: 0575 847065
FAX 0575 847054   WEB SITE www.gargonza.it

OPEN Restaurant lunch and dinner   **CLOSED** Restaurant Tuesday; January and February   **CREDIT CARDS** Visa, MC, Amex   **DIRECT SALE** Yes; wine and oil available from the castle reception   **ENGLISH SPOKEN** Yes   **RESERVATIONS** Recommended   **PRICE** $$$ **OTHER** Apartments available for holiday rentals   **DIRECTIONS** From the top of Monte San Savino, take SS 73 toward Siena; Gargonza is 7 kms up the hill, signposted

---

In 1304 the Castle of Gargonza hosted a gathering of Ghibellines that included the poet Dante Alighieri. One hundred thirty years later a Florentine decree ordered that the walls of some of the Val di Chiana castles taken as war booty from the Aretines be knocked down, Gargonza among them. And so they were, though parts of the original structure were left. Subsequently, the castle and the buildings within its circular walls were rebuilt and used for agricultural purposes. It now belongs to Florentine count Roberto Guicciardini. He has, in recent years, set about fixing it up, revitalizing its vineyards and olive groves and creating a restaurant and a well-appointed "residence."

The castle commands breathtaking views of the Val di Chiana—after all, castles were usually built to that end. The restaurant is on the long approach close to the castle. It is a nice setting, with a pretty courtyard for eating outside in summer. Inside, I spotted some of Rampini's beautiful hand-painted platters from Chianti (see p 212). The count's idea for the restaurant is to return to the uncomplicated but satisfying country fare that Tuscany is famous for. "The Mediterranean diet is increasingly popular," he affirmed. "The basic elements of olive oil, wine, simple meats, and seasonal vegetables: these are the building blocks of this healthy home-cooked cuisine."

    The restaurant offers a range of pastas and soups, followed by meats (including Chianina beef) grilled over wood embers. There is a nice choice of side dishes, including grilled mixed vegetables, stewed peppers or haricot beans, and various salads. Cheeses and desserts follow, accompanied by the Chianti Putto of the castle, though there is a fuller wine list.

Giovi

ANTICA TRATTORIA AL PRINCIPE   52010 GIOVI
RESTAURANT   TELEPHONE 0575 362046

OPEN Lunch and dinner   **CLOSED** Monday; holidays in summer   **CREDIT CARDS** Visa, MC, Amex   **ENGLISH SPOKEN** No   **RESERVATIONS** Recommended Thursday and on weekends
PRICE $$$ **DIRECTIONS** From SS 71 about 8 kms north of Arezzo, follow signs to Borgo a Giovi and Giovi; the restaurant is in the center of the old village

---

Don't be put off by the "suburb" you must drive through to get into the old part of Giovi. At its heart is a medieval square, remarkably intact, with a Romanesque church and a cluster of what were once coach houses for the travelers stopping between the Casentino and Arezzo. Back then, this small square had enough passing trade to fill three restaurants. Al Principe is the only one left. It is the oldest trattoria in Arezzo, founded more than 180 years ago. Inside, a series of small rooms have been opened up to form the dining rooms, as a patchwork of beamed ceilings reveals.

    At lunchtime the trattoria is filled with local businessmen and farmers, many of whom spend a good part of the meal talking about food. There is nothing unusual in that: Italian men love discussing the foods they love.

    I arrived in November, and the new season's olive oil was being pressed throughout the surrounding hills. As each group of diners sat down they were offered a bottle of thick green oil, a pepper mill, and a basket of bread. They took a slice, drizzled on some oil, and ground pepper over it. With this *fettunta* (and no further ado) the meal had begun.

    Along with the classic Tuscan starters of *crostini* and *affettati* (platters of cured meats), the season afforded the rare *ovoli* mushrooms, served raw. There was a choice of meat- or fish-based *primi* and *secondi*. My neighbors started with a creamy risotto with mixed *frutti di mare,* followed by an unusual dish of squid, celery, and *cannellini* beans. My *passato di fagioli* was a creamy purée of beans and vegetables with a handful of very fine pasta thrown in. A little "raw" oil and two large scallions went with it. Handmade pastas included *maccheroni,* which here were noodles almost as wide as *pappardelle,* with a hearty meat and mushroom sauce.

Main courses went beyond the usual grilled meats, *alla brace.* The unusual *anguilla al coccio*—tender eel in a spicy tomato sauce—came bubbling hot in a terra-cotta pot. It was served with *cannellini* beans boiled with sage. There was a good selection of fresh seasonal vegetables, including braised artichokes and stewed *coste* (Swiss chard). The desserts were homemade. The wine list includes a lot of big names as well as a drinkable local *sfuso.*

Gorgiti

FORNO COCOLLINI
BREAD

GORGITI 52024 LORO CIUFFENNA
TELEPHONE 055 9704001

OPEN 8:00–20:00   **CLOSED** Wednesday   **CREDIT CARDS** None   **DIRECT SALE** Yes
ENGLISH SPOKEN No   **DIRECTIONS** From Loro Ciuffenna, follow signs to Gorgiti

Anyone who has had the pleasure of reading Burton Anderson's book *Pleasures of the Italian Table,* about Italy's artisan foods and their makers, will remember his evocative description of a predawn visit to this bakery to watch Carlo Cocollini making bread in his wood-burning oven. The *pane Toscano* is worth a trip to the tiny village; the informative book is worth reading.

Loro Ciuffenna

COOPERATIVA VECCHIO FRANTOIO "IL FONTINO"
OLIVE OIL

VIA SETTEPONTI LEVANTE, 30 52024 LORO CIUFFENNA
TELEPHONE 055 9172259

OPEN End of October to end of December; otherwise, sales by appointment only
CREDIT CARDS None   **DIRECT SALE** Yes   **ENGLISH SPOKEN** No   **DIRECTIONS** On the
Setteponti road between Loro Ciuffenna and San Giustino; the mill is on the right, 1.2 kms after Loro

In late autumn, when you see the olives being hand-picked from the trees by men and women on ladders, you can take your clean empty bottles and buy the new season's extra-virgin oil directly from this small mill. It is always a wonderful spectacle to see the giant stone wheels grinding the olives to a paste: the air is filled with a fragrant mist of oil.

This cooperative has about twenty members—all independent olive cultivators within a two-kilometer radius of the mill. The olive harvest is a joyous time;

visitors to the *frantoio* can sample the just-pressed spicy green oil on slices of country bread, washed down with a little local wine.

Also

MULINO PARIGI

Under Loro Ciuffenna's high bridge at the entrance to the town is a miller who still uses the powerful river water to drive his grinding wheels. This seventeenth-century mill was on the verge of closing, but it has since been saved with landmark status. It is well worth seeing for anyone interested in the history of Tuscan food making. Chestnut and other flours are on sale, freshly ground.

Manzano

TENIMENTI LUIGI D'ALESSANDRO WINE	VIA MANZANO, 15 52042 CAMUCIA TELEPHONE 0575 618667 FAX 0575 618411 E-MAIL tenimenti.dalessandro@flashnet.it

OPEN Sales 9:00–12:00, 15:00–19:00; tastings and visits by appointment only   **CLOSED** Never
CREDIT CARDS Visa, MC, Amex   **DIRECT SALE** Yes   **ENGLISH SPOKEN** Yes
DIRECTIONS On the road between Camucia (Cortona) and Foiano della Chiana

"This is an area without winemaking traditions," explained Massimo d'Alessandro, "so we have been free to create our own." One of three Roman brothers who own this estate at Manzano, d'Alessandro is an architect who, since the early 1980s, has become increasingly involved with winemaking. The estate, with more than 50 hectares (125 acres) of vineyards and a remarkable eighteenth-century villa, is beautifully positioned on a small rise in the Chiana plain. The d'Alessandros' father bought the estate in 1967, planting it all to Sangiovese and Trebbiano, Tuscany's classic red and white grapes. The results were mediocre.

"When I took over we did some experimentation," Massimo continued, "and discovered that the modern system of high-density planting of hot-climate grape varieties—especially Syrah and Chardonnay—gave great results here." The vineyards were replanted: from sixteen hundred plants per hectare, they increased to seven thousand. If before, each plant had produced 10 kgs (22 lbs) of grapes, each now produces only 800 grams (less than 2 lbs). "The French have a saying: one plant, one glass of wine. This way there is incredible concentration of flavor in the fruit, as all the plant's energy goes into it."

Indeed, Manzano's wines, which in 1999 all became Cortona DOC, are praised for their terrific intensity. The estate's primary red, Il Bosco, of 90 percent Syrah and 10 percent Sangiovese, is a wine of elegance and structure. Fontarca is a modern-style Chardonnay with Viognier; aged mostly in *barriques*, it, too, is a powerful, harmonious wine with a floral bouquet brought to it by the Viognier. There is also a lovely sweet Vin Santo, but all other vineyards have now been replanted to Syrah. A second line of Syrah, Vescovo Secondo, will offer a younger wine to drink sooner.

D'Alessandro's investments have included the cellars. They are now filled with legions of small French oak *barriques;* a distillery has been installed for the making of the winery's two grappas. There are plans for a very modern *cantina* designed by d'Alessandro—if he can get permission to build.

Meliciano

FATTORIA LA VIALLA	**VIA DI MELICIANO, 26 52029 MELICIANO**
OLIVE OIL, SPECIALTY FOODS	TELEPHONE 0575 364372 FAX 0575 364623

OPEN 9:00–12:30, 15:00–18:00   **CLOSED** Saturday and Sunday   **CREDIT CARDS** Visa
DIRECT SALE Yes   **ENGLISH SPOKEN** Yes   **OTHER** Rooms to rent
DIRECTIONS From Castiglion Fibocchi, go toward Meliciano; the farm is on the left after about 4 kms

This interesting and large organic farm produces extra-virgin olive oil in its own stone mill. The small mill building is in a rural setting: an unpaved road barely reaches it. The hand-picked olives—black Morellino, green Raggiaia, and mottled Frantoiano—are ground and pressed the day they are picked. If the air in the mill is too chill, a small wood-burning stove is lit in the corner.

"If the olives are allowed to go below 6°C [42°F] they freeze," explained Piero Lo Franco, the farm's owner, "and oil extraction is difficult under 15°C [59°F]. So some heat must be applied, if only to the room."

The farm's wines, jams, vegetable preserves, and other products are on sale from its pleasant shop.

Monte San Savino

MACELLERIA ALDO	**PIAZZA GAMURRINI, 31 52048 MONTE SAN SAVINO**
MEAT: PORCHETTA	TELEPHONE 0575 844098

OPEN 8:00–13:00, 16:00–19:30   **CLOSED** Wednesday afternoon; Sunday; first two weeks of July
CREDIT CARDS None   **ENGLISH SPOKEN** No   **DIRECTIONS** In the town's central square

Monte San Savino is known for *porchetta*—whole roasted pig. This is a very popular food in Tuscany: even the smallest markets have stalls selling the crispy-skinned meat sliced from the animal, which is proudly on display, head and all. This cheery butcher's shop, run by Aldo Jacomoni and his wife, Giorgina, makes the finest *porchetta* in Monte San Savino. Signora Jacomoni explained how it is done.

"We start with large animals weighing around 75 kilos [165 lbs]. The pig is washed and the skin pricked at intervals, to let the hot fat out as it cooks. The major bones and organs are carefully removed from inside, leaving the skin intact. The cavity is stuffed with our special mixture of seasonings, which includes wild fennel and garlic, and is then sewn up."

Meanwhile, the huge wood-burning oven is prepared. Branches of dried broom (*erica*) are stacked in the oven to start the fire; they will confer a particular aroma to the meat. The refractory brick oven is heated for about two hours, until it reaches 300°C (572°F). Then the prepared pig is placed inside. "The first half hour is crucial," Signora Jacomoni continued. "You have to make sure the temperature is right. Then you leave the pig to roast for ten hours, until it is beautifully browned on the outside and cooked right through."

The shop features homemade *salumi* and fresh meats, including a line of organic *salumi*, and Chianina steaks vacuum-packed for anyone who has far to go. Monte San Savino holds its annual *sagra della porchetta*—roasted pig fair—in September.

RISTORANTE BELVEDERE　　　　　BANO, 226 52048 MONTE SAN SAVINO
RESTAURANT　　　　　　　　　TELEPHONE 0575 849588　　FAX 0575 844262
　　　　　　　　　　　　　　　　E-MAIL massimo.rossi 4@tin.it

OPEN Lunch and dinner　**CLOSED** Monday　**CREDIT CARDS** Visa, MC, Amex
ENGLISH SPOKEN A little　**FEATURES** Summer terrace, miniature golf, children's playground
RESERVATIONS Necessary on weekends　**PRICE** $$; pizza $　**DIRECTIONS** From Monte San Savino, take the road up toward Gargonza; the restaurant is signposted

---

Positioned way up above the Val di Chiana, this spacious family-run restaurant and pizzeria is a relaxed place to take the whole family. Not only is it very reasonably priced, but parents can let their kids play outside while they linger over a nice bottle of wine. The restaurant offers free miniature golf to its patrons, as well as other outdoor games.

Massimo Rossi, the Belvedere's young owner, is a qualified sommelier and an active champion of local artisan-made foods and olive oils. He organizes tastings and has researched a fine selection of wine and oil for the restaurant, with a smaller markup than usual.

The full menu includes a range of pizzas. Try a platter of mixed *crostini* to start—most Tuscans do. The egg pasta is homemade; baked ricotta *gnocchetti* are a house special. Meats grilled over a wood fire (*alla brace*) are always good. *Straccetti* (little rags) are thin strips of beef cooked with softened onions and balsamic vinegar. There is a wide choice of desserts (important for kids), including homemade gelati.

ORIETTA LAPUCCI   CORSO SANGALLO, 8/10 52048 MONTE SAN SAVINO
TABLE CRAFTS: POTTERY   TELEPHONE 0575 844375

OPEN 9:00–13:00, 15:00–19:30; at other times, ring bell for sales   **CLOSED** Saturday and Sunday
in winter   **CREDIT CARDS** None   **ENGLISH SPOKEN** No   **DIRECTIONS** Off Piazza Gamurrini

Working with red and white clay from Empoli, the Lapuccis and Chelis create unusual ceramics traditional only to Monte San Savino. The clay is cut away by hand (*traforato*) to look almost like lace, then glazed white or colored. The work is very detailed; the objects—bowls, plates, vases—are precious yet rustic enough to look handmade. *Scaldini* are earthenware pots with high handles; they held glowing embers and served as hand warmers. In November a *festa* in the town is dedicated to them.

Montevarchi

LA BOTTEGA DI VANNA   LE LOGGE, 11 52025 MONTEVARCHI
FARM PRODUCE: ORGANIC   TELEPHONE 055 982391

OPEN 8:00–13:00, 17:00–20:00   **CLOSED** Sunday; Saturday afternoon in summer, Wednesday
afternoon in winter   **CREDIT CARDS** None   **ENGLISH SPOKEN** No
DIRECTIONS Under the portico in Piazza Mazzini, near the station

This wonderful shop began as the outlet for the Paterna farm at Terranuova Bracciolini (p 373). It sells fresh organic produce, preserved vegetables and fruits (including Sandra Masi's fine range), pulses, organic wine, and some organic dairy foods—from farm to consumer, without middlemen. The staff is friendly, the vegetables and fruit are delicious—and it's all good for us!

PASTICCERIA BONCI   VIALE DIAZ, 49 52025 MONTEVARCHI
PASTRY, BAR   TELEPHONE 055 982308 SHOP
                                                    FAX 055 981225

OPEN 7:00–13:30, 16:00–20:00   **CLOSED** Monday; Sunday afternoon in summer; August
CREDIT CARDS None   **ENGLISH SPOKEN** Yes   **DIRECTIONS** On SS 69 *circonvallazione*,
or ring road, through outer Montevarchi, by Via Piave

This attractive pastry shop is run by the Bonci family. They have their own bakery nearby producing pastries, cakes, *panforte*, and chocolates. The Bonci's *panforte* weighs 500 grams (1 lb); it comes in a pretty wrapping and makes a good present to take home. This version is lightly spiced, soft, and fresh-tasting, with almonds and candied melon rind in it. Recently the Boncis have won prizes with their pastries.

The chocolates are made by young Michele Mezzasoma, who was trained in the Piemontese manner of cream and liquid fillings. There are candied fruits and *confetti*—the hard candy-covered seeds of coriander, anise, cumin, and cardamom that make nice breath-fresheners.

Pergine Valdarno

"PERGENTINO" OIL COOPERATIVE
OLIVE OIL

PIAZZA DELLA CHIESA, 10
52020 PERGINE VALDARNO
TELEPHONE 0575 896020   FAX 0575 897045

OPEN November–January and June–August 17:30–19:00; the rest of the year by appointment only
CREDIT CARDS None   DIRECT SALE Yes   ENGLISH SPOKEN Yes   OTHER The cooperative's *frantoio* is at Pieve a Presciano. It is open to visitors in November and December
DIRECTIONS The shop is in the center of the village

The lovely hills around Pergine are terraced with olive groves, and the town's extra-virgin olive oil is considered to be among Tuscany's finest. This small cooperative was formed in 1983—just two years before the winter that froze most of central Italy's olive trees. It was not until 1991 that the group was able to begin production.

"Despite 1985, we are lucky here," explained Arturo Ghezzi, a member of the cooperative. "This area is north facing, so the most serious olive parasite gets killed off in winter. Consequently, we do very little spraying."

Each tree yields about 15 kgs (33 lbs) of olives, which translates into only about 2 kgs (4½ lbs) of oil—just two or three bottles per plant. The olives are picked by hand before being taken to the nearby modern-style *frantoio*. The oil has very low acidity.

The cooperative has produced an artist-designed bottle for their gift packs; it comes in its own wooden carrying box. The oil is available in regular bottles, too. Artichoke hearts preserved in oil are also on sale from the little shop.

Ponte a Chiani

FRANTOIO E CANTINA VINI TIPICI ARETINO
OLIVE MILL, WINE

PONTE A CHIANI, 57F 52040 PONTE A CHIANI
TELEPHONE 0575 363038   FAX 0575 363950
E-MAIL vita@frael.it

OPEN Shop 8:00–12:30, 14:30–18:00   CLOSED Saturday afternoon; Sunday
CREDIT CARDS None   DIRECT SALE Yes   ENGLISH SPOKEN No
DIRECTIONS On the main road between Ponte a Chiani and Indicatore

This *Frantoio* and Cantina Sociale produces oil and wine for its many small members from the surrounding *Colline Aretine*. The two modern buildings, the oil mill and the wine cellar, are side by side, and they share a shop selling their reasonably priced oils and wines. The *cantina's* range of wines has improved in recent years and includes the local white Bianco Valdichiana DOC, of primarily Trebbiano, with added Grechetto, Chardonnay, and Pinots Bianco and Grigio. There is a Chianti

DOCG and its Riserva—which contains some Merlot and Cabernet and is aged partly in *barriques*—as well as the Chianti Colli Aretini DOCG.

The *frantoio* is of the modern type, with steel hammers to pound the olives to a pulp and centrifugal separators. In November, when the harvest is on, the parking lot is full of *api*, the three-wheeled vehicles so popular in the countryside. Inside, the farmers watch over their olives like anxious parents as the bitter green and black fruit is so mysteriously transformed into golden oil.

Poppi

AZIENDA AGRICOLA MULINO ROSSI
CHEESE: GOAT'S

FILETTO, 21 52014 POPPI
TELEPHONE 0575 500163

OPEN Sales by appointment only   CREDIT CARDS None   DIRECT SALE Yes; the cheese is also sold from Easter to October at Ponte a Poppi market on Tuesday mornings
ENGLISH SPOKEN A little   OTHER Organic produce in summer   DIRECTIONS From Ponte a Poppi, cross the bridge toward Poppi. After the bridge turn right toward Quorle. After 700 meters turn right toward Quorle for 2 kms. After a small stone bridge, take the right fork toward Filetto (yellow sign). The road becomes unpaved, and after a very sharp left bend, the house is on the left after 1 km

If you are a fan of goat's cheese and like to explore the countryside, you will enjoy the drive up into the hills above Poppi to this small farm. The views are spectacular and the dirt roads are passable if your car's clearance off the ground is high enough.

Arianna Adani and Angelo Rossini have a herd of thirty-five goats grazing the pastures around their house. Their creamy, unpasteurized organic cheeses are made in the French style, as Arianna explained: "Unlike pecorino-style cheeses, which are made in about one hour at fairly high heat [30°C/86°F], *caprino* goat's cheese requires a *cagliatura* [addition of rennet] at lower temperatures [18°C/64°F], which must be sustained for a full twenty-four hours." She explained that goat's milk is closer to human milk than cow's and has a lower fat content.

Arianna makes a fresh curd *caprino* that resembles quark, as well as herbed and matured cheeses. She also sells her cheeses at Firenze's Fierucola and Fierucolina markets (see p 92).

PLATEAU PASTA
PASTA

VIA DEI GUAZZI, 8 PONTE A POPPI 52014 POPPI
TELEPHONE 0575 529507

OPEN 8:30–19:00   CLOSED Saturday afternoon; Sunday   CREDIT CARDS None
DIRECT SALE Yes   ENGLISH SPOKEN No   DIRECTIONS From Bibbiena, go toward Poppi, turning right toward Cesena before Poppi; the factory is on the right after 20 meters

This small, semi-industrial pasta factory makes handy packages of vacuum-packed pasta that keep in the refrigerator for up to two months. The *tortelli di patate*, a favorite Casentino recipe, are stuffed with a delicious potato filling.

There are several types of tagliatelle noodles, as well as *ravioli* filled with nettle (*ortica*) and ricotta, or truffle-scented ricotta.

Pratovecchio

L'OSTERIA DI GIOVANNI PRETAGLIA
SNACK BAR

VIA ROMA, 57 52015 PRATOVECCHIO
TELEPHONE 0575 583843

OPEN Monday, Wednesday–Saturday 6:00–22:00; Sunday 8:00–13:30, 15:00–22:00
CLOSED Tuesday; August   **CREDIT CARDS** None   **ENGLISH SPOKEN** A little
DIRECTIONS Just beyond Pratovecchio, on the road to Stia

For the past ten years Giovanni Petraglia's bar has provided a stopping place for people journeying to and from the Casentino. They come in for a coffee or a glass of wine, or for one of his sandwiches made from fragrant, unsalted local bread and his special *prosciutto affumicato al ginepro,* ham seasoned with salt, pepper, chili, and garlic before being lightly smoked over a fire of juniper branches and then matured for eight months. The *prosciutto* is wonderfully moist and tender and not overly salty, with a slight sweetness from the smoke.

"In the old days this was a common *salume* in these parts," Giovanni told me. "People used to hang up their hams near the fireplace to dry out, and they took on this smoky flavor." Giovanni also stocks a few cheeses, including those made by the Talla Cooperative on the Pratomagno (p 373).

Also

LA TANA DEGLI ORSI

VIA ROMA, 1. 0575 583377
OPEN FOR DINNER ONLY, CLOSED WEDNESDAY

With six hundred Italian wines to choose from, the finest artisan-made *salumi* and cheeses, local dishes cooked well and imaginatively, this friendly restaurant has won a reputation for high standards and fair prices.

Rendola

OSTERIA DI RENDOLA
RESTAURANT

VIA DI RENDOLA RENDOLA 52025 MONTEVARCHI
TELEPHONE 055 9707491   FAX 055 9707490

OPEN Lunch and dinner   **CLOSED** Wednesday; holidays in winter   **CREDIT CARDS** Visa, MC
ENGLISH SPOKEN Yes   **RESERVATIONS** Recommended on weekends and for dinner
PRICE $$$$ **DIRECTIONS** From Montevarchi, go south toward Mercatale Valdarno; Rendola is signposted from there

This *osteria* has a rural setting, overlooking olive groves and vineyards. It is within the grounds of the Fattoria di Rendola, in what were the blacksmith and carpentry workshops. The buildings were refurbished when the restaurant opened in 1993. The interior has been tastefully stripped to reveal wood beams, brick, and stone. There is a large open fireplace.

The menu has been devised in a similar way: traditional and contemporary dishes have been selected with care and pared down to accentuate their primary flavors. The chef, Francesco Berardinelli, whose experience includes a stint at San Domenico's in New York, and who recently opened Beccofino in Firenze (see p 97), has sought out fine local ingredients.

In autumn, my lunch began with slices of home-smoked tuna served with a compote of Mediterranean vegetables—eggplant, peppers, beans—and a garlic-less basil pesto. A *fonduta di finocchio* was a well-seasoned stiff purée of fennel seasoned with newly pressed olive oil. It was garnished with grilled shrimp. Other, more typically Tuscan, options change with the seasons.

A very fine *passato* (puréed soup) of *fagioli* beans was scented with rosemary and given texture by plumped grains of *farro* and tiny diced pieces of pancetta bacon. It was drizzled with oil and nicely peppered. Smoky-sweet *pappardelle* noodles were made with chestnut flour and topped with a chunky wild boar sauce. Stewed rabbit was served here with an aromatic *bramata* (medium grind) polenta enhanced with fresh herbs. A *feuilleté* tart of pears had a surprising rosemary accent. There are well-chosen wines to accompany these well-cooked foods.

Rimbocchi

AZIENDA AGRICOLA
GABRIELE MATEUCCI
CHEESE

CANVECCHIO, 26 BIFORCO 52011 RIMBOCCHI
TELEPHONE 0575 599261

OPEN Telephone appointment preferred for sales   **CREDIT CARDS** None   **DIRECT SALE** Yes
ENGLISH SPOKEN No   **DIRECTIONS** From Bibbiena, go toward Chiusi della Verna and then follow signs for Rimbocchi. From Rimbocchi, take the road for La Verna. The farm is on the right after about 3 kms; it is the first cluster of buildings after Montefatucchio

A drive up the mountain to this cheesemaker reveals some spectacular scenery. Gabrielle Mateucci and his lovely wife, Gina, overlook a landscape of unusual striated rock formations that change continually as the light moves across them. Their flock of 180 sheep grazes in sloping fields full of wild herbs.

"Our pecorino is so flavorful because of these aromatic pastures," Gabrielle said. "The biggest problem we have are the wolves. They are a protected species and are increasing in number. We guard our flock with big Maremman sheepdogs. Otherwise our sheep would be killed off."

As well as her prize-winning fresh and semiaged (aged from three to eight weeks) *pecorini*, Gina makes a small amount of fragrant ricotta, which should be preordered, because of the high demand. The cheeses, on sale directly from the farm, are at their most plentiful from April through October. The couple is always there, but it is best to phone, preferably at mealtimes, before going up.

San Giovanni Valdarno

IVV
TABLE CRAFTS: GLASSWARE

LUNGARNO GUIDO RENI, 60
52027 SAN GIOVANNI VALDARNO
TELEPHONE 055 942619
E-MAIL info@ivvnet.it

OPEN 9:00–13:00, 16:00–19:30 **CLOSED** Sunday, Monday morning **CREDIT CARDS** Visa, MC **ENGLISH SPOKEN** Yes **DIRECTIONS** On the east bank of the Arno River (across from the town), 1 km from the Valdarno *autostrada* exit

This glass factory has updated its image and now produces some stylish colored glass pieces at affordable prices. Glasses, vases, and other objects are blown or blown and then pressed into molds. There are good discounts on many items. Shoppers at Williams-Sonoma and Pottery Barn will recognize some of the pieces, as IVV produces glassware for them.

Sansepolcro

UN PUNTO MACROBIOTICO
HEALTH FOODS, RESTAURANT

VIA GIORDANO BRUNO, 48/A
52037 SANSEPOLCRO
TELEPHONE 0575 735544

OPEN Lunch Monday–Saturday, dinner Thursday–Saturday **CLOSED** Sunday **CREDIT CARDS** None **ENGLISH SPOKEN** A little **DIRECTIONS** In the town center, near Porta Fiorentina

Like its sister stores in Arezzo (see p 342) and Firenze (see p 108), Un Punto Macrobiotico sells macrobiotic and other health foods and offers a reasonably priced restaurant serving vegetarian meals made with organic produce.

CARNI SHOP
MEAT

VIA DEI LORENA, 32 52037 SANSEPOLCRO AREZZO
TELEPHONE 0575 742924

OPEN 7:30–13:00, 15:30–19:30 **CLOSED** Wednesday afternoon in winter; Monday in summer; August **CREDIT CARDS** None **ENGLISH SPOKEN** No **DIRECTIONS** On the main road into Sansepolcro from Anghiari and the *superstrada*

Antimo Buzzichini's butcher's shop has specialized in Chianina beef for nearly twenty years. This local breed is considered to be among the finest beef in the world. "The Chianina are very low in fat, so their meat is lean and tender," explained Antimo. "You can tell by looking at a raw steak: the Chianina's color is less deeply red than other beef and has a nice layer of pure white fat around its edge. Recently even the Americans have been importing them to breed at home. In Italy the animals are controlled by veterinary inspectors who also ensure that no hormones have been administered. We know what they eat, so there should be no danger of disease."

The most popular cut is the *Fiorentina*, a T-bone, but others are available from the shop, which also sells a small range of ready-to-cook meats.

MACELLERIA MARTINI VIA XX SETTEMBRE, 95 52037 SANSEPOLCRO
MEAT TELEPHONE 0575 742310
WEB SITE www.altavaltiberina.it

OPEN 8:00–13:00, 16:00–20:00 **CLOSED** Sunday; Monday in summer; Wednesday afternoon in winter; July **CREDIT CARDS** None **ENGLISH SPOKEN** A little **DIRECTIONS** In the town center, by Piazza Torre di Berta

Aldo Martini is the quintessential butcher: red-faced, robust, and cheery. The attractive tiled shop he runs with his family is full of enticing goodies, some of which are special only to Sansepolcro.

Martini and his sons, Ivano and Marcello, produce an excellent *lombo di suino sott'olio*—lean loin of pork that is salt-cured before being sliced thick and preserved in herb-scented extra-virgin olive oil. It is sold in jars and makes a fine antipasto. There is chopped chicken and pigeon liver paste for topping *crostini*, a rich goose sauce (*sugo d'oca*) for pasta, well-flavored *prosciutto Toscano*, and a range of *salumi*, some of which are preserved in oil.

The fresh-meat counter features Chianina steaks and locally bred pork. A true Casentino rarity is the stuffed goose or chicken's neck (*collo ripieno*). It is filled with a mixture of ground veal, béchamel, liver, and egg, and baked in meat sauce or broth.

ROSA GORI VIA DEL PRUCINO, 2/E 52037 SANSEPOLCRO
PASTA TELEPHONE 0575 742606

OPEN Winter 8:00–13:00, 16:30–19:30; summer 8:00–13:00, 17:00–20:00
CLOSED Monday; holidays in summer **CREDIT CARDS** None **ENGLISH SPOKEN** A little
DIRECTIONS The *pastificio* is outside the old part of town, to its west

Fresh pasta is popular in this part of the Aretino, and this *pastificio* has been a fixture in Sansepolcro since 1968. It sells a range of egg pastas—flat noodles and stuffed. Ravioli are filled with herbs, ricotta, and Parmesan; *agnolotti* with mixed ground meats, such as *mortadella*, veal, and pork with Parmesan; and *cappelletti* with ground beef or pork. For an easy dinner there are oven-ready cannelloni and lasagne, potato or spinach gnocchi, and sauces. *Bringoli* are a local eggless pasta—like thick spaghetti—of durum wheat and water. They are traditionally served with *sugo finto* (fake sauce), which is made of vegetables, offcuts of meat and offal, and cheese.

PASTICCERIA CHIELI
PASTRY

VIA FRATERNITÀ, 12 52037 SANSEPOLCRO
TELEPHONE 0575 742026   FAX 0575 735507

OPEN 8:00–13:30, 16:30–20:00   **CLOSED** Monday   **CREDIT CARDS** Visa, MC
ENGLISH SPOKEN A little   **OTHER** Chieli's other *pasticceria* is on Via XX Settembre, 8; the dessert wine shop is on Via Fraternità, 5   **DIRECTIONS** Off Piazza Torre di Berta, in the town center

---

Rosangela Chieli runs the finest pastry shops in Sansepolcro. I was struck by her lively intelligence. It was refreshing to meet such a positive modern-food artisan. "The *pasticceria* was started by my father in 1948," she explained, "with the local repertoire of butter cream tarts, 'dry' biscuits, and fried *bomboloni*. He lacked formal training but used fine ingredients, and his pastries were a success." Now, fifty years later, the future of the family business lies with Rosangela's brother Daniele and her son Alessio Conti.

"These days there are many options for young pastry chefs wanting to master the specializations. We wanted our son to benefit from them." Alessio attended courses on chocolate, yeasts, candied fruits, and sugar sculpture. The Chielis also invite *maestri* to work in Sansepolcro. The day I was there a *marron glacé* specialist was giving a workshop. "Our clients now appreciate many northern specialties, like fine chocolates or French-style mousses. And of course we still prepare all the local favorites."

The elegant shop is filled with tempting confections. There are *pinoli*-studded ricotta tarts and puff-ball cakes called *cartoccio*, with jam and almond paste in their batter. Small cookies include the light, chewy *brutti ma buoni* (ugly but good) almond macaroons. There are fine chocolates in the Piemontese or Belgian tradition, with sumptuously sweet *fourré* fillings of nut, cocoa, or liqueur creams and contrasting decorative casings.

Fresh fruits are "transformed" into jams, jellies, and preserved in syrup. Herbed jellies of *melissa* (balm) and mint are fragrant pastes for spreading on toast. Anyone who hankers for the aniseed balls of their youth should try *confetti*, the hard sugar balls whose centers contain aromatic seeds. Across the street, the Chielis have opened a small showcase of (mainly) dessert wines to go with their pastries.

DA VENTURA
RESTAURANT

VIA N. AGGIUNTI, 30 52037 SANSEPOLCRO
TELEPHONE 0575 742560

OPEN Lunch and dinner   **CLOSED** Saturday; January and August   **CREDIT CARDS** Visa, MC,
Amex   **ENGLISH SPOKEN** Yes   **RESERVATIONS** Recommended Sunday and holidays
PRICE $$ **OTHER** Da Ventura also has a few rooms to let
DIRECTIONS In the center of town, down the street from the museum

Da Ventura is a family-run restaurant popular on the Piero della Francesca "circuit." Situated on one of Sansepolcro's main walking streets, it has lovely terracotta ceilings with old beams and carved wainscoting. As you step down from the sidewalk, you are greeted by mounds of fresh noodles drying on the entrance table. During the meal, the hot pasta and a choice of sauces is served from an amusing trolley. Diners can determine how much of each they want.

Trolleys return throughout the meal. One appears with mixed antipasti of preserved and pickled vegetables, *lombo di maiale sott'olio* (slices of lean pork loin preserved in oil), and other *salumi*. Later, a *secondi* trolley brings roasted meats and wonderful accompanying vegetables. A final dessert *carrello* comes laden with sweets.

FIORENTINO
RESTAURANT

VIA LUCA PACIOLI, 60 52037 SANSEPOLCRO
TELEPHONE RESTAURANT 0575 742033;
HOTEL 0575 740350   FAX 0575 740370

OPEN Lunch and dinner   **CLOSED** Friday; early July   **CREDIT CARDS** Visa, MC
ENGLISH SPOKEN Yes   **RESERVATIONS** Recommended on weekends   **PRICE** $$
DIRECTIONS The restaurant is in the Hotel Fiorentino, one flight up from the street, in the
town center, off Via XX Settembre

Though I have eaten many good meals since my last dinner at Fiorentino, I cannot forget the quality of this restaurant's food. It is like when a wonderful cook invites you over for dinner and prepares special dishes for the occasion that reveal the sensibility of a true artist. The artists in this case are an elderly woman, Signora Uccellini, and her friend. They maintain a tradition of home cooking few are lucky enough to grow up with.

The restaurant, upstairs in Sansepolcro's oldest hotel, is full of character. And so is its host, the *signora*'s son, Alessio Uccellini. This portly gentleman, sporting a bow tie and colorful waistcoat, moves around the dining room with feline dexterity. A man of wit and culture, he dominates the lofty salons of the historic building's *piano nobile*. The brightly lit rooms, with their decorated, timbered ceilings, are filled with an eclectic array of treasures and trophies.

The menu resembles many others I have read; the difference is the quality. *Salumi* for antipasti are Martini's (see p 367). Here, when a simple meat broth is offered, you can be sure it is the real thing—served plain or with a handful of pasta or beans. The homemade egg pasta is excellent. In autumn, I tried tender noodles of a palpably fine texture served with a meltingly soft, savory artichoke sauce. Broad *pappardelle* were paired, as usual, with *lepre*. But this freshly cooked hare sauce had a meaty depth, a tenderness to it that was neither greasy nor heavy. There are no freezers in this kitchen.

An abundant choice of *secondi* included lamb baked with tomato and olives, turkey breast studded with truffles, veal stuffed with artichokes, pork liver with bay, and kidneys with sage. Plump wood pigeon were stewed with big green olives in a liver-enriched sauce, while tender rabbit was cooked with ripe tomatoes and rosemary. There was an unusual *caponata* of carrots, celery, potato, and yellow pepper; there was also caramelized sweet and sour onions. Everything was fresh, justly seasoned, light, and appetizing—Tuscan cooking at its best.

A memorable tiramisù had a froth-light egg-yolk sauce. Crème caramel mousse was voluptuous with toasted almonds folded into it. The dish of prickly pears (*fichi d'India*), persimmons (*cachi*), pomegranates, and figs was painterly. Delicious food, fine wines, an unhurried, convivial atmosphere—my ingredients for a favorite restaurant.

Also

Those who were brought up in the United States on good-tasting Buitoni macaroni may be interested to find that some of Sansepolcro's most important streets are named after the Buitonis. I discovered that Sansepolcro was the home of this mighty pasta producer: Buitoni was the town's principal employer and performed many philanthropic deeds at the beginning of the twentieth century. In 1939 Giovanni Buitoni went to the United States and founded this favorite American food empire. (Another Buitoni started Perugina, the chocolate makers famous for Baci, or kisses.) A Buitoni factory still exists on the outskirts of town, now part of the multinational Nestlé corporation.

PANIFICIO LA SPIGA   VIA SANTA CATERINA, 76. 0575 740522

Using a wood oven fired with oak, beech, broom, and juniper, the young Valerio Caroscioli has made a name for himself baking Tuscany's classic breads. The shop is in the semibasement of a beautiful fifteenth-century building, complete with arched *loggia*, within Sansepolcro's historic walls.

GELATERIA GHIGNONI   VIA TIBERINA SUD, 85. DOGANA. 0575 741900

In 1994, this *gelateria* won a national gelato competition with its *pinolata* flavor. Since then it has really expanded its repertoire and now boasts thirty-three flavors, including shrimp, salmon, porcini, and truffle. More palatable flavors include a nicely deep chocolate, and *cavallucci*, named for the popular Tuscan cookies. The *gelateria* is at Dogana, 1 km from Sansepolcro's center, on the road toward Città di Castello (Perugia); its ices are also available in Firenze, at Hemingway (see p 106).

Stia

FILETTO
RESTAURANT

PIAZZA B. TANUCCI, 28 52017 STIA
TELEPHONE 0575 583631

OPEN Lunch and dinner in summer; lunch only in winter **CLOSED** Saturday in winter; November and June **CREDIT CARDS** None **ENGLISH SPOKEN** No **RESERVATIONS** Recommended on Sunday **PRICE** $$ **DIRECTIONS** In Stia's top piazza

---

This old-fashioned trattoria is strategically placed in Stia's highest and prettiest square, Piazza Tanucci, by the Romanesque church. In summer a few tables are set outside. The Francalanci family has run it for four generations. Next door, Filetto's *tabaccheria* also sells local *salumi*.

The dining area occupies a series of low rooms on the square. There are terra-cotta floors, pitchers of spring water, and a kitchen with a large open wood fire. The food is simple but satisfying. Meals start with mixed *salumi*, or on weekends, *crostini* canapés. In autumn, the abundantly portioned homemade *primi* include *pappardelle* noodles with wild boar sauce, tagliatelle, ravioli, and the local specialty, *tortelli di patate*—tender squares of egg pasta enclosing a pale orange filling of potato, garlic, cheese, parsley, and tomato. They are best eaten simply with melted butter. *Penne strascinate* (dried pasta quills in a piquant meat sauce) are served from a Tuscan terra-cotta pot. When it is available, *la zuppa ripiena* is a hearty peasant soup made from chicken innards.

Filetto is known for its succulent meats, roasted or grilled over wood embers. For those who prefer vegetables, there are stewed *fagioli*, chickpeas, peppers, or spinach. Ask for Filetto's own olive oil to drizzle over the vegetables. Desserts include tender *panna cotta* with sweet black-currant sauce, creamy *mascarpone* pudding, and *cantucci* biscuits dipped in Vin Santo.

Subbiano

TORRE SANTA FLORA
HOTEL RESTAURANT

IL PALAZZO, 169 52010 SUBBIANO
TELEPHONE 0575 421045   FAX 0575 489607
WEB SITE www.cedi.ats.it/santa.flora/

OPEN Lunch and dinner **CLOSED** Monday lunch in summer; all day Monday in winter; January **CREDIT CARDS** All **ENGLISH SPOKEN** Yes **RESERVATIONS** Recommended **PRICE** $$$–$$$$ **OTHER** Garden terrace for summer dining **DIRECTIONS** The hotel is off the SS 71 between Subbiano and Castelnuovo; it is signposted

---

This small but elegant *relais* hotel is situated in the country alongside the Arno River as it runs down from the Casentino hills toward Firenze. Its restaurant is open also to nonguests of the hotel, and it offers some of the most genuine food near Arezzo. The young chef, Michela Bianconi, has a talented, natural way with the ingredients of this area, and you can taste it in her dishes.

In spring, an airy zucchini *timballo* was served with a coral-red tomato sauce and garnished with fresh zucchini flowers. Pasta lovers should try the *pappardelle* with duck—handmade noodles with a chunky sauce. A more delicate seafood "broth" was topped by a spectacular pastry dome that revealed an array of fresh Mediterranean fish. A traditional side dish from the Casentino is celery: boiled, shredded, formed into balls, then deep-fried and served in a tomato sauce. It accompanied guinea fowl flavored with a wild thyme that is known in dialect as *peporino*. The desserts are all homemade, and there are some fine wines to go along with the meal. Worth a detour if you are in or around Arezzo.

ZOLFINO: THE BEAN COLUMBUS DIDN'T FIND?

"Christopher Columbus brought many bean varieties back to Europe from the Americas," explained Marco Noferi, an organic grower from the Paterna cooperative, "but a few were indigenous to Europe, and formed part of the genetic dowry of legumes used by the Etruscans and Romans centuries earlier." Local legend has it that the *zolfino* was one of these indigenous varieties—but most likely it too came to us via Columbus.

The *zolfino* is pale yellow in color (*zolfo* means "sulphur" in Italian) and is famous for its creamy texture, richness of flavor, and almost imperceptibly thin skin, making it easier to digest than other beans.

"These beans are strange," Noferi added. "It's as if they disdained any but the ground here in the Valdarno—all efforts to grow them elsewhere have failed. They are quite tricky to cultivate: they don't like anything but rainwater, and they rot if you try irrigation."

Ten years ago the *zolfino* had all but disappeared, cultivated only by a handful of growers. After a mention on a television food program, they became all the rage among wealthy Florentines and fancy restaurants—and their wholesale price tripled.

"Our beans are naturally dried [as opposed to kiln-dried] and need no soaking before cooking. You just boil them until tender and eat them with some good olive oil; their *profumo* fills the table—we wouldn't think of eating any other kind."

Talla

COOPERATIVA ZOOTECNICA DEL PRATOMAGNO TERRA DI PETRARCA
VIA DI BICCIANO. TALLA. 0575 597680

This artisan cheesemaker is on the Pratomagno mountain, and its sheep's cheeses, either of raw milk or pasteurized, are excellent. Its shop hours are 8:00–13:00, 15:00–17:30; closed Saturday afternoon and Sunday. Wines and *salumi* from other Aretino cooperatives are also on sale.

Terranuova Bracciolini

**COOPERATIVA
AGRICOLA VALDARNESE**
FARM PRODUCE: ORGANIC

PATERNA VIA SETTEPONTI, 96
52028 TERRANUOVA BRACCIOLINI
TELEPHONE/FAX 055 977052
WEB SITE www.paterna.it

OPEN 8:00–13:00, 17:00–20:00 **CLOSED** Sunday **CREDIT CARDS** None **DIRECT SALE** Yes
MAIL ORDER Yes **ENGLISH SPOKEN** No **OTHER** Paterna has an outlet store in Montevarchi
(p 361) **DIRECTIONS** On Setteponti road between Loro Ciuffenna and San Giustino Valdarno

The Valdarno Cooperative, Paterna, began more than fifteen years ago and is one of Tuscany's most important organic producers. Its 40 hectares (100 acres) of land are under the auspices of the Tuscan branch of AIAB, the Italian organic growers' association.

"Paterna brought people together who believed in the possibility of reversing the bad habits of Tuscany's postwar farmers," explained Marco Noferi, its dynamic young director. "Much of the land was cultivated by uneducated *contadini*, peasants. They were pushed into buying and using chemical pesticides and weed-killers by promises of better yields, and unfortunately the mentality was often the more, the better. So the land really took a beating."

The association requires that land be left alone for five years after it has been chemically treated before it can be called chemical-free, or organic (*biologico*). On-site controls are carried out yearly.

Marco Noferi and his partner, Tamara Scarpellini, produce organic vegetables and fruits, extra-virgin olive oil, wines, pulses, and grains, including chestnuts and wheat ground at Loro Ciuffenna's water mill (see p 358). Paterna's produce is sold fresh or preserved under oil or vinegar or as jam. The farm's shop is lined with jars: baby artichokes, sliced zucchini or eggplant in olive oil, chestnut purées, fruit jams, tomato sauces.

Noferi is actively safeguarding the Valdarno's indigenous, but almost extinct, plant species, including the *zolfino* bean; he successfully brought organic produce to the area's kindergartens. The farm and its shop are lovely to visit, and the organic cause is undoubtedly worth supporting.

OSTERIA "IL CANTO DEL MAGGIO"
RESTAURANT

PENNA ALTA, 30/D PENNA 52028
TERRANUOVA BRACCIOLINI
TELEPHONE/FAX 055 9705147
WEB SITE www.cantodelmaggio.com

OPEN Summer: Dinner Tuesday–Sunday and Sunday lunch; winter: dinner Thursday–Sunday and Sunday lunch; snack lunches in wine bar all year   **CLOSED** Monday; Tuesday and Wednesday in winter; ten days in October; one week in January   **CREDIT CARDS** Visa, MC, Amex
ENGLISH SPOKEN Yes   **FEATURES** Outdoor summer terrace   **RESERVATIONS** Recommended
PRICE $$–$$$ **OTHER** The *osteria* has rooms for holiday rentals   **DIRECTIONS** From Terranuova Bracciolini, go toward Loro Ciuffenna. Penna Alta is on the left after 1 km. The *osteria* is signposted; park at the top of the drive

---

Mauro Quirini describes his *osteria*'s delicious cuisine as "the happy encounter between the poor food of Arezzo and the rich food of Firenze." His country cooking features fine artisan-made ingredients and seasonal produce. Many vegetables and herbs are homegrown; he has built a room for aging *salumi* and a pit for maturing cheeses—all in the tiny hamlet that is Penna Alta, which, until Quirini arrived, had been abandoned since the 1950s.

Il Canto del Maggio is situated in the small rooms of a small house. There are many personal touches: sculptures and decorative objects are tucked on door ledges or into niches. The menu offers some of the area's culinary rarities: home-cured *salame*, thin-skinned yellowish *zolfino* beans (see p 372), country prosciutto aged for more than two years—twice that of its commercial counterparts.

In autumn the antipasti included this full-flavored, peppered prosciutto, thin slices of *capocollo* (salt-cured pork shoulder) served with orange-scented butter, Quirini's coarsely ground *finocchiona,* and slices of *salame* accompanied by a paste of crushed figs and nuts. Toasted bread was topped simply with Tuscan black cabbage and fragrant new olive oil. The flavors were pure and decisive—an excellent start to the meal.

The *zuppa di fagioli* was a thick purée of herbed beans, with whole beans and chopped scallions added for texture. Herb *strozzapreti* were like the filling to ravioli without the pasta: tender green dumplings under a blanket of melted, truffled *fonduta* cheese. Wide *pappardelle* noodles were sauced with a coarsely chopped *battuto grosso* of vegetables and chicken livers. Capon came with fried cardoons, a bitter vegetable in the artichoke family. Duck was tender and served in a jelly dominated by citrus zest.

For dessert, a chilled chestnut mousse was soft, creamy, and smoky from the chestnuts' drying; white chocolate mousse was more compact. A well-selected wine list completed this fine gastronomic experience.

OSTERIA COSTACHIARA
RESTAURANT

BADIOLA 52027 TERRANUOVA BRACCIOLINI
TELEPHONE 055 944318

OPEN Lunch and dinner   **CLOSED** Tuesday; second half of August   **CREDIT CARDS** Visa, MC
ENGLISH SPOKEN No   **FEATURES** Garden tables in summer   **RESERVATIONS** Always
recommended   **PRICE** $$ **OTHER** Four rooms available for summer rental
DIRECTIONS From the Valdarno exit of the *autostrada* A1, go left toward San Giovanni Valdarno
for 3.5 kms. Turn right into Badiola. Go straight through the village, cross a river, then turn right
toward Montemarciano and Persignano. The restaurant is on the right after 800 meters

This *osteria's* cuisine is *cucina contadina*—peasant cooking. The setting is certainly rural: a large *casa colonica* (farmhouse) situated in a garden over the river from San Giovanni Valdarno. With his family, the affable Aldo Betti has run this lively, atmospheric restaurant since 1991. He is a great host: dressed in his white half apron he describes the foods as if he himself couldn't resist them.

And you can't help feeling hungry seeing his big display of unusual homemade antipasti. There are bowls of olives and *sott'aceti* (pickled vegetables), steamed greens, boiled *fagioli*, twists of crispy pork fat (*ciccioli*), tomatoes stuffed with tuna and capers. Meats include sliced tongue, a deep-pink country *prosciutto Toscano* on the bone, and a range of locally cured *salumi*.

Primi are rustic and appetizing. Betti's *"bella" zuppa di fagioli* comes steaming hot in an earthenware bowl. A fine, *piccante* purée of beans, it is thickened with thin noodles, *taglierini*. *Pici*, like thick spaghetti, is topped with a meaty sauce of pigeon and guinea fowl flavored with rosemary, without tomato.

Meats grilled over the wood fire are a specialty: chops, steaks, and sausages. Whole pork livers (*fegatelli*) are spit-roasted with bay (*alla Fiorentina*) or fennel (*all'Aretina*). Aldo Betti told me that Giorgio Vasari, the Renaissance painter and author of the 1550 *Lives of the Painters,* was born in Arezzo and was very partial to these *fegatelli*. Home-killed wild boar is served with corn-yellow polenta, stewed in a peppery sauce with sage. This is robust country cooking that is best enjoyed with a group of friends and some good Tuscan wine.

Vitiano

FRANTOIO OLEARIO GIANCARLO GIANNINI

VITIANO, 227A. 0575 97370

This modern-style *frantoio*, or olive mill, may be visited during the olive pressing season—November and December. Oil may be bought directly from the mill during that time. At other times, phone ahead for an appointment to visit.

Tuscan Market Days, Town by Town

These are the weekly or monthly market days for each town listed. Some markets have large food sections; others may have only a few stalls. Most big towns also have at least one or more permanent covered markets, usually open every morning except Sunday.

The Lunigiana and Versilia (CHAPTER 1)

AULLA   Saturday morning

BAGNONE   Monday morning

CAMAIORE   Monday morning, Friday morning

CARRARA   Monday morning

FIVIZZANO   Tuesday morning

FORTE DEI MARMI   Wednesday morning

MASSA   Tuesday morning, Friday morning

PIETRASANTA   Saturday morning

PONTREMOLI   Wednesday morning, Saturday morning

SERAVEZZA   Saturday morning

VIAREGGIO   Piazza Santa Maria, daily

VILLAFRANCA IN LUNIGIANA   Friday morning

Lucca and the Garfagnana (CHAPTER 2)

ALTOPASCIO   Thursday morning

BARGA   Friday morning

CAPANNORI   Friday morning

CASTELNUOVO DI GARFAGNANA   Thursday morning

LUCCA   Mercato del Carmine daily except Wednesday and Sunday; antiques market third Saturday and Sunday of each month

MASSAROSA   Tuesday morning

PIAZZA AL SERCHIO   Tuesday morning

PIEVE FOSCIANA   Saturday morning

PORCARI   Saturday morning

Pistoia and Mount Abetone   (CHAPTER 3)

AGLIANA   Thursday morning

CUTIGLIANO   Tuesday morning

LAMPORECCHIO   Saturday morning

MONSUMMANO TERME   Monday morning

MONTECATINI TERME   Thursday morning

PESCIA   Saturday morning

PISTOIA   Wednesday and Saturday mornings

PONTE BUGGIANESE   Friday morning

QUARRATA   Saturday morning

SAN MARCELLO PISTOIESE   Thursday morning

Firenze (Florence), Prato, and Their Provinces   (CHAPTER 4)

BAGNO A RIPOLI   Wednesday morning

BORGO SAN LORENZO   Tuesday morning

CALENZANO   Wednesday morning

CAMPI BISENZIO   Saturday afternoon

CASTELFIORENTINO   Saturday morning

CERTALDO   Wednesday morning

EMPOLI   Thursday morning

FIGLINE VALDARNO   Tuesday morning

FIRENZE VIALE LINCOLN   Tuesday morning, and see p 92–93

FUCECCHIO   Wednesday morning

IMPRUNETA   Saturday morning

INCISA VAL D'ARNO   Friday morning

MONTELUPO FIORENTINO   Saturday morning

MONTESPERTOLI   Tuesday morning

POGGIO A CAIANO   Thursday morning

PONTASSIEVE   Wednesday morning

PRATO   Monday morning

REGGELLO   Saturday morning

RÙFINA   Saturday afternoon

SCANDICCI   Saturday

SESTO FIORENTINO   Saturday

SIGNA   Friday morning

TAVARNUZZE   Wednesday morning

VICCHIO   Thursday morning

VINCI   Wednesday morning

Pisa and Its Hills   (CHAPTER 5)

BIENTINA   Tuesday morning

CAPANNOLI   Tuesday morning

CASCINA   Thursday morning

CASTELFRANCO DI SOTTO   Monday morning

CASTELNUOVO VAL DI CECINA   Wednesday morning

PISA   Piazza Duomo, daily, and see p 136

POMARANCE   Thursday morning

PONSACCO   Wednesday morning

PONTEDERA   Friday morning

SAN GIULIANO TERME   Tuesday morning

SAN MINIATO   Tuesday morning

SAN ROMANO   Wednesday morning

SANTA CROCE SULL'ARNO   Saturday morning

VOLTERRA   Saturday morning

Livorno and Its Coast   (CHAPTER 6)

CECINA   Tuesday morning

COLLESALVETTI   Thursday morning

DONORATICO   Thursday morning

LIVORNO   Via dei Pensieri, Friday morning, and see p 160–161

MARINA DI BIBBONA   Wednesday morning in summer

PIOMBINO   Wednesday morning

ROSIGNANO SOLVAY   Monday morning

SAN VINCENZO   Saturday morning

The Island of Elba   (CHAPTER 7)

CAMPO NELL'ELBA   Wednesday morning

PORTOFERRAIO   Friday morning

RIO MARINA   Monday morning

Chianti Classico and Its Wines   (CHAPTER 8)

CASTELLINA IN CHIANTI   Saturday morning

CASTELNUOVO BERARDENGA   Thursday morning

GAIOLE IN CHIANTI   Second Tuesday afternoon of the month

GREVE IN CHIANTI   Saturday morning

PANZANO   Sunday morning

POGGIBONSI   Tuesday morning

RADDA IN CHIANTI   Fourth Monday afternoon of the month
SAN CASCIANO IN VAL DI PESA   Monday morning
STRADA IN CHIANTI   Tuesday morning
TAVARNELLE VAL DI PESA   Thursday morning

Grosseto and the Maremma   (CHAPTER 9)

CAPALBIO   Wednesday morning
CASTIGLIONE DELLA PESCAIA   Saturday morning
FOLLONICA   Friday morning
GROSSETO   Thursday morning
MANCIANO   Saturday morning
MASSA MARITTIMA   Wednesday morning
ORBETELLO   Saturday morning
PITIGLIANO   Wednesday morning
PORTO ERCOLE   Monday morning
PORTO SANTO STEFANO   Tuesday morning
RIBOLLA   Tuesday morning
ROCCASTRADA   Wednesday morning
SCANSANO   Friday morning

Mount Amiata   (CHAPTER 10)

ABBADIA SAN SALVATORE   Monday–Saturday mornings
CAMPIGLIA D'ORCIA   First Tuesday morning of the month
CASTEL DEL PIANO   First Wednesday of the month
CASTIGLIONE D'ORCIA   Fourth Saturday morning of the month
PIANCASTAGNAIO   Alternate Saturday mornings
RADICOFANI   Alternate Thursday mornings

Siena and the Crete Senesi   (CHAPTER 11)

BUONCONVENTO   Saturday morning
CETONA   Saturday morning
CHIANCIANO TERME   Wednesday morning
CHIUSI SCALO   Monday morning
COLLE DI VAL D'ELSA   Friday morning
MONTEPULCIANO   Thursday morning
MONTERONI D'ARBIA   Tuesday morning
PIENZA   Friday morning

RAPOLANO TERME   Thursday and Friday mornings
SAN GIMIGNANO   Thursday morning
SAN QUIRICO D'ORCIA   Alternate Tuesday mornings
SARTEANO   Friday mornings
SIENA   Wednesday morning
SINALUNGA   Tuesday morning
TORRITA DI SIENA   Friday morning
TREQUANDA   First Thursday afternoon of the month

Montalcino and Its Wines   (CHAPTER 12)
MONTALCINO   Friday morning

Arezzo, Its Hills and Valleys   (CHAPTER 13)
ANGHIARI   Wednesday morning
AREZZO   Saturday morning, and see p 345
BIBBIENA   Thursday morning
CAMUCIA   Thursday morning
CASTELFRANCO DI SOPRA   Friday morning
CORTONA   Saturday morning
FOIANO DELLA CHIANA   Monday morning
LORO CIUFFENNA   Monday morning
MONTE SAN SAVINO   Wednesday morning
MONTEVARCHI   Thursday morning
PIEVE SANTO STEFANO   Monday morning
POPPI   Tuesday morning
PRATOVECCHIO   Friday morning
SAN GIOVANNI VALDARNO   Saturday morning
SANSEPOLCRO   Saturday morning
STIA   Tuesday afternoon
TERRANUOVA BRACCIOLINI   Friday morning

Glossary

acciaio inossidabile stainless steel

acciuga, acciughe (pl) anchovy

aceto vinegar

acquacotta rustic Maremman soup of vegetables and egg

acquavite brandy

affettati sliced cured meats, a common antipasto

affogato al caffè a popular dessert: ice cream "drowned" in espresso coffee

agnello lamb

agriturismo holiday rentals on farms or in country houses

alimentari grocery store

alla brace cooked over wood embers

allevamento animal breeding; farm

amaretto macaroon made with bitter and sweet almonds

amaro bitter; an herbal liqueur used as a *digestivo*

anguilla eel

annata year of vintage

antipasto hors d'oeuvre, the appetizer course of a meal

aperitivo predinner drink

apicoltura beekeeping

aragosta clawless spiny lobster

arrabbiata a spicy, hot tomato-based pasta sauce (literally, "angry")

astice lobster

azienda company, business

azienda agricola farm

baccalà salt cod

bar bar serving coffee, alcoholic beverages, and snacks

barriques small barrels usually of French oak popular in modern winemaking. American oak *barriques* impart a stronger taste

bianco white

bicchiere glass

borgo village, especially medieval

bottarga (di tonno) dried roe (of tuna)

botte, botti (pl) large wooden barrels, usually of Slavonian oak or chestnut

bottiglia bottle

brace   wood embers

branzino   sea bass; it may be wild or farmed (*di allevamento*)

brioche   generic Italian name for breakfast pastry, including croissant

bruschetta   grilled bread usually rubbed with garlic and drizzled with olive oil

budino   sweet or savory "pudding"

caffè   coffee; if you order *un caffè,* you will be served an espresso

camino   fireplace

cannellini   white beans popular in Tuscany

cantina   cellar, wine cellar, or winery

cantucci, cantuccini   hard almond biscuits often dunked in Vin Santo

caponata   sweet-and-sour Sicilian vegetable dish, usually with eggplants

capperi   capers

caprino   goat's cheese

capriolo   roebuck

caratello   small wooden cask used for making Vin Santo

carciofi   artichokes

cardo   cardoon, a vegetable in the thistle family

carne   meat

carpaccio   as commonly used, very thinly sliced raw meat or fish with
a lemon and oil marinade

carta dei vini   wine list

cartoccio   a method of baking in paper or foil

caseificio   cheese factory

castagna   chestnut

cefalo   gray mullet

cervo   venison

Chianina   a breed of cattle formerly used to pull the plough, now regarded
as the finest eating beef

chiodini   two types of small edible wild mushrooms, *Armillariella mellea*
or *Clitocybe tabescens*

ciclo continuo   modern style of olive-oil mill (literally, "continuous cycle")

cinghiale   wild boar

companatico   "to go with bread"

confetti   hard sugar candies

coniglio   rabbit

consorzio   consortium of food or wine producers; it oversees production and sales

contadino   peasant, farmworker, or tenant farmer

contorno   used on menus to signify side dishes

cotoletta alla Milanese   breaded veal chop popular in Milan

coulis   a thick purée or sauce, usually of fruit

crostata   open-faced tart, especially fruit or jam filled *crostini, crostoni*   canapés

cru   French term used in Italy to indicate a superior single vineyard and its wine

cucina povera   simple, peasant cookery (literally, "poor cooking")

cultura promiscua   the traditional style of interplanting crops with vines and olive and fruit trees

damigiana   demijohn, large glass wine flask

degustazione   tasting (of wine or food)

digestivo   digestive, liqueur to aid digestion

DOC, DOCG   denominations used in wine zones, see p 23–24

dolce   sweet, dessert

dolci   desserts, sweets

DOP   denomination "of protected origin," used for foods

drogheria   grocery store selling imported spices and other specialized ingredients

enologist, enologo   winemaker

enoteca   wine bar, wine collection, usually for sale, as in a wine shop

erbe   herbs, grasses, or wild leaves

erboristeria   shop selling herbal products

etichetta   label

ettaro   hectare; measure of land used in farming, equivalent to 2.47 acres

fagiano   pheasant

fagioli   beans

fagiolini   string beans

faraona   guinea fowl

farro   spelt wheat, *Tritticum dicoccum*, see p 48

fattoria   farm or estate

fava   fava or broad bean

fettunta   like *bruschetta*, grilled bread drizzled with olive oil

fiaschetteria   wine bar and shop

fiasco   flask, as in the old-style, half-straw-covered Chianti bottles

finocchiona   a salt-cured sausage of coarsely ground pork scented with wild fennel seeds, in Tuscany usually eaten fresh

Fiorentina   T-bone steak, at its best when of Chianina beef

Firenze   Florence

focaccia, focaccina   flat, crusty yeast bread, often topped with salt, olive oil, and other savory toppings

frantoio   olive oil mill

frittata   Italian slow-cooked omelette, often eaten at room temperature as a snack or antipasto

fritto misto   mixed fried food

frizzante   lightly fizzy, semi-sparkling

fruttato   fruity, said of wine
frutti di bosco   wood fruits, especially berries
frutti di mare   seafood
fungo, funghi   mushrooms

gallinella   Mediterranean fish in the gurnard family
ganache   a chocolate and whipping cream filling for chocolates
gelateria   ice cream parlor
gelato   ice cream
giovane   young
gnocchi, gnocchetti   small dumplings, usually of potato and flour, eaten as a *primo*
governo Toscano   fermentation method once popular in Tuscan winemaking, see p 62
gramolatrice   a machine used to churn ground olive paste before the oil can be extracted
grappa   distilled spirit made from the grape residues after the winemaking process
grappolo   grape bunch
grigliata mista   mixed grill (of meats, etc.)

hectare   see *ettaro*, a measure of land used in farming equivalent to 2.47 acres

IGT   denomination used for wine, see p 24
integrale   whole wheat (of bread or pasta)
invaiatura   the changing of color of grapes or olives
invecchiamento   aging, of wine
invecchiato   aged, said of cheese or wine

latte   milk
legno   wood
lepre   hare
litro   liter (1.065 U.S. quarts)
lombo   loin

macchia Mediterranea   scrub, the stunted plants that grow wild around
   the Mediterranean basin
macine   stone wheels, especially for grinding olives
mallegato   blood sausage
manzo   beef
mare   sea
mascarpone   Italian cream cheese
mezzadria   system of sharecropping common in Tuscany until after World War II
miele   honey
minestra   soup or first course

misto   mixed
morbido   mellow, said of wine
mostarda   sweet-and-hot fruit preserve from Cremona
muffa   mold

normale   the basic DOC wine, as opposed to the Riserva

olio   oil
oliva   olive
olivastra   a variety of olive tree found especially on Mount Amiata
orata   gilt-head bream
orecchiette   small "earlike" bunches at the top of bunches of grapes; type of short pasta
ortica, ortiche (pl)   stinging nettles
ossi di morto   very brittle egg white and almond biscuits (literally, "dead man's bones")
osteria   inn, now commonly used for informal restaurants
ovolo   orange-capped wild mushroom, *Amanita caesarea*

padrone   landlord, owner
pancetta   salt-cured pork belly, like bacon
pane sciocco   unsalted Tuscan bread
panettiere   baker
panforte   medieval spiced honey confection studded with fruits and nuts, typical of Siena
panna cotta   baked cream pudding
panzanella   bread and vegetable salad
pappa al pomodoro   rustic bread and tomato soup
pappardelle   wide egg noodles
parago, pagello   Mediterranean fish in the bream family
parfait   in Italian used for pâtélike savory dishes as well as desserts
passata, passato   purée, especially of tomato
passito, passiti (pl)   semidried grapes and the sweet wine made from them
pasticceria   pastry shop, pastry
pasticceria mignon   petits fours or bite-size pastries
pasticciere   pastry chef or baker
pecorino   cheese made from sheep's milk
peperoncino   hot chili pepper
pernice   partridge
pesce   fish
pesce spada   swordfish
pesto   Genovese ground basil, garlic, and cheese sauce for pasta
piazza   place, square
piccante   hot, spicy
piccola pasticceria   petit fours, bite-size pastries

pinci, pici   thick handmade pasta like spaghetti

pinoli   pine nuts

podere   farm

poggio   hill

polenta   ground cornmeal and the dish made from it

pollo   chicken

polpo, polipo   octopus

pomodoro   tomato

porcino, porcini (pl)   wild mushroom, *Boletus edulis*

potatura verde   "green" pruning, carried out during the plant's growing season

primi   first courses

prodotto   product, produced

produttore   producer

profumo   bouquet, perfume, scent

prosciutto   ham

prosciutto crudo   salt-cured ham

prosciutto Toscano   Tuscan salt-cured ham, usually saltier and more robust in flavor than the Parma

quintale   quintal, equivalent to a hundred kgs

ragù (Bolognese)   meat sauce for pasta

retrogusto   aftertaste

ribollita   twice-cooked hearty Tuscan soup of vegetables, pulses, and bread (literally, "reboiled")

ricciarelli   soft marzipan cookies of Siena

ricotta   soft curd cheese made from whey, usually of cow's or sheep's milk

rimontaggio   the action of pumping the must over the "cap" in winemaking

ripieno   filling

riserva   reserve, applies to DOC or DOCG wines

riso   rice

risotto   rice dish

ristorante   restaurant

rombo   turbot or brill

rosato   rosé wine

rosso   red

rovere   oak

salame, salamella   salt-cured salami

sale   salt

salsiccia, salsicce (pl)   sausages

salumi ready-to-eat salt-cured meats, usually of pork, including prosciutto

salumiere maker of *salumi*

salumificio factory producing *salumi*

salvia sage

sapore flavor

scampo, scampi (pl) large shrimp or Dublin Bay prawn

schiacciata (also *ciaccia*) see focaccia

sciocco see *pane sciocco*

secco dry

secondi second or main course

semifreddo dessert frozen after it has been made

sfuso loose; refers to unbottled wine or liquids

sommelier wine waiter or expert; French word used in Italy

soppressata head cheese, also known as *biroldo*

sott'aceto, sott'aceti (pl) preserved under vinegar, usually vegetables

sott'olio, sott'olii (pl) preserved under oil

spalla shoulder

spigola sea bass (also called *branzino*)

spumante sparkling (wine)

stoccafisso stockfish

super-Tuscan modern-style wine, see p 26

tabaccheria tobacconist's shop

tagliatelle, tagliatelline, tagliolini egg noodles

tappo cork, bottle top

tartufo truffle, also an ice cream

tartufo di mare shellfish in the clam family

tavola calda informal eatery selling hot foods

tenuta farm or estate

terroir French word that denotes an area in winemaking

timo thyme

tiramisù a coffee- and mascarpone-based dessert (literally "pick me up")

tonno tuna fish

tortelli a type of stuffed pasta

tortelli di patate potato-filled egg pasta squares

totano long-bodied "flying" squid

trattoria a family-run country restaurant

triglia red mullet

tufo tufa, a yellowish volcanic soil

uva   grape
uvetta   dried raisin

vassoio   tray
vecchio   old
vendemmia   harvest, or grape harvest
verdura   vegetable
vigna, vigneto   vineyard
vino   wine
vino da meditazione   a contemplative wine that is drunk by itself, without food
vino da tavola (vdt)   table wine
vino passito   usually sweet wine made from semidried grapes
vinsantaia   room used to store *caratelli* of Vin Santo; it is often the attic
Vin Santo   a Tuscan dessert wine, see p 24
vite   vine
vitello tonnato   thinly sliced veal with tuna sauce, usually served cold
viticoltore   grape grower
vitigno   grape variety or type

zabaglione, zabaione   egg and sweet-wine custard
zafferano   saffron
zona artigianale, industriale   industrial or artisanal zones (of a town)
zuppa   soup
zuppa inglese   a kind of Italian trifle

Index

b